W9-BLE-831

GREAT SPY STORIES

GREAT

SPY STORIES

Edited by ALLEN DULLES

CASTLE

ACKNOWLEDGMENTS

"The Recruitment of the Archtraitor," from *The Panther's Feast*, by Robert Asprey. Copyright © 1959 by Robert Asprey. Reprinted by permission of the author.

"The Defection of Kuznetov," from *Topaz*, by Leon Uris. Copyright © 1967 by Leon Uris. McGraw-Hill edition, 1967. Bantam Books edition, 1968. Reprinted by permission of Bantam Books, Inc.

"Happy, the Joe," from *Call It Treason*, by George Locke Howe. Copyright 1948, 1949 by George Locke Howe. Reprinted by permission of The Viking Press, Inc.

"The Stockings of Major André," from *The Secret Road*, by Bruce Lancaster. Copyright © 1952 by Bruce Lancaster. Reprinted by permission of Atlantic–Little, Brown and Co.

"Conspiracy up to the Ears," from *Azef*, Roman Goul, translated by Mirra Ginsburg. Copyright © 1962 by Roman Goul. Reprinted by permission of Doubleday & Company, Inc.

"A Conversation on the Train," from *The Birds Fall Down*, by Rebecca West. Copyright © 1966 by Rebecca West. All rights reserved. Reprinted by permission of The Viking Press, Inc., and The Macmillan Company of Canada.

"Mr. Vladimir and Mr. Verloc," from *The Secret Agent*, by Joseph Conrad. By permission of J. M. Dent & Sons, Ltd., Trustees to the Joseph Conrad Estate.

"Entrapping a Lady," from *The Scarlet Pimpernel*, by Baroness Orczy. By permission of Mr. J. Orczy-Barstow and Hodder & Stoughton, Ltd.

Continued on next page

87   9 8 7 6

Copyright © 1969 by the Estate of Allen W. Dulles. All rights reserved.

Arrangement to publish this book has been made by Castle, a division of Book Sales, Inc., 110 Enterprise Avenue, Secaucus, N.J. 07094
ISBN 0-89009-717-8

The CASTLE trademark is registered in the U.S. Patent and Trademark Office.

"The Bruce-Partington Plans," from *The Later Adventures of Sherlock Holmes,* by A. Conan Doyle. Reprinted by permission of the Estate of Sir Arthur Conan Doyle and John Murray, Ltd.

"Guarding the Zeppelins," from *Drink to Yesterday,* by Manning Coles. Copyright © 1940, 1941 by Cyril Henry Coles and Adelaide Frances Oke Manning. Reprinted by permission of Curtis Brown, Ltd.

"A Defector Who Didn't Make It," from *Dark Duet,* by Peter Cheyney. Reprinted by permission of Peter Cheyney Ltd.

"A Message to Umballa," from *Kim* by Rudyard Kipling. Reprinted by permission of Mrs. George Bambridge, Doubleday & Company, Inc., and The Macmillan Company of Canada.

"I.A.," condensed from the book *Mountolive,* by Lawrence Durrell. Copyright © 1958 by Lawrence Durrell. Reprinted by permission of E. P. Dutton & Co., Inc., and Faber & Faber, Ltd.

"Far from Home," from *Spylight,* by James Leasor. Copyright © 1966 by James Leasor. Published by permission of J. B. Lippincott Company and William Heinemann, Ltd.

"The Assistant Producer," from *Nabokov's Dozen,* by Vladimir Nabokov. Copyright 1943 by The Atlantic Monthly Company. Reprinted by permission of Doubleday & Company, Inc.

"Betrayal," from *Darkness at Noon,* by Arthur Koestler. Copyright © 1949 by Arthur Koestler. Reprinted by permission of A. D. Peters & Co. and Jonathan Cape, Ltd.

"Belgrade, 1926," from *A Coffin for Dimitrios,* by Eric Ambler. Copyright © 1939 by Eric Ambler and renewed 1966. Reprinted by permission of Alfred A. Knopf, Inc. and Hodder & Stoughton, Ltd.

"A Problem of Identity," from *The Great Impersonation,* by E. Phillips Oppenheim. Copyright 1920 by Little, Brown and Company. Copyright 1948 by Gerald Tooth. Reprinted by permission of Little, Brown and Co.

"A Confusion of Celts," from *Assignment in Brittany,* by Helen MacInnes. Copyright © 1941 by Helen Highet. Reprinted by permission of Ashley Famous Agency, Inc.

"The Trojan Horse," from *The Aeneid of Virgil,* translated by Rolfe Humphries. Copyright 1951 by Charles Scribner's Sons. Reprinted by permission of the publisher.

"A Belated Promotion," from *Operation Heartbreak,* by Duff Cooper. Copyright © 1954 by John Julius Norwich. Reprinted by permission of John Julius Norwich, c/o Marvin Josephson Associates.

"A Little Piece of Hungary," from *The Ipcress File,* by Len Deighton. Copyright © 1963 by Len Deighton. Reprinted by permission of Simon & Schuster, Inc. and Hodder & Stoughton, Ltd.

"The Trigger," from *The Manchurian Candidate,* by Richard Condon. Copyright © 1959 by Richard Condon. Reprinted by permission of Harold Matson Co., Inc.

"Taylor's Run," from *The Looking Glass War,* by John le Carré. Copyright © 1965 by D. J. M. Cornwell. Reprinted by permission of Coward-McCann, Inc. and William Heinemann, Ltd.

"The End of James," from *From Russia with Love,* by Ian Fleming. Copyright © 1957 by The Macmillan Company. Reprinted by permission of The Macmillan Company and Glidrose Productions Limited.

"Giulia Lazzari," excerpts from "A Trip to Paris" and "Giulia Lazzari," from *Ashenden*, by W. Somerset Maugham. Copyright © 1927, 1928 by W. Somerset Maugham. Reprinted by permission of Doubleday & Company, Inc., William Heinemann, Ltd., and Executors to Estate of W. Somerset Maugham.

"All's Well," from *On Hazardous Duty*, by David St. John. Copyrght © 1965 by David St. John. Reprinted by permission of The New American Library, Inc., New York.

"The Recruitment of Major Blenkinsop," from *Water on the Brain*, by Sir Compton MacKenzie. Published by Chatto & Windus, Ltd., 1954. Reprinted by permission of the author.

"The Inventive Mr. Wormold," adapted from *Our Man in Havana*, by Graham Greene. Copyright © 1958 by William Heinemann, Ltd. Reprinted by permission of The Viking Press, Inc. and William Heinemann, Ltd.

Contents

Foreword

Every age has its literature of the improbable, a favorite form of fantasy peculiar to it. This is usually a literature of action and adventure, rarely thoughtful or analytical. In our time, it seems, the spy story—or, more broadly put, the story of secret agents and secret missions—has become the favorite literature of the improbable, filling the age-old needs of an adventure-hungry reading public.

Why the spy should have come to be the hero of this particular kind of literature in our day, replacing the knight errant, the swashbuckler, the cowboy, and all the rest of the old gallery, is not so easy to explain. Eric Ambler points out that until recent times the spy was generally thought of as a rather sneaky and socially unacceptable figure, associated in most people's minds with unwashed terrorists and anarchists. It is true that World War II and the Cold War served to elevate the reputation of spying in the public mind and to make it socially acceptable because a more attractive and more highly motivated type of individual appeared to be engaged in it. Yet this does not fully account for the fact that a seemingly inexhaustible literary format has come into being in which the spy is the adventure hero of our time.

My own theory is that the conflict in all adventure tales is the ancient one between good and evil presented in its simplest and most primitive form—"the good guys" against "the bad guys." But we have run out of evil princes usurping the crown, princesses who need champions, captives who must be ransomed, and all the other combinations and situations which gave substance to the popular fiction of other ages, mirroring in simplified fashion erstwhile political, social, and religious conflicts. Today we live in a time of serious contention and competition among great nations, in the political, military, and technological spheres. For reasons too obvious to explain, the efforts of the major nations in all these areas are characterized more than at any other time in history by one thing—secrecy. Given this state of affairs, can you think of any figure other than the spy, allowing for all the distortion and unreality in which that figure is clothed, who can come forward and embody so vividly and understandably the contest of nations in its simplest terms?

The statesman, the diplomat, and the scientist may be the decisive figures in the real history of our time, but from the point of view of fiction they are colorless compared with the spy. Usually older gentlemen of settled mien, they sit in offices and laboratories. But the spy has the muscle and the daring to take the place of the discarded hero of yore. He is the new-model musketeer, and his adventures are but newly furbished tussles between the Queen's men and the Cardinal's, the Crusaders and the Saracens, the cowboys and the Indians.

Inspect, if you will, as I have just been doing, a goodly number of these spy tales and reduce their plots and entanglements to the bare bones. As you will discover, most of them devote rather little space to the real business of espionage, to "the craft of intelligence," as I have called it elsewhere—the assessment of the target, the vetting and recruitment of agents, and, finally, the acquisition of secret information. They are really about a man who is asked to go on a mission which must be accomplished in secrecy, and about what happened to him on his way out and on his way back. What we have is that most ancient of tales, the Quest, the hero on the road to Castle Perilous meeting dragons and witches, often followed by that other ancient tale, the Chase, because on the way back the hero has the papers or the abducted daughter of the Prime Minister, or whatever the target he was sent to reach, and the bad guys are after him. The creation of suspense is almost automatic. If you look at a work like Ian Fleming's *From Russia with Love,* you will see that it consists almost entirely of the elements I have mentioned above: the quest, reaching the target, and the chase.

This brings me to that interesting point where the operations of an intelligence service and the plots of most spy stories part company, never to meet again. If the spy adventure didn't take a certain basic liberty with the facts of the business, it could hardly exist. You have noted, of course, if you are a reader of spy tales or have watched the run-of-the-mill spy episode on television, that the hero, the spy, is "one of our men"; that is to say, he is of the same nationality as the reading or television audience. His capacity in the intelligence organization of his home country is rarely clearly defined. He is an "agent," a troubleshooter. He has been on many previous missions and he is a man with experience. His identity is known to the enemy. He may have disguises or other names, but they dissolve readily. In some tales he may be going on his first mission, but if the book succeeds he will no doubt go on some later ones .

Now, this is one thing no intelligence service in its right mind will ever do (except in time of war). It will not send one of its own officers or even one of its own nationals as an agent into enemy territory if there is the slightest chance that his identity or his affiliation with an intelligence organization is known anywhere in the outside world. The essence of successful espionage is secrecy; the idea is not to attract the hounds but to put them off the track or never to let them get on it. But, of course, if the agent were successful in doing this, as every real-life agent wishes to be, there would be no adventure.

If I seem to have been a little hard on the popular spy-romance-adventure story, the reader may wonder just what he is going to find in this volume. If it is a fact that a great many spy tales are not devoted to depicting the intelligence business as it really is practiced, there is still no reason why they cannot be good stories. Many are, and I have included some of the good ones in this collection. But there is another body of spy fiction.

After spending a good part of a lifetime in intelligence work, you cannot blame me if I like the work of authors who have taken some pains to depict espionage and other intelligence enterprises accurately, and at the same time do their best to tell a good story. It is this body of spy fiction on which I have also drawn in assembling this anthology.

There seem to be three kinds of authors who have accomplished this: those who have spent some time in intelligence service and have seen it from the inside, those who have no personal experience but have made it their business to find out what it is really like, and those authors who have attempted to fictionalize actual cases. Who they are and how well they succeeded becomes apparent, I hope, in the stories I have chosen and the prefatory notes to them. I have, of course, not limited myself to espionage but have included almost anything that comes within the purview of the modern intelligence organization.

Espionage fiction, good and bad, reflects, as one would expect, the political conflicts and the social and scientific upheavals peculiar to the epoch in which it was written. In this volume I have included representative pieces from each of the last seven or eight decades. There are also a few pieces from or about still earlier epochs, but these are largely curiosities or landmarks in the history of spy fiction, such as *The Scarlet Pimpernel.*

In choosing contemporary spy tales for this volume, I tried chiefly to pick them, aside from their readability, for the divergence of their themes, but it would have been impossible in a volume of this scope to represent all the best of them or all the themes.

There is a great dearth of good short stories about spies and spying. It may be because espionage in fiction always depends upon a certain degree of complexity to be intriguing and it takes a good deal of exposition to set all the wheels in motion. Only in a novel can the full tale be told with all its trappings. But this means that the anthologist has the challenging task of extracting episodes and standing them on their own feet. Many of the selections in this volume are excerpts from novels; they are samples, crosscuts, call them what you will. I have in many cases chosen the very opening of a novel, where the scene is set and the wheels first begin to turn, because, as also with non-spy novels, the opening scene is usually one on which the author has lavished a great portion of care and love. I have in most cases avoided using the climaxes, endings, and dénouements of books, as being perhaps most unfair to their authors. Also there is usually too much to explain to the reader before he can get his teeth into it. The major exception is the piece I chose from *From Russia with Love,* because it is such a good and typically James Bond scene.

I would like to thank the many persons who have been helpful in assembling this volume: Howard Roman, for his literary assistance and advice, Walter Pforzheimer for again making the material of his extensive library available to me, Ladislas Farago, Burke Wilkinson and Robert Deindorfer, for pointing out certain stories to me with which I was previously unacquainted, Cass Canfield and Mrs. Margaret Butterfield of Harper & Row and Kenneth Giniger of The K. S. Giniger Co. for their editorial and moral support. And without the constant and loyal efforts of my secretary, Marjorie Cowan Miduch, this volume could hardly have come into being.

ALLEN DULLES

1. *Told As It Was*

"Truth is stranger than fiction" is a saying that could have been invented by someone who was thinking of the world of espionage. If the recent cases of the British traitor and spy Kim Philby and the Soviet intelligence officer Penkovskiy had first been thought up by an imaginative author as works of fiction, many a publisher might have rejected them as improbable and too great a strain on the credulity of the reader.

Certainly no one has concocted any spy tales as daring, spine-chilling, and complex in both plot and psychology as the many major spy cases which have been revealed to the public in the years since World War II—those of Klaus Fuchs, Guy Burgess and Donald Maclean, Otto John, George Blake, to name only a few. It is no wonder, then, that certain authors have drawn upon actual cases such as these instead of inventing characters and plots out of whole cloth.

This is not a new development. One of the first American novels, James Fenimore Cooper's *The Spy* (1821), was based on a story Cooper heard from John Jay, some forty years after the American Revolution, about a spy of George Washington's. The exploits of Civil War spies (often ladies of the Confederacy) gave rise to a crop of spy romances after that war was over. Following both World Wars, a large number of men and women who actually took part in intelligence operations in those wars— some of them authors by trade—produced a flood of fiction based

1

on personal experience. The British author Bernard Newman, who was himself a British spy in Ludendorff's headquarters, gathered enough material during World War I to turn out spy tales for the next twenty years.

There is, of course, a difference between the work of the author who was on the scene and the one who was not. The former is likely to stick to the facts; the latter may feel freer to tamper with them. One has the impression that Somerset Maugham's *Ashenden* stories are very close to the actual events that inspired them. For Joseph Conrad or Rebecca West, a spy story which they heard or read about merely served to fire their imaginations, and they often transformed the crass happenings into works of art.

It is likely, too, that many of the lesser works of fiction based on actual happenings are in the form of fiction rather than factual reporting simply because the author was unable to get his hands on the full story and used his imagination to supply what was missing.

ROBERT ASPREY

▼

1 The Recruitment of the Archtraitor

This book by Captain Robert Asprey, a former American Marine officer turned author, about Colonel Alfred Redl, a notorious Austrian double agent before World War I, stays very close to the historical facts and is based on documentary research, much of it dug up for the first time in the Vienna state archives by Captain Asprey. Many would contend that his book is not a novel at all, yet it certainly departs from being a biography and becomes imaginative literature when Asprey ventures to create episodes for which there is no documentary evidence, as he does in the excerpt which follows.

This describes the recruitment of Redl in 1902 by the Russian Military Intelligence. The means used by the Russians to exert pressure on Redl are historically accurate. At the time, Redl was a captain occupying a very high post in the Imperial Austro-Hungarian Military Intelligence Service. In the years that followed, he was promoted to colonel and became the chief of the service. It was not until 1913, ten years after the recruitment Asprey reconstructs for us, that Redl's infamous treachery was uncovered. Its disclosure caused, naturally enough, a nationwide scandal at the time and is described in the latter part of Asprey's book.

The most fascinating part of Redl's performance, of which we are given an inkling in the last pages of the present excerpt, was the arrangement he made with his Russian masters for swapping spies. Redl, who was later in charge of Austrian counterintelligence in Prague, had occasionally to catch a Russian agent in order to look efficient. However, it was not necessary for him to go

---

FROM *The Panther's Feast.*

3

find the agents, although he would make it look as though he had. The Russians served agents up to him in return for his doing the same favor for them. The greatest damage Redl did, however, was in handing over Austrian General Staff plans, to which he had access, to the Russians—and it was for this that the Russians prized his services. Thanks to Redl's perfidy and the fact that the Austrians did not revise their staff plans before the outbreak of World War I, thousands of Austrian lives were lost on the battlefield.

The "Katrina" mentioned at the opening of the excerpt is a female Russian agent who managed to become friendly with Redl in the preliminary Russian attempt to compromise him. She did not get very far, for reasons which are later made abundantly clear.

The reader will note how, with great literary skill, the author makes the scene where Redl is recruited on the hills outside Vienna reminiscent of a famous Biblical setting in which the Devil, pointing to the countryside below and the world, offers his prime temptation.

The index finger of Major Batjuschin's hand probed deep in his black beard for an irritant whisker. On his desk was a vodka bottle and beside it a half-filled glass. Immediately before him lay an opened correspondence folder which now and again his fist struck. His small eyes had reddened from the vodka; when they glared at the folder they looked unusually piggish.

Sitting across from him was a man also holding a glass of vodka which he had not touched. The most striking characteristic of this man was his anonymity. Nothing about him—not his skin, his face, his build, his clothing—suggested any impression contrary to that of the opaqueness at once offered by his eyes. Fluent in a dozen languages, this man rarely spoke. When he did, his native tongue carried the same nondescript accent that characterized his total being. He was an undercover agent. His name was Pratt. He was one of the finest intelligence agents in the world.

For some minutes the most noticeable sound in the room had been Major Batjuschin's sharp breaths, the aftermath of a furious outburst. Pratt, discerning that his employer was again under control, broke the silence.

"You imply, then, that they have doubled her?"

"No," Major Batjuschin snapped. "I admit it is possible because in this business anything is possible. I do not really think it is that bad, not yet. But she has failed. That is bad." He picked up the correspondence folder and slammed it to the desk. "Oh, yes, he buys her expensive gifts, he entertains her. She learns something: he is in the Intelligence Bureau, he evidently has been given the Counterintelligence Section, he travels a great deal. He is popular in the General Staff: he was elected a member of the Cavalry Fund last January, Baron von Giesl is friendly with him, he is often seen with young officers. Bah! This is not the old Katrina. Where is she who snaps her fingers and the man falls cringing in his passion for her? There is none of that here"— he tapped the folder—"here in this mess of words." Major Batjuschin snatched at his glass, gulped its contents, coughed and leaned back in his chair. "This Redl may become a menace. He has already inconvenienced my operations in Galicia; new border patrols, more careful scrutiny of documents, increased security in military installations. He is probably behind the arrest of Alexander von Carina. He may arrest more of my agents. I do not like it. This man could embarrass me. I will not—"

He was interrupted by a knock on the door. "What is it?" he called gruffly.

Lieutenant Pawlow walked to him with a large envelope. "I think the Major will find everything in order."

When Pawlow left the room, Batjuschin opened the envelope. As he spoke, he passed separate items across the desk to Pratt. "Here are your identity papers. Here is money—you can draw more from Colonel de Roop in our Vienna Embassy if you need it. But only in an emergency—I would prefer he does not learn you are in Vienna. Here is what we know about Redl. Here are photographs of him. The first thing I want you to do is to learn if Katrina is crossing me. If she is she will be dead in a week. Then get to Redl. I don't know what is going on but my nose tells me something is peculiar." Major Batjuschin stood up. "I want Redl. I am willing to pay for him. I would prefer him alive." His tiny red eyes flicked over the formless face. "If necessary, I will take him dead."

Pratt rose, folded the papers and put them in his pocket. In his flat voice, he said, "I shall get him for you—one way or the other."

As instructed by the writer of the anonymous letter, Alfred Redl left the fiacre in Mödling, walked two blocks along the main road leading up the valley, turned off on a smaller road that soon dwindled to a path winding to the Vienna hills. He was dressed in civilian clothes. Against the cold air he wore a heavy overcoat with fur collar, and to counter the frostslip of the steep slope he carried a heavy walking stick. Halfway up the path at a junction he stopped, removed a glove, pulled a piece of paper from his pocket. It was the letter he had received the previous evening—on the back of it was a crude map. He oriented himself, chose the path to the right and began climbing. He was breathing heavily. He was frightened.

The trees thinned out along the new path and he could hear the gentle whine of wind through their barren trunks. He stopped at the next junction, referred quickly to the map, chose one of four paths before him and began a fresh ascent. He thought: This person is no amateur; he is up there watching me, watching to see if I am followed. The trees were very thin now and he could see a hundred yards in any direction through their winter nakedness. Bending into the wind he walked until a hundred yards farther he reached a small plateau, a height that commanded the local terrain. In the center of the plateau was an iron cross. A man stood beside it.

Alfred walked across the flat until he faced the man. The man wore a black overcoat with its collar turned up and a hat pulled low over his face. Only the redness of cold distinguished the few flaccid features that showed, but they were enough to jar Redl's memory to recognition. "Herr Diplomat Ingenieur Kaufmann," he accused.

"Yes, that name is sufficient," Pratt said. He looked swiftly down the slopes. "No one is following you, Captain Redl?"

"No one is following me, but if I should not return within—"

"You will return, my dear Captain. I mean no harm."

"What do you want, Kaufmann?"

The man pointed northeast to the Kahlenberg, then to the spire of St. Stephen's Cathedral rising like a needle from the inner city of Vienna. He indicated the expanse by slicing a flat hand through the air, then he cupped this hand and held it to Redl. "I want to give you all that, Redl. Everything you can see and much more besides."

"What do you want, Kaufmann?"

"An arrangement, Redl. You have debts, I believe?"

"Of course," Alfred snapped. "A few—nothing exceptional."

The man pulled a paper from his coat and handed it to Redl. "Surely the General Staff would consider your debts exceptional. If you were to devote your salary for the next three years to their payment, you would still owe considerable money. And my list is far from being complete, I am sure."

Alfred shrugged. "I have means," he said. "An inheritance is due. . . ."

"You have nothing, Redl. Your father died all but a pauper. Your brothers: a minor civil servant, an army officer; your sisters teaching school in Galicia; your mother dying in a sanitarium, a free one at that."

Without changing expression Alfred said, "General Beck would understand. He expects his officers to live well."

"That may be so," Pratt said. He handed Alfred a second sheaf of papers. "Perhaps the Chief of the General Staff would understand the major reason for your debts?"

Alfred's mouth contracted as he glanced through the pages. "You are very thorough, Herr Kaufmann," he said.

"I am paid to be thorough, Captain Redl. Shall we talk business?"

"Apparently we must," Alfred said. "How much are you asking for these papers?"

"Only your future co-operation—I am prepared to pay for that in cash as well."

"Could cash not otherwise dispose of this tedious matter?"

"It could," the man said easily, "if you had enough money."

"How much would that be?"

Pratt laughed a short, hard sound. "More than you have ever seen, Redl. More than you ever will see. Let me tell you something. You are new in this business of espionage but I am not. Oh, you are clever, you have already worried some important persons. Still, you are new, you lack experience, particularly in dealing with professionals. There are not many of us. I am one."

"Who are you, Kaufmann?"

"I do not know myself, Redl. Sometimes I think I am everyone, sometimes no one. To your hotel clerk, I am Kaufmann, an engineer from Potsdam who, not liking street noises, preferred rooms on the third floor which happen to be directly under your apartment. To one of your friends, never mind who, I am Schmidt, a detective from the State Police. To the innkeeper in St. Veit I am a harmless Munich Bürger who just happens to sit with his wine where he can observe who enters and leaves that interesting little villa run by your friend, Herr Rudolf Reiner. To some in Paris I am Guillard, an Alsatian winegrower; to those in Belgrade I am a Prague publisher with Slav sympathies; in Warsaw, I am Pratt, an Estonian. That last is the most accurate, but the name is wrong. I was raised in an orphanage—my real name was lost."

"You have a price?"

"Yes, I have a price. Every man has a price. But I have contracted already for this job. A good professional, Redl, will never double . . . and live to enjoy it."

"I am sorry to hear that," Alfred said. He had removed his glove. With his free hand he scratched an eye, then began lowering the hand casually toward his overcoat pocket. Pratt's rapid words halted the movement. "I am holding a pistol aimed at your stomach, Redl. Now give me your weapon, butt first." He took the revolver. "You can't buy me and you can't kill me, so perhaps you are ready to listen to me." He pulled an envelope from an inside pocket. "Here are ten thousand crowns which I shall pay you for the plans of three fortresses: Cracow, Halicz and Zaleszczyki—the plans that Alexander Carina had been told to secure. Do not try a bluff—your reports will be compared with information already in our files."

"In whose files?"

"Russian Army Intelligence," Pratt said. "My employer is Major Batjuschin, Chief of Espionage Center West, Headquarters, Warsaw. You will find Batjuschin a generous man. He wants information, he will pay for it. He is also a dangerous man to cross."

"If I refuse your Major Batjuschin?"

"I will mail a report directly to General Beck."

"He would not believe it," Alfred said.

"But he would be forced to investigate. An investigation would prove that you have male lovers."

"Do you think they would admit it, ruin their own careers?"

"A few would, to save themselves. Your servant, Joseph, has no career to ruin. An ignorant, eighteen-year-old peasant. To keep from going to jail during the Carina investigation, he accommodated himself to your pleasure. To keep from going to jail during the Redl investigation, he would accommodate himself to another's pleasure. He would talk—that peculiar habit of yours, Redl, the one Joseph does not like, transvestitism I believe it is called."

Alfred flinched. "Did Joseph tell—"

"No, Redl, I have never spoken to Joseph. When you return to your apartment, look behind the stove in your bedroom. Look on the floor under the porcelain connection to the chimney. There you will find my ear—a piece of pipe that leads to my own sitting room. I have recorded your interesting conversations, Redl, both with Joseph and others."

Redl's tongue wet his lips. "I could go to the Chief myself," he said. "I would tell him everything. To avoid a scandal I would be allowed to resign without trial. I would remain a free man."

Pratt removed a flask from his pocket. He drank from it and handed it to Redl. "A free man, Redl? A free man has never lived on this earth. Even birth carries its basic obligations. We must eat, sleep,

be sheltered—all so that we may grow to harbor other more complicated desires within our minds, desires which in turn enchain us in
pursuance of their fulfillment. Not being a free man, Redl, you cannot
remain a free man. If your Chief were especially kind, if instead of a
choice between a pistol or a trial he gave you your liberty, you could
go on as you have been until now seeking comfort, fame, success. But
where would you find it? If you were to remain in the Empire, you
would find nothing because you would be a social pariah. Where
would you go, where could you go? England, America, South
America? You do not know the languages. You are thirty-seven years
old, you are trained only for the military. What would you do?"

Alfred stared at the trees that lined the slopes like so many
thousand soldiers standing stupidly at attention. "I do not know," he
said. "I do not know what I would do."

"Don't you understand the dirty trick society has played on you,
Redl? What do you owe it, what do I owe it, this nebulous mass of
hypocrisy that would dance us like on the strings of its precious will?
Duty, honor, loyalty, flag, country—bah! Concepts as empty as the
consciences of those who created them, words used by the few to
exploit the many, words to gain and hold and wield the power denied
to us by poor birth. Do you think I care if you are homosexual? Do you
think I care if you dress Joseph like a woman and make love to him?
Do you think I stand here to trap you like some forlorn animal?
Society has trapped you, Alfred Redl. I am offering you escape."

Alfred turned from the man. He looked at the gray sky, the trees
massed like regiments waiting for a final order on a formal battlefield.
"I must think," he said. "I must have time to think."

"There is no time," Pratt said. "There is only this way out. Take it,
Redl. Take the money, the power I am offering you. It is your only
hope, Redl."

Alfred turned slowly until he was facing Pratt. "Give me the
envelope," he said. "I shall get you the plans."

Pratt handed him the envelope along with a small piece of paper.
"Meet me at this address, the day after tomorrow. Four P.M. sharp. I
will take the night train to Warsaw." . . .

Alfred sat in his office in the Bureau, his brow furrowed in concentration. Any notion that he may have held about the simplicity of
contracting with the devil had soon been dispelled by the demands
levied on him by Batjuschin. And then the courier last night—Batjuschin wants this, Batjuschin wants that, Batjuschin is very interested in
your mobilization plans. Mobilization plans! The most carefully

guarded secret in the General Staff. Did Batjuschin think that he had this kind of information at his finger tips? He of all people should know that time was needed, that haste could only mean exposure.

Idly fingering his mustache, Alfred tried to forget the unpleasant interview of the previous evening. His eye fell on the Carina file that he had just been discussing with Colonel von Giesl. "I do hope we get a conviction," the old man had said, "I would like to teach that fellow in Warsaw a lesson—you know, the one you say is behind this case." "Major ˙Batjuschin, sir?" "Yes, that fellow, Batjuschin—whoever the devil he is." Who is Batjuschin? . . . Alfred's error suddenly leaped at him: he had allowed the shock of his exposure to jar him from a logical course, to mislead him into regarding Batjuschin as some kind of inhuman behemoth, omnipotent in this world. And all the time Batjuschin was nothing but another man, albeit a clever and cunning one, who had concentrated on Redl while Redl had ignored him. Batjuschin was a human being, he must be vulnerable to something. His hands trembling in excitement, Alfred drafted the message that would send his agents in search of the information he so desperately needed. He read over his words, made a few corrections and pressed a button. "Have this coded and sent off immediately," he told his corporal.

It was snowing when he arrived at the estate in the woods outside Kowno. An·armed sentry scrutinized the driver of the sleigh, grunted, then pushed open the wide wooden gate.

"Ah, so it is good," Major Batjuschin said when Captain Redl was ushered into his office. "Come, my dear Captain, sit here before the fire where the Russian cold will vanish in the warmth of my pleasure at seeing you. Vodka? Good. We drink vodka, then tea comes. Tell me now about your trip."

While Alfred sketched his recent movements, he studied the small figure pacing back and forth before the fire. Without the fierce black beard, he concluded, Batjuschin would look like a worried farmer.

"So, now," Batjuschin said when Alfred had finished. "I am deeply honored you come so far to see me. Too, I am impressed by your excellent Russian. I see you are a clever man, Captain Redl. I am not surprised—I have followed your career for many years." He refilled their glasses and sat opposite his guest. A note of impatience appeared in his next question: "Tell me, you have brought something for me?"

"I have," Alfred said.

The little eyes narrowed. "What you suggested in your letter? Some papers from your General Staff, perhaps?"

"No, I have brought no documents, Major."

Batjuschin frowned. "Then what is it, what brings you this uncomfortable way at great risk to yourself?"

Alfred smiled. "A greater risk to myself by remaining in Vienna. I have come to see if we could reach an understanding, Major."

"We have an understanding, Redl. You do as I say and we shall—"

"That is a Russian understanding, Batjuschin. If I continue to do as you say, I will be playing your brand of roulette with all chambers loaded."

"If you do not, you will be exposed!"

Alfred bit out his next words: "Then where will you get the important information which you must have?"

"What are you talking about?"

"About a powerful clique in your General Staff in St. Petersburg which would like to see you relieved and sent to Siberia. I have learned that certain of your associates are asking embarrassing questions, for example what happened to fifty thousand rubles that you claim to have paid the Bohemian-Russian Cultural Society in Prague."

"I paid it," Batjuschin growled.

"Perhaps your Chief believes that," Alfred said, "but I do not. I penetrated that organization six months ago. I know everything about it, including your payment of only ten thousand rubles."

Major Batjuschin stared at his guest. "You are a clever man, Redl. You would not be so stupid as to try to blackmail me?"

"I am in no position to blackmail you. I am trying to save both of us, if you will let me. The situation is obvious: unless you offer your superiors a startling espionage coup you will be finished. I suppose that is the reason you are putting so much pressure on me right now. Is that correct?"

"If it is?"

"Then you would do well to hear me out. I cannot deliver our mobilization plans to you. My Chief has never mentioned them to me, much less discussed them with me. He will in time, of that I am quite certain. In the interim I can provide information that would prove a sop to your General Staff."

Interest flickered across Batjuschin's pinched face. "And what is that?"

"The name of one of my informants. He is a senior officer in the Imperial Russian General Staff!"

"Who is he?"

Alfred laughed. "It is not quite so easy, my dear Major. Our present situation calls for what I have been taught is a Russian characteristic: patience."

"Go on, go on," Batjuschin said.

"You have ordered me to deliver the plans of the fortress at Przemysl. To avoid raising suspicion, I must have a reason for personal investigation of this fortress just as the Carina case allowed access to the other fortresses. You could provide that reason."

"I am beginning to understand," Batjuschin said.

Alfred smiled. "You undoubtedly have agents at work in the Przemysl area."

"An exchange of spies," Batjuschin said.

"Precisely. Our reputations profit as a result. No one likes a spy. The man who catches spies is a hero. Decorations, promotions. He will be trusted. Doors, secret doors, will be opened to him. He will learn plans, General Staff plans, Batjuschin. And there is other profit. The funds you normally expend to catch spies will be yours to retain."

Batjuschin licked his lips. "Yours as well."

"Oh, yes, mine as well." Alfred leaned forward in his chair. "My plan will profit us both. But it is a long-range plan. If we hurry, we are ruined."

"That General Staff officer you mention. What is his name?"

Alfred removed a small book and a pencil from his pocket. You will learn that on the day your spy in Przemysl confesses to me."

"You are careful, Captain Redl."

"We have a word in German: *Rückversicherung*. It means 'back insurance.' Do we understand each other, Major?"

Major Batjuschin slapped his palms against his legs. "All right. We understand each other. In Przemysl you will find a master locksmith named Zaleski, Joseph, born 1872, former Austrian subject, now a Russian national. He began working for me six years ago after he contacted our border watch and delivered a marked map of the Przemysl installations to my officer in Kiev, General Staff Captain Tolmaczew. His accomplice is his stepfather, Schuster, Peter, born 1861, Austrian subject. They have reported on roads, railroads, canals, regimental depots, supply centers. . . ."

Soon after tea, Alfred left the estate in the woods. He returned to Lemberg that night.

▼

2 The Defection of Kuznetov

What follows is the opening chapter of Leon Uris's best-seller Topaz, in which he describes the defection of the KGB officer Kuznetov. The information which Kuznetov later gives the Americans sets the rest of the plot in violent motion.

What made the book more than ordinarily interesting, what aroused a furor on both sides of the Atlantic, was the factual information which lay behind it, for it is one of the many novels of espionage based, in part at least, on fact. In the case of Topaz, however, the facts which it dramatized had not previously been aired (most historical spy novels treat of material which is already in the public domain) and a most unusual thing happened. It was the cause rather than the result of a public revelation.

Uris had been acquainted with the former French diplomat Philippe de Vosjoli and had made use in his novel of some stories which de Vosjoli had told him. After the publication of the novel, de Vosjoli wrote, for Life, his own memoir of the events Uris had put into his novel, and anyone who wanted to could compare the two versions. Readers of Topaz who may have thought it was merely a highly contemporary-sounding romance suddenly woke up to the fact that they had been reading about recent historic events of great pith and moment. The rather bold scene showing President Kennedy writing a letter to President de Gaulle, in which, on the basis of Kuznetov's information, the American President warns the French President that one of his closest advisers is in the pay of the KGB, was, according to de Vosjoli's revelations, drawn from history.

Some of the most important information acquired by the

FROM *Topaz*.

Western intelligence services in the post-World War II period,
especially in the counterespionage field, has come from defectors
from the intelligence services of both Soviet Russia and the
Eastern European satellite countries. As the Life *article put it,*
speaking of the defector whom Uris calls Kuznetov: "He killed a
whole generation of KGB men—not physically, but as intelligence
operatives."

The headwaiter approached. "Is one of you gentlemen Mr. Nordstrom?"

"Yes."

"Telephone, sir."

"Excuse me," he said, folding his napkin and following the headwaiter from the terrace into the enormity and plushness of the Wivex. The orchestra played the "Colonel Bogie" march from *The Bridge Over the River Kwai,* and the Danes kept jovial time by clapping in rhythm.

The waiter pointed to a phone booth in the lobby.

"Thank you." Michael closed the door behind him. "Nordstrom," he said.

"My name means nothing to you," a heavily accented Russian voice spoke, "but I know who you are."

"You've got the wrong party."

"You are Michael Nordstrom, the American Chief of ININ, Inter-NATO Intelligence Network. You sign your cables with the code name 'Oscar,' followed by the numerals six, one, two."

"I said you've got the wrong party."

"I have some papers of extreme interest," the voice on the other end persisted. "NATO papers in the four-hundred series. Your contingency plans for a counterattack if the Soviet Union invades through Scandinavia. I have many other papers."

Nordstrom squelched a deep sigh by placing his hand quickly over the mouthpiece. He caught his bearings immediately. "Where are you?"

"I am calling from a phone booth over the Raadhuspladsen."

Nordstrom glanced at his watch. One o'clock. It would take several hours to formulate a plan. "We can set up a meeting for this evening. . . ."

"No," the voice answered sharply. "No. I will be missed. It must be done immediately."

"All right. Glyptoteket Museum in a half-hour. On the third floor there's an exhibit of Degas wire statuettes," Nordstrom instructed.

"I am familiar with it."

"How can you be identified?"

"Under my arm I carry two books, *Laederhalsene* in Danish and *The Rise and Fall of the Third Reich* in English."

"A man named Phil will contact you." Nordstrom hung up.

The first obvious thought that crossed his mind was a rendezvous trap in which the Russians could photograph him contacting a Soviet agent for future blackmail use. He would send his deputy in Denmark, Sid Hendricks, to make the contact, then lead the man to a place which he could cover against being followed or photographed. The pressing time factor annoyed him, but bait or not the Russian's opening gambit was taken.

Michael placed a coin in the phone box and dialed.

"American Embassy."

"Nordstrom. Get the ININ office."

"Mr. Hendricks' office, Miss Cooke speaking."

"Cookie, this is Mike Nordstrom. You're buddies with the manager of the Palace Hotel . . . what's his name?"

"Jes Hansen."

"Get him on the horn and tell him we need a favor. Large suite at the end of a hallway. Something we can block off and cover from all directions."

"How soon?"

"Now. Send four or five of the boys down, tape machine and cameras. I'll meet them there in twenty minutes."

"Got it."

Michael Nordstrom was a bit heftier than he would have liked but he still moved with deftness and grace. He wove his way back to the terrace quickly. A scream shrilled out from the roller coaster. "Sorry, fellows, office wants Sid and me back right away."

The Danish and Norwegian ININ chiefs stood and they all shook hands.

"Have a good trip back to the States," H. P. Sorensen said.

"See you in Oslo, Mike," Per Nosdahl said.

Sid Hendricks reminded Sorensen they had a meeting next day and the two Americans departed.

They got into Sid's car on H. C. Boulevard. "What's up, Mike?"

"Russian. Maybe a defector. Go right away to the Glyptoteket's Degas exhibition on the third floor. He'll be carrying two books, *Laederhalsene*—and, uh, *Rise and Fall*, the Shirer book, in English. Identify yourself as Phil, then have him follow you. Waltz him around the Tivoli a few times to make sure he isn't being tailed by his own people. End up at the Palace Hotel. One of the boys from your office will be waiting and tell you where to take him. If you don't show in an hour, we'll know it was a setup. Check him out carefully as you can."

Sid nodded and got out of the car. Nordstrom watched him cross the avenue. The curtain, a mass of bicycles, closed behind him. Nordstrom emerged from the other side of the car for the short walk to the Palace, then grumbled beneath his breath. This sudden turn of events would force him to cancel a date with a lovely Danish miss.

Fifteen minutes had elapsed when Sid Hendricks entered the block-long red brick building housing a conglomeration of art treasures, sponsored by a Danish brewery.

He paid a krone admission, bought a catalogue, then made directly up a long flight of stairs on the right side of the main lobby.

The room was empty. Hendricks studied it for unwanted guests but could spot none. He thumbed through the catalogue, then moved around the dozens of Degas wire studies of horses and ballet dancers, each an experiment to capture phases of motion. He stopped before a glass case and looked long at a particularly magnificent piece, a rearing horse.

"Unfortunately, we do not see much Degas in the Soviet Union."

Hendricks squinted to try to catch in the glass the reflection of the man who had slipped up behind him, but all he could make out was a transparent disfiguration.

"A few pieces in the Pushkin Museum in Moscow," the Russian accent labored, "and somewhat better in the Hermitage, but I do not get to Leningrad often."

Hendricks turned the page in the catalogue. "Never been there," he answered, keeping his eyes straight ahead.

"I have. I'd like to leave."

"I don't think we've met."

"Not formally. You are Sidney Hendricks, in charge of the American ININ Division in Denmark."

"Anyone can get that information out of the Embassy Directory."

"Then, how about this information? Your boss, Michael Nordstrom, is in Copenhagen to meet the Danish and Norwegian ININ counterparts. Nosdahl and Sorensen, to discuss expansion of an espionage ring of Scandinavian students studying in the Soviet Union."

With that, Sid Hendricks turned and faced his adversary.

The two stipulated books nestled tightly under the arm of a man of shorter than average height. Russians look like Russians, Hendricks thought. High forehead, suffering brown eyes of a tortured intellectual, uneven haircut, prominent cheekbones, knobby fingers. His suit showed Western styling but was sloppily worn.

"Follow me and keep a hundred-foot interval."

Hendricks passed from the room through a group of incoming art students and their instructor.

On the street he waited on the corner of Tietgensgade until the Russian emerged from the museum, then crossed to the Tivoli Gardens and paid an admission into the Dansetten.

Cha-cha-cha music favored the midafternoon dancers. Sid sighted in on a pair of unescorted girls sitting hopefully in a corner, and invited one to dance. His Cha-cha-cha left much to be desired but it did give him a total vantage. The Russian entered, watched, did not appear to have followers.

Hendricks abruptly left the astonished girl and plunged into the maze of zigzag paths, hawkers, strollers, the labyrinth of glass buildings, the blaze of flowers, the multitude of restaurants, exhibits, fun and amusement booths, the fairyland that made up the wonderment of Tivoli.

Sid Hendricks led the Russian in circles. Along the artificial boat lake he doubled back so that he walked past his pursuer, then made up the steps of the multitiered Chinese pagoda. From here he could look down and study all the activity below. Only the single Russian clung to his trail.

He was now satisfied that the Russian was not being followed, and he passed from the Tivoli, crossing the teeming Raadhuspladsen filled with the usual complement of pigeons that inhabit city-hall squares throughout the world.

His deputy, Dick Stebner, waited in the lobby of the Palace Hotel. Without further word, the three walked the stairs to the third floor. The long corridor was covered by Hendricks' men. Stebner made down the carpeted hall to an end suite, opened the door and the three of them entered.

Harry Bartlett, another deputy, waited by the false fireplace. The Russian stood in the center of the room. The lock clicked behind him.

"Who are you? What do you want?" Bartlett asked.

"I want to see Nordstrom," the Russian retorted. "You are not Nordstrom. You are one of the ININ men in Hendricks' office."

The bedroom door opened slowly. Michael Nordstrom entered. His bulk made the Russian seem even smaller. "Yes," the latter whispered, "you are the one I wish to see."

"Shoot."

"Shoot?"

"Who are you? What do you want?"

The Russian studied Stebner and Hendricks at the door and the other one, Bartlett. "My compliments to you, Nordstrom. You are very good. You did this quickly and your Hendricks is clever. Do you have a cigarette?"

Michael cupped his hands to hold the flame and his eyes met the Russian's. The man was frightened despite his professional poise. He sucked deeply on the cigarette as though calling on a friend and he licked his lips in a gesture of fear.

"I am Boris Kuznetov," he said, "chief of a division of KGB. I wish to defect."

"Why?"

"I have reason to suspect I am going to be liquidated."

"What reasons?"

"Two close comrades in KGB who shared my views have been purged recently. I travel in the West often. This time surveillance on me is unusually heavy. And then," he sighed, "a close dear friend told me before I came to Copenhagen that if I have a chance to clear out, I had better make the break."

Kuznetov pulled hard again on the cigarette. He knew the men arrayed before him would naturally suspect he was a plant.

"This friend of yours," Hendricks said, "wasn't it dangerous for him to warn you?"

"It makes no difference if you are a Russian or an American, Mr. Hendricks. Our profession is cruel, yet . . . they cannot take from us all that is human. Humans, in the end, are compassionate. Someday you may need a friend. Someday a friend will need you. Do you understand?"

"If you are under such tight watch," Nordstrom challenged, "how did you cut yourself loose just now?"

"I am in Copenhagen with my wife and daughter. I left them at the restaurant. As long as they have guards on my family they know I will return, so it is normal for me to be away for a few hours, perhaps to make an intelligence contact, perhaps to shop, perhaps even to visit a woman. But I am a devoted family man and I always come back."

"How did you know I would be at the Wivex Restaurant?"

"Because of your basic intelligence attitude. We Russians hide our intelligence people and never let it be known who they are. You Americans advertise who is CIA, who is ININ, on the theory that people will come to you with informatiom. In this case, your theory works. It is not secret you are in Copenhagen. You always eat at Wivex or Langelinie near the Little Mermaid. You like Danish seafood. It is not hard to find out. Today I checked your reservation at Wivex and so I ate at Seven Nations just over the square."

"You said you carried documents."

"Yes. They are hidden in Copenhagen. I will tell you where they are when we make our agreement."

"All right, Kuznetov. I'm impressed. We'll get back to you in twenty-four hours."

"No!"

"What do you mean?"

The Russian's breath quickened. Fright, real or played, was in him. "I am afraid now to return to my embassy. We must do it right away . . . today, and my wife and daughter must come with me."

Kuznetov studied the skeptical American eyes. They all glowered in suspicion at the man who called himself Kuznetov, watched him fidget and breathe deeply over and over. The clock from the city hall tolled the hour, massively.

"How long can you stay out now?" Mike Nordstrom asked.

"A few more hours."

"Get back to your wife and daughter, then go shopping or do the Tivoli for a few hours. I'm going to make a try at putting it together. Do you know Den Permanente?"

"Yes. The building that houses the permanent exhibits of Danish arts and crafts."

"It closes at five-thirty. Be there at the counter of the silversmith, Hans Hansen. It's near the main door. Now, take a good look at these three gentlemen. One of them will be standing by to lead you to a waiting car."

"You must not fail!"

"There's a fifty-fifty chance we can do it."

"My guards . . ."

"We'll handle them."

The Russian called Kuznetov walked slowly to a seat, sank into it, held his face in his hands and sobbed.

Nordstrom dispatched Stebner and another deputy to tail the Russian, then sped back to the embassy with the rest of his people, locking the ININ offices behind them.

TOP SECRET EYES ONLY TO SAILBOAT 606. CONTACT MADE COPENHAGEN WITH BORIS KUZNETOV. CLAIMS TO BE KGB DIVISION CHIEF. DESIRES TO DEFECT WITH FAMILY. PLANS UNDER WAY. I WILL TAKE FULL RESPONSIBILITY. NEED GREEN LIGHT IMMEDIATELY OR NO GO. OSCAR 612.

Coats off, ties open, sleeves rolled, Michael Nordstrom and his men plunged into formulating a quick but foolproof plan. They set into motion the obtaining of cars without diplomatic plates, finding a hideaway on the northern coast, getting a light plane on stand-by and flying Nordstrom's own plane out of Denmark to a German airfield. Individual assignments were passed out and rehashed. The minutes ticked off too quickly, and as the hour neared five o'clock, ashtrays brimmed and the tension rose to fever pitch.

The phone rang.

"Mr. Hendricks' office. Miss Cooke speaking."

"Cookie, this is Stebner. Boss there?"

She handed the phone to Michael. "Nordstrom."

"Stebner. Do we go?"

"No word back from Washington yet. If I don't hear in ten minutes, we cancel. What's your picture?"

"He just entered Den Permanente with his wife and daughter. We've spotted four guards working in two pairs."

"Did the guards go inside the building?"

"They sure did."

"Beautiful. I'm sending a half-dozen of the fellows down now. Stake them out around the entrance. If we get a cable to go, watch for Bartlett driving a blue 1960 four-door Ford sedan with German plates. You make the hookup with Kuznetov and get in with him."

"Got it."

Nordstrom set the phone down and sent the men off to cover the Den Permanente entrance. He and Miss Cooke waited alone in the office. They both lit cigarettes. He paced. She tapped her long-nailed fingers on the desk. All around Copenhagen, bells rang out the hour of five.

"I guess we're out of business," Nordstrom mumbled.

Sid Hendricks tore in from the code room and set the cable before his boss.

TOP SECRET TO OSCAR 612. GREEN LIGHT. SAILBOAT 606.

Den Permanente houses the works of Danish artisans from crystal and silver to modern teak furniture and wild patterns in fabrics. Like Denmark itself, the place was not large, but its wares were magnificent.

Near the building, Stebner and a half-dozen ININ agents waited for Bartlett and the blue Ford. Stebner took a position so that he could clearly see Boris Kuznetov with his wife and daughter. They came down from the second floor. Mrs. Kuznetov read the time from a lavaliere watch. Stebner wondered why her husband loved her so. She was a drab and dumpy woman. The daughter, he estimated, was about twenty. A fine figure, but it ended right there. Severe hairdo, no make-up, flat shoes.

Stebner glanced over to the first set of guards. He was positive of them because he knew that one was an Assistant Resident of the Soviet Embassy. This pair lolled about a table filled with carved wooden figurines of comic Vikings, those monkeys who hang arm to leg in a chain, and several families of teakwood ducks.

The second set of guards was a pair of women hovering over a fabric counter. They used females, no doubt, to be able to keep tabs on the Kuznetov women, even in the public toilets. The Russian women stuck out like a pair of sore thumbs among the lovely Danish creatures around them.

Boris Kuznetov pointed to the display counter of the silversmith, Hans Hansen, and they walked toward it, containing their tensions admirably.

Down the block, a blue Ford turned the corner.

The ININ agents closed in on the entrance as the car moved into the curb lane and inched through the ever-present sea of bicycle riders.

Now it was halfway down the block.

In the building, the five-thirty closing bell rang.

Kuznetov looked desperately toward the door.

Stebner took a step inside and nodded. The Russian offered his arm to his wife and daughter, took the few steps outside quickly.

The guards dropped the merchandise they were fingering and followed.

Stebner slammed the doors of Den Permanente in their faces, shoved Kuznetov and his family into the rear of the blue Ford and got into the front beside Bartlett.

Kuznetov's guards flung the doors of Den Permanente open and rushed to the sidewalk, only to collide with an ININ man on a bicycle who rode into them. Everyone sprawled to the ground, and as they scrambled to their feet the other ININ agents jostled and bumped them creating an instant of confusion, just long enough for the car to turn the corner and go out of sight.

It sped north out of Copenhagen along the coastal road with the Kuznetovs crouched in the back. Beyond the suburb, Bartlett turned the Ford off the highway and onto the pier at Taarbaek to switch cars.

Nordstrom and Hendricks were waiting in the front seat of a Mercedes. Stebner transferred the Kuznetovs and Bartlett returned toward Copenhagen again.

Nordstrom turned to the shaken family. "Everything's going to be all right," he soothed. "Try to keep calm."

Kuznetov nodded that he understood.

"You owe me something. Some documents."

Kuznetov took a baggage claim check from his wallet. "At the luggage storage at the main railroad station."

The sharp ring of the phone startled them all.

"Hello."

"Sam?"

"Speaking."

"This is George. Cessna 310 is at the Elsinore Airport, cleared, warmed up and ready to go."

"We're on the way."

The flight was choppy. The damnable northern European weather moved in and flung them around. Tamara Kuznetov became sick, adding to everyone's discomfort in the small craft.

It turned dark and the weather had fallen nearly to the ground as they approached the British air base at Celle, in northern Germany.

From the Ground Controlled Approach shack on the strip, the voice of a British airman talked them down through the clouds and cross winds.

"Flaps down . . . glide . . ." The lights of the field burst through the fog. A sigh of relief as the little bird touched down. A FOLLOW ME jeep led the Cessna back out to the end of the strip where Nordstrom's plane with Department of the Interior markings was revved up and waiting.

In moments, his Convair was airborne, pushing through the turbulence toward the Atlantic . . . America . . . and Andrews Air Force Base.

▼

3 Happy, the Joe

George Howe was a former OSS officer attached to the American Seventh Army in Alsace during that last winter of World War II when the final push into the heartland of Germany was under way. In his novel Call It Treason, *he gives an authentic picture of an OSS unit whose job it was to locate and recruit German prisoners of war who would be willing to parachute into Germany behind the lines for the purpose of gathering military information.*

The larger part of the book is devoted to the actual mission of Karl Maurer, whose code name is Happy. It is undoubtedly a composite of much that really happened to certain such agents, plus a good deal that was invented. In the excerpt I have chosen, from an earlier part of the book, the picture of the recruitment and preliminary handling of the new agent is quite true to life, and its value lies almost entirely in its portrayal of the psychology of the recruiter and his recruit. A "Joe" was wartime intelligence slang for an agent and a "Joe-house" was where the agents were put up while in training. At the beginning of the excerpt, the Army medic Dr. Brophy, to whom the German prisoner of war Maurer has been assigned as an orderly, suggests to the intelligence unit that Maurer might be good agent material.

I have the smartest kid working for me, smarter than you or any-one else I've seen since I left Hartford, and he wants to end the war. I don't want to lose him, but if he's in your line maybe I'd better give him up and find another orderly."

Pete nodded. The recruits always wanted to end the war—who

FROM *Call It Treason.*

didn't—whatever their real motives might be, greed or fun or faith. He pushed the Camels toward Brophy. "What's his name?"

"Karl Maurer."

"Oh, yeah, the Luftwaffe corporal who serenaded the MPs. I thought he must be smart. The one the OD called Happy."

"It's a good word for him." Brophy nodded. "Fred told me about him. I should have got around to him before. If you think you can spare him, we might have a job for him. But don't ask what kind of job, and if you send him in he can't go back even if we don't take him."

"You'll take him all right, and a little appreciation to me, please, for being willing to give up my prize assistant."

"Gee, thanks. Now you won't have so much time to write V-mail to your girl in Hartford. Such self-sacrifice deserves at least a Silver Star. I'll mention it to the general next time he comes to call. Greater love than this hath no man."

Brophy brought him into Pete's office the next afternoon at closing time, so as to make the visit seem casual, then tactfully disappeared, leaving the corporal standing awkwardly among the half-dozen who had heard the rumor there might be a new German Joe. He looked around the room shyly, like a schoolboy, but proudly, like a soldier of the Wehrmacht in the propaganda books.

"Sit down, Corporal," Pete said. "You needn't be bashful with us. I want you to feel you are among friends."

He spoke in German. The corporal sat down, not to make himself comfortable but to obey an order. He sat upright, with his hands on his knees. He looked respectful and attentive and alert, wary even. They could tell he was nervous, for his knuckles were whiter than they should have been. Who wouldn't be nervous? He declined Pete's offer of a cigarette. He wanted it, for even the cadre didn't get much tobacco, and ordinary PWs got none. But he wasn't ready yet to accept a favor. He looked from one to the other of them like a kid waiting for the hard question in an exam. Pete blew smoke rings from his own cigarette.

"Now don't tell me why you want to work for us, Corporal, if you don't choose to. I have no right to ask"—and indeed this was the first time he had ever even wondered—"but you can tell me if you feel like it."

Corporal Maurer shut his eyes and frowned. "I want to work for freedom, sir," he said, "that's all. *Für die Freiheit.*"

There was an awkward pause. Freedom was a word used in orders of the day, and sometimes in the editorials of *Stars & Stripes*. There is a soldier's vocabulary at each extreme: the monosyllables he speaks but never writes, and the long words he reads but never utters. "Freedom," dropped into that barred prison room, was as shocking as smut in a parlor, and it was an American who blushed.

The boy opened his eyes and ended the pause himself. "I don't want to pull a gun, though I suppose it might be necessary for my own safety sometimes."

Pete smiled. "It might, but we wouldn't ask you to go out of your way for sabotage or assassination. We're not gunmen ourselves. Just information."

"It sounds worse, Captain," he smiled back, "when you word it that way than when Fritz Gruber sits at the controls of our Vierling. Before I was captured I kept thinking how little he understood what he shot at. Since I was captured I have been thinking that most of your troops, if you will excuse me, know too little about us. Only what you hear from Doctor Goebbels. He is not a medical doctor."

"You see," someone whispered from the shadows, "he wants to educate us. That's always the way with amateurs."

"You know, I suppose," Pete suggested, "that you would be a traitor to your own country?"

"Excuse me, Herr Kapitän," he broke out, "I do not agree. My father would not agree. I should be more loyal to Germany than Doctor Goebbels has been."

"Perhaps not," Pete said drily, "but the Gestapo would certainly agree, and they are the ones that might count."

"Do you Germans really think you have a chance to win?" boomed the colonel from his dark observant corner of the room. "Psychologically it is an interesting delusion, and a tenacious one."

The boy flushed. He wheeled toward the voice. "I don't know, sir. I don't think so myself, but that has nothing to do with my being here. If He deserved to win, I should still fight for Him, no matter what the chances. As to that, the boys in the battalion think what the officers tell us."

"And the officers?"

"They have to sound confident, sir; it's their business. I have never heard the true opinion of any officer."

"Touché, Colonel," croaked Documents.

"How much pay would you expect, Corporal?" asked Finance.

"I don't expect any, sir. I could not accept it."

"Oh, yes, you have to take some money. The United States government won't hire anyone without pay. Our usual salary is —— dollars a month. That is —— Reichsmarks."*

* Deleted by request.

The boy stared. His corporal's pay was seventy-three Reichsmarks. "We can keep it for you till the end of the war, Corporal," Pete said awkwardly. "It will help you when you get back to medical school."

"He can't have insurance, though," muttered Finance. "It isn't regulation unless they have dependents, and he's too young to be married."

"Pipe down, Shylock," Security whispered to him. "Do you want to make sure of losing a good man?"

After a moment Pete spoke up. "How do we know we can trust you, Corporal? Maybe our colleague Colonel Skorzeny sends you to us."

The corporal spread his hands. It was clear he did not recognize Skorzeny's name, just as few GIs would have recognized the name of 109.

"I don't suppose you can know," he answered, "but you could find out something about my father from the doctors of France and maybe of America. He is known everywhere. He even has a friend who lives in your capital. At least, he was a friend before the war."

They pricked up their ears. All of them had taken their training in Washington and in the woods around it, the same training they were passing on to the Joes.

"I don't know him myself, but I have heard my father speak of him. His name is Doctor Schober. He is not a physican but an economist. I think he works in your State Department."

"And you would be willing to jump into Germany in your own uniform to find out what information we might ask of you?" the colonel badgered him.

"Yes, sir. That is what I came to say."

"And you know you would be shot or hanged if you were caught?" He nodded.

"And you would give away to us the location of your own 852nd Battalion? If we didn't know it already, I mean," he added hastily.

"Yes, sir."

"Knowing that it would be bombed?"

The corporal did not answer, but he nodded, with his eyes on the ground.

"And without pay?"

"I decline to be paid for it," he said harshly. "If you must allot money, keep if for my father so that he can buy equipment for our clinic after the war."

At a nod from the colonel, Pete stood up. "Well, Corporal, write down your father's and Doctor Schober's names and addresses for us here. We will think for a while. Meanwhile, I am afraid we cannot send you back to the dispensary or out into the barracks with the other prisoners. You will have a room of your own for a week, till we decide. And above all, don't speak of this conversation to anyone, understand? I mean not to any American. You won't see any Germans for a while."

"*Zu Befehl*," which means "At your orders."

He stood at the door, ready to be guided out. Pete punched the desk bell for the guardhouse. A sergeant of the guard came in.

"Take this prisoner to the cell on the third floor."

"Yes, sir."

As the door closed on the khaki and the blue-gray, Pete smiled. "There you are at last, Colonel. The Christlike Joe you spoke about the other day. The pure-hearted traitor."

"You needn't laugh," the colonel answered. "I don't expect you know much about music, but Wagner has a phrase that seems to describe this kid. The pure in heart made wise by love."

He hummed the theme from *Parsifal:* "*Durch Mitleid wissend, der reine Thor.*"

"I don't understand you young cynics." He sighed. "There are people who take risks for their beliefs, you know, without thinking of reward or excitement. It isn't stylish, but I hope my own son may have enough honesty—"

"To spy on F.D.R.?"

"Watch your step, Captain!"

"Well," shrugged Pete, "we have certainly picked up the whole range lately, what with a crook like the Tiger and a Tarzan like Paluka, and now this innocent."

Corporal Maurer walked up the three flights of worn granite steps ahead of the American sergeant. Through the window on the landing he could see a thousand compatriots shuffling in the line to the mess shack, tinkling their zinc kits. Supper would probably be not much different from the supper thousands of American PWs were getting at the same time beyond the Rhine, except for real coffee.

The cell itself was built of wattled steel; the two dormers were barred with iron rods. But it had its own stove, with a binful of wood beside it, and a real two-by-six cot covered with United States Army blankets, instead of a roll laid on the stone floor.

"*Das ist prima!*" The corporal laughed to the sergeant.

The sergeant closed the steel door and threw the bolt from outside, then opened the wicket and leaned on the little shelf.

"Don't worry, buddy. Nobody ever stays in this cell very long. You can use the bucket in the corner, but put the lid back. Sorry to speak of it to a guest, but some of your pals in barracks aren't too careful. I'll send you up some chow. But don't expect sympathy from an American KP like you get from me. A new set of Uncle Sam's fatigues, too, so you can get rid of that old fleasack you've been wearing the last few years."

He clanged the wicket shut. His prisoner nodded absently; he was gazing down at the crowd in the compound.

That night the colonel made an entry in his notebook: "No. 7. Subversion NG. Admits fear. Too honest for job? If so, reliable for followup. Query: mental courage vs. physical?"

Corporal Maurer stayed on ice only four days. Security had a German *Who's Who* which told about the doctor and even named his two sons. Someone in Washington got hold of Schober, who had a title something like Special Assistant in the Division of Economic Coordination, and a Canadian wife. The combination sounded reliable. Switzerland confirmed by code cable that the doctor was an anti-Nazi as a German could be and still survive. So his son was in.

Fred spirited him out of the cell the night his clearance came through, with the Luftwaffe uniform in a barracks bag over his shoulder. At night, so there would be no prisoners around to recognize him, and so he could not remember the way from the cage down to the Schloss and the Golden Well. All traffic on the ten-mile convoy route was blacked out. The jeep showed nothing but the little cat's eyes. Even if there had been a moon the firs would have hidden it. The road was full of potholes tailored to remind the spine that the truck, quarter ton, has no springs. Sometimes Fred had to get out and make sure he was really on the road, wondering whether a few lampposts would not have been worth in time and material what they might have given away to snipers and the Luftwaffe. A kilometer ahead of the Schloss he tied a handkerchief over the boy's eyes. He had to guide him like a blind man up the spiral stone stairs to the field office. The Schloss was three hundred years old, but no one had got around to putting a rail on those stairs; they were a hazard in the dark, even with your eyes open and a flashlight in your hand.

He took off the handkerchief and sat the boy on the sofa. The contract was waiting, a contract between Karl Maurer and the Government of the United States of America which WITNESSETH:

that employer shall pay employe the sum of —— dollars* each month while said contract is in force;

* Deleted by request.

that employe shall faithfully perform all duties which may be assigned
to him by the employer;

that employe further agrees a) to subscribe freely and without reservation to any oath of office prescribed by employer and b) to keep forever
secret this employment and all information which he may obtain by reason
thereof; and further that this contract is a voluntary act of employe, undertaken without duress.

"Voluntary." The corporal put his finger on the word, smiling up at
Fred over the schnapps-candle, as if he had scored a point in a close
deal. He affixed his fingerprints to the bottom of the sheet, and they
both signed it. "In the Reich," he laughed, "criminals are fingerprinted,
not soldiers. I guess I am a criminal now."

"Maybe so," said Fred, "but we're calling you Happy from now on,
so that no one need ever know your real name."

He reflected that the officer of the day had chosen the perfect
adjective, for "happy," like the French "exalté," carries just that note of
vision which adds gaiety to faith.

The storekeeper, without curiosity, carried his barracks bag to the
raftered attic where the GIs slept, to hang with the bags of the other
Joes who had joined before. Six of them hung from the collarbeams,
swaying a little when a gust hit the roof. Like Bluebeard's closet. Next
morning he would stencil on the bag the single name "Happy."

Fred locked the contract and the snapshots in the field safe, under
a new manila file headed with the same name. Happy had passed from
the service of the Third Reich to the service of the United States. From
now on, till he was repatriated at the end of the war, nobody who did
not know the combination of that safe would know his name was Karl
Maurer. From now on he was anonymous.

"You will take care of my pictures, please?" He smiled as Fred tied
the handkerchief again. "I shall want them when I come back from my
mission. If I should not come back, tell my father that I volunteered.
You did not force me, as the regime does by threatening one's family."

"Don't worry, kid." Fred patted him on the back. "You'll come
back all right. They always do."

But they didn't, not always.

He followed Fred down the stairs again, blindfolded, his hand on
Fred's shoulder, hugging the wall, and into the jeep. They started the
winding two miles up to the German Joe-house. When they were out
of sight of the Schloss Fred let him take off the blindfold.

"I am not ashamed of signing," he blurted suddenly.

So Fred knew he was, a little. "We couldn't exchange you back to the Luftwaffe now anyway; you'd have to return to the cell and wait a couple of weeks for a labor detail, after all the prisoners now in the cage have been processed. If you want to do that, let me know before we reach the next house. After that it will be too late to change your mind. No more dispensary detail, however you decide. They would not be too easy on you in the road gang either, if they knew you had run out on us."

Happy began counting the alternatives on his fingers, keeping his eyes open for a house. "But it is plenty tough. If He should win, it would be—the way it is, forever, in Germany. He can't win anyway, as the officer in the dark said. Without Him the end will be easier for us. He has done much for Germany, I don't deny, like building the Autobahns, but it is slavery. I can't have anyone think, even in the regime, that I am afraid. You know, don't you, Herr Leutnant, that I am not afraid?"

"Everyone knows you're not afraid; you're braver than I am."

Fred knew he sounded pompous. He knew Happy was not afraid of the Gestapo and still less of the road gang. He was afraid of something in his own mind. He was afraid of the word spy.

BRUCE LANCASTER

▼

4 The Stockings of Major André

Bruce Lancaster has written many historical novels, chiefly about the American past. The Secret Road is about George Washington's intelligence operations during the latter part of the American Revolution. From it, I have chosen an excerpt which depicts a famous pair of related incidents, the arrest of the British spy and go-between Major John André, and the last-minute escape of the traitor General Benedict Arnold.

The Lieutenant Colonel John Jameson who appears in Lancaster's story was in command of the cavalry post at Northcastle, New York, to which André was brought after his capture by a group of militiamen. It is historical fact that on the morning of September 23, 1780, Jameson sent a dispatch to General Washington reporting that a prisoner had just been taken with plans of the West Point fortifications concealed in his stockings and with a pass from General Arnold in the name of John Anderson. Jameson wrote Washington that he was sending him the plans but was sending the prisoner himself to Arnold. Jameson did not yet know that the prisoner was André.

For some unknown reason, Jameson then changed his mind, had Anderson brought back to Northcastle, and instead sent a courier to Arnold to tell him of Anderson's arrest. Lancaster supplies us with certain imaginary events to explain what history has not yet explained; namely, why Jameson recalled his prisoner and did not send him to Arnold. Lancaster invented his hero, Grant Ledyard, though most of his other characters are historical, including Colonel Benjamin Tallmadge, Washington's intelligence chief in the New York area, and the Culpers, a network of efficient spies

---

FROM *The Secret Road.*

working under Tallmadge. It is also historically correct that Arnold's treasonable correspondence with the British, in which he signed himself "Gustavus" or "Mr. Moore," had been intercepted, but until André's capture no one had yet ascertained that the writer of the letters was Arnold.

At the beginning of our excerpt, Grant Ledyard, returning to his post, is riding across the so-called Neutral Ground (Westchester) where American and British partisans roamed at will, since neither party was in control of the area. It was here that André was picked up by Revolutionary militia while making his way back to British headquarters in New York after a secret visit to Benedict Arnold at West Point.

Through the morning hours, Grant waited on the hill above the Tarrytown road. Occasional carts rolled down the highway below him, their dust rising into the clear September air, but except for them, the roads and fields lay empty and silent. At ten o'clock, Grant considered saddling up his horse and riding south in the hope of coming on Tallmadge and his men and putting an end to the interminable waiting. He walked slowly toward his grazing horse, still irresolute.

There was metal gleaming down on the road, the dull sheen of a musket barrel. Grant drew his pistols, made his way quickly but silently down the slope. A tall, bareheaded man was ambling along in the direction of Northcastle, pitted musket slung over his back. He wore a green Hessian coat with faded red facings. Grant glided onto the road, pistols leveled. "Hands up!" he snapped.

The man flung his arms high above his head. "Sure, if it pleasures you, mister," said the man.

"Who are you?" asked Grant quickly.

"John Paulding, mister. Farm near Tarrytown."

"What's your party?"

"The Upper party.* What you think?"

Pistols still level, Grant said, "Got anything to show it?"

"Not with my hands like this."

"A paper?" asked Grant, watching him carefully. "Get it out with one hand. Toss it onto the road."

With wonderful contortions of a long arm, Paulding extracted a soiled paper from his coat and dropped it. Grant picked it up and over the signature of Lieutenant Colonel Jameson read that John Paulding

---

* The revolutionary party.

was a duly enrolled member of the volunteer militia. A brief and unmistakable description of the bearer followed. Grant nodded. "That's all right. Drop your arms. What are you doing in a Hessian coat?"

Paulding looked sadly at him. "I wear what I can find."

"Where have you been?"

"Lot of us have been ranging up the hills these last two nights. The Commander's due back from Hartford any day now. We didn't want no mishaps to him."

"Many of you?"

"I'd say every able-bodied man from here to the Fairfield line. Mister, these hills has been busting with us."

"Under orders?"

"Unofficial as hell."

Grant remembered his feeling during the night that men were moving about him, never close, never seen or heard, a feeling that had persisted in his mind. An unofficial guard of honor for the Commander. He addressed Paulding again. "Did you come across any of our cavalry?"

Paulding shook his head. "The boys said that Benny Tallmadge was out with his iron heads, but I ain't seen 'em."

"If Tallmadge were heading for Northcastle, he'd have to pass along here, wouldn't he?"

"He'd sort of have to, unless he'd struck in way east of here, and that ain't likely," answered Paulding.

"Want to take a scout south for me and see if you find him?"

"Can't hardly," said Paulding. "I'm Northcastle-bound. I got a prisoner to give Jameson there."

Grant stared at him. "You've got a prisoner? For God's sake where?"

Paulding jerked a grimy thumb. "Down the road a piece. Ike van Wart and Dave Williams have got him. Seems his feet hurt, and they stopped to let him dabble 'em in a brook."

"What is he? British or Hessian?"

"Don't rightly know, but mister, has he got pretty clothes! Blue overcoat, claret undercoat. Kind of elegant."

"A civilian? Are you sure you've got the right to hold him?"

"Ample right, mister. With his own breath he told us he held to the Lower party."

"What's his name?"

"Oh, that's all right too. It's writ out pretty. The name's John Anderson."

"I see," said Grant slowly. "John Anderson. Of course." His palms were suddenly moist, and he was conscious of his heart beating rapidly.

"Know him?" asked Paulding in mild surprise.

"I've heard the name," answered Grant, his mind still repeating "Anderson" over and over.

"Look here," said Grant. "You say you're taking him to North-castle? I'll ride on with you. I'll see that you turn your man over to Jameson and get credit for him. My horse is up the hill. I'll bring him down here." He ran up the slope while Paulding sat patiently on a boulder, waiting for his comrades and the prisoner.

Under the pines, Grant adjusted his bridle, tightened the girth and led his mount downward, weaving carefully between tree trunks and boulders. Through the interlaced branches he caught glimpses of the road below him. He was close enough to hear the crunch of boots. A few more steps and he would be face to face with John Anderson, would know for sure who John Anderson was.

He gave a wrench to his bridle, dragged his horse out of the last bushes. Paulding was talking with two well-set-up countrymen, one of whom led a riderless horse. Between them stood a man in a claret-colored coat, a long blue overcoat across one arm, a small, slim man with carefully dressed hair.

The group shifted and Grant saw the man in the claret-colored coat. Major John André, adjutant general to Sir Henry Clinton, looked calmly about him, then his eyes fell on Grant. There was a quick flicker of recognition in the major's expression. Then it was carefully masked.

Grant said, "Good evening, Major. Our positions seem to be changed since our last meeting."

André's laugh seemed utterly natural. "Good evening, Captain. I'm greatly flattered at your giving me military rank. My name is—"

"I know," said Grant. "John Anderson."

A light shadow came over André's face. Then he laughed again. "Of course. These men here must have told you."

"Just where had you been when they halted you?"

"I?" André gave a careless gesture. "Walking for my health. It's something my physician recommends."

"In what direction?"

"Oh, as to that," André began airily. "I was—but look here. This is a damned uncomfortable place to stand quizzing. These young friends of mine had talked of taking me on to Colonel Jameson. I hope you won't think me rude if I suggest that further questioning be postponed until we are in his presence."

"I can hardly force you to talk against your will," said Grant.

André smiled engagingly. "I knew you'd be reasonable about it." He glanced at his captors. "Now, let's get on to Northcastle."

Grant mounted reluctantly and the little group set off through the cool, sunny afternoon. Paulding, van Wart and Williams plodded along, dogged and workmanlike. Their prisoner, still tethered to his horse, walked among them with a light, dancer's step. His head was high, and he kept looking to right and left as though enjoying a pleasant outing. A dozen yards in the rear, Grant watched the four with an uneasy eye. But those men would never let André slip through their fingers. They wanted credit at headquarters for his capture as well as the reward that would come to them from André's valuables, theirs, under law. Other militiamen joined Paulding and his friends, and formed a sort of escort for them.

When from a low rise the scattered houses of Northcastle appeared, Grant felt a deep sense of relief. Bright-helmeted troopers moved briskly about a white farmhouse standing in a field. Others were gathering at a shed that jutted out from a low yellow house in a hollow, and Grant could make out the pale flicker of flame under slung camp kettles. "Jameson's quarters," thought Grant. John Anderson would be turned over to Jameson. He stirred impatiently in the saddle, eager to begin the questioning. The colonel, of course, would conduct matters, but no one in the American Army, except perhaps Tallmadge, could guide that questioning better than Grant. He gathered his reins, ready to ride up and lead the party.

A pleasant-looking man with short, curly hair reached up and caught Grant's bridle. "Don't want to make trouble, Cap, but John Paulding and the others kind of aim to take their prize in alone."

Grant tried to free his reins. "Don't be fools! I've got business with Colonel Jameson. Come on. Let me go."

The smiling man spoke soothingly. "In a little while, Cap. Say maybe a half-hour. Easy! We don't want to play rough but if need be, we'll have to rope you up and sit on you. There's six of us. Ain't it better to be reasonable?"

Sudden anger, intensified by the long night ride, flared in Grant's brain. He snatched at his reins. "God damn it, stand clear. I'm going through. Hinder me, and you'll find yourselves standing court-martial on about ten counts."

"Oh, no, Cap." The man's smile broadened. "No soldier law for us. We're volunteer militiamen. No regiment, no officers. Just us." Still holding the reins, he leaned an arm confidentially on the horse's neck. "It's like this, Cap. Been more'n once that the soldier-suit boys have taken prisoners away from us and we don't see a cracked farthing of what's due us by law. I don't say you'd do that, but Paulding just wants to feel safe."

Grant said resignedly, "All right. But I know a lot about that prisoner that Jameson's got to hear. Besides, I'm getting hungry."

The man beside him nodded approvingly. "Now that's what I call reasonable, seasonable and feasonable of you, Cap. You won't have to tarry too long. Hey, Lem. You can spare a slice of that cold beef and a little bread from your wallet. Eph Tucker, you give him a pull at that rum bottle we took off'n the old farmer down to Buttermilk Hill."

While the men watched him closely, Grant ate a slice of rare roast beef wedged between two chunks of bread, drank sparingly of the thick, under-aged rum. Between bites, he studied the distant village. Paulding and his men were guiding André to the white farmhouse. He saw the group halted by a mounted guard, then passed on to two men by the door. There was a brief pause, after which they all disappeared into the farmhouse. As he ate, Grant felt increasingly easier. It was just as well to let the preliminary routine questioning go on. He could add nothing to that. Then, with André under secure guard, Grant would have a confidential talk with Jameson after which the major would be held to wait the Commander's pleasure.

He spoke to the nearest guard. "Are you timing this half-hour? Have you got a watch?"

"Sun's good enough for me, Cap. More rum?"

Grant shook his head, his eyes on the farmhouse. What was Jameson saying to John Anderson? It was probable that André would not identify himself, at least for the present. The news of the capture of one suspicious civilian with a very ordinary name would not spread from Northcastle, probably would not reach the ears of the "fairly important American officer" of whom Culper had written, the officer known as Gustavus or Mr. Moore. That gentleman would, for a while at least, feel secure in his treachery.

The man who had stopped Grant peered toward Northcastle. "Guess you can amble any time you got a mind to, Cap," he remarked.

His thoughts interrupted, Grant looked up. There was a stir about the door of the white farmhouse. An orderly appeared, more troopers, followed by Paulding, van Wart and Williams. Then John André stepped easily and confidently into the sunshine, a trooper on either side of him. One of them held a stirrup for him, and he mounted the same horse to which he had been tethered earlier by Paulding. Grant's jaw dropped. "God Almighty! They're letting him go!" he cried.

As though in answer to his words, there was a stir by the picket lines and ten troopers rode up to the house, a junior officer or a sergeant guiding them. The detail formed a double file about André and the leader seemed to be shouting instructions to his men. Another trooper emerged from the doorway, mounted and galloped off, this time taking the road that led north to the Hudson and the high lands about Peekskill. The detail surrounding André milled about, then started off in the wake of the last orderly.

"Where the devil are they taking the prisoner?" shouted Grant.

"Him? Oh, to the red barn. It's a sight stronger than it looks. He won't get free."

Grant barely heard the last words. He touched his mount with his spurs and raced off toward the white house, where he pulled up abruptly. As he dismounted he saw that André and his escort were coming abreast of the barn. An impatient voice from the doorway made him turn. "Something you want, Captain?"

"Captain Ledyard, from Fairfield. I'd like to see Colonel Jameson at once."

The other answered, "I'm Captain Miller, adjutant to the colonel. What do you want to see him about?"

"That prisoner," said Grant quickly. "The man called John Anderson."

Miller shook his head. "The colonel is busy. Maybe he can see you later. From Fairfield, are you?" He began to laugh. "A lot of use you and your crowd are. We've had to send our best men and horses to Tallmadge down there to chase spies. By God, it's good! Then we catch a really big one right up here, someone who must have been running around under your noses all the time!"

Grant started to answer angrily, but checked himself. He said smoothly, "I guess the credit's yours all right, if he really is a spy."

"Ho!" cried Miller, nettled. "You should have seen the papers that I saw, papers that Paulding and his boys found in his stockings."

Grant laughed. The idea that the astute André had incriminating papers on his person was absurd.

Miller began tapping a thin forefinger into his other palm. "Listen to this: Item No. 1. There was Major Bauman's report of the ordnance in all the forts and batteries around West Point. Item No. 2. A report on the number of men needed to man the works. Item No. 3. An account of the weak spots in the defenses. Item No. 4. A transcript of a statement about defense made by the Commander at a council of generals. Of course he's a spy." He glared in triumph at Grant, who could only stare dumfounded.

Miller was enjoying his triumph. "Oh, we've got him all right. And do you know who had signed Anderson's pass? Do you know who signed those reports?" He laughed harshly. "No. You don't. Maybe you'll hear some day."

Grant nodded absently while his mind, almost unbidden, began its own process of elimination. Major Bauman? Yes, for the ordnance report. The Frenchman Villefranche? Yes, for the works, but not the guns. General Knox? Hardly. He was concerned with the field guns rather than fortress artillery. Then all at once he knew and the knowledge shook him so deeply that he could feel his shoulders trembling.

Benedict Arnold had sent hundreds of good Massachusetts infantrymen far away from the fort on the pretext of woodcutting. He had ordered the chain lifted from the Hudson—to afford passage to His Majesty's ships. He had asked for the names of men engaged in confidential work. Grant spoke through stiff lips. "I want permission to talk to John Anderson. Now!"

Miller blinked in amazement. "He's not here! God no! He's been sent away, of course."

"I know," Grant's voice cracked. "To the red barn."

"No. To his Excellency General Benedict Arnold and, by God, Arnold will make him sweat, I tell you."

"You—you've sent him to Arnold?" Grant took a step backward, then butted past Miller into the house. "Out of my way." He brushed past a gaping orderly and opened the door at the end of the hall. In the bare room a weary-looking lieutenant colonel of cavalry was bent over a pile of papers. Grant cried, "Colonel Jameson! Stop him. For God's sake stop him!"

Colonel Jameson raised his head and said icily, "Appointments are made through my adjutant. Kindly close the door as you leave."

"Sir, I've seen your adjutant. This matter can't wait. The man Anderson—"

Jameson rose slowly, obviously controlling himself with difficulty. He cleared his throat and Grant saw that his hands were trembling with fatigue. "You'll leave the name of your commanding officer with my adjutant. I shall recommend disciplinary action, most strongly."

Grant cried, "I know this is irregular, sir. As for reporting me, I'm under your own command. Captain Ledyard, attached to Major Tallmadge at Fairfield. I had no business pushing Captain Miller aside and I'll apologize to him. But for God's sake, Colonel, recall the man Anderson."

Jameson reseated himself. "Ledyard. Of course. Sit down, Captain. Didn't mean to storm at you. What about Anderson?"

"Yesterday afternoon, a letter came to Fairfield, asking us to be on the lookout for him," Grant began, as he seated himself.

Jameson shook his head. "Only yesterday? I had one some days ago. So did Colonel Sheldon. The matter is being seen to."

Grant was on his feet again. "That's what I'm afraid of, sir. It's not only that letter. There's so much more. Warnings have come to us, bit by bit, from the other side. We've picked up a little ourselves in Fairfield. It builds up into something damnable, something that can be fatal. For God's sake, sir, take my word that trouble's afoot and moving faster and faster that'll blow us, all of us, right off the continent. If you want to save what we believe in, for Heaven's sake call back your troopers and Mr. Anderson!"

Jameson studied Grant carefully and approval came into his weary eyes. "I'm going to commend you in orders, Captain, for strict attention to duty. But don't worry about Mr. Anderson. I'm sending him on to General Arnold. If you know the general as well as I do, you'll stop fretting."

Grant exploded. "That's just it. I'll go over the whole matter with you later but—" his fist beat out the words on the table—"but John Anderson must not meet Benedict Arnold."

Jameson frowned dubiously. "The West Point command's just the place for Anderson, just the place where he'll have to answer a lot of damned embarrassing questions. Do you know—" he put his elbows on the table and looked seriously at Grant—"do you know that the fellow actually had a pass, signed by General Arnold? I'd not want to be in his shoes when he faces Arnold, especially in the general's present temper. Oh, Anderson'll be even safer, from our standpoint, at West Point than here. Now if you'll excuse me, Captain."

Grant's fists clenched in exasperation. "Once again, sir, recall Anderson or—" Voices sounded out in the hall. Spurs clanked and there was a rap on the door. Jameson spoke wearily, "Would you mind opening it, Ledyard?" Grant flung the door open and stepped back, staring at Benjamin Tallmadge who stood erect on the other side of the threshold. Then Tallmadge spoke quickly. "I got your messages from the Green Farms posts. What's happened?"

"Everything, sir. I've been trying to explain to Colonel Jameson—"

Tallmadge, hard-faced and unsmiling, laid a hand on Grant's cuff. "I see. Wait right here. I've got to report." He strode into the room, unruffled and courteous, and saluted his superior. "Patrol completed, sir. To White Plains and beyond. Nothing significant in the area. Now, sir, with your permission, I'd like to question Captain Ledyard in your presence." Jameson, still puzzled, nodded assent. Tallmadge turned to Grant. "That identification you wrote about. Your Oyster Bay acquaintance. You're sure?"

Grant felt a great weight lifted from him. "There's not the least doubt. More than that, I saw Anderson within the last hour. He's been sent on to West Point."

Jameson broke in, "Under heavy guard. My orders. He'll be turned over to General Arnold."

"To Gustavus! Or to Mr. Moore! One and the same!" Grant shouted.

"Yes," said Tallmadge slowly. "I've come to that conclusion, too. Brewster forwarded another message from Culper after you'd left Fairfield."

Jameson, his head in his hands, sighed. "Would you gentlemen mind explaining to me just what you're talking about?"

"You've not gone into details, Grant?" asked Tallmadge.

"There's not been time. I've been urging the colonel to recall Anderson."

"Of course," said Tallmadge tersely. "May I ask, Colonel, if you talked with the man Anderson?"

"Certainly," answered Jameson. "He wouldn't say much." He mentioned the pass signed by Arnold in Anderson's name, the reports on the defenses, garrison and armament of the Hudson forts, the résumé of the Commander's conference with his generals.

"And those papers, Colonel?" asked Tallmadge. "May I see them?"

Jameson looked surprised. "The papers? My dear major, I had no right to keep them. I sent them, with a brief account of Anderson's arrest, to the Commander. They'll reach him somewhere this side of the Connecticut line."

"To the Commander?" exclaimed Tallmadge. "Not to Arnold?"

"No. He'd know their contents anyway. But I did send him, by special courier, a copy of my letter to the Commander. It has a description of the papers of course."

Tallmadge turned on his heel and walked to the window, chin on his chest. For a moment he stood looking out over the sunlit meadow to the west. Then he faced Jameson. "Excuse me, Colonel, but the matter is of great urgency. Recall Anderson. Above all, recall that courier with the letter to West Point."

Jameson bristled. "Why?"

"Because, sir, if you don't, you'll be compounding the blackest, most damnable bit of treason that's ever touched this continent."

Jameson got to his feet. "Watch your tongue, Major."

Tallmadge went on. "Listen. We've known for a long time that something's been brewing. Most we had from, let us say, a friend outside our lines. I found out a few things. Ledyard, at great personal risk, discovered more. It involves the sale to our enemies of the West Point forts. John Anderson, Colonel, is actually Major John André, adjutant general to Sir Henry Clinton. The captain will confirm that."

Grant nodded. "I met Major André at Oyster Bay, where he got a letter addressed to John Anderson. There's no mistake, Colonel."

"Thanks, Captain," said Tallmadge. "Now, Colonel, we also learned that this plan for the treacherous sale of West Point was the result of a dicker between André, acting for Clinton, and an American officer who signed himself as either Gustavus or Mr. Moore."

There was a tragic, stunned look in Jameson's eyes. He seemed to force himself upright in his chair. "No. It's too fantastic. Too utterly damnable. Treason! We've had incompetent fools in high places, we've had vacillation, timidity, but never treason." His voice sank to a dry rustle. "Never!"

"We have it now," said Tallmadge. "What we lack is time. We must have John Anderson here. Bring him back!"

"Suppose you're wrong?" muttered Jameson.

"Then no harm's done," said Tallmadge. "We still have a bona-fide prisoner. A few hours to consider his disposition won't do any harm."

"All right," said Jameson reluctantly. He wrote a few lines on a sheet of paper, stepped to the door. "Captain Miller! Have Lieutenant Cox and two troopers overtake the prisoner and his escort and bring them back here."

Grant and Tallmadge exchanged glances. The major said earnestly, "Believe me, sir, you'll never regret this. Did your order include the recall of the courier to General Arnold?"

"No!" Jameson's jaw snapped on the word. "It's my duty to notify my superior officer. I've gone farther than I want in recalling the prisoner."

There was a silence in the room. Grant felt empty and defeated. Then Tallmadge spoke and the tone of his voice shot sudden hope through Grant. The major was saying, "With all due respect, Colonel, is that your final decision?"

"Utter and absolute," answered Jameson.

"In that case, sir," said Tallmadge and there was a serene confidence in his face, "may I withdraw? I'm going to take my troopers, ride on to West Point and—"

"And what?"

"Arrest General Benedict Arnold on charges of high treason!"

Jameson went white as Grant gave an exclamation of joy and hitched at his saber, shouting, "I'm with you, sir."

Jameson's jaw sagged. "Arrest—arrest General Arnold?"

"Or Gustavus or Mr. Moore, as you please. They're all the same person. We know it. With your permission, sir, I'll leave at once. Ready, Grant?"

Jameson was leaning forward over the table, incredulous. "You can't do that. I certainly won't sanction it."

"You don't have to, sir. I'll take full responsibility. Your name needn't even appear in any later inquiries. Just Ledyard and myself!"

Grant moved toward the door. "I'll warn the troopers, Major."

"You stay where you are," barked Jameson. "Now look here, Major. I've got respect for your judgment and integrity. But I can't permit this. General Arnold's my superior. How'll I look if you've made a mistake? Men of my regiment arresting a full major general. Oh, no!"

"As I said, Colonel, officially you'll know nothing about this."

Jameson said firmly, "Give over this plan of yours, Tallmadge. If you don't give me your word you'll make no such attempt—I'd hate to have to put you under arrest, but I'd have to."

Grant, his hand on the latch of the door, watched Tallmadge.

The major seemed to freeze and all expression left his face. He said, "You leave me no choice, Colonel. I'll not make the attempt." He glanced toward Grant whose hand was still on the latch. "Don't press the matter, Grant. We'll just have to pray that American luck will hold for us, somehow."

Jameson struck his hands together in approval. "Now that's being sensible, both of you. Ready to talk about the posts and the horses, Major? Then pull up a chair. Glad to have the chance of meeting you, Captain Ledyard."

Grant took a last look at Tallmadge, but the major had drawn up to the table apparently absorbed in thoughts of the coming discussion. Grant touched the brim of his helmet and left the room. Without knowing just where he was going, he walked dully out across the meadows.

Chewing a blade of grass, he tried to rally from the shock of the colonel's refusal either to intercept the messenger to Arnold or to allow Tallmadge to ride to the Hudson with his troopers. Time was slipping away. The prisoner had been recalled, but two couriers were riding out the sun, one to the east and one to the west. Of course, if the east-bound rider met the Commander returning from Hartford, the situation might be saved. But supposing the Commander did not follow the southern route. Supposing he stopped to inspect depots. "We're counting on luck and nothing else," he thought.

Troopers were leading their horses to water at a brook that

wandered through the field. Almost unconsciously he recognized the bandy-legged stride of the officer in charge of the group. It was Lieutenant Gunnison. The troopers with him must be Tallmadge's patrol. Picked men, of course, some of the best in the regiment. Good man, Gunnison, by Tallmadge's accounts. Ready for any kind of service, resourceful. "I'm senior to Gunnison," thought Grant. Slowly he rose from the stone wall and began walking, uncertainly at first, then with gathering speed. He broke into a trot, calling, "Gunnison!"

Gunnison recognized him. "Hello, Captain. What are you brewing now?"

"Let your sergeant see to the watering. Come over here out of earshot. Are your men fresh?"

Gunnison raised his eyebrows. "Had quite a ride with Major Ben. But they're middling."

"You in command in the major's absence?"

Gunnison laughed. "Sure I am."

"Then listen to me. Get through your watering quickly, then mount up your men. No bugles, no noise. You've got to take me on faith. Take your detail west, heading for the ground above Peekskill. Don't pass that white house where Jameson is. I'll ride with you, at the head of the column, with one of your troopers for a guide."

Gunnison still looked troubled. "Is this something Tallmadge wants done?" he asked.

Grant hesitated. "He—yes. He wants it done. You take my word that he wants it. We've got big stakes, Gunnison. We're going to arrest a general."

Gunnison brightened. "What? Arrest a general? Fine! Never done that before. Which one?"

Grant stepped still closer and dropped his voice. "Arnold."

Gunnison's eyes bulged. "Arnold?" Then he made flipping motions with his hands. "Pick up the cards. You're dealing a game I don't know."

Grant spoke with earnestness. "This has got to be done. If you want to back out, all right. In that case, I'll relieve you from command and take your detail. But the detail's going and I'm going."

Gunnison dug his spur into the ground. "God Almighty! I might as well come along. Going to tell me anything more?"

"Better not. I'll be in command, and the troopers mustn't know a thing. All that matters to them is that they're riding to Arnold's headquarters at the Robinson house."

"Here we go," groaned Gunnison. "I'll pass the word along, quietly. The boys are used to this sort of thing."

"And find me a mount," added Grant. "My own's up there by Jameson's and I don't dare go after it."

"Of course—you're such a stickler for regulations," said Gunnison dryly.

The troopers formed quietly in a hollow beyond the far bank of the stream. Grant, mounted on a spare horse, nodded to the guide. "Stay by me and don't ask questions. All I want is to sight Sugar Loaf Mountain, this side of General Arnold's quarters. Understand?"

The trooper nodded. Grant raised his arm, dropped it, and the column moved silently off, keeping a stretch of rising ground between it and the windows of the white house where Jameson and Tallmadge still talked.

The sun set and shadows fell deep over the hills. Grant rode on through the night, fretting at each halt that the strength of the horses demanded. If he succeeded, if by a sudden swift dash he was able to seize Arnold's person, what would the next step be? He would somehow have to hold him until the arrival of the Commander, who by then would presumably have had Jameson's letter. If he failed— That didn't bear thinking about.

During a halt late the following afternoon, Gunnison drew Grant aside. "Sure you don't want to tell me anything more?"

"No. The less you know, the safer you are if things go wrong for me. But here's what you're to do when we sight the Robinson house above Sugar Loaf. Have your men mark where the guards are and be ready to disarm them. The guards won't be suspecting anything. Then—"

"Guards?" exclaimed Gunnison. "There are only a dozen men, and just a few of them on duty at one time."

"Then we'll bring our troop right to the door. I'll go in alone and you surround the house. If I come out with Arnold, have your troopers seize him. If he comes out alone—" he paused, "if he comes out alone, use your own judgment."

"Hold him and wait for further orders from you?"

Grant shook his head. "If he's alone, I won't be around to give any. I hope you'll arrest him. That's all I can tell you. Damn it, haven't those horses rested enough? Come on, mount up." And on they rode through the night.

It was well past dawn when the high peak of Sugar Loaf rose over the trees that choked the wild, tumbled valleys, a lowering overcast morning. "There she is," observed the sergeant who had acted as Grant's guide.

"Know just where the house is?" Grant asked.

"Ought to. Been here often enough."

"Then take your bearings. I want to come in from the shore side, and I don't want our troop to be seen until we're right there. Do you know a way?"

"Cart path they use for bringing in firewood from the hills," answered the sergeant. "Kind of curves in past the sheds and around to the kitchen door."

Sugar Loaf towered at the left as they rode on through the trees. Then the trees stopped and Grant saw a squarish house with a long, low ell jutting from the northern end. Smoke rose from two chimneys, eddied sluggishly and rolled away west toward a break in the Hudson cliffs where a gentler slope, scarred by a path, led to the river. Grant held up his arm, glanced at Gunnison who began cautiously shifting his troopers preparatory to surrounding the house.

Grant dismounted, drew a loaded pistol from his holster, took a deep breath and strode toward the low veranda. On all sides he could hear a muted thud and jingle as Gunnison's men deployed. By the corner of the house, Grant stopped. A horse was tethered to a post by the far end of the ell and even at that distance he could make out a big white "2" on the blue saddle cloth. Jameson's courier to Arnold had arrived!

There were no guards in sight. As Grant sprang onto the veranda, the front door opened and a fine-looking man in artillery blue and red stepped out. Grant's heart gave a great leap. Alexander Hamilton! If Hamilton were here, then the Commander must be nearby.

Grant called, "Colonel Hamilton!"

Hamilton smiled. "Oh, you must be Ledyard. Got anything for me from Tallmadge?"

Grant spoke quickly. "The Commander, Colonel. Where is he? It's urgent."

"He's inspecting some of the river forts with General Knox."

"The Commander had no courier en route from Colonel Jameson?"

"Jameson? No. We left Hartford much earlier than we expected, coming by the northern route."

Grant felt a sudden hollowness. Jameson's courier had taken the southern road, and thus missed meeting Washington. Grant pointed to the horse with the 2nd Dragoon saddle cloth. "Whose is that?"

"That? Oh, that's another Jameson courier, I suppose. Came in not long ago with a letter for General Arnold."

"Did you see the general read the letter? What did he do?" Grant's voice was husky with growing shock.

Hamilton laughed. "What is this? Are you cross-examining the general? Why, he didn't do much of anything, Ledyard. Read it, stuffed it in his pocket. Then he went upstairs, to speak to Mrs. Arnold, I guess. When he came down he told me that he was called across to West Point and that he'd see the Commander on his return." He smiled again. "Any more questions?"

"Sorry, Colonel. I should have said this concerns Culper."

Hamilton looked astonished. "Yes, you should have said so, I think. The general went down that path there. His barge's at a private landing by the cliffs. You might catch him if you hurry. I'd— Hi! Wait a minute."

Grant had already jumped from the porch. Forgetting Hamilton, forgetting Gunnison and his troopers, he set off down the twisting path at a full gallop. Then a rickety landing swayed before him. Immediately in front of him, the river was empty. Fifty yards away to the left, a dozen oars winked, dipped, winked as they drove a heavy barge downstream with the strong current towards Teller's point where His Majesty's sloop *Vulture* waited. The oars flickered on as Grant stared at the barge. A cloaked figure in the stern sheets turned, looking back at West Point, then at the Robinson house. Even at that distance, Grant recognized Arnold. With a sudden desperate gesture, Grant raised his pistol and fired. The ball hissed away over the water, splashed harmlessly a few yards short of the barge. In the stern a hand lifted in a gesture that might have been contemptuous derision. The oars pulled on and the barge grew smaller and smaller as it shot away to the shelter of the *Vulture*.

11. *Cloak and Bomb*

Toward the end of the nineteenth century, a new kind of spy literature began to make its appearance. It was inspired by a very real and sinister menace of the time—the bomb-throwing, cloak-wearing anarchists and revolutionaries of Czarist Russia, some of whom had spilled over into Western Europe or found their partisans and imitators there.

One of the earliest serious novels of this kind was Dostoevski's *The Possessed*, first published in 1873. For the climactic event of his plot, Dostoevski made some use of an actual case in which a student was murdered by his fellows. The victim wanted to withdraw from a political conspiracy because he was disillusioned. The murder was committed because it was feared he would betray the group sooner or later. A popular theme in novels of this period, because it was so common an occurrence, was the betrayal of a secret group to the police by members who had turned informer.

What fascinated the authors whose works appear in this section was not only the wild irrational personalities of the actors, but the tangled play of duplicity and treason. It is interesting to note that three different novels written at quite different times have each made use of material drawn from the most famous police-spy case of the period just before World War I. This was the case of Ievno Azef, who for a long period was both the chief of the Battle Organization (the assassin squad) of the

Russian Social Revolutionary Party and an agent of the police, to whom he betrayed the Battle Organization's plans. Conrad drew on part of the Azef story in *Under Western Eyes;* Roman Goul compressed the whole tale into his novel *Azef,* and most recently Rebecca West recast the climactic discovery of Azef's duplicity in an entirely new mold in *The Birds Fall Down.* One could hardly invent a more baffling villain than Azef was in life, nor weave more complex, mysterious, and twisted plots than he actually did.

ROMAN GOUL

▼

Conspiracy up to the Ears

Roman Goul's treatment of the Azef story stays very close to history and invents little except for the presumed thoughts of the characters. Azef's usefulness to the police was immense. He could identify every member of the revolutionary organization and could inform on their plots in advance, since he himself frequently insti-gated them or at least planned them. But there was one problem: if the police closed in on the conspirators too often, the conspira-tors could not help suspecting that someone was betraying them. Thus Azef frequently had to persuade the police to refrain from arrests in order to protect himself. On the occasions when the suspicion of the revolutionaries was aroused, Azef, a genius at manipulation, was usually able to direct it away from himself and toward someone else. He was able to continue his double game for so long because at heart his colleagues found it unthinkable that he could be a traitor, so well did he play the role of the dauntless and devoted assassin. There is a certain similarity in the case of the British traitor and spy Kim Philby, many of whose colleagues found it impossible to imagine that he could have betrayed his country.

The excerpt I have chosen from Goul's book describes one of the occasions when Azef's duplicity was voiced by a fellow revolu-tionary who had good reason to know of it, since he himself was a traitor working for the police. The fact that he had learned of Azef's relations to the police reflects on the rather loose security within the police organization. But since the accusation stemmed from a traitor, Azef, as the author shows us, had little to fear. In this translation, the Battle Organization is called the Fighting

FROM *Azef.*

49

Organization. The scene of the action in the excerpt is Geneva, Switzerland.

The meeting was stormy. But not because news of revolutionary unrest had come from Russia, confirmed by a high official who had informed the party about the panic and confusion in the highest circles. Nor because of the money offered through Koni Zilliacus. The meeting was thrown into an uproar by the sudden realization that the party was in the hands of a provocateur.

It began when the chairman, Gotz, looking tired and drawn as he sat wrapped in a warm plaid shawl in his chair, announced in a hurried, breaking voice:

"Comrades, we have just received important news. On March 16 the members of the Fighting Organization, Boris Moyseenko, Dulebov, and Podvitsky, were arrested in Moscow. On March 17 the comrades Ivanovskaya, Barykov, Zagorodny, Nadezhdina, Leontieva, Barykova, Shneerov, Novomeysky, Shergov, Efrussi, and Katz were arrested in Petersburg. Borishansky was seized, carrying dynamite, at the Petersburg-Warsaw railroad station. Dynamite was also found at the home of Tatyana Leontieva in Petersburg. Comrades," said Gotz, and his hands shook, "inside of a few days we have lost our dearest, our most devoted comrades. The Fighting Organization in Russia is smashed! Comrades, this is terrible news. But there are things even worse than the defeat we have just suffered. There are most alarming facts, comrades, which demand immediate investigation. I am not afraid to say it, and I am sure I am not mistaken: there is a provocateur at the very heart of our party!"

A hush fell on the crowded room. Everyone looked at Gotz. Directly opposite him sat the hulking figure of Azef.

"Comrades," Gotz cried in a trembling voice, rich with intonations. "It is not only the disaster of the Fighting Organization in Petersburg and Moscow that compels us to give utmost attention to this question. There are incontrovertible facts which confirm the presence of a major provocateur in our midst. First let me tell you: comrade Nikolay Sergeevich Tyutchev, who has just arrived and is present here, has given us facts which lead to sad conclusions."

An elderly man of aristocratic appearance, dressed modestly but elegantly, with silvery-gray hair, a pointed beard, and an intelligent, energetic face, asked from the corner:

"Will you permit me, Mikhail Raphailovich?"

"Please, Nikolay Sergeevich." Gotz leaned back brokenly in his wheelchair.

"About two days before the Petersburg arrests," Tyutchev spoke calmly and distinctly, "I received a telephone call at the editorial office of *Russian Wealth*. A voice which I did not recognize said: 'Give warning—all the rooms are infected.' "

There was unbroken silence in the room. Azef clumsily shifted in his chair. Leaning on his hand, he stared at Tyutchev. His low forehead was wrinkled, the eyes frowned. Tyutchev did not look at him. His eyes were on the other comrades, and most of all on the agitated, exhausted face of Gotz.

"I asked: 'Can I speak to you personally?' Evidently, this was unexpected. There was a pause, and it even seemed to me that my informant at the other end was conferring with someone. Then he asked hesitantly: 'But it is late. Besides, where?' I answered, 'Here.' The reply was, 'No, it is inconvenient,' and the receiver was put down."

Tyutchev finished. It seemed that heartbeats could be heard in the room. Then the silence was broken by short exclamations.

"Quiet, comrades!" Gotz rapped with his bony hands.

"A question to Nikolay Sergeevich." Azef raised his hand.

"Go on, Ivan."

Azef turned toward Tyutchev clumsily, heavily, with his whole body; he could not turn his neck.

"Nikolay Sergeevich, you could not recognize the speaker by his voice?"

"No, but I must say, I have heard it somewhere before. It reminded me by its rather unusual timbre of a voice I have not heard for ten years."

"Pardon me, Nikolay Sergeevich, was it a man's voice or a woman's?" Everyone turned to Chernov.

"Well, Victor Mikhailovich," Tyutchev said, smiling. "This does not seem so very important. After all we do not know who telephoned, and probably never shall. Why indulge in guesswork? It was a man's voice."

Chernov gestured vaguely.

"Comrades, we are going into this incident in too much detail," said Gotz. "This is neither the time nor the place for it. You can't suck information from your thumb. Nikolay Sergeevich did not recognize the voice. I merely wanted to inform you about this call. Besides, we have still more convincing data in our hands, of a much more concrete character."

Azef stared at Gotz's distracted face with dark, calm, steady eyes.

Savinkov nudged Azef, bending over:

"Do you believe it?"

"It's possible," Azef grunted.

"We have received a letter at the address of *Revolutionary Russia*. I shall read it, and we'll comment later." Raising his vibrating, agitated voice, Gotz read:

"Esteemed comrades, the Police Department has received information concerning the following Socialist Revolutionaries: (1) Herman, has a passport in the name of Boris Dmitrievich Neradov, lived in Switzerland, at present in Russia (illegally), has probably come on a different passport. (2) Mikhail Ivanovich Sokolov, lived in Switzerland under a passport in the name of a German subject, Ludwig Cain, will soon leave for Russia. (3) Sokolov will be followed into Russia by: (a) Grisha, who calls himself Chernov, Vasnetsov, or Bordzenko; (b) Prince Dmitry Alexandrovich Khilkov (two weeks later); and (c) the former student Mikhail Alexandrovich Vedenyapin, about two months later (will leave illegally from Switzerland). With comradely greetings. . . ."

Azef mumbled sideways to Savinkov: "No signature."

"Is there a signature?" Savinkov asked loudly.

"There is, but I shall withhold it," Gotz replied excitedly, covering the sheet of paper on the table with his hand. "Comrades! It is entirely clear that the police could have received this information only from a provocateur. I have thought about it for a long time. The situation is most serious. We must take the only possible revolutionary point of view: no name or authority can be too sacrosanct for scrutiny. The whole party is in danger. Let us start with the extreme assumption—that each of us is suspect. Let the comrades speak up. Does anyone have any suspicions? And against whom?"

There was an agonizing silence. No one dared to raise his eyes to his neighbor.

"I do not want to conceal my suspicions, comrades," Gotz spoke quietly into the silence. "I may be committing a wrong, but let the proper court judge this. I must say that I have grounds for suspecting a certain member of the party."

There was dead silence.

"I suspect . . . Tatarov. . . ."

The silence deepened. Gotz understood that his suspicions were shared.

"To begin with, according to my calculations, Tatarov has spent more than six thousand rubles on his new publishing house in six weeks. Where did he get the money? He commands neither personal nor party funds. If he received a contribution, he should have reported it to the Central Committee. I asked him where he got this money. He said he received it from the well-known editor Charnolussky. I must confess, I have begun to doubt this. I suggest that someone be sent to Petersburg to ask Charnolussky whether he had given any money, and how much. Besides, Tatarov will be coming to Geneva in a few days. He must be placed under surveillance here. I repeat: if Tatarov spoke the truth about the source of the money, and the surveillance by the comrades reveals nothing, I shall withdraw my suspicions. But, comrades, I feel that I must share my doubts with you. . . ."

"You are right, Misha!" cried Chernov.

"It sounds likely," Azef rumbled to Savinkov.

"Who will undertake to watch Tatarov in Geneva, comrades?"

"I nominate Savinkov!" cried Azef.

"Savinkov," several voices supported him.

"There must be three."

"Sukhomlin! Alexander Gurevich!"

"And so, comrades Savinkov, Sukhomlin, and Gurevich will have to assume this unpleasant but indispensable duty. As for the journey to Petersburg, to see Charnolussky, I propose comrade Argunov."

"Yes, yes, Argunov!"

Argunov, who had recently escaped from Siberian exile, stood up to say something. But it was clear that he did not object. And Gotz called out, raising his voice:

"No one against? Then comrade Argunov will go to Petersburg."

The day's agenda was completed.

At night Azef walked alone, a huge, dark, bowed carcass, down the Boulevard des Philosophes. Puffing at his cigarette, he reviewed all the facts he could recall. He had decided to take his time with the Petersburg terrorists. There was no doubt—someone else was informing the police. His shoes creaked on the gravel. With unerring instinct, Azef knew: it was Tatarov.

He would not sleep that night. He turned in to the English Gardens and sat down, muttering something hoarsely as he smoked. In the chilling wind from Lake Leman he decided that Tatarov must die. But the fear that Tatarov might still have time enough to denounce and expose him persisted. Azef heard his teeth chatter with the cold. At times his thick lips stretched into a semblance of a grin. He muttered to himself.

The wind grew colder. Excursion steamers, gay with lights and music, were returning across the dark lake. Azef felt cold. He rose and, swaying his dark bulk, walked down the path across the English Gardens to his hotel. But he did not go to bed. Apart from Tatarov, there was danger from another, unknown hand, and this danger also had to be averted. Azef wrote a letter.

First he cited the document read by Gotz, signed, "With comradely greetings, V. Kosovsky." Then, breathing heavily, he went on, line after sprawling line:

This document will show you, Leonid Alexandrovich, how deplorable things are in your Police Department, and how careful one must be in giving you information. Here in Geneva this letter has convinced everyone in the Socialist Revolutionary group of the existence of a provocateur who is very close to the center of activity. Is it impossible for the Police Department to conduct its work in such a way that its memoranda will not fall into the hands of revolutionary organizations? The result will be that Prince Khilkov, who is still in England, visiting his relatives, will not return to Russia, since he was immediately informed about the document. The same is true of Vedenyapin. I am really astonished at the department's inability to maintain adequate secrecy in its work. I have not received either money or letters. Please send the money at once. And, for God's sake, be careful. One misstep, and I am lost.

Sincerely,
Your Ivan

The dawn was bright over the lake. Fishing boats sailed away into the red-blue distance. Azef, still dressed in his black suit, slept on the sofa, moaning, grinding his teeth, and crying out, as if he desperately wanted to say something and could not.

In the morning Savinkov was told that Tatarov had arrived. Tatarov was a tall man, typically Russian, with a square, strong, curly beard, rather short legs, and dark hair parted in the middle. Rawboned and broad he moved noisily, spoke loudly, and looked like an unfrocked deacon.

Savinkov remembered him from childhood, when they had played stickball and skittles together. As soon as Tatarov learned that Savinkov was in Geneva, he came to see him. They would not have recognized each other now. Savinkov was a European, and much too elegant for a revolutionary. Tatarov, though he was fond of wearing modish ties and suits, still looked like a village priest or a peasant. Thumping with his shoes and shouting loudly, Tatarov was obviously feeling fine.

"It's been a long, long time, Boris Victorovich, since we last met!

Well, won't you tell me how you are doing? Where have you come from now? Moscow?"

"Kiev."

"Kiev? I was told you've been in Moscow."

"Perhaps."

"Ha-ha-ha! Secrets and secrets! Conspiracy up to the ears! You aren't talking to a provocateur, but to a comrade who has been in the party a bit longer than you!"

"Sorry, Nikolay Yurievich. The chiefs are strict."

"Chiefs! Who are the chiefs? But, of course, our lips are sealed. But I know everything myself. Abroad, it's Mishka Gotz! In Russia, you're the exalted chief of the terrorists! Trying to throw dust in my eyes! But never mind."

Tatarov paced the room noisily, his hands twisting his wide-brimmed, light-colored hat, of the kind often worn by bad artists.

Tatarov was stupid and insensitive. Jabbering on, he did not even look at Savinkov. "I will kill this big man," thought Savinkov. "I will kill him because he is rotten and stupid, because he is wearing this gaudy tie; I will kill him like an ox. But how huge he is! He'll make a lot of noise when he falls."

"I am so glad to see you," went on Tatarov. "Tyutchev is also here. We were in exile in Siberia together! Generally Geneva is full of our people, wherever you turn. But I'd like to see Baska. Do you know where she is?"

"Who is this 'Baska'?"

"Why, Yakimova!"

"Ah, I've heard of her. No, I don't know. But tell me, Nikolay Yurievich, I was told you'll be in publishing now?"

"Yes, yes, I will. Why? Do you have anything for publication? You do write?"

"I have a thing or two."

"Let me have it, with pleasure, with pleasure."

Savinkov thought, "I will kill him."

"If you'll permit me, I shall give you a manuscript in a few days."

"Memoirs?"

"Not exactly. Something along that line."

"Very interesting, very. I'll tell you what, Boris Victorovich, the comrades will have dinner with me Sunday—I'll be going on soon, you know. Why don't you come, too, and bring along the manuscript, will you?"

"*Bon*," said Savinkov, striking his hand against Tatarov's and pressing it more firmly than usual.

Tatarov invited fifteen persons to dinner to a private room at the Angleterre Restaurant. Azef sent his excuses. Fourteen guests were at the table, all of them party leaders. The white-haired Tyutchev sat next to Breshkovskaya. Shaking his red mane over the new collar that seemed to bind his fat neck, Chernov was laughing. Savinkov, the old Minor, Rakitnikov, Bach, Natanson, Avksentiev, and Potapov were also there. Only three of the guests—Tyutchev, Savinkov, and Chernov —knew that the host was a provocateur. The table was bright and festive, with silver, flowers, wines, and delicacies. Tatarov recalled how he founded the "Workers' Banner" group eight years previously. The comrades spoke of his hunger strike at the Fortress of St. Peter and Paul, when he refused food for twenty-two days. Tatarov modestly waved them off, saying:

"What is twenty-two days? Others struck longer than that." Raising his glass, he stood up:

"Comrades, let us drink to the revolution! It is near, its footsteps can be heard approaching! Let us drink to our party, which leads the revolution, and above all to our comrades of the Fighting Organization. Hurrah!"

The slender goblets rang on many notes as the guests clinked and drank. Clinking with Chernov, Tatarov emptied his glass and felt a pleasant, heady warmth spread through his body. Someone quickly raised an answering toast, waving his glass and shouting:

"A happy journey to Nikolay Yurievich! To the success of his work in Russia—hurrah!"

After dinner, when everyone was noisy and gay, Chernov approached Tatarov with a smile and asked, twisting a large button on his coat:

"And when are you planning to leave, Nikolay Yurievich?"

Grasping Chernov by his powerful arms and drawing him nearer, Tatarov said:

"This evening, Victor Mikhailovich, at 11:30."

"Impossible."

"Why?"

"The Central Committee has some business with you."

"I must go. What business?"

Chernov spoke, smiling: "I am instructed by the Central Committee to ask you to remain a day longer."

"Very well," Tatarov shrugged, "if there is business, I'll stay. Until tomorrow?"

Chernov said simply and warmly, "Until tomorrow."

Passing near Savinkov, he breathed:
"He is staying. Keep an eye on him."

Tatarov entered gaily, smoothing out his beard, which had gotten rumpled in the wind.

"Good morning," he said, glowing with sanguine energy as he passed from Tyutchev to Savinkov, from Savinkov to Bach. There seemed to be a trace of chill in Tyutchev's greeting. "He is always like that," Tatarov reassured himself and joined Savinkov at the table. On the table there was a photograph of a plump brunette in a gold frame. They looked at her, but neither of them knew her.

"What is it about?"

"We are waiting for Chernov; he is the chairman."

At that moment the door opened and Victor Mikhailovich entered, smiling.

"Harmony and affection to all!" he said from the threshold. "What weather, my friends, straight out of Pushkin! Clear, transparent, a heavenly breeze. Ah, Nikolay Yurievich, good morning, I thought you might have left. Excellent, excellent! Well then, comrades, were you waiting for me? If you don't mind," and Victor Mikhailovich pulled over a comfortable armchair.

Savinkov, Tyutchev, Bach, and Tatarov sat down. Minor lowered his old bones into a chair. But from the way they were sitting down, Tatarov sensed something wrong. "I should have left," he thought. Concealing his anxiety, he asked, stroking his beard:

"What's the question before us, Victor Mikhailovich?" He was pleased that his voice was steady.

"One moment, Nikolay Yurievich," said Chernov, writing something rapidly in a tiny round hand. "The question?" Chernov laid aside the pen and raised one eye at Tatarov, while the other stared off somewhere past him. "The question, you see, is quite serious. Well, not so serious, really, but the Central Committee is making an audit of party affairs, and so I have asked you in the name of the committee to remain and help us to clear up the financial and censorship aspects of your new publishing venture. Of course you will understand the desire of the Central Committee to maintain control of the publishing work?"

Tatarov looked at his hand, lying on the table. It was clear that they suspected him. "The main thing is to be absolutely calm," he said to himself as Chernov went on.

"But before we take up this matter, Nikolay Yurievich, I would like to . . . I mean, this committee would like to clarify certain details. . . ."

Tatarov strained to guess where this was leading. He knit his brows over his dark Gypsy eyes and stroked his beard. Their purpose still eluded him.

"I shall ask you to answer the first point." Chernov's squint became wilder. "Who gave you the money for the publishing house? But you know the wise old folk saying, Nikolay Yurievich," Chernov said pleasantly. " 'He who shuns the truth takes the longest route.' Just give us straight facts, I beg you."

"Of course, Victor Mikhailovich," laughed Tatarov. "You simply were not informed. I told Gotz: I received the sum of fifteen thousand rubles from Charnolussky and was promised further aid by Charnolussky and Zitron. He is the Odessa publisher," Tatarov added.

There was a moment's pause. Chernov's blurred eye came to rest on some point under the ceiling. Then, shaking his red mane and stroking it, Chernov drawled:

"I see, I see. Well, this is something I did not know. But tell me," he suddenly turned upon Tatarov, and his voice was sharp, "are you staying at the Hotel des Voyageurs under the name of Plevinsky?"

Tatarov should have burst out laughing. He should have banged his fist on the table and shouted: This is outrageous! But he saw the icy stares of his comrades. "I'm lost," flashed through his mind. His heart turned over twice and seemed to drop to his soles.

"Yes, under the name of Plevinsky."

"And the room number?"

"Twenty-eight, I think."

Chernov's face swam up very near, smiling, distorted. His words came slowly, distinctly:

"This is not true. We have inquired. There is no Plevinsky either in Room 28, or anywhere in the Hotel des Voyageurs."

Someone's breath was drawn sharply. Minor's chair creaked as he crossed his legs.

"I don't remember the name of the hotel. Perhaps it isn't the Hotel des Voyageurs." Tatarov understood that he was speaking stupidly, destroying himself, but he was now rolling irresistibly into some horrible abyss. Another moment, and they would kill him as they killed Sudeykin. Savinkov was tracing a curly feminine profile on a scrap of paper.

"Try to recall it," said Chernov. "Boris Victorovich, please write down for the record: does not remember the name of the hotel, the street, or the number."

Savinkov's pen screeched on the paper.

"But we are not children," said Tatarov. "I lied about the hotel because I am living with a woman and wanted to protect her."

"Oh?"

"I'll name her, if you wish."

"No, no, Nikolay Yurievich, it isn't necessary. You should have said so at once. We'll simply drop it. Do forgive me; so that's it! I am sorry. But now let's go on to business. Tell us, Nikolay Yurievich, how is your publishing house protected against the censorship?"

Tatarov wanted to interrupt him, to shout, but he saw it would be futile.

"I was promised protection by a powerful personage," and he heard his breaking voice betraying him.

"Who is he?" Chernov's voice hammered at him now as if driving nails into something soft, so that they sank in down to their heads.

"A certain prince."

"What prince?"

"Why? I said a prince. That's enough."

"By authority of the Central Committee I suggest that you give us the name."

"Very well. It is a count," Tatarov said in a low voice.

"A count?"

"But this is unimportant—a count, a prince. Why do you need the name?"

"The Central Committee orders you to give it."

Tatarov wrinkled his face and passed his hand over his forehead. "Count Kutaisov," he said quietly.

"Kutaisov?" Chernov stood up. "You were in contact with him? Don't you know that the party has been planning an attempt upon Count Kutaisov?"

Tatarov's head sank low; his hands convulsively gripped the edge of the table.

"You have lied," he heard Chernov's voice coming near, "in concealing your address. You have lied about the source of your money. Charnolussky did not give you any; we checked it. You have never met Zitron. You heard his name for the first time from Minor three days ago. Do you admit it?"

Tatarov shook himself and raised his head. With a last flare-up of energy, he thought, "Get away, escape!" He shouted:

"What do you accuse me of? What does this mean?"

"Of treachery!" Tyutchev could no longer restrain himself.

There was a long, terrible silence.

"It will be better if you confess. You will relieve us of the trouble of exposing you," said Chernov.

"Degayev was offered conditions to redeem himself. Would you like us to put conditions to you?" asked Bach.

Savinkov was drawing a daisy on the margin of his notes.

The door opened and they saw Azef on the threshold. He was scowling angrily. Those who knew him saw that he was extremely perturbed.

"Forgive me, comrades, I was delayed," he mumbled under his breath.

"We are finishing, Ivan; sit down," said Chernov.

A quick glance at Tatarov told Azef everything. He walked in and squeezed himself heavily into an armchair in the corner.

In a breaking voice, which threatened momentarily to turn into a sob, Tatarov said:

"You can kill me. You can force me to kill. I am not afraid. But I am innocent. I give you the word of a revolutionary."

Chernov leaned over to Tyutchev, who nodded his silvery close-cropped head. Chernov wrote something, then passed the paper to Tyutchev, Savinkov, and Bach.

Tatarov looked down at his shoes; the laces seemed too tight. Chernov rose and, addressing Tatarov, read:

"In view of the fact that N. Yu. Tatarov lied to the comrades about affairs concerning the party, in view of the fact that he had personal contact with Count Kutaisov without utilizing it for revolutionary purposes, and without even informing the Central Committee about it, and in view of the fact that Tatarov failed to reveal the source of his considerable funds, the investigating committee decrees that Tatarov be removed from all party offices and committees, and that the inquiry be continued."

Tatarov did not raise his head.

"You are free for today, but the Central Committee forbids you to leave Geneva without its permission. Your departure will be regarded as flight."

Tatarov walked out with lowered head, without saying good-by. In the hallway he realized he was trembling. It was raining outside. Tatarov did not notice it, although he turned up his collar.

"But his guilt is proven!" exclaimed someone. There were cries in the room: "Comrades have died!" "He must be killed!" "On these grounds?" "Provocateurs were killed for less!"

Azef screamed with rage: "And you let him go!? You let him go! He should have been crushed on the spot like a viper!" Azef's face was twisted with such fury as none of them had ever seen before.

"But you must understand, we couldn't, not here, not at the home of Osip Solomonovich!" cried Chernov.

"You gaping crows! Jabbering fools! Idiots! You couldn't! But it is all right for him to send us to the gallows? Do you know how many comrades he has killed? Is that like water off a duck's back to you?" Azef shouted, flinging out of the room and slamming the door without a good-by to anyone.

In the morning there was a knock on Tatarov's door. He was sitting up, unwashed, his shirt creased under his suspenders. Chernov entered. Without offering his hand, he sat down in an armchair. Tatarov was seized with new anxiety.

"You don't even shake hands?"

"Nikolay Yurievich! We shall not shake your hand until you have cleared yourself of suspicion," began Chernov. "Tell me," he said more kindly, "why did you lie? Why this story about Kutaisov? And Charnolussky? And the hotel? What does it all mean?"

Tatarov's thoughts throbbed with confusion.

"Victor Mikhailovich, do you realize what I am going through?" His voice shook; that was good. "After years of prison and exile, after eight years of dangerous revolutionary work, to be faced with such inhuman accusations!"

Tatarov's lips were trembling. Chernov thought he might start crying.

"I cannot face a court; it is too painful. But I have something to tell. Everyone speaks of the disasters in Petersburg and Moscow, about provocateurs. But don't I feel myself that there is a provocateur at work?" Tatarov said. "I know there is. And I see it was a mistake not to have informed the comrades. I've been investigating on my own for a long time as best I could, and now I've succeeded. . . ."

"In discovering the provocateur?"

"Yes."

"His name?" Chernov leaned toward him excitedly.

"Victor Mikhailovich, you will not believe it, but it's a fact! It's a fact!" Tatarov struck himself on the chest. "The party is being betrayed . . . by Azef. . . ."

"Wha-at!" Chernov jumped up. "You dare to insult Azef! The leader of our party?! Trying to hit back in this way? I've come for a frank confession! But your role is clear now. You will please report to give further evidence!"

"But it is true, I assure you, Victor Mikhailovich, it is true!" cried Tatarov, advancing on Chernov. "I shall bring you facts!"

"Swine!" Chernov clenched his fists and ran out of the room.

Tatarov hurriedly packed his suitcases. "It means death! Yes, yes, death!" He rushed back and forth in his locked room. And at the hour when he was to appear to testify, Tatarov was already near Munich, on his way to Russia.

REBECCA WEST

▼

2 A Conversation on the Train

It was with some trepidation that I chose an episode from Rebecca West's recent novel, The Birds Fall Down, *for this collection. The plot of this magnificent work, inspired by the Azef story, is so tightly woven that it is almost impossible to extract from it and to enlighten the reader sufficiently in an introductory note such as this one for him to follow the story. On the other hand, I felt I could not forgo representing it here because it has no equal in the field of novels about spies and provocateurs. Few writers have ever tried to depict the tangled web of the double and triple agent in fiction in its true complexity. Certainly no one has ever succeeded in making a literary masterpiece of such material. The only comparable work is Conrad's* Under Western Eyes, *but his plot is almost transparent compared with Dame Rebecca's.*

The full extent of Azef's duplicity was clarified once and for all in the course of an amazing conversation between two men that took place during a long railroad journey in Germany in the year 1908. One of the men was a former Russian revolutionary, Burt-zeff, who had suspected Azef and was making it his business to unmask him. He had gathered and analyzed all the incidents in the history of the Battle Organization which pointed the finger of suspicion at Azef, but he did not yet have final proof that Azef was the culprit. The other man was a certain Lopuhin, a former high official of the Czar's secret police, who, Burtzeff was certain, knew in detail of Azef's services to the police. The meeting in the railway compartment was not accidental. Burtzeff knew that Lopuhin was traveling on that particular train, and he made it his business to confront him there. What came out in this conversation, besides

FROM *The Birds Fall Down.*

the ultimate and unimpeachable evidence that Azef was the culprit, was the astounding revelation, previously unknown to Lopuhin, that Azef had also betrayed the police by the simple device of not betraying certain revolutionary plots to them when it suited him not to. Thus the two famous assassinations which rocked Russia and much of Europe in the eighteen-nineties, namely those of the Czar's Minister of the Interior Plehve (which Conrad makes use of in Under Western Eyes) *and of the Grand Duke Sergei, had succeeded because Azef not only did not inform the police that they were being planned (he later claimed total ignorance of them) but also gave the revolutionaries information concerning the security measures taken by the police to guard these dignitaries.*

This historic meeting in the railway compartment inspired the central scene in Rebecca West's novel, the one which culminates in the excerpt that follows. In her transformation of this material, Chubinov, a revolutionary intellectual, has sought out the aged Nikolai Diakonov, the former Minister of Justice under the Czar, now in exile and disgrace, who is traveling from Paris to the coast in a train with his granddaughter Laura. Chubinov wants to warn him of a discovery he has just made and to confirm its correctness. This discovery is that Kamensky, the devoted secretary of Diakonov who has followed him into exile, is one and the same person as Gorin, the chief of the assassination department of the Social Revolutionary Party. It was because of the successful assassination of a brace of dukes and generals that Diakonov, who was responsible for their protection, has been disgraced and exiled. Diakonov has never understood how it could have happened. But Dame Rebecca has added an additional complication to the original story. Kamensky is not only still playing his double game. He is even spying on Diakonov in exile for the Czar. The discovery of his duplicity endangers the lives of all who know of it and becomes the mainspring for the rest of the action of the novel, which departs then from historical fact. At the time of the Burtzeff-Lopuhin conversation, Azef had already removed himself from revolutionary circles. He died a natural death some years later, which is not the way it happens with Kamensky in The Birds Fall Down.*

IF Kamensky was Gorin, Laura thought, it was terrible that he had used the same forks and spoons, eaten off the same plates, and drunk

out of the same glasses as the Diakonov family, and sat at the table
as it had been furnished by their dead. The silver equipage had been
given to an ancestor by Catherine the Great: a string of silver ele-
phants trod a narrow silver track on the shining white cloth round a
larger elephant on a column, like the one in the square in Rome. The
forks and spoons were different from the Georgian ones they used at
home in Radnage Square, they were French. Another ancestor had
taken his bride to Paris just before Louis XV had issued his decree
requisitioning his subjects' silver to pay for his wars, and they had
taken back to Russia two great chests of it. The glasses had come from
Prague, from another honeymoon, and they had survived a hundred
years, only because they were always washed in a basin lined with
several layers of flannel. People had forgotten what the plates were,
and there were so many services nobody bothered whether they were
Meissen or Sèvres. Some were Chelsea but were painted with Japanese landscapes. They had the childish look that belongs to a
picture of a place by someone who has never been there. All were
so beautiful she looked at them every time. Now, if Nikolai went
into the dining-room and said, "Take all these things away for ever,
they are spoiled," he would be right. It would be no use just washing
them. At home in Radnage Square they would pretend there was no
problem, everyone would eat off the polluted ware, and it would be a
sort of poisoning. There was some good in being Russian. But perhaps
Kamensky was not Gorin.

Nikolai and Chubinov were talking languidly, two tired men,
about the origins of Kamensky and Gorin. Chubinov was saying that
Gorin was forty-three years old and was born at Lyskovo in the
Grodnensko province, and had studied at the University of St. Petersburg until the police began to harry them, then at Karlsruhe, and later
at Darmstadt, where he had taken his diploma in engineering. Nikolai
was saying that Kamensky was forty-one, was born at Kharkov, and
had taken his degrees in engineering at Moscow and Berlin. That was
certain. The Ministry had checked. "And Darmstadt too," said Chubinov, "we checked that." They were silent.

"What does Gorin look like?" Laura asked.

"He is dark. His eyes and hair are dark, and his face is unlined,
considering his age."

"Kamensky is dark, dark and short, pleasing but not distinguished,"
said Nikolai.

"Gorin is not short," said Chubinov, "he is not much shorter than I
am."

"But you are short."

"For you who are abnormally tall, it's difficult to get a conception of normal height."

"But what's Gorin like?" asked Laura. "What would you tell somebody to look out for, if they had to meet him at a railway-station?"

"Well, he's a Russian. It isn't only that his cheekbones are high, he's got the Slav signature on his face. If you met him anywhere you'd say, 'Ah, here's one of us.' I really can't think of anything else. I've often thought it strange that such a remarkable man should have such an ordinary appearance, for to tell the truth hundreds of thousands look exactly as he does."

"Millions of Russians look exactly like Kamensky, provided they're not of noble birth," said Nikolai. "But God forbid we should hang a man because he looks so like a great many other Russians that maybe he might be another man who also looks like a great many other Russians." He spoke with a hint of cunning.

"Gorin also looks as if he wasn't noble," meditated Chubinov. "I should think his father was probably a minor functionary in a not very large town, or perhaps a merchant, but in a small way of business. But he has, now I come to think of it, one physical trait as outstanding as his mental endowments. He has the eyes of an eagle. I've never known a man in middle life with such sight. Walking on the hills above Zurich, I've known him tell the time by the clock on a tower in the heart of the city, though not the youngest among us could see anything but the round dial."

"Then Gorin's not Kamensky," said Nikolai in calm and disagreeable triumph. "Kamensky's almost blind. I've never seen him without his spectacles. He's helpless without them."

"No, Grandfather," Laura said, "he isn't."

He looked at her out of the corner of his eye as if they were both Orientals and should not be speaking so directly.

"Don't you remember that the other day I tried on Monsieur Kamensky's spectacles?"

His glance did not soften.

"I tried to tell you, but you were angry with me. What I wanted to say was that Monsieur Kamensky's spectacles are glass, plain glass. He can see as well as anybody."

Without a pause Nikolai answered, "Thousands of our minor functionaries do that. Wear spectacles which are plain glass. I've come across the practice again and again among those not well-born. It's a sign of distinction among the undistinguished. A claim that one's not coarsely perfect, like one's cousin the peasant. That my friend Kamensky, of whom I know nothing ill, wears such spectacles is no proof that he's Chubinov's friend Gorin, who seems to be all one might expect of his pack of enlightened scoundrels."

Chubinov said gently, "So, you're determined not to ask, just to die. I can't do so. I feel it's my duty to live until I've discovered the truth and proclaimed it."

"There's no need for anyone but God to know the truth," said Nikolai. "The part of man is to obey, and for obedience one does not have to know the truth. One has only to pay attention to the command."

"Please, Monsieur Chubinov," said Laura, "does Gorin put anything on his hands? Monsieur Kamensky uses an ointment which his grandmother made for him when he got chilblains, with a herb in it which has a very strong smell." She stopped, astonished, even after all that had happened, by the horror on his face.

"In winter-time his rooms reeks with the stuff."

"People of that class always smell to high heaven from October to April, with the salves and messes made up for them by their old women," said Nikolai. "It's no proof of anything."

"Gorin's salve," said Chubinov, "is made from a herb we call *pizhina* in Russian."

"We call it tansy. It's very green and it doesn't grow very high but it isn't flat on the ground either. Would that be *pizhina?*"

"I've never seen it," said Chubinov. "For me it's a puff of steam from a bathroom door. When I was a little boy my mother and my aunts used to put *pizhina* leaves in their baths, and my German tutor used to sniff and say, '*Ach, der gute Rainfarn,*' and I recognized the smell again in Gorin's room."

"*Rainfarn.* I don't know that word. In French it's *la barbotine,* that's what Mummie calls it."

"We're lost unless a cook comes into the carriage, or someone carrying a German-French dictionary," said Nikolai. "This is an absurd conversation, belittling to us all. If one's stabbed, one doesn't spend one's last breath guessing what tradesman sold the dagger."

"But of course Kamensky's Gorin," said Laura, and shook with fury. "There's something that makes it certain. Grandfather, don't you remember? The way he got free this morning when he was bringing us down to the station. . . . Monsieur Chubinov, my grandfather has a little footman, he's just a boy, you must have seen him with us at the station, he's really too young to be a footman. He's very nice. He's devoted to Monsieur Kamensky, he says he's been very kind to him. When we were all getting into the carriage outside my grandfather's apartment, Monsieur Kamensky pretended that the little footman had slammed the door on his hand and hurt him. The poor boy said he hadn't, but Kamensky pretended he was in great pain and went on humbugging and humbugging, shamming not only that he was hurt, but shamming too that he was making light of it, and that for the boy's sake. I wish this wasn't true." She stopped for a minute and prayed, "God, let all this not have happened." But there was no answer. She went on, "Finally he pretended he was in such pain he had to get out of the carriage and go to a pharmacy where he could get his hand bandaged. But of course he was going off to the Café Viborg. And the boy was terribly upset. Oh, certainly Kamensky's Gorin, and he ought to be killed."

Nikolai was staring out of the windows at the fields. "It's not so bright as it was," he said. "Every time the sun goes behind a cloud in France you see the country's damp as a sponge." He shuddered, dropped his chin on his chest, closed his eyes, and softly asked a question.

"Oh, speak clearly!" groaned Chubinov. But it was not for him to complain. He had covered his ears as if he did not want to hear.

"I asked you," said Nikolai, "whether the name of Kaspar meant anything to you?"

"Nikolai Nikolaievitch, why did you not ask that question an hour ago?"

"For the same reason that you're not answering it now."

They sat side-by-side in silence, looking out at the dull day. When the sun came out of the clouds they turned their faces away from the brightness.

"Well, here it is, the bitter morsel," sighed Chubinov. "Kaspar is the Party name of Gorin. Only those of us who know him intimately call him Gorin. To all others he is Kaspar. Since you've asked this question, I suppose that Kaspar is the name used by Kamensky when he acts as a police spy." He broke the silence that followed by crying out quite loudly, "Nikolai Nikolaievitch, this is all your fault. None of this would have happened if you had been true to your own class, to your own kind. How could you take a police spy into your home? Blind as you are with bigotry, infatuated with your imagined duty to defend reaction, how could you let a police spy sit on your chairs, breathe the same air, talk with you, eat with you, meet your women folk? Even if the jackal cleans the gutters outside your house, the jackal is a jackal."

"But he wasn't a police spy like other police spies," said Nikolai. "Perhaps being with your kind corrupted him. He used not to be vile,

he was a good, good man. He came to my notice first when I was at
the Ministry of Ways and Communications. He was in charge of some
important pumping operations which had to be done when they laid a
railway-line over that marshland down by Vologda. Good God, he
cannot be a villain, he simply can't. Up there we had an epidemic of
typhus among the workers, and he behaved like a saint, he was fear-
less, he was a father to the sick, he caught the sickness himself, and all
this when he might have got leave to come back to Moscow, for he was
among the experts whom we could not afford to lose. When the
doctors sent him to us to convalesce he wanted to return long before
he was fit; I had to keep him with me by pretending I needed an extra
secretary for the moment, and in a very short time I realized he was a
subordinate beyond one's dreams. An excellent engineer, with much
knowledge of the newer work done in Germany and France, particularly in the field of hydraulics, and so good, so pious, so gracious.
Charity bubbled up in him, the janitors and the cleaners and the old
clerks all loved him, and if he came to me one day weeping, to tell me
that he could give information regarding the iniquitous proceedings in
certain revolutionary circles, you, Vassili Iulievitch, you know quite
well why that was, and that it was neither unnatural nor dishonourable. How can you have the impudence to transfer to him the shame
that lies on you!"

"I've not the slightest idea what you're talking about," said
Chubinov.

"I'm talking about his brother," said Nikolai, heavily.

"Gorin's brother? He hasn't got one."

"Not now. But he had one."

"No, never. Three sisters, yes. But I've heard him say several times
that he had never had a brother. Indeed, when we were at Montreux
he told me that it had always been his great desire to have a brother,
and that he'd found a substitute in me."

Trembling, Nikolai hissed, "Kamensky had a brother. Younger
than himself. He was enticed into joining your organization when he
was a student at Kharkov. Suddenly the boy appeared in Petersburg at
Kamensky's lodgings and begged his older brother for his protection,
saying that he'd been ordered by your Committee to shoot the Governor of Kharkov, and that he'd suddenly realized he could not kill, he
could not break the law of God. So he refused. No actual threat was
made by your committee, but he'd become aware that he was going to
be punished for his resistance to evil, and he feared the worst.
Kamensky left the boy in his lodgings, went to the house of a friend
who had a telephone, and tried to ring me up to ask for an appoint-

ment next day, but I was out. When he returned to his lodgings the boy was gone. Vassili Iulievitch, have you so many crimes on your conscience that you do not remember this one?"

"I don't remember it because it never happened. It couldn't have happened. For some reason which I can't bring to mind at the moment, we've never contemplated murdering the Governor of Kharkov."

"An odd omission. You must try to recall the reason, and tell me about it some time. But either you are lying, or you know nothing about the workings of your own organization. Your father was quite right in all he said about you. For there was such a boy. We found him. When Kamensky, in a frenzy of grief, was so far beyond himself that he ventured to come to my house in the middle of the night, a great liberty for a man in his position, we alerted the police both in Petersburg and back in Kharkov. After four days a peasant reported to the police that at a time which was a few hours after Kamensky's brother had disappeared, he had seen three men carrying a young man whom he supposed to be drunk into a villa on the Peterhof Road. A couple of nights later he passed the villa and it was in darkness, and a neighbour told him that the family was away on a long visit to the Crimea. That puzzled him, and he told the police, who went in and found the body of Kamensky's brother in the kitchen. A noose had been thrown round his neck and the rope had been slung on to a meat-hook in the ceiling. The wretched boy had been slowly strangled. Be careful how you speak of this. I went with Kamensky. I saw the boy's tongue lolling from his mouth. I am a soldier. But I had not seen any such thing before."

Chubinov stammered, "What was the name of the villa?"

"What a thing to ask. I don't remember. It was ten miles out on the Peterhof Road."

"Ten miles out on the Peterhof Road. A corpse hung from a meat-hook in the ceiling. The tongue. Nikolai Nikolaievitch, that wasn't Kamensky's brother. It was a student named Valentine. A traitor. A shameful traitor. He had led the police straight to one of our printing-presses. It was no mistake. Gorin took his papers off the body."

"The police found papers on the body which showed he was Kamensky's brother." Nikolai's voice fell to a whisper. "If you had seen how Kamensky wept."

The train stopped at a station and the two men did not speak again until the guard's trumpet sent it pushing on.

"This is the end of my life," said Chubinov.

"If I say that, it has no meaning, simply because it is true," said

Nikolai Nikolaievitch. "But in any case, I do not feel what you convey when you say that. It keeps on running through my head that the messengers came to Job and told him that fire had come down from heaven and burned up his servants. I do not feel that my servant Kamensky has done anything. I feel something has been done to him."

Presently they began to talk like policemen again. "I have to admit," said Chubinov hesitantly, "that there was always something mysterious about the case. We never actually knew who had performed the deed of vengeance, and it was premature. The committee was in the course of examining the proofs of Valentine's treachery, but it had not come near to the stage of giving orders for his punishment. Then Gorin found an unsigned note at his lodgings telling that three of our members could wait no longer and had trodden the viper under their heel, and it gave the address of the villa on the Peterhof Road. Gorin picked me up at my home and we went there at once. It was a terrible scene. Gorin is exquisitely sensitive. I've often heard him say that while he would dare to commit any murder in order that the tyrants who are strangling Russia should pay for their crimes, he can never reconcile himself to the harsh necessity that to make a murder, a sentient being has to be murdered."

"I see that's awkward for him," said Nikolai Nikolaievitch. "But don't worry. He showed himself quite robust that night. For if he took Valentine off the meat-hook for you, he must have put him back on it for me."

"I had forgotten, I had forgotten. But you don't mend anything by your mockery," said Chubinov.

"From our side," said the other, "there was something odd. We found Valentine's baptismal certificate in the Kharkov church records, and his school registration, but he had never attended Kharkov University. It turned out that Kamensky had never seen him there or had any proof that he was enrolled there. You see, I am like you, I slip back into thinking that he was honest. Well, the tale Kamensky then told us was that he supposed that the boy's revolutionary friends had seduced him into consenting to spend his days on some illegal activity before the term started, so he never went there at all."

"You should have known what could have been behind that," said Chubinov. "Some boy called Kamensky died after leaving high school and before getting to the university, and our people stole his identity for one of our workers."

"Yes, that ghoulish trick I should have recognized by this time. But to get back to our loved one. He came into my office the next day, grief-stricken, enraged, alone, helpless, weeping—weeping again—and with a peculiarly touching quality about his tears. He asked if he might join your organization and report on its doings, so that he could expiate the guilt which lay on him for not having protected his young brother from your devilry. Well, as I said before, this reaction seemed neither unnatural nor dishonourable. I was then given to understand, and until you came into this compartment it was never suggested to me that I should doubt it, that he presented himself to your organization, pretended that he believed his brother's disappearance was due to the Secret Police, gained your confidence, and thus enabled us to punish many criminals and avert many crimes. In my personal relations with him I experienced a curious pleasure. Now I know all about him, or more about him, the only virtue I can credit him with is courage, but he seemed to have all the virtues, and one more than is named, a kind of gaiety. And when I was disgraced he did not waver. I have come to love him. And I am not such a fool as you think," he suddenly roared, "for he was on our side. Assuredly he was on our side. He must have been on our side, he gave us your Vesnin, Patopenko, and Komissaroff. Yes, and many others of your abominable breed."

"He was on our side," said Chubinov, changing his glasses. "He in his own person planned the executions of Dubassoff and Sipyagin and Plehve—yes, it was he who coached the cab-driver in getting his horse to move on slowly while he seemed to be trying to restrain it, so that Sazonoff could use it as cover up to the very last moment, when he ran out and threw the bomb which freed us from the butcher of Kishinev, the past master of pogroms. Without him the Grand Duke Sergei would be alive today—"

"Do not speak to me of that death," Nikolai begged him, with sudden gentleness. "Every time I hear of it I sin. I loathed the Grand Duke Sergei, he was the incarnation of that evil which must not be blamed, since it arises out of stupidity, and is thus, God help us all to understand, plainly God's will. When there is any mention of his assassination I fall straight into sin, I blaspheme, before I know what I'm doing. I thank God he is dead. Again and again I've done penance for this, and again and again I offend. This too is part of the trouble you've made for all of us, you accursed murderers."

"But it's you, not we, who are the murderers. We are the instruments of justice. No guilt rests on us. There is blood on our hands, but it is turned to glory by the rectitude of our cause. How strange it is that one of us two should have lived a life which is like a noble poem and the other a life which is that poem's ignoble parody."

"One day you'll learn which side it was that produced the parody," Nikolai promised, "from the lips of the Lord himself," he added spitefully. He called to an attendant who was going down the corridor. "What's the next station we stop at? Grissaint? It is a big station? With frequent trains back to Paris? Good." His eyes went back to Chubinov. "Forgive me, I shouldn't mock a dead man. And you're a dead man, Vassili Iulievitch."

"No," said Chubinov. "Not yet."

"I think you will be very soon. I'm going to die quite soon. Not at once, but quite soon. My granddaughter and I will get out at the next station, this Grissaint, or whatever it's called, and take the next train back to Paris. My duty dictates that step, because there's no more direct route I know of between Northern France and St. Petersburg, and that's where I must go. If the Tsar wishes me to return to Russia in order to humiliate me and accuse me of a crime I have not committed, and insult me by pardoning my innocence, then to Russia I must go."

"No," said Laura, "no. Can't you think for one single moment of Grandmother?"

"I've spent my whole life telling my inferiors that the Tsar's will is sacred, even when it ordered their destruction. There's no reason I can see why I should alter my attitude when it is myself whom he wants to destroy. So I must return to Russia and there I will die, either in prison or out of it, from rage. But it will take some time to wear me down to that. But you, Vassili Iulievitch, you will be dead quite soon."

JOSEPH CONRAD

▼

3 Mr. Vladimir and Mr. Verloc

In a sense, the world in which the action of Conrad's novel The
Secret Agent *takes place is not far removed from that of the
preceding pieces although geographically the scene is England.
Conrad's Mr. Verloc is, like Azef, a provocateur in the employ of
the Czar's secret-police system. The aim of the provocation is not,
as in Azef's case, to expose and apprehend the revolutionaries
within Russia but rather to make the democratic English aware of
the danger from revolutionaries and anarchists that threatens the
stability of empire throughout Europe. Mr. Vladimir, the new
emissary of the Czar's police in London, wants to incite the
anarchists, through the instrument of Mr. Verloc, to some outrageous act which will make the English bear down more ruthlessly on the troublemakers whom they are otherwise inclined to
ignore. Just what this act should be is eventually put forward by
Mr. Vladimir after much circumlocution. As far-fetched and outrageous as the plan seems, Conrad based it on an event which had
actually taken place at Greenwich in 1894, an attempt to blow up
the observatory. As happens later in* The Secret Agent, *the conspirator who carried the bomb was blown to pieces, but not the
observatory.*

*The reader soon senses from Conrad's depiction of the secret-
police officer and his lackadaisical agent that he is holding up both
sides to ridicule, the Czarist autocracy (which as a Pole he knew
and hated) and the disruptive and asinine machinations of the
anarchists who, like a character in Dostoevski's* The Possessed,
*wished to bring about "the downfall of everything." Yet despite
the caricature, it is astonishing how well Conrad, who to the best*

FROM *The Secret Agent.*

74

of my knowledge never had contact with the secret world of espionage, manages to give the flavor of an exchange between a supercilious intelligence officer and his unsatisfactory agent.

Mr. Vladimir, First Secretary, had a drawing-room reputation as an agreeable and entertaining man. He was something of a favorite in society. . . .

But there was no trace of merriment or perplexity in the way he looked at Mr. Verloc. Lying far back in the deep arm-chair, with squarely spread elbows, and throwing one leg over a thick knee, he had, with his smooth and rosy countenance, the air of a preternaturally thriving baby that will not stand nonsense from anybody.

"You understand French, I suppose?" he said.

Mr. Verloc stated huskily that he did. His whole vast bulk had a forward inclination. He stood on the carpet in the middle of the room, clutching his hat and stick in one hand; the other hung lifelessly by his side. He muttered unobtrusively somewhere deep down in his throat something about having done his military service in the French artillery. At once, with contemptuous perversity, Mr. Vladimir changed the language, and began to speak idiomatic English without the slightest trace of a foreign accent.

"Ah! Yes. Of course. Let's see. How much did you get for obtaining the design of the improved breech-block of their new field-gun?"

"Five years' rigorous confinement in a fortress," Mr. Verloc answered unexpectedly, but without any sign of feeling.

"You got off easily," was Mr. Vladimir's comment. "And, anyhow, it served you right for letting yourself get caught. What made you go in for that sort of thing—eh?"

Mr. Verloc's husky conversational voice was heard speaking of youth, of a fatal infatuation for an unworthy—

"Aha! *Cherchez la femme,*" Mr. Vladimir deigned to interrupt, unbending, but without affability; there was, on the contrary, a touch of grimness in his condescension. "How long have you been employed by the Embassy here?" he asked.

"Ever since the time of the late Baron Stott-Wartenheim," Mr. Verloc answered, in subdued tones, and protruding his lips sadly, in sign of sorrow for the deceased diplomat. The First Secretary observed this play of physiognomy steadily.

"Ah! ever since . . . Well! What have you got to say for yourself?" he asked, sharply.

Mr. Verloc answered with some surprise that he was not aware of having anything special to say. He had been summoned by a letter— And he plunged his hand busily into the side-pocket of his overcoat, but before the mocking cynical watchfulness of Mr. Vladimir, concluded to leave it there.

"Bah!" said the latter. "What do you mean by getting out of condition like this? You haven't got even the physique of your profession. You—a member of a starving proletariat—never! You—a desperate socialist or anarchist—which is it?"

"Anarchist," stated Mr. Verloc, in a deadened tone.

"Bosh!" went on Mr. Vladimir, without raising his voice. . . . "You wouldn't deceive an idiot. They all are that, by the by; but you seem to me simply impossible. So you began your connection with us by stealing the French gun designs. And you got yourself caught. That must have been very disagreeable to our Government. You don't seem to be very smart."

Mr. Verloc tried to exculpate himself huskily.

"As I've had occasion to observe before, a fatal infatuation for an unworthy—"

Mr. Vladimir raised a large white, plump hand.

"Ah, yes. The unlucky attachment—of your youth. She got hold of the money, and then sold you to the police—eh?"

The doleful change in Mr. Verloc's physiognomy, the momentary drooping of his whole person, confessed that such was the regrettable case. Mr. Vladimir's hand clasped the ankle reposing on his knee. The sock was of dark-blue silk.

"You see, that was not very clever of you. Perhaps you are too susceptible."

Mr. Verloc intimated, in a throaty, veiled murmur, that he was no longer young.

"Oh! That's a failing which age does not cure," Mr. Vladimir remarked, with sinister familiarity. "But no! You are too fat for that. You could not have come to look like this if you had been at all susceptible. I'll tell you what I think is the matter: you are a lazy fellow. How long have you been drawing pay from this Embassy?"

"Eleven years," was the answer, after a moment of sulky hesitation. "I've been charged with several missions to London while His Excellency Baron Stott-Wartenheim was still Ambassador in Paris. Then by his Excellency's instructions I settled down in London. I am English."

"You are! Are? Eh?"

"A natural-born British subject," Mr. Verloc said, stolidly. "But my father was French, and so—"

"Never mind explaining," interrupted the other. "I dare say you could have been legally a Marshal of France and a Member of Parliament in France and a Member of Parliament in England—and then, indeed, you would have been of some use to our Embassy."

This flight of fancy provoked something like a faint smile on Mr. Verloc's face. Mr. Vladimir retained an imperturbable gravity.

"But, as I've said, you are a lazy fellow; you don't use your opportunities. In the time of Baron Stott-Wartenheim we had a lot of soft-headed people running this Embassy. They caused fellows of your sort to form a false conception of the nature of a secret service fund. It is my business to correct this misapprehension by telling you what the secret service is not. It is not a philanthropic institution, I've had you called here on purpose to tell you this."

Mr. Vladimir observed the forced expression of bewilderment on Verloc's face, and smiled sarcastically.

"I see that you understand me perfectly. I dare say you are intelligent enough for your work. What we want now is activity—activity."

On repeating this last word Mr. Vladimir laid a long white forefinger on the edge of the desk. Every trace of huskiness disappeared from Verloc's voice. The nape of his gross neck became crimson above the velvet collar of his overcoat. His lips quivered before they came widely open.

"If you'll only be good enough to look up my record," he boomed out in his great, clear, oratorical bass, "you'll see I gave a warning only three months ago, on the occasion of the Grand-Duke Romuald's visit to Paris, which was telegraphed from here to the French police, and—"

"Tut, tut!" broke out Mr. Vladimir, with a frowning grimace. "The French police had no use for your warning. Don't roar like this! What the devil do you mean?"

With a note of proud humility Mr. Verloc apologized for forgetting himself. His voice, famous for years at open-air meetings and at workmen's assemblies in large halls, had contributed, he said, to his reputation of a good and trustworthy comrade. It was, therefore, a part of his usefulness. It had inspired confidence in his principles. "I was always put up to speak by the leaders at a critical moment," Mr. Verloc declared, with obvious satisfaction. There was no uproar above which he could not make himself heard. . . .

"Well, I am going to speak plain English to you" [Mr. Vladimir said]. "Voice won't do. We have no use for your voice. We don't want a voice. We want facts—startling facts, damn you!" he added, with a sort of ferocious discretion, right into Mr. Verloc's face. . . .

"You give yourself for an 'agent provocateur.' The proper business of an 'agent provocateur' is to provoke. As far as I can judge from your record kept here, you have done nothing to earn your money for the last three years."

"Nothing!" exclaimed Verloc, stirring not a limb, and not raising his eyes, but with the note of sincere feeling in his tone. "I have several times prevented what might have been—"

"There is a proverb in this country which says prevention is better than cure," interrupted Mr. Vladimir, throwing himself into the arm-chair. "It is stupid in a general way. There is no end to prevention. But it is characteristic. They dislike finality in this country. Don't you be too English. And in this particular instance, don't be absurd. The evil is already here. We don't want prevention—we want cure."

He paused, turned to the desk, and turning over some papers lying there, spoke in a changed businesslike tone, without looking at Mr. Verloc.

"You know, of course, of the International Conference assembled in Milan?"

Mr. Verloc intimated hoarsely that he was in the habit of reading the daily papers. To a further question his answer was that, of course, he understood what he read. At this Mr. Vladimir, smiling faintly at the documents he was still scanning one after another, murmured: "As long as it is not written in Latin, I suppose."

"Or Chinese," added Mr. Verloc, stolidly.

"H'm. Some of your revolutionary friends' effusions are written in a charabia every bit as incomprehensible as Chinese—" Mr. Vladimir let fall disdainfully a gray sheet of printed matter. "What are all these leaflets headed F.P., with a hammer, pen, and torch crossed? What does it mean, this F.P.?" Mr. Verloc approached the imposing writing-table.

"The Future of the Proletariat. It's a society," he explained, standing ponderously by the side of the arm-chair, "not anarchist in principle, but open to all shades of revolutionary opinion."

"Are you in it?"

"One of the vice-presidents," Mr. Verloc breathed out heavily; and the First Secretary of the Embassy raised his head to look at him.

"Then you ought to be ashamed of yourself," he said, incisively. "Isn't your society capable of anything else but printing this prophetic bosh in blunt type on this filthy paper—eh? Why don't you do something? Look here. I've this matter in hand now, and I tell you plainly that you will have to earn your money. The good old Stott-Wartenheim times are over. No work, no pay."

Mr. Verloc felt a queer sensation of faintness in his stout legs. He stepped back one pace, and blew his nose loudly.

He was, in truth, startled and alarmed. The pale London sunshine, struggling clear of the London mist, shed a lukewarm brightness into the First Secretary's private room; and, in the silence, Mr. Verloc heard, against a window-pane, the faint buzzing of a fly—his first fly of the year—heralding, better than any number of swallows, the approach of spring. The useless fussing of that tiny, energetic organism affected unpleasantly this big man, threatened in his indolence.

In the pause Mr. Vladimir formulated in his mind a series of disparaging remarks concerning Mr. Verloc's face and figure. The fellow was unexpectedly vulgar, heavy, and impudently unintelligent. He looked uncommonly like a master plumber come to present his bill. The First Secretary of the Embassy, from his occasional excursions into the field of American humor, had formed a special notion of that class of mechanic as the embodiment of fraudulent laziness and incompetency.

This was, then, the famous and trusty secret agent, so secret that he was never designated otherwise but by the symbol △. in the late Baron Stott-Wartenheim's official, semi-official, and confidential correspondence; the celebrated agent △., whose warnings had the power to change the schemes and the dates of royal, imperial, grand-ducal journeys, and sometimes caused them to be put off altogether! This fellow! And Mr. Vladimir indulged mentally in an enormous and derisive fit of merriment, partly at his own astonishment, which he judged naïve, but mostly at the expense of the universally regretted Baron Stott-Wartenheim. His late Excellency, whom the august favor of his Imperial master had imposed as Ambassador upon several reluctant Ministers of Foreign Affairs, had enjoyed in his lifetime a fame for an owlish, pessimistic gullibility. His Excellency had the social revolution on the brain. He imagined himself to be a diplomatist set apart by a special dispensation to watch the end of diplomacy, and pretty nearly the end of the world in a horrid democratic upheaval. His prophetic and doleful despatches had been for years the joke of Foreign Offices. He was said to have exclaimed on his death-bed (visited by his Imperial friend and master): "Unhappy Europe! Thou shalt perish by the moral insanity of thy children!" He was fated to be the victim of the first humbugging rascal that came along, thought Mr. Vladimir, smiling vaguely at Mr. Verloc.

"You ought to venerate the memory of Baron Stott-Wartenheim!" he exclaimed, suddenly.

The lowered physiognomy of Mr. Verloc expressed a sombre and weary annoyance.

"Permit me to observe to you," he said, "that I came here because I was summoned by a peremptory letter. I have been here only twice before in the last eleven years, and certainly never at eleven in the morning. It isn't very wise to call me up like this. There is just a chance of being seen. And that would be no joke for me."

Mr. Vladimir shrugged his shoulders.

"It would destroy my usefulness," continued the other, hotly.

"That's your affair," murmured Mr. Vladimir, with soft brutality. "When you cease to be useful, you shall cease to be employed. Yes, Right off. Cut short. You shall—" Mr. Vladimir, frowning, paused, at a loss for a sufficiently idiomatic expression, and instantly brightened up, with a grin of beautifully white teeth. "You shall be chucked!" he brought out, ferociously.

Once more Mr. Verloc had to react with all the force of his will against that sensation of faintness running down one's legs which, once upon a time, had inspired some poor devil with the felicitous expression: "My heart went down into my boots." Mr. Verloc, aware of the sensation, raised his head bravely.

Mr. Vladimir bore the look of heavy inquiry with perfect serenity.

"What we want is to administer a tonic to the Conference in Milan," he said, airily. "Its deliberations upon international action for the suppression of political crime don't seem to get anywhere. England lags. This country is absurd with its sentimental regard for individual liberty. It's intolerable to think that all your friends have got only to come over to—"

"In that way I have them all under my eye," Mr. Verloc interrupted, huskily.

"It would be much more to the point to have them all under lock and key. England must be brought into line. The imbecile bourgeoisie of this country make themselves the accomplices of the very people whose aim is to drive them out of their houses to starve in ditches. And they have the political power still, if they only had the sense to use it for their preservation. I suppose you agree that the middle classes are stupid?"

Mr. Verloc agreed hoarsely.

"They are."

"They have no imagination. They are blinded by an idiotic vanity. What they want just now is a jolly good scare. This is the psychological moment to set your friends to work. I have had you called here to develop to you my idea."

And Mr. Vladimir developed his idea from on high, with scorn and condescension, displaying at the same time an amount of ignorance as to the real aims, thoughts, and methods of the revolutionary world which filled the silent Mr. Verloc with inward consternation. He confounded causes with effects more than was excusable; the most distinguished propagandists with impulsive bomb-throwers; assumed organization where, in the nature of things, it could not exist; spoke of the social revolutionary party one moment as of a perfectly disciplined army, where the word of chiefs was supreme, and, at another, as if it had been the loosest association of desperate brigands that ever camped in a mountain gorge. Once Mr. Verloc had opened his mouth for a protest, but the raising of a shapely, large white hand arrested him. Very soon he became too appalled to even try to protest. He listened in a stillness of dread which resembled the immobility of profound attention.

"A series of outrages," Mr. Vladimir continued, calmly, "executed here in this country; not only *planned* here—that would not do—they would not mind. Your friends could set half the Continent on fire without influencing the public opinion here in favor of a universal repressive legislation. They will not look outside their back yard here."

Mr. Verloc cleared his throat, but his heart failed him, and he said nothing.

"These outrages need not be especially sanguinary," Mr. Vladimir went on, as if delivering a scientific lecture, "but they must be sufficiently startling—effective. Let them be directed against buildings for instance. What is the fetish of the hour that all the bourgeoisie recognize—eh, Mr. Verloc?"

Mr. Verloc opened his hands and shrugged his shoulders slightly.

"You are too lazy to think," was Mr. Vladimir's comment upon that gesture. "Pay attention to what I say. The fetish of to-day is neither royalty nor religion. Therefore the Palace and the Church should be left alone. You understand what I mean, Mr. Verloc?"

The dismay and the scorn of Mr. Verloc found vent in an attempt at levity.

"Perfectly. But what of the Embassies? A series of attacks on the various Embassies—" he began. But he could not withstand the cold, watchful stare of the First Secretary.

"You can be facetious, I see," the latter observed, carelessly. "That's all right. It may enliven your oratory at socialistic congresses. But this room is no place for it. It would be infinitely safer for you to follow carefully what I am saying. As you are being called upon to furnish facts instead of cock-and-bull stories, you had better try to make your profit of what I am taking the trouble to explain to you. The sacrosanct fetish of to-day is science. Why don't you get some of your friends to go for that wooden-faced panjan-drum—eh? Is it not part of these institutions which must be swept away before the F.P. comes along?"

Mr. Verloc said nothing. He was afraid to open his lips, lest a groan should escape him.

"This is what you should try for. An attempt upon a crowned head or on a president is sensational enough in a way, but not so much as it used to be. It has entered into the general conception of the existence of all chiefs of state. It's almost conventional—espe-cially since so many presidents have been assassinated. Now let us take an outrage upon—say, a church. Horrible enough at first sight, no doubt, and yet not so effective as a person of an ordinary mind might think. No matter how revolutionary and anarchist in incep-tion, there would be fools enough to give such an outrage the character of a religious manifestation. And that would detract from the especial alarming significance we wish to give to the act. A murderous attempt on a restaurant or a theatre would suffer in the same way from the suggestion of non-political passion: the exas-peration of a hungry man, an act of social revenge. All this is used up; it is no longer instructive as an object-lesson in revolutionary anarchism. Every newspaper has ready-made phrases to explain such manifestations away. I am about to give you the philosophy of bomb-throwing from my point of view; from the point of view you pretend to have been serving for the last eleven years. I will try not to talk above your head. The sensibilities of the class you are attack-ing are soon blunted. Property seems to them an indestructible thing. You can't count upon their emotions either of pity or fear for very long. A bomb outrage to have any influence on public opinion now must go beyond the intention of vengefulness or terrorism. It must be purely destructive. It must be that, and only that, beyond the faintest suspicion of any other object. You anarchists should make it clear that you are perfectly determined to make a clean sweep of the whole social creation. 'But how to get that appallingly absurd notion into the heads of the middle classes so that there should be no mistake?' That's the question. 'By directing your blows at something outside the ordinary passions of humanity' is the answer. Of course, there is art. A bomb in the National Gallery would make some noise. But it would not be serious enough. Art has never been their fetish. It's like breaking a few back windows in a man's house; whereas, if you want to make him really sit up, you must try at least to raise the roof. There would be some screaming, of course, but from whom? Artists, art critics, and such like—people of no account. Nobody minds what they say. But there is learning—science. Any imbecile that has got an income believes in that. He does not know why, but he believes it matters somehow. It is the sacrosanct fetish. All the damned professors are radicals at heart. Let them know that their great panjandrum has got to go, too, to make room for the Future of the Proletariat. A howl from all these intellectual idiots is bound to help forward the labors of the Milan Conference. They will be writing to the papers. Their indignation would be above suspicion, no material interests being openly at stake, and it will alarm every selfishness of the class which should be impressed. They believe that in some mysterious way science is at the source of their material prosperity. They do. And the absurd ferocity of such a demonstration will affect them more profoundly than the mangling of a whole street—or theatre—full of their own kind. To the last they can always say: 'Oh, it's mere class hate.' But what is one to say to an act of destructive ferocity so absurd as to be incomprehensible, inexplicable, almost unthinkable—in fact, mad? Madness alone is truly terrifying, inasmuch as you cannot placate it either by threats, persuasion, or bribes. Moreover, I am a civilized man. I would never dream of directing you to organize a mere butchery, even if I expected the best results from it. But I wouldn't expect from a butchery the result I want. Murder is always with us. It is almost an institution. The demonstration must be against learning—science. But not every science will do. The attack must have all the shocking senselessness of gratuitous blasphemy. Since bombs are your means of expression, it would be really telling if one could throw a bomb into pure mathematics. But that is impossible. I have been trying to educate you; I have expounded to you the higher philosophy of your usefulness, and suggested to you some serviceable arguments. The practical application of my teaching interests you mostly. But from the moment I have undertaken to interview you I have also given some attention to the practical aspect of the question. What do you think of having a go at astronomy?"

For some time Mr. Verloc's immobility by the side of the arm-chair resembled a state of collapsed coma—a sort of passive insensibility interrupted by slight convulsive starts, such as may be observed in the domestic dog having a nightmare on the hearth-rug. And it was in an uneasy, doglike growl that he repeated the word:

"Astronomy."

He had not recovered thoroughly as yet from that state of

bewilderment brought about by the effort to follow Mr. Vladimir's rapid, incisive utterance. It had overcome his power of assimilation. It had made him angry. This anger was complicated by incredulity. And suddenly it dawned upon him that all this was an elaborate joke. Mr. Vladimir exhibited his white teeth in a smile, with dimples on his round, full face posed with a complacent inclination above the bristling bow of his necktie. The favorite of intelligent society women had assumed his drawing-room attitude accompanying the delivery of delicate witticisms. Sitting well forward, his white hand upraised, he seemed to hold delicately between his thumb and forefinger the subtlety of his suggestion.

"There could be nothing better. Such an outrage combines the greatest possible regard for humanity with the most alarming display of ferocious imbecility. I defy the ingenuity of journalists to persuade their public that any given member of the proletariat can have a personal grievance against astronomy. Starvation itself could hardly be dragged in there—eh? And there are other advantages. The whole civilized world has heard of Greenwich. The very boot-blacks in the basement of Charing Cross Station know something of it. See?"

The features of Mr. Vladimir, so well known in the best society by their humorous urbanity, beamed with cynical self-satisfaction, which would have astonished the intelligent women his wit enter-tained so exquisitely. "Yes," he continued, with a contemptuous smile, "the blowing up of the first meridian is bound to raise a howl of execration."

"A difficult business," Mr. Verloc mumbled, feeling that this was the only safe thing to say.

"What is the matter? Haven't you the whole gang under your hand? The very pick of the basket? That old terrorist, Yundt, is here. I see him walking about Piccadilly in his green havelock almost every day. And Michaelis, the ticket-of-leave apostle—you don't mean to say you don't know where he is? Because if you don't, I can tell you," Mr. Vladimir went on, menacingly. "If you imagine that you are the only one on the secret fund list, you are mistaken."

This perfectly gratuitous suggestion caused Mr. Verloc to shuffle his feet slightly.

"And the whole Lausanne lot—eh? Haven't they been flocking over here at the first hint of the Milan Conference? This is an absurd country."

"It will cost money," Mr. Verloc said, by a sort of instinct.

"That cock won't fight," Mr. Vladimir retorted, with an amazingly genuine English accent. "You'll get your screw every month, and no more till something happens. And if nothing happens very soon, you won't get even that. What's your ostensible occupation? What are you supposed to live by?"

"I keep a shop," answered Mr. Verloc.

"A shop! What sort of shop?"

"Stationery, newspapers. My wife—"

"Your what?" interrupted Mr. Vladimir, in his guttural Central-Asian tones.

"My wife." Mr. Verloc raised his husky voice slightly. "I am married."

"That be damned for a yarn!" exclaimed the other, in unfeigned astonishment. "Married! And you a professed anarchist, too! What is this confounded nonsense? But I suppose it's merely a manner of speaking. Anarchists don't marry. It's well known. They can't. It would be apostasy."

"My wife isn't one," Mr. Verloc mumbled, sulkily. "Moreover, it's no concern of yours."

"Oh yes, it is," snapped Mr. Vladimir. "I am beginning to be convinced that you are not at all the man for the work you've been employed on. Why, you must have discredited yourself completely in your own world by your marriage. Couldn't you have managed without? This is your virtuous attachment—eh? What with one sort of attachment and another, you are doing away with your usefulness."

Mr. Verloc, puffing out his cheeks, let the air escape violently, and that was all. He had armed himself with patience. It was not to be tried much longer. The First Secretary became suddenly very curt, detached, final.

"You may go now," he said. "A dynamite outrage must be provoked. I gave you a month. The sittings of the Conference are suspended. Before it reassembles again something must have happened here, or your connection with us ceases."

He changed the note once more with an unprincipled versatility.

"Think over my philosophy, Mr.—Mr.—Verloc," he said, with a sort of chaffing condescension, waving his hand towards the door. "Go for the first meridian. You don't know the middle classes as well as I do. Their sensibilities are jaded. The first meridian. Nothing better, and nothing easier, I should think."

III. *Mask and Intrigue*

Once you start looking for spies in literature, you find them everywhere, especially if you allow a broad enough interpretation of the term—informers, eavesdroppers, conspirators, traitors, spinners of intrigue, keepers and sellers of secrets. There is a bit of spying or, rather, counterspying (in the form of postal censorship) in Shakespeare's *Henry V*, when the three emissaries to the French court are discovered to be traitors to the king after their treasonable mail has been read (Act II, Scene 2):

> "The king hath note of all that they intend,
> By interception which they dream not of."

In Dickens' *A Tale of Two Cities*, as you may recall, the climactic event, in which Sydney Carton substitutes himself for Charles Darnay as a candidate for the guillotine, is made possible by the fact that the turnkey at the prison is a certain John Barsad, whose unsavory history as a professional spy and informer for a series of different employers gives Carton a hold over him. All in all, you could put together a whole collection of spy stories, in the broadest sense of the word, just by drawing on Sir Walter Scott, Robert Louis Stevenson, and the host of other nineteenth-century novelists.

What you will not find in these earlier works is a continuous spy story, one in which the spy is the protagonist or even a major character, nor will you find much in which the idea of an intelligence organization plays any role, although such organizations, loosely construed, have existed since the earliest times. In both the excerpts which follow, these elements play a rather larger role than they do in most historical romances, which is not the only reason I chose them. Since we have finally moved away from tales based on fact and into pure fiction, the author's ability to invent a good tale was in the end what counted for most.

ALEXANDRE DUMAS

▼

1 The General of the Order

The Vicomte de Bragelonne *is a sequel to* The Three Musketeers *and takes place ten years later. In it Athos, Porthos, Aramis, and D'Artagnan all appear again, not much changed from the gilded buckoes we first knew, except for Aramis. He, as you may recall, entered the priesthood at the end of the earlier book. In ten years he has become the Bishop of Vannes in Brittany. In our excerpt he manages with one frightening leap to reach the dizzy heights of ecclesiastical power.*

Looking back on the seventeenth century, the writers of the eighteenth and nineteenth centuries (and not only in Protestant countries) saw in the Jesuits a sinister secret society, dedicated not just to strengthening the church but to political dominance of all Europe. Their methods, it was popularly thought, were much as Dumas describes them in this remarkable scene—to come into possession of valuable state secrets and to use them to control the kings and princes of the world. The Jesuits were or had, in a sense, an international intelligence system, its members and associates delivering their information to headquarters for whatever use it might have. The theme of the excerpt is, however, not so much espionage itself—we are not told (except in the case of Aramis) how the holders of the secrets came to possess them—but rather the power of the secret.

Some explanatory aids: The dying General of the Order is disguised as a Franciscan. At that time, secular persons could be associated with the Jesuit order, as is the doctor who treats the supposed Franciscan. In case the reader, at the end, feels he has been cheated by our cutting him off, I can tell him that Dumas never does explain why poison was used.

FROM *The Vicomte de Bragelonne.*

During the week, seven travelers [besides Aramis and the Franciscan] had taken up their abode in the inn. . . . These seven persons, accompanied by a suitable retinue, were the following;—

First of all, a brigadier in the German army, his secretary, physician, three servants, and seven horses. The brigadier's name was the Comte de Wostpur.—A Spanish cardinal, with two nephews, two secretaries, an officer of his household, and twelve horses. The cardinal's name was Monseigneur Herrebia.—A rich merchant of Bremen, with his man-servant and two horses. This merchant's name was Meinheer Bonstett.—A Venetian senator with his wife and daughter, both extremely beautiful. The senator's name was Signor Marini.—A Scotch laird, with seven highlanders of his clan, all on foot. The laird's name was MacCumnor.—An Austrian from Vienna without title or coat-of-arms, who had arrived in a carriage; a good deal of the priest, and something of the soldier. He was called the Councilor.—And, finally, a Flemish lady, with a man-servant, a lady's maid, and a female companion, a large retinue of servants, great display, and immense horses. She was called the Flemish lady.

All these travelers had arrived on the same day, and yet their arrival had occasioned no confusion in the inn, no stoppage in the street; their apartments had been fixed upon beforehand, by their couriers or secretaries, who had arrived the previous evening or that very morning. . . .

[It was late at night.] While the innkeeper stood respectfully near the door, the Franciscan collected himself for a moment. He then passed across his sallow face a hand which seemed dried up by fever, and rubbed his nervous and agitated fingers across his beard. His large eyes, hollowed by sickness and inquietude, seemed to pursue in the vague distance a mournful and fixed idea.

"What physicians have you at Fontainebleau?" he inquired, after a long pause.

"We have three, holy father."

"What are their names?"

"Luiniguet first."

"The next one?"

"A brother of the Carmelite order, named Brother Hubert."

"The next?"

"A secular member, named Grisart."

"Ah! Grisart?" murmured the monk. "Send for Monsieur Grisart immediately."

The landlord moved in prompt obedience to the direction. "Tell me, what priests are there here?"

"What priests?"

"Yes; belonging to what orders?"

"There are Jesuits, Augustines, and Cordeliers; but the Jesuits are the closest at hand. Shall I send for a confessor belonging to the order of Jesuits?"

"Yes, immediately."

It will be imagined that, at the sign of the cross which they had exchanged, the landlord and the invalid monk had recognized each other as two affiliated members of the well-known Society of Jesus. Left to himself, the Franciscan drew from his pocket a bundle of papers, some of which he read over with the most careful attention. The violence of his disorder, however, overcame his courage; his eyes rolled in their sockets, a cold sweat poured down his face, and he nearly fainted, and lay with his head thrown backwards and his arms hanging down on both sides of his chair. For more than five minutes he remained without any movement, when the landlord returned, bringing with him the physician, whom he hardly allowed time to dress himself. The noise they made in entering the room, the current of air which the opening of the door occasioned, restored the Franciscan to his senses. He hurriedly seized hold of the papers which were lying about, and with his long and bony hand concealed them under the cushions of the chair. The landlord went out of the room, leaving patient and physician together.

"Come here, Monsieur Grisart," said the Franciscan to the doctor; "approach closer, for there is no time to lose. Try, by touch and sound, and consider, and pronounce your sentence."

"The landlord," replied the doctor, "told me that I had the honor of attending an affiliated brother."

"Yes," replied the Franciscan, "it is so. Tell me the truth, then; I feel very ill, and I think I am about to die."

The physician took the monk's hand and felt his pulse. "Oh, oh," he said, "a dangerous fever."

"What do you call a dangerous fever?" inquired the Franciscan, with an imperious look.

"To an affiliated member of the first or second year," replied the physician, looking inquiringly at the monk, "I should say—a fever that may be cured."

"But to me?" said the Franciscan. The physician hesitated.

"Look at my gray hair, and my forehead, full of anxious thought," he continued: "look at the lines in my face, by which I reckon up the trials I have undergone; I am a Jesuit of the eleventh year, Monsieur Grisart." The physician started, for, in fact, a Jesuit of the eleventh year was one of those men who had been initiated in all the secrets of the order, one of those for whom science has no more secrets, the society no further barriers to present—temporal obedience, no more trammels.

"In that case," said Grisart, saluting him with respect, "I am in the presence of a master?"

"Yes; act, therefore, accordingly."

"And you wish to know?"

"My real state."

"Well," said the physician, "it is a brain fever, which has reached its highest degree of intensity."

"There is no hope, then?" inquired the Franciscan, in a quick tone of voice.

"I do not say that," replied the doctor; "yet, considering the disordered state of the brain, the hurried respiration, the rapidity of the pulse, and the burning nature of the fever which is devouring you—"

"And which has thrice prostrated me since this morning," said the monk.

"All things considered, I shall call it a terrible attack. But why did you not stop on your road?"

"I was expected here, and I was obliged to come."

"Even at the risk of your life?"

"Yes, at the risk of dying on the way."

"Very well. Considering all the symptoms of your case, I must tell you that your condition is almost desperate."

The Franciscan smiled in a strange manner.

"What you have just told me is, perhaps, sufficient for what is due to an affiliated member, even of the eleventh year; but for what is due to me, Monsieur Grisart, it is too little, and I have a right to demand more. Come, then, let us be more candid still, and as frank as if you were making your own confession to Heaven. Besides, I have already sent for a confessor."

"Oh! I have hopes, however," murmured the doctor.

"Answer me," said the sick man, displaying with a dignified gesture a golden ring, the stone of which had, until that moment, been turned inside, and which bore engraved thereon the distinguishing mark of the Society of Jesus.

Grisart uttered a loud exclamation. "The general!" he cried.

"Silence," said the Franciscan, "you now understand that the whole truth is all important."

"Monseigneur, monseigneur," murmured Grisart, "send for the confessor, for in two hours, at the next seizure, you will be attacked by delirium, and will pass away in its course."

"Very well," said the patient, for a moment contracting his eyebrows, "I have still two hours to live then!"

"Yes; particularly if you take the potion I will send you presently."

"And that will give me two hours of life?"

"Two hours."

"I would take it, were it poison, for those two hours are necessary not only for myself, but for the glory of the order."

"What a loss, what a catastrophe for us all!" murmured the physician.

"It is the loss of one man—nothing more," replied the Franciscan, "for Heaven will enable the poor monk, who is about to leave you, to find a worthy successor. Adieu, Monsieur Grisart; already even, through the goodness of Heaven, I have met with you. A physician who had not been one of our holy order would have left me in ignorance of my condition; and, confident that existence would be prolonged a few days further, I should not have taken the necessary precautions. You are a learned man, Monsieur Grisart, and that confers an honor upon us all; it would have been repugnant to my feelings to have found one of our order of little standing in his profession. Adieu, Monsieur Grisart; send me the cordial immediately."

"Give me your blessing, at least, monseigneur."

"In my mind, I do; go, go; in my mind, I do so, I tell you— *animo*, Maître Grisart, *viribus impossible*." And he again fell back on the armchair, in an almost senseless state. M. Grisart hesitated, whether he should give him immediate assistance, or should run to prepare the cordial he had promised. He decided in favor of the cordial, for he darted out of the room and disappeared down the staircase.

A few moments after the doctor's departure, the confessor arrived. He had hardly crossed the threshold of the door when the Franciscan fixed a penetrating look upon him, and, shaking his head, murmured—"A weak mind, I see; may Heaven forgive me if I die without the help of this living piece of human infirmity." The confessor, on his side, regarded the dying man with astonishment, almost with terror. He had never beheld eyes so burningly bright at the very moment they were about to close, nor looks so terrible at the moment they were about to be quenched in death. The Franciscan made a rapid and imperious movement of his hand. "Sit down, there, my father," he said, "and listen to me." The Jesuit confessor, a good priest, a recently initiated member of the order, who had merely seen the beginning of its mysteries, yielded to the superiority assumed by the penitent.

"There are several persons staying in this hotel," continued the Franciscan.

"But," inquired the Jesuit, "I thought I had been summoned to listen to a confession. Is your remark, then, a confession?"

"Why do you ask?"

"In order to know whether I am to keep your words secret."

"My remarks are part of my confession; I confide them to you in your character of a confessor."

"Very well," said the priest, seating himself on the chair which the Franciscan had, with great difficulty, just left, to lie down on the bed.

The Franciscan continued,—"I repeat, there are several persons staying in this inn."

"So I have heard."

"They ought to be eight in number."

The Jesuit made a sign that he understood him. "The first to whom I wish to speak," said the dying man, "is a German from Vienna, whose name is the Baron de Wostpur. Be kind enough to go to him, and tell him the person he expected has arrived." The confessor, astounded, looked at his penitent; the confession seemed a singular one.

"Obey," said the Franciscan, in a tone of command impossible to resist. The good Jesuit, completely subdued, rose and left the room. As soon as he had gone, the Franciscan again took up the papers which a crisis of the fever had already, once before, obliged him to put aside.

"The Baron de Wostpur? Good!" he said; "ambitious, a fool, and straitened in means."

He folded up the papers, which he thrust under his pillow. Rapid footsteps were heard at the end of the corridor. The confessor returned, followed by the Baron de Wostpur, who walked along with his head raised, as if he were discussing with himself the possibility of touching the ceiling with the feather in his hat. Therefore, at the appearance of the Franciscan, at his melancholy

look, and seeing the plainness of the room, he stopped, and inquired,—"Who summoned me?"

"I," said the Franciscan, who turned toward the confessor,
saying, "My good father, leave us for a moment together; when this
gentleman leaves, you will return here." The Jesuit left the room,
and, doubtless, availed himself of this momentary exile from the
presence of the dying man to ask the host for some explanation
about this strange penitent, who treated his confessor no better than
he would a man-servant. The baron approached the bed, and wished
to speak, but the hand of the Franciscan imposed silence upon
him.

"Every moment is precious," said the latter, hurriedly. "You
have come here for the competition, have you not?"

"Yes, my father."

"You hope to be elected general of the order?"

"I hope so."

"You know on what conditions only you can possibly attain this
high position, which makes one man the master of monarchs, the
equal of popes?"

"Who are you," inquired the baron, "to subject me to these
interrogatories?"

"I am he whom you expected."

"The elector-general?"

"I am the elected."

"You are—"

The Franciscan did not give him time to reply; he extended his
shrunken hand, on which glittered the ring of the general of the
order. The baron drew back in surprise; and then, immediately
afterwards, bowing with the profoundest respect, he exclaimed,—
"Is it possible that you are here, monseigneur; you, in this wretched
room; you, upon this miserable bed; you, in search of and selecting
the future general, that is, your own successor?"

"Do not distress yourself about that, monsieur, but fulfil immediately the principal condition, of furnishing the order with a
secret of importance, of such importance that one of the greatest
courts of Europe will, by your instrumentality, forever be subjected
to the order. Well! do you possess the secret which you promised, in
your request, addressed to the grand council?"

"Monseigneur—"

"Let us proceed, however, in due order," said the monk. "You
are the Baron de Wostpur?"

"Yes, monseigneur."

"And this letter is from you?"

The general of the Jesuits drew a paper from his bundle, and presented it to the baron, who glanced at it, and made a sign in the affirmative, saying, "Yes, monseigneur, this letter is mine."

"Can you show me the reply which the secretary of the grand council returned to you?"

"Here it is," said the baron, holding towards the Franciscan a letter bearing simply the address, "To his excellency the Baron de Wostpur," and containing only this phrase, "From the 15th to the 22d May, Fontainebleau, the hotel of the Beau-Paon.—A.M.D.G."*

"Right," said the Franciscan, "and now speak."

"I have a body of troops, composed of 50,000 men; all the officers are gained over. I am encamped on the Danube. In four days I can overthrow the emperor, who is, as you are aware, opposed to the progress of our order, and can replace him by whichever of the princes of his family the order may determine upon." The Franciscan listened, unmoved.

"Is that all?" he said.

"A revolution throughout Europe is included in my plan," said the baron.

"Very well, Monsieur de Wostpur, you will receive a reply; return to your room, and leave Fontainebleau within a quarter of an hour." The baron withdrew backwards, as obsequiously as if he were taking leave of the emperor he was ready to betray.

"There is no secret there," murmured the Franciscan, "it is a plot. Besides," he added, after a moment's reflection, "the future of Europe is no longer in the hands of the House of Austria."

And with a pencil he held in his hand, he struck the Baron de Wostpur's name from the list.

"Now for the cardinal," he said; "we ought to get something more serious from the side of Spain."

Raising his head, he perceived the confessor, who was awaiting his orders as respectfully as a school-boy.

"Ah, ah!" he said, noticing his submissive air, "you have been talking with the landlord."

"Yes, monseigneur; and to the physician."

"To Grisart?"

"Yes."

"He is here, then?"

"He is waiting with the potion he promised."

* *Ad majorem Dei gloriam.*

"Very well; if I require him, I will call; you now understand the great importance of my confession, do you not?"

"Yes, monseigneur."

"Then go and fetch me the Spanish Cardinal Herrebia. Make haste. Only, as you now understand the matter in hand, you will remain near me, for I begin to feel faint."

"Shall I summon the physician?"

"Not yet, not yet . . . the Spanish cardinal, no one else. Fly."

Five minutes afterwards, the cardinal, pale and disturbed entered the little room.

"I am informed, monseigneur,—" stammered the cardinal.

"To the point," said the Franciscan, in a faint voice, showing the cardinal a letter which he had written to the grand council. "Is that your handwriting?"

"Yes, but—"

"And your summons?"

The cardinal hesitated to answer. His purple revolted against the mean garb of the poor Franciscan, who stretched out his hand and displayed the ring, which produced its effect, greater in proportion to the greatness of the person over whom the Franciscan exercised his influence.

"Quick, the secret, the secret!" said the dying man, leaning upon his confessor.

"*Coram isto?*" inquired the Spanish cardinal.

"Speak in Spanish," said the Franciscan, showing the liveliest attention.

"You are aware, monseigneur," said the cardinal, continuing the conversation in Castilian, "that the condition of the marriage of the Infanta with the king of France was the absolute renunciation of the rights of the said Infanta, as well as of King Louis XIV, to all claim to the crown of Spain." The Franciscan made a sign in the affirmative.

"The consequence is," continued the cardinal, "that the peace and alliance between the two kingdoms depend upon the observance of that clause of the contract." A similar sign from the Franciscan. "Not only France and Spain," continued the cardinal, "but the whole of Europe even, would be violently rent asunder by the faithlessness of either party." Another movement of the dying man's head.

"It further results," continued the speaker, "that the man who might be able to foresee events, and to render certain that which is no more than a vague idea floating in the mind of man, that is to say, the idea of future good or evil, would preserve the world from a great catastrophe; and the event, which has no fixed certainty even in the brain of him who originated it, could be turned to the advantage of our order."

"Closer!" murmured the Franciscan, in Spanish, who suddenly became paler, and leaned upon the priest. The cardinal approached the ear of the dying man, and said, "Well, monseigneur, I know that the king of France has determined that, at the very first pretext, a death for instance, either that of the king of Spain, or that of a brother of the Infanta, France will, arms in hand, claim the inheritance, and I have in my possession, already prepared, the plan of policy agreed upon by Louis XIV for this occasion."

"And this plan?" said the Franciscan.

"Here it is," returned the cardinal.

"In whose handwriting is it?"

"My own."

"Have you anything further to say to me?"

"I think I have said a good deal, my lord," replied the cardinal.

"Yes, you have rendered the order a great service. But how did you procure the details, by the aid of which you have constructed your plan?"

"I have the under-servants of the king of France in my pay, and I obtain from them all the waste papers, which have been saved from being burnt."

"Very ingenious," murmured the Franciscan, endeavoring to smile; "you will leave this hotel, cardinal, in a quarter of an hour, and a reply shall be sent you." The cardinal withdrew.

"Call Grisart, and desire the Venetian Marini to come," said the sick man.

While the confessor obeyed, the Franciscan, instead of striking out the cardinal's name, as he had done the baron's, made a cross at the side of it. Then, exhausted by the effort, he fell back on his bed, murmuring the name of Dr. Grisart.

When he returned to his senses, he had drunk about half of the potion, of which the remainder was left in the glass, and he found himself supported by the physician, while the Venetian and the confessor were standing close to the door. The Venetian submitted to the same formalities as his two predecessors, hesitated as they had done at the sight of the two strangers, but his confidence restored by the order of the general, he revealed that the pope, terrified at the power of the order, was weaving a plot for the general expulsion of the Jesuits, and was tampering with the different courts of Europe in order to obtain their assistance. He described the pontiff's auxiliaries, his means of action, and indicated the particular locality in the Archipelago where, by a sudden surprise, two cardinals, adepts of the eleventh year, and, consequently, high in authority, were to be transported, together with thirty-two of the principal affiliated members of Rome. The Franciscan thanked the Signor Marini. It was by no means a slight service he had rendered the society by denouncing this pontifical project. The Venetian thereupon received directions to set off in a quarter of an hour, and left as radiant as if he already possessed the ring, the sign of the supreme authority of the society. As, however, he was departing, the Franciscan murmured to himself: "All these men are either spies, or a sort of police, not one of them a general; they have all discovered a plot, but not one of them a secret. It is not by means of ruin, or war, or force, that the Society of Jesus is to be governed, but by that mysterious influence moral superiority alone confers. No, the man is not yet found, and to complete the misfortune, Heaven strikes me down, and I am dying. Oh! must the society indeed fall with me for want of a column to support it? Must death, which is waiting for me, swallow up with me the future of the order; that future which ten years more of my own life would have rendered eternal? For that future, with the reign of the new king, is opening radiant and full of splendor." These words, which had been half-reflected, half-prounced aloud, were listened to by the Jesuit confessor with a terror similar to that with which one listens to the wanderings of a person attacked by fever, whilst Grisart, with a mind of a higher order, devoured them as the revelations of an unknown world, in which his looks were plunged without ability to comprehend. Suddenly the Franciscan recovered himself.

"Let us finish this," he said; "death is approaching. Oh! just now I was dying resignedly, for I hoped . . . while now I sink in despair, unless those who remain . . . Grisart, Grisart, give me to live a single hour longer."

Grisart approached the dying monk, and made him swallow a few drops, not of the potion which was still left in the glass, but of the contents of a small bottle he had upon his person.

"Call the Scotchman!" exclaimed the Franciscan; "call the Bremen merchant. Call, call, quickly. I am dying. I am suffocated."

The confessor darted forward to seek assistance, as if there had been any human strength which could hold back the hand of death, which was weighing down the sick man; but, at the threshold of the door, he found Aramis, who, with his finger on his lips, like the statue of Harpocrates, the god of silence, by a look motioned him back to the end of the apartment. The physician and the confessor, after having consulted each other by looks, made a movement as if to push Aramis aside, who, however, with two signs of the cross, each made in a different manner, transfixed them both in their places.

"A chief!" they both murmured.

Aramis slowly advanced into the room where the dying man was struggling against the first attack of the agony which had seized him. As for the Franciscan, whether owing to the effect of the elixir, or whether the appearance of Aramis had restored his strength, he made a movement, and his eyes glaring, his mouth half open, and his hair damp with sweat, sat up on the bed. Aramis felt that the air of the room was stifling; the windows were closed; the fire was burning upon the hearth; a pair of candles of yellow wax were guttering down in the copper candlesticks, and still further increased, by their thick smoke, the temperature of the room. Aramis opened the window, and, fixing upon the dying man a look full of intelligence and respect, said to him:

"Monseigneur, pray forgive my coming in this manner, before you summoned me, but your state alarms me, and I thought you might possibly die before you had seen me, for I am but the sixth upon your list."

The dying man started and looked at the list.

"You are, therefore, he who was formerly called Aramis, and since, the Chevalier d'Herblay? You are the bishop of Vannes?"

"Yes, my lord."

"I know you, I have seen you."

"At the last jubilee, we were with the Holy Father together."

"Yes, yes, I remember; and you place yourself on the list of candidates!"

"Monseigneur, I have heard it said that the order required to become possessed of a great state secret, and knowing that from modesty you had in anticipation resigned your functions in favor of the person who should be the depositary of such a secret, I wrote to say that I was ready to compete, possessing alone a secret I believe to be important."

"Speak," said the Franciscan; "I am ready to listen to you, and to judge of the importance of the secret."

"A secret of the value of that which I have the honor to confide to you cannot be communicated by word of mouth. Any idea which, when once expressed, has thereby lost its safeguard, and has become vulgarized by any manifestation or communication of it whatever, no longer is the property of him who gave it birth. My words may be overheard by some listener, or perhaps by an enemy; one ought not, therefore, to speak at random, for, in such a case, the secret would cease to be one."

"How do you propose, then, to convey your secret?" inquired the dying monk.

With one hand Aramis signed to the physician and the confessor to withdraw, and with the other he handed to the Franciscan a paper enclosed in a double envelope.

"Is not writing more dangerous still than language?"

"No, my lord," said Aramis, "for you will find within this envelope characters which you and I alone can understand." The Franciscan looked at Aramis with an astonishment which momentarily increased.

"It is a cipher," continued the latter, "which you used in 1655, and which your secretary, Ivan Injan, who is dead, could alone decipher, if he were restored to life."

"You knew this cipher, then?"

"It was I who taught it him," said Aramis, bowing with a gracefulness full of respect, and advancing towards the door as if to leave the room: but a gesture of the Franciscan, accompanied by a cry for him to remain, restrained him.

"*Ecce homo!*" he exclaimed; then reading the paper a second time, he called out, "Approach, approach quickly!"

Aramis returned to the side of the Franciscan, with the same calm countenance and the same respectful manner, unchanged. The Franciscan, extending his arm, burnt by the flame of the candle the paper which Aramis had handed him. Then, taking hold of Aramis's hand, he drew him towards him, and inquired: "In what manner and by whose means could you possibly become acquainted with such a secret?"

"Through Madame de Chevreuse, the intimate friend and confidante of the queen."

"And Madame de Chevreuse—"

"Is dead."

"Did any others know it?"

"A man and a woman only, and they of the lower classes."

"Who are they?"

"Persons who had brought him up."

"What has become of them?"

"Dead also. This secret burns like vitriol."

"But you survive?"

"No one is aware that I know it."

"And for what length of time have you possessed this secret?"

"For the last fifteen years."

"And you have kept it?"

"I wished to live."

"And you give it to the order without ambition, without acknowledgment?"

"I give it to the order with ambition and with a hope of return," said Aramis; "for if you live, my lord, you will make of me, now you know me, what I can and ought to be."

"And as I am dying," exclaimed the Franciscan, "I constitute you my successor. . . . Thus." And drawing off the ring, he passed it on Aramis's finger. Then, turning towards the two spectators of this scene, he said: "Be ye witnesses of this, and testify, if need be, that, sick in body, but sound in mind, I have freely and voluntarily bestowed this ring, the token of supreme authority, upon Monsieur d'Herblay, bishop of Vannes, whom I nominate my successor, and before whom I, an humble sinner, about to appear before Heaven, prostrate myself, as an example for all to follow." And the Franciscan bowed lowly and submissively, whilst the physician and the Jesuit fell on their knees. Aramis, even while he became paler than the dying man himself, bent his looks successively upon all the actors of this scene. Profoundly gratified ambition flowed with lifeblood towards his heart.

"We must lose no time," said the Franciscan; "what I had still to do on earth was urgent. I shall never succeed in carrying it out."

"I will do it," said Aramis.

"It is well," said the Franciscan, and then turning towards the Jesuit and the doctor, he added, "Leave us alone," a direction they instantly obeyed.

"With this sign," he said, "you are the man needed to shake the world from one end to the other; with this sign you will overthrow; with this you will edify; *in hoc signo vinces!*"

"Close the door," continued the Franciscan after a pause. Aramis shut and bolted the door, and returned to the side of the Franciscan.

"The pope is conspiring against the order," said the monk; "the pope must die."

"He shall die," said Aramis, quietly.

"Seven hundred thousand livres are owing to a Bremen mer-

chant of the name of Bonstett, who came here to get the guarantee
of my signature."

"He shall be paid," said Aramis.

"Six knights of Malta, whose names are written here, have
discovered, by the indiscretion of one of the affiliated of the
eleventh year, the three mysteries; it must be ascertained what these
men have done with the secret, to get it back again and bury it."

"It shall be done."

"Three dangerous affiliated members must be sent away into
Thibet, there to perish; they stand condemned. Here are their
names."

"I will see that the sentence be carried out."

"Lastly, there is a lady at Anvers, grand-niece of Ravaillac: she
holds certain papers in her hands that compromise the order. There
has been payable to the family during the last fifty-one years a
pension of fifty thousand livres. The pension is a heavy one, and the
order is not wealthy. Redeem the papers for a sum of money paid
down, or, in case of refusal, stop the pension—but run no risk."

"I will quickly decide what is best to be done," said Aramis.

"A vessel chartered from Lima entered the port of Lisbon last
week; ostensibly it is laden with chocolate, in reality with gold.
Every ingot is concealed by a coating of chocolate. The vessel
belongs to the order; it is worth seventeen millions of livres; you will
see that it is claimed; here are the bills of lading."

"To what port shall I direct it to be taken?"

"To Bayonne."

"Before three weeks are over it shall be there, wind and weather
permitting. Is that all?" The Franciscan made a sign in the affirmative, for he could no longer speak; the blood rushed to his throat
and his head, and gushed from his mouth, his nostrils, and his eyes.
The dying man had barely time to press Aramis's hand, when he fell
in convulsions from his bed upon the floor. Aramis placed his hand
upon the Franciscan's heart, but it had ceased to beat. As he
stooped down, Aramis observed that a fragment of the paper he
had given the Franciscan had escaped being burnt. He picked it up,
and burnt it to the last atom. Then, summoning the confessor and the
physician, he said to the former: "Your penitent is in heaven; he
needs nothing more than prayers and the burial bestowed upon the
pious dead. Go and prepare what is necessary for a simple inter-
ment, such as a poor monk only would require. Go."

The Jesuit left the room. Then, turning towards the physician,
and observing his pale and anxious face, he said, in a low tone of

voice: "Monsieur Grisart, empty and clean this glass; there is too much left in it of what the grand council desired you to put in."

Grisart, amazed, overcome, completely astounded, almost fell backwards in his extreme terror. Aramis shrugged his shoulders in sign of pity, took the glass, and poured out the contents among the ashes of the hearth. He then left the room, carrying the papers of the dead man with him.

EDITOR'S NOTE: *Aramis's secret was that the King of France, Louis XIV, had a twin brother, who was kept hidden in the Bastille—the Man in the Iron Mask.*

▼

2 Entrapping a Lady

*The Scarlet Pimpernel was published in 1905 by the Baroness
Emmuska Orczy, a Hungarian noblewoman, whose belated sympathies for the French aristocracy of the time of the Revolution
can no doubt be explained by her own origins. She wrote a
number of aristocratic romances, but the* Pimpernel *was the only
book she is remembered for. It went through some forty editions,
was dramatized and enjoyed a good run on the London stage, and
became a movie starring Leslie Howard. If it sounds somewhat
stilted, long-winded, and slow-moving to us today, it had the merit
of an excellent plot full of robust action with twists and surprises
galore.*

*Marguerite Blakeney, née St. Just, a Frenchwoman by birth, is
married to Sir Percy Blakeney, an English nobleman of the best
society, who, to Marguerite's disappointment, has become in recent years a lazy do-nothing who spends all his time at cards,
parties, or with his horses and dogs—or so it seems. The Scarlet
Pimpernel, on the other hand, is a brave, anonymous, and elusive
hero whose exploits are universally admired. At the head of a
small band of fellow English aristocrats he devotes his energies to
helping the persecuted aristocracy escape from France to safety in
England. No one except his immediate associates knows who he is.
On the scene comes Chauvelin, the representative of the French
Republic in England, but in reality an official of the secret police
with a special mission in England. In the excerpt which follows, he
tries to enlist the services of Marguerite in this mission by recourse
to a very old tactic.*

If you have never read The Scarlet Pimpernel, *and are not*

FROM *The Scarlet Pimpernel.*

likely to, but if your curiosity is aroused as to the identity of this worthy, I can give you a little hint. His name is mentioned in this note. You can imagine in what a pickle our heroine Marguerite finds herself after she has been forced to help Chauvelin apprehend him.

Chauvelin looked at Marguerite long and scrutinisingly. It seemed as if those keen, pale eyes of his were reading every one of her thoughts. They were alone together; the evening air was quite still, and their soft whispers were drowned in the noise which came from the coffee-room. Still, Chauvelin took a step or two from under the porch, looked quickly and keenly all round him, then, seeing that indeed no one was within earshot, he once more came back close to Marguerite.

"Will you render France a small service, *citoyenne?*" he asked, with a sudden change of manner, which lent his thin, fox-like face singular earnestness.

"La, man!" she replied flippantly, "how serious you look all of a sudden. . . . Indeed I do not know if I would render France a small service—at any rate, it depends upon the kind of service she—or you—want."

"Have you ever heard of the Scarlet Pimpernel, Citoyenne St. Just?" asked Chauvelin, abruptly.

"Heard of the Scarlet Pimpernel?" she retorted with a long and merry laugh, "Faith, man! We talk of nothing else. . . . We have hats 'à la Scarlet Pimpernel'; our horses are called 'Scarlet Pimpernel'; at the Prince of Wales' supper party the other night we had a 'soufflé à la Scarlet Pimpernel.' . . . Lud!" she added gaily, "the other day I ordered at my milliner's a blue dress trimmed with green, and bless me, if she did not call that 'à la Scarlet Pimpernel.' "

Chauvelin had not moved while she prattled merrily along; he did not even attempt to stop her when her musical voice and her childlike laugh went echoing through the still evening air. But he remained serious and earnest whilst she laughed, and his voice, clear, incisive, and hard, was not raised above his breath as he said,—

"Then, as you have heard of that enigmatical personage, *citoyenne,* you must also have guessed, and known, that the man who hides his identity under that strange pseudonym, is the most bitter enemy of our republic, of France . . . of men like Armand St. Just."

"La!" she said, with a quaint little sigh, "I dare swear he is. . . . France has many bitter enemies these days."

"But you, *citoyenne*, are a daughter of France, and should be ready to help her in a moment of deadly peril."

"My brother Armand devotes his life to France," she retorted proudly: "as for me, I can do nothing . . . here in England. . . ."

"Yes, you . . ." he urged still more earnestly, whilst his thin fox-like face seemed suddenly to have grown impressive and full of dignity, "here in England, *citoyenne* . . . you alone can help us. . . . Listen!—I have been sent over here by the Republican Government as its representative: I present my credentials to Mr. Pitt in London to-morrow. One of my duties here is to find out all about this League of the Scarlet Pimpernel, which has become a standing menace to France, since it is pledged to help our cursed aristocrats—traitors to their country, and enemies of the people—to escape from the punishment which they deserve. You know as well as I do, *citoyenne*, that once they are over here, those French émigrés try to rouse public feeling against the Republic. . . . They are ready to join issue with any enemy bold enough to attack France. . . . Now, within the last month, scores of these émigrés, some only suspected of treason, others actually condemned by the Tribunal of Public Safety, have succeeded in crossing the Channel. Their escape in each instance was planned, organized and effected by this society of young English jackanapes, headed by a man whose brain seems as resourceful as his identity is mysterious. All the most strenuous efforts on the part of my spies have failed to discover who he is; whilst the others are the hands, he is the head, who beneath this strange anonymity calmly works at the destruction of France. I mean to strike at that head, and for this I want your help—through him afterwards I can reach the rest of the gang: he is a young buck in English society, of that I feel sure. Find that man for me, *citoyenne!*" he urged, "find him for France!"

Marguerite had listened to Chauvelin's impassioned speech without uttering a word, scarce making a movement, hardly daring to breathe. She had told him before, that this mysterious hero of romance was the talk of the smart set to which she belonged; already, before this, her heart and her imagination had been stirred by the thought of the brave man, who, unknown to fame, had rescued hundreds of lives from a terrible, often an unmerciful fate. She had but little real sympathy with those haughty French aristocrats, insolent in their pride of caste, of whom the Comtesse de Tournay de Basserive was so typical an example; but, republican and liberal-minded though she was from principle, she hated and loathed the methods which the young Republic had chosen for establishing itself. She had not been in Paris for some months; the horrors and bloodshed of the Reign of Terror, culminating in the September massacres had only come across the Channel to her as a faint echo. Robespierre, Danton, Marat, she had not known in their new guise of bloody justiciaries, merciless wielders of the guillotine. Her very soul recoiled in horror from these excesses, to which she feared her brother Armand—moderate republican as he was—might become one day the holocaust.

Then, when first she heard of this band of young English enthusiasts, who, for sheer love of their fellowmen, dragged women and children, old and young men, from a horrible death, her heart had glowed with pride for them, and now, as Chauvelin spoke, her very soul went out to the gallant and mysterious leader of the reckless little band, who risked his life daily, who gave it freely and without ostentation, for the sake of humanity.

Her eyes were moist when Chauvelin had finished speaking, the lace at her bosom rose and fell with her quick, excited breathing; she no longer heard the noise of drinking from the inn, she did not heed her husband's voice or his inane laugh, her thoughts had gone wandering in search of the mysterious hero! Ah! There was a man she might have loved, had he come her way: everything in him appealed to her romantic imagination; his personality, his strength, his bravery, the loyalty of those who served under him in the same noble cause, and, above all, that anonymity which crowned him, as if with a halo of romantic glory.

"Find him for France, *citoyenne!*"

Chauvelin's voice close to her ear roused her from her dreams. The mysterious hero had vanished, and, not twenty yards away from her, a man was drinking and laughing, to whom she had sworn faith and loyalty.

"La! man," she said with a return of her assumed flippancy, "you are astonishing. Where in the world am I to look for him?"

"You go everywhere, *citoyenne*," whispered Chauvelin, insinuatingly. "Lady Blakeney is the pivot of social London, so I am told . . . you see everything, you hear everything."

"Easy, my friend," retorted Marguerite, drawing herself up to her full height and looking down, with a slight thought of contempt, on the small, thin figure before her. "Easy! you seem to forget that there are six feet of Sir Percy Blakeney, and a long line of ancestors to stand between Lady Blakeney and such a thing as you propose."

"For the sake of France, *citoyenne!*" reiterated Chauvelin, earnestly.

"Tush, man, you talk nonsense anyway; for even if you did know who this Scarlet Pimpernel is, you could do nothing to him—an Englishman!"

"I'd take my chance on that," said Chauvelin, with a dry, rasping little laugh. "At any rate we could send him to the guillotine first to cool his ardour, then, when there is a diplomatic fuss about it, we can apologise—humbly—to the British Government, and if necessary, pay compensation to the bereaved family."

"What you propose is horrible, Chauvelin," she said, drawing away from him as from some noisome insect. "Whoever the man may be, he is brave and noble, and never—do you hear me?—never would I lend a hand to such villainy."

"You prefer to be insulted by every French aristocrat who comes to this country?"

Chauvelin had taken sure aim when he shot this tiny shaft. Marguerite's fresh young cheeks became a thought more pale and she bit her under lip, for she would not let him see that the shaft had struck home.

"That is beside the question," she said at last with indifference. "I can defend myself, but I refuse to do any dirty work for you—or for France. You have other means at your disposal; you must use them, my friend."

And without another look at Chauvelin, Marguerite Blakeney turned her back on him and walked straight into the inn.

"That is not your last word, *citoyenne*," said Chauvelin, as a flood of light from the passage illumined her elegant, richly-clad figure, "we meet in London, I hope!"

"We meet in London," she said, speaking over her shoulder at him, "but that is my last word."

She threw open the coffee-room door and disappeared from his view, but he remained under the porch for a moment or two, taking a pinch of snuff. He had received a rebuke and a snub, but his shrewd, fox-like face looked neither abashed nor disappointed; on the contrary, a curious smile, half sarcastic and wholly satisfied, played around the corners of his thin lips.

(*Some days later, at the opera in London.*)

He paused a moment, like a cat which sees a mouse running heedlessly by, ready to spring, yet waiting with that feline sense of enjoyment of mischief about to be done. Then he said quietly—

"Your brother, St. Just, is in peril."

Not a muscle moved in the beautiful face before him. He could only see it in profile, for Marguerite seemed to be watching the stage intently, but Chauvelin was a keen observer; he noticed the sudden rigidity of the eyes, the hardening of the mouth, the sharp, almost paralysed tension of the beautiful, graceful figure.

"Lud, then," she said, with affected merriment, "since 'tis one of your imaginary plots, you'd best go back to your own seat and leave me to enjoy the music."

And with her hand she began to beat time nervously against the cushion of the box. Selina Storace was singing the "*Che faro*" to an audience that hung spellbound upon the prima donna's lips. Chauvelin did not move from his seat; he quietly watched that tiny nervous hand, the only indication that his shaft had indeed struck home.

"Well?" she said suddenly and irrelevantly, and with the same feigned unconcern.

"Well, *citoyenne?*" he rejoined placidly.

"About my brother?"

"I have news of him for you which, I think, will interest you, but first let me explain. . . . May I?"

The question was unnecessary. He felt, though Marguerite still held her head steadily averted from him, that her every nerve was strained to hear what he had to say.

"The other day, *citoyenne*," he said, "I asked for your help. . . . France needed it, and I thought I could rely on you, but you gave me your answer. . . . Since then the exigencies of my own affairs and your own social duties have kept us apart . . . although many things have happened. . . ."

"To the point, I pray you, *citoyen*," she said lightly; "the music is entrancing, and the audience will get impatient of your talk."

"One moment, *citoyenne*. The day on which I had the honour of meeting you at Dover, and less than an hour after I had your final answer, I obtained possession of some papers, which revealed another of those subtle schemes for the escape of a batch of French aristocrats —that traitor de Tournay amongst others—all organized by that arch-meddler, the Scarlet Pimpernel. Some of the threads, too, of this mysterious organization have come into my hands, but not all, and I want you—nay! you must help me to gather them together."

Marguerite seemed to have listened to him with marked impatience; she now shrugged her shoulders and said gaily—

"Bah! man. Have I not already told you that I care nought

about your schemes or about the Scarlet Pimpernel. And had you
not spoken about my brother . . ."

"A little patience, I entreat, *citoyenne*," he continued imperturbably. "Two gentlemen, Lord Antony Dewhurst and Sir Andrew
Ffoulkes were at 'The Fisherman's Rest' at Dover that same night."

"I know. I saw them there."

"They were already known to my spies as members of that
accursed league. It was Sir Andrew Ffoulkes who escorted the
Comtesse de Tournay and her children across the Channel. When
the two young men were alone, my spies forced their way into the
coffee-room of the inn, gagged and pinioned the two gallants, seized
their papers, and brought them to me."

In a moment she had guessed the danger. Papers? . . . Had
Armand been imprudent? . . . The very thought struck her with
nameless terror. Still she would not let this man see that she feared;
she laughed gaily and lightly.

"Faith! and your impudence passes belief," she said merrily.
"Robbery and violence!—in England!—in a crowded inn! Your men
might have been caught in the act!"

"What if they had? They are children of France, and have been
trained by your humble servant. Had they been caught they would
have gone to jail, or even to the gallows, without a word of protest
or indiscretion; at any rate it was well worth the risk. A crowded inn
is safer for these little operations than you think, and my men have
experience."

"Well? And those papers?" she asked carelessly.

"Unfortunately, though they have given me cognisance of certain names . . . certain movements . . . enough, I think, to thwart
their projected coup for the moment, it would only be for the
moment, and still leaves me in ignorance of the identity of the
Scarlet Pimpernel."

"La! my friend," she said, with the same assumed flippancy of
manner, "then you are where you were before, aren't you? and you
can let me enjoy the last strophe of the aria. Faith!" she added,
ostentatiously smothering an imaginary yawn, "had you not spoken
about my brother . . ."

"I am coming to him now, *citoyenne*. Among the papers there
was a letter to Sir Andrew Ffoulkes, written by your brother, St.
Just."

"Well? And?"

"That letter shows him to be not only in sympathy with the

enemies of France, but actually a helper, if not a member, of the League of the Scarlet Pimpernel."

The blow had been struck at last. All along, Marguerite had been expecting it; she would not show fear, she was determined to seem unconcerned, flippant even. She wished, when the shock came, to be prepared for it, to have all her wits about her—those wits which had been nicknamed the keenest in Europe. Even now she did not flinch. She knew that Chauvelin had spoken the truth; the man was too earnest, too blindly devoted to the misguided cause he had at heart, too proud of his countrymen, of those makers of revolutions, to stoop to low, purposeless falsehoods.

That letter of Armand's—foolish, imprudent Armand—was in Chauvelin's hands. Marguerite knew that as if she had seen the letter with her own eyes; and Chauvelin would hold that letter for purposes of his own, until it suited him to destroy it or to make use of it against Armand. All that she knew, and yet she continued to laugh more gaily, more loudly than she had done before.

"La, man!" she said, speaking over her shoulder and looking him full and squarely in the face, "did I not say it was some imaginary plot. . . . Armand in league with that enigmatic Scarlet Pimpernel! . . . Armand busy helping those French aristocrats whom he despises! . . . Faith, the tale does infinite credit to your imagination!"

"Let me make my point clear, *citoyenne*," said Chauvelin, with the same unruffled calm, "I must assure you that St. Just is compromised beyond the slightest hope of pardon."

Inside the orchestra box all was silent for a moment or two. Marguerite sat, straight upright, rigid and inert, trying to think, trying to face the situation, to realise what had best be done.

In the house Storace had finished the aria, and was even now bowing in her classic garb, but in approved eighteenth-century fashion, to the enthusiastic audience, who cheered her to the echo.

"Chauvelin," said Marguerite Blakeney at last, quietly, and without that touch of bravado which had characterised her attitude all along, "Chauvelin, my friend, shall we try to understand one another? It seems that my wits have become rusty by contact with this damp climate. Now, tell me, you are very anxious to discover the identity of the Scarlet Pimpernel, isn't that so?"

"France's most bitter enemy, *citoyenne* . . . all the more dangerous, as he works in the dark."

"All the more noble, you mean. . . . Well!—and you would now force me to do some spying work for you in exchange for my brother Armand's safety?—Is that it?"

"Fie! two very ugly words, fair lady," protested Chauvelin, urbanely. "There can be no question of force, and the service which I would ask of you, in the name of France, could never be called by the shocking name of spying."

"At any rate, that is what it is called over here," she said drily. "That is your intention, is it not?"

"My intention is, that you yourself win a free pardon for Armand St. Just by doing me a small service."

"What is it?"

"Only watch for me to-night, Citoyenne St. Just," he said eagerly. "Listen: among the papers which were found about the person of Sir Andrew Ffoulkes there was a tiny note. See!" he added, taking a tiny scrap of paper from his pocket-book and handing it to her.

It was the same scrap of paper which, four days ago, the two young men had been in the act of reading, at the very moment when they were attacked by Chauvelin's minions. Marguerite took it mechanically and stooped to read it. There were only two lines, written in a distorted, evidently disguised, handwriting; she read them half aloud—

"Remember we must not meet more often than is strictly necessary. You have all the instructions for the 2nd. If you wish to speak to me again, I shall be at G.'s ball."

"What does it mean?" she asked.

"Look again, *citoyenne,* and you will understand."

"There is a device in the corner, a small red flower. . . ."

"Yes."

"The Scarlet Pimpernel," she said eagerly, "and G.'s ball means Grenville's ball. . . . He will be at my Lord Grenville's ball to-night."

"That is how I interpret the note, *citoyenne,*" concluded Chauvelin, blandly. "Lord Antony Dewhurst and Sir Andrew Ffoulkes, after they were pinioned and searched by my spies, were carried by my orders to a lonely house on the Dover Road, which I had rented for the purpose: there they remained close prisoners until this morning. But having found this tiny scrap of paper, my intention was that they should be in London, in time to attend my Lord Grenville's ball. You see, do you not? that they must have a great deal to say to their chief . . . and thus they will have an opportunity of speaking to him to-night, just as he directed them to do. Therefore, this morning, those two young gallants found every bar and bolt open in that lonely house on the Dover Road, their jailers disappeared, and two good horses standing ready saddled and tethered in the yard. I have not seen them yet, but I think we may safely conclude that they did not draw rein until they reached London. Now you see how simple it all is, *citoyenne!*"

"It does seem simple, doesn't it?" she said, with a final bitter attempt at flippancy, "when you want to kill a chicken . . . you take hold of it . . . then you wring its neck . . . it's only the chicken who does not find it quite so simple. Now you hold a knife at my throat, and a hostage for my obedience. . . . You find it simple. . . . I don't."

"Nay, *citoyenne,* I offer you a chance of saving the brother you love from the consequences of his own folly."

Marguerite's face softened, her eyes at last grew moist, as she murmured, half to herself:

"The only being in the world who has loved me truly and constantly. . . . But what do you want me to do, Chauvelin?" she said, with a world of despair in her tear-choked voice. "In my present position, it is well-nigh impossible!"

"Nay, *citoyenne,*" he said drily and relentlessly, not heeding that despairing, childlike appeal, which might have melted a heart of stone, "as Lady Blakeney, no one suspects you, and with your help to-night I may—who knows?—succeed in finally establishing the identity of the Scarlet Pimpernel. . . . You are going to the ball anon. . . . Watch for me there, *citoyenne,* watch and listen. . . . You can tell me if you hear a chance word or whisper. . . . You can note everyone to whom Sir Andrew Ffoulkes or Lord Antony Dewhurst will speak. You are absolutely beyond suspicion now. The Scarlet Pimpernel will be at Lord Grenville's ball to-night. Find out who he is, and I will pledge the word of France that your brother shall be safe."

Chauvelin was putting the knife to her throat. Marguerite felt herself entangled in one of those webs from which she could hope for no escape. A precious hostage was being held for her obedience: for she knew that this man would never make an empty threat. No doubt Armand was already signalled to the Committee of Public Safety as one of the "suspect"; he would not be allowed to leave France again, and would be ruthlessly struck, if she refused to obey Chauvelin. For a moment—woman-like—she still hoped to temporise. She held out her hand to this man, whom she now feared and hated.

"If I promise to help you in this matter, Chauvelin," she said pleasantly, "will you give me that letter of St. Just's?"

"If you render me useful assistance to-night, *citoyenne,*" he replied with a sarcastic smile, "I will give you that letter . . . to-morrow."

"You do not trust me?"

"I trust you absolutely, dear lady, but St. Just's life is forfeit to his country . . . it rests with you to redeem it."

"I may be powerless to help you," she pleaded, "were I ever so willing."

"That would be terrible indeed," he said quietly, "for you . . . and for St. Just."

Marguerite shuddered. She felt that from this man she could expect no mercy. All-powerful, he held the beloved life in the hollow of his hand. She knew him too well not to know that, if he failed in gaining his own ends, he would be pitiless.

She felt cold in spite of the oppressive air of the opera-house. The heart-appealing strains of the music seemed to reach her, as from a distant land. She drew her costly lace scarf up around her shoulders, and sat silently watching the brilliant scene, as if in a dream.

IV. *"The Dangerous German Spy"*

In the first decades of the new century and up to the
outbreak of the First World War, the saber-rattling and the
diplomatic intrigues of the great European powers loosed a
small avalanche of international spy fiction in which that persistent ogre "the dangerous German spy" first raised his
close-cropped head and his imperial mustache. A great business of purloining important diplomatic documents, secret
treaties, and war plans, and of spying with field glass, pencil,
and pad upon fortifications and naval shipyards got under
way in fiction.

William Le Queux, now almost entirely forgotten, was one
of the foremost producers in this department and he had many
imitators. Even writers like Conan Doyle, who otherwise specialized chiefly in detective stories, felt bound to handle this topic
of the day. But it was the war itself which really put spy fiction
on the map, because for the first time people who had been in
intelligence took to writing novels based on their experiences,
some of them thinly veiled memoirs, some of them not so thinly
veiled. The list is long and many are still remembered as well as
read: Somerset Maugham, Sir Compton Mackenzie, John Buchan,
A. E. W. Mason, Bernard Newman, and the inimitable E. Phillips
Oppenheim. All English, of course. The Americans hadn't been
in the business long enough to start writing about it.

I find it interesting to note that a similar fad did *not* follow

117

on the heels of World War II. At least not immediately. It is only during the last few years, amidst the recent upswing in the production of all kinds of spy fiction, that writers have been turning back to World War II and discovering or rediscovering the espionage and subversion practiced by the Axis powers at that time, a much more sinister and lethal business which makes anything practiced during World War I look rather sporting in comparison. I can think of some reasons for this. The fearful taste left in the mouth of the world after the years of Nazi cruelty and oppression was perhaps not conducive to the creation of popular entertainment. Then, too, the rapidity with which the Cold War overtook us turned attention away from the subject of the war itself and presented writers of spy fiction with a brand-new field to conquer.

A. CONAN DOYLE

▼

1 The Bruce-Partington Plans

*I know I tread on dangerous ground when I write on the subject
of Sherlock Holmes. There are too many experts around. It is
dangerous even to say that such-and-such a tale is the best one in
a certain category, because there are thousands of partisans with
their own favorites who will not agree. However, when it comes to
the adventures in which Conan Doyle turned the attention of his
master sleuth to spies—there are not very many of them—I think
that* The Bruce-Partington Plans *is the one which stands up best.
In it, a piece of complex detection worthy of the great Holmes is
carried out and as a result an international spy is trapped. It is
really the only tale of which this can be said.*

*Doyle did not really interest himself in spies until the menace
of World War I and of the German espionage which preceded it
had become the subject of the times. There are earlier stories in
which important government documents disappear, like* The Naval
Treaty, *but the spy who might purchase them is off the scene and
only a potential actor. Even in* The Adventure of the Second Stain,
written not long before Bruce-Partington, *in which a French agent
blackmails the wife of a British statesman in order to get his hands
on an important letter (written by William II), the element of
espionage is rather minor and subordinated to the drama of the
blackmailed lady. (Doyle blithely glosses over the means by which
the French agent found out about the existence of the letter by
saying in one short sentence: "He had some spy in the office who
knew of its existence.") And in the one story which is entirely
about German spies,* His Last Bow, *there is unfortunately no
detection at all.*

FROM *The Later Adventures of Sherlock Holmes.*

119

But Bruce-Partington *has everything in it—an unexpected culprit in the best tradition of the mystery story, that villain of the day the German spy, and, most important of all, detection and analysis of a sort which makes Watson say to Holmes, "A masterpiece. You have never risen to a greater height."*

In the third week of November, in the year 1895, a dense yellow fog settled down upon London. From the Monday to the Thursday I doubt whether it was ever possible from our windows in Baker Street to see the loom of the opposite houses. The first day Holmes had spent in cross-indexing his huge book of references. The second and third had been patiently occupied upon a subject which he had recently made his hobby—the music of the Middle Ages. But when, for the fourth time, after pushing back our chairs from breakfast we saw the greasy, heavy brown swirl still drifting past us and condensing in oily drops upon the window-panes, my comrade's impatient and active nature could endure this drab existence no longer. He paced restlessly about our sitting-room in a fever of suppressed energy, biting his nails, tapping the furniture, and chafing against inaction.

"Nothing of interest in the paper, Watson?" he said.

I was aware that by anything of interest, Holmes meant anything of criminal interest. There was the news of a revolution, of a possible war, and of an impending change of Government; but these did not come within the horizon of my companion. I could see nothing recorded in the shape of crime which was not commonplace and futile. Holmes groaned and resumed his restless meanderings.

"The London criminal is certainly a dull fellow," said he, in the querulous voice of the sportsman whose game has failed him. "Look out of this window, Watson. See how the figures loom up, are dimly seen, and then blend once more into the cloud-bank. The thief or the murderer could roam London on such a day as the tiger does the jungle, unseen until he pounces, and then evident only to his victim."

"There have," said I, "been numerous petty thefts."

Holmes snorted his contempt.

"This great and sombre stage is set for something more worthy than that," said he. "It is fortunate for this community that I am not a criminal."

"It is, indeed!" said I, heartily.

"Suppose that I were Brooks or Woodhouse, or any of the fifty men who have good reason for taking my life, how long could I survive against my own pursuit? A summons, a bogus appointment, and all would be over. It is well they don't have days of fog in the Latin countries—the countries of assassination. By Jove! here comes something at last to break our dead monotony."

It was the maid with a telegram. Holmes tore it open and burst out laughing.

"Well, well! What next?" said he. "Brother Mycroft is coming round."

"Why not?" I asked.

"Why not? It is as if you met a tram-car coming down a country lane. Mycroft has his rails and he runs on them. His Pall Mall lodgings, the Diogenes Club, Whitehall—that is his cycle. Once and only once, he has been here. What upheaval can possibly have derailed him?"

"Does he not explain?"

Holmes handed me his brother's telegram.

MUST SEE YOU OVER CADOGAN WEST. COMING AT ONCE. MYCROFT.

"Cadogan West? I have heard the name."

"It recalls nothing to my mind. But that Mycroft should break out in this erratic fashion! A planet might as well leave its orbit. By the way, do you know what Mycroft is?"

I had some vague recollection of an explanation at the time of the *Adventure of the Greek Interpreter.*

"You told me that he had some small office under the British Government."

Holmes chuckled.

"I did not know you quite so well in those days. One has to be discreet when one talks of high matters of state. You are right in thinking that he is under the British Government. You would also be right in a sense if you said that occasionally he is the British Government."

"My dear Holmes!"

"I thought I might surprise you. Mycroft draws four hundred and fifty pounds a year, remains a subordinate, has no ambitions of any kind, will receive neither honour nor title, but remains the most indispensable man in the country."

"But how?"

"Well, his position is unique. He has made it for himself. There has never been anything like it before, nor will be again. He has the tidiest and most orderly brain, with the greatest capacity for storing

facts, of any man living. The same great powers which I have
turned to the detection of crime he has used for this particular
business. The conclusions of every department are passed to him,
and he is the central exchange, the clearing-house, which makes out
the balance. All other men are specialists, but his specialism is
omniscience. We will suppose that a Minister needs information as
to a point which involves the Navy, India, Canada and the bi-
metallic question; he could get his separate advices from various
departments upon each, but only Mycroft can focus them all, and
say off-hand how each factor would affect the other. They began by
using him as a short-cut, a convenience; now he has made himself
an essential. In that great brain of his everything is pigeon-holed, and
can be handed out in an instant. Again and again his word has
decided the national policy. He lives in it. He thinks of nothing else
save when, as an intellectual exercise, he unbends if I call upon him
and ask him to advise me on one of my little problems. But Jupiter
is descending today. What on earth can it mean? Who is Cadogan
West, and what is he to Mycroft?"

"I have it," I cried, and plunged among the litter of papers upon
the sofa. "Yes, yes, here he is, sure enough! Cadogan West was the
young man who was found dead on the Underground on Tuesday
morning."

Holmes sat up at attention, his pipe half-way to his lips.

"This must be serious, Watson. A death which has caused my
brother to alter his habits can be no ordinary one. What in the
world can he have to do with it? The case was featureless as I
remember it. The young man had apparently fallen out of the train
and killed himself. He had not been robbed, and there was no
particular reason to suspect violence. Is that not so?"

"There has been an inquest," said I, "and a good many fresh
facts have come out. Looked at more closely, I should certainly say
that it was a curious case."

"Judging by its effect upon my brother, I should think it must
be a most extraordinary one." He snuggled down in his armchair.
"Now, Watson, let us have the facts."

"The man's name was Arthur Cadogan West. He was twenty-
seven years of age, unmarried, and a clerk at Woolwich Arsenal."

"Government employ. Behold the link with brother Mycroft!"

"He left Woolwich suddenly on Monday night. Was first seen
by his fiancée, Miss Violet Westbury, whom he left abruptly in the
fog about 7:30 that evening. There was no quarrel between them
and she can give no motive for his action. The next thing heard of

him was when his dead body was discovered by a plate-layer named Mason, just outside Aldgate Station on the Underground system in London."

"When?"

"The body was found at six on the Tuesday morning. It was lying wide of the metals upon the left hand of the tracks as one goes eastward, at a point close to the station, where the line emerges from the tunnel in which it runs. The head was badly crushed—an injury which might well have been caused by a fall from the train. The body could only have come on the line in that way. Had it been carried down from any neighbouring street, it must have passed the station barriers, where a collector is always standing. This point seems absolutely certain."

"Very good. The case is definite enough. The man, dead or alive, either fell or was precipitated from a train. So much is clear to me. Continue."

"The trains which traverse the lines of rail beside which the body was found are those which run from west to east, some being purely Metropolitan, and some from Willesden and outlying junctions. It can be stated for certain that this young man, when he met his death, was travelling in this direction at some late hour of the night, but at what point he entered the train it is impossible to state."

"His ticket, of course, would show that."

"There was no ticket in his pockets."

"No ticket! Dear me, Watson, this is really very singular. According to my experience it is not possible to reach the platform of a Metropolitan train without exhibiting one's ticket. Presumably, then, the young man had one. Was it taken from him in order to conceal the station from which he came? It is possible. Or did he drop it in the carriage? That also is possible. But the point is of curious interest. I understand that there was no sign of robbery?"

"Apparently not. There is a list here of his possessions. His purse contained two pounds fifteen. He had also a cheque-book on the Woolwich branch of the Capital and Counties Bank. Through this his identity was established. There were also two dress-circle tickets for the Woolwich Theatre, dated for that very evening. Also a small packet of technical papers."

Holmes gave an exclamation of satisfaction.

"There we have it at last, Watson! British Government—Woolwich Arsenal—technical papers—Brother Mycroft, the chain is complete. But here he comes, if I am not mistaken, to speak for himself."

A moment later the tall and portly form of Mycroft Holmes was ushered into the room. Heavily built and massive, there was a suggestion of uncouth physical inertia in the figure, but above this unwieldy frame there was perched a head so masterful in its brow, so alert in its steel-grey, deep-set eyes, so firm in its lips, and so subtle in its play of expression, that after the first glance one forgot the gross body and remembered only the dominant mind.

At his heels came our old friend Lestrade, of Scotland Yard—thin, austere. The gravity of both their faces foretold some weighty quest. The detective shook hands without a word. Mycroft Holmes struggled out of his overcoat and subsided into an armchair.

"A most annoying business, Sherlock," said he. "I extremely dislike altering my habits, but the powers that be would take no denial. In the present state of Siam it is most awkward that I should be away from the office. But it is a real crisis. I have never seen the Prime Minister so upset. As to the Admiralty—it is buzzing like an overturned bee-hive. Have you read up the case?"

"We have just done so. What were the technical papers?"

"Ah, there's the point! Fortunately, it has not come out. The Press would be furious if it did. The papers which this wretched youth had in his pocket were the plans of the Bruce-Partington submarine."

Mycroft Holmes spoke with a solemnity which showed his sense of the importance of the subject. His brother and I sat expectant.

"Surely you have heard of it? I thought everyone had heard of it."

"Only as a name."

"Its importance can hardly be exaggerated. It has been the most jealously guarded of all Government secrets. You may take it from me that naval warfare becomes impossible within the radius of a Bruce-Partington's operation. Two years ago a very large sum was smuggled through the Estimates and was expended in acquiring a monopoly of the invention. Every effort has been made to keep the secret. The plans, which are exceedingly intricate, comprising some thirty separate patents, each essential to the working of the whole, are kept in an elaborate safe in a confidential office adjoining the Arsenal, with burglar-proof doors and windows. Under no conceivable circumstances were the plans to be taken from the office. If the Chief Constructor of the Navy desired to consult them, even he was forced to go to the Woolwich office for the purpose. And yet here we find them in the pockets of a dead junior clerk in the heart of London. From an official point of view it's simply awful."

"But you have recovered them?"

"No, Sherlock, no! That's the pinch. We have not. Ten papers were taken from Woolwich. There were seven in the pockets of Cadogan West. The three most essential are gone—stolen, vanished. You must drop everything, Sherlock. Never mind your usual petty puzzles of the police-court. It's a vital international problem that you have to solve. Why did Cadogan West take the papers, where are the missing ones, how did he die, how came his body where it was found, how can the evil be set right? Find an answer to all these questions, and you will have done good service for your country."

"Why do you not solve it yourself, Mycroft? You can see as far as I."

"Possibly, Sherlock. But it is a question of getting details. Give me your details, and from an armchair I will return you an excellent expert opinion. But to run here and run there, to cross-question railway guards, and lie on my face with a lens to my eye—it is not my métier. No, you are the one man who can clear the matter up. If you have a fancy to see your name in the next honours list—"

My friend smiled and shook his head.

"I play the game for the game's own sake," said he. "But the problem certainly presents some points of interest, and I shall be very pleased to look into it. Some more facts, please."

"I have jotted down the more essential ones upon this sheet of paper, together with a few addresses which you will find of service. The actual official guardian of the papers is the famous Government expert, Sir James Walter, whose decorations and sub-titles fill two lines of a book of reference. He has grown grey in the service, is a gentleman, a favoured guest in the most exalted houses, and above all a man whose patriotism is beyond suspicion. He is one of two who have a key of the safe. I may add that the papers were undoubtedly in the office during working hours on Monday, and that Sir James left for London about three o'clock taking his key with him. He was at the house of Admiral Sinclair at Barclay Square during the whole of the evening when this incident occurred."

"Has the fact been verified?"

"Yes; his brother, Colonel Valentine Walter, has testified to his departure from Woolwich, and Admiral Sinclair to his arrival in London; so Sir James is no longer a direct factor in the problem."

"Who was the other man with a key?"

"The senior clerk and draughtsman, Mr. Sidney Johnson. He is a man of forty, married, with five children. He is a silent, morose man, but he has, on the whole, an excellent record in the public service. He is unpopular with his colleagues, but a hard worker. According to his own account, corroborated only by the word of his wife, he was at home the whole of Monday evening after office hours, and his key has never left the watch-chain upon which it hangs."

"Tell us about Cadogan West."

"He has been ten years in the service, and has done good work. He has the reputation of being hot-headed and impetuous, but a straight, honest man. We have nothing against him. He was next Sidney Johnson in the office. His duties brought him into daily, personal contact with the plans. No one else had the handling of them."

"Who locked the plans up that night?"

"Mr. Sidney Johnson, the senior clerk."

"Well, it is surely perfectly clear who took them away. They are actually found upon the person of this junior clerk, Cadogan West. That seems final, does it not?"

"It does, Sherlock, and yet it leaves so much unexplained. In the first place, why did he take them?"

"I presume they were of value?"

"He could have got several thousands for them very easily."

"Can you suggest any possible motive for taking the papers to London except to sell them?"

"No, I cannot."

"Then we must take that as our working hypothesis. Young West took the papers. Now this could only be done by having a false key—"

"Several false keys. He had to open the building and the room."

"He had, then, several false keys. He took the papers to London to sell the secret, intending, no doubt, to have the plans themselves back in the safe next morning before they were missed. While in London on this treasonable mission he met his end."

"How?"

"We will suppose that he was travelling back to Woolwich when he was killed and thrown out of the compartment."

"Aldgate, where the body was found, is considerably past the station for London Bridge, which would be his route to Woolwich."

"Many circumstances could be imagined under which he would pass London Bridge. There was someone in the carriage, for example, with whom he was having an absorbing interview. This interview led to a violent scene, in which he lost his life. Possibly he tried to leave the carriage, fell out on the line, and so met his end. The other closed the door. There was a thick fog, and nothing could be seen."

"No better explanation can be given with our present knowledge; and yet consider, Sherlock, how much you leave untouched. We will suppose, for argument's sake, that young Cadogan West had determined to convey these papers to London. He would naturally have made an appointment with the foreign agent and kept his evening clear. Instead of that he took two tickets for the threatre, escorted his fiancée half-way there, and then suddenly disappeared."

"A blind," said Lestrade, who had sat listening with some impatience to the conversation.

"A very singular one. That is objection No. 1. Objection No. 2: We will suppose that he reaches London and sees the foreign agent. He must bring back the papers before morning or the loss will be discovered. He took away ten. Only seven were in his pocket. What had become of the other three? He certainly would not leave them of his own free will. Then, again, where is the price of his treason? One would have expected to find a large sum of money in his pocket."

"It seems to me perfectly clear," said Lestrade. "I have no doubt at all as to what occurred. He took the papers to sell them. He saw the agent. They could not agree as to price. He started home again, but the agent went with him. In the train the agent murdered him, took the more essential papers, and threw his body from the carriage. That would account for everything, would it not?"

"Why had he no ticket?"

"The ticket would have shown which station was nearest the agent's house. Therefore he took it from the murdered man's pocket."

"Good, Lestrade, very good," said Holmes. "Your theory holds together. But if this is true, then the case is at an end. On the one hand the traitor is dead. On the other the plans of the Bruce-Partington submarine are presumably already on the Continent. What is there for us to do?"

"To act, Sherlock—to act!" cried Mycroft, springing to his feet. "All my instincts are against this explanation. Use your powers! Go to the scene of the crime! See the people concerned! Leave no stone unturned! In all your career you have never had so great a chance of serving your country."

"Well, well!" said Holmes, shrugging his shoulders. "Come, Watson! And you, Lestrade, could you favour us with your company for an hour or two? We will begin our investigation by a visit to Aldgate Station. Good-bye, Mycroft. I shall let you have a report before evening, but I warn you in advance that you have little to expect."

An hour later, Holmes, Lestrade and I stood upon the underground railroad at the point where it emerges from the tunnel immediately before Aldgate Station. A courteous red-faced old gentleman represented the railway company.

"This is where the young man's body lay," said he, indicating a spot about three feet from the metals. "It could not have fallen from above, for these, as you see, are all blank walls. Therefore, it could only have come from a train, and that train, so far as we can trace it, must have passed about midnight on Monday."

"Have the carriages been examined for any sign of violence?"

"There are no such signs, and no ticket has been found."

"No record of a door being found open?"

"None."

"We have had some fresh evidence this morning," said Lestrade. "A passenger who passed Aldgate in an ordinary Metropolitan train about 11:40 on Monday night declares that he heard a heavy thud, as of a body striking the line, just before the train reached the station. There was dense fog, however, and nothing could be seen. He made no report of it at the time. Why, whatever is the matter with Mr. Holmes?"

My friend was standing with an expression of strained intensity upon his face, staring at the railway metals where they curved out of the tunnel. Aldgate is a junction, and there was a network of points. On these his eager, questioning eyes were fixed, and I saw on his keen, alert face that tightening of the lips, that quiver of the nostrils, and concentration of the heavy tufted brows which I knew so well.

"Points," he muttered; "the points."

"What of it? What do you mean?"

"I suppose there are no great number of points on a system such as this?"

"No; there are very few."

"And a curve, too. Points, and a curve. By Jove! if it were only so."

"What is it, Mr. Holmes? Have you a clue?"

"An idea—an indication, no more. But the case certainly grows in interest. Unique, perfectly unique, and yet why not? I do not see any indications of bleeding on the line."

"There were hardly any."

"But I understand that there was a considerable wound."

"The bone was crushed, but there was no great external injury."

"And yet one would have expected some bleeding. Would it be possible for me to inspect the train which contained the passenger who heard the thud of a fall in the fog?"

"I fear not, Mr. Holmes. The train has been broken up before now, and the carriages redistributed."

"I can assure you, Mr. Holmes," said Lestrade, "that every carriage has been carefully examined. I saw to it myself."

It was one of my friend's most obvious weaknesses that he was impatient with less alert intelligences than his own.

"Very likely," said he, turning away. "As it happens, it was not the carriages which I desired to examine. Watson, we have done all we can here. We need not trouble you any further, Mr. Lestrade. I think our investigations must now carry us to Woolwich."

At London Bridge, Holmes wrote a telegram to his brother, which he handed to me before dispatching it. It ran thus:

SEE SOME LIGHT IN THE DARKNESS, BUT IT MAY POSSIBLY FLICKER OUT. MEANWHILE, PLEASE SEND BY MESSENGER, TO AWAIT RETURN AT BAKER STREET, A COMPLETE LIST OF ALL FOREIGN SPIES OR INTERNATIONAL AGENTS KNOWN TO BE IN ENGLAND, WITH FULL ADDRESS. SHERLOCK.

"That should be helpful, Watson," he remarked, as we took our seats in the Woolwich train. "We certainly owe brother Mycroft a debt for having introduced us to what promises to be a really very remarkable case."

His eager face still wore that expression of intense and high-strung energy, which showed me that some novel and suggestive circumstance had opened up a stimulating line of thought. See the foxhound with hanging ears and dropping tail as it lolls about the kennels, and compare it with the same hound as, with gleaming eyes and straining muscles, it runs upon a breast-high scent—such was the change in Holmes since the morning. He was a different man to the limp and lounging figure in the mouse-coloured dressing-gown who had prowled so restlessly only a few hours before round the fog-girt room.

"There is material here. There is scope," said he. "I am dull indeed not to have understood its possibilities."

"Even now they are dark to me."

"The end is dark to me also, but I have hold on one idea which may lead us far. The man met his death elsewhere, and his body was on the roof of a carriage."

"On the roof!"

"Remarkable, is it not? But consider the facts. Is it a coincidence that it is found at the very point where the train pitches and sways as it comes round on the points? Is not that the place where an object upon the roof might be expected to fall off? The points would affect no object inside the train. Either the body fell from the roof, or a very curious coincidence has occurred. But now consider the question of the blood. Of course, there was no bleeding on the line if the body had bled elsewhere. Each fact is suggestive in itself. Together they have a cumulative force."

"And the ticket, too!" I cried.

"Exactly. We could not explain the absence of a ticket. This would explain it. Everything fits together."

"But suppose it were so, we are still as far as ever from unravelling the mystery of his death. Indeed, it becomes not simpler, but stranger."

"Perhaps," said Holmes, thoughtfully; "perhaps." He relapsed into a silent reverie, which lasted until the slow train drew up at last in Woolwich Station. There he called a cab and drew Mycroft's paper from his pocket.

"We have quite a little round of afternoon calls to make," said he. "I think that Sir James Walter claims our first attention."

The house of the famous official was a fine villa with green lawns stretching down to the Thames. As we reached it the fog was lifting, and a thin, watery sunshine was breaking through. A butler answered our ring.

"Sir James, sir!" said he, with solemn face. "Sir James died this morning."

"Good heavens!" cried Holmes, in amazement. "How did he die?"

"Perhaps you would care to step in, sir, and see his brother, Colonel Valentine?"

"Yes, we had best do so."

We were ushered into a dim-lit drawing room, where an instant later we were joined by a very tall, handsome, light-bearded man of fifty, the younger brother of the dead scientist. His wild eyes, stained cheeks, and unkempt hair all spoke of the sudden blow which had fallen upon the household. He was hardly articulate as he spoke of it.

"It was this horrible scandal," said he. "My brother, Sir James, was a man of very sensitive honour, and he could not survive such an affair. It broke his heart. He was always so proud of the efficiency of his department, and this was a crushing blow."

"We had hoped that he might have given us some indications which would have helped us to clear the matter up."

"I assure you that it was all a mystery to him as it is to you and to all of us. He had already put all his knowledge at the disposal of the police. Naturally, he had no doubt that Cadogan West was guilty. But all the rest was inconceivable."

"You cannot throw any new light upon the affair?"

"I know nothing myself save what I have read or heard. I have no desire to be discourteous, but you can understand, Mr. Holmes, that we are much disturbed at present, and I must ask you to hasten this interview to an end."

"This is indeed an unexpected development," said my friend when we had regained the cab. "I wonder if the death was natural, or whether the poor old fellow killed himself! If the latter, may it be taken as some sign of self-reproach for duty neglected? We must leave that question to the future. Now we shall turn to the Cadogan Wests."

A small but well-kept house in the outskirts of the town sheltered the bereaved mother. The old lady was too dazed with grief to be of any use to us, but at her side was a white-faced young lady, who introduced herself as Miss Violet Westbury, the fiancée of the dead man, and the last to see him upon that fatal night.

"I cannot explain it, Mr. Holmes," she said. "I have not shut an eye since the tragedy, thinking, thinking, thinking, night and day, what the true meaning of it can be. Arthur was the most singleminded, chivalrous, patriotic man upon earth. He would have cut his right hand off before he would sell a State secret confided to his keeping. It is absurd, impossible, preposterous to anyone who knew him."

"But the facts, Miss Westbury?"

"Yes, yes; I admit I cannot explain them."

"Was he in any want of money?"

"No; his needs were very simple and his salary ample. He had saved a few hundreds, and we were to marry at the New Year."

"No signs of any mental excitement? Come, Miss Westbury, be absolutely frank with us."

The quick eye of my companion had noted some change in her manner. She coloured and hesitated.

"Yes," she said, at last. "I had a feeling that there was something on his mind."

"For long?"

"Only for the last week or so. He was thoughtful and worried. Once I pressed him about it. He admitted that there was something, and that it was concerned with his official life. 'It is too serious for me to speak about, even to you,' said he. I could get nothing more."

Holmes looked grave.

"Go on, Miss Westbury. Even if it seems to tell against him, go on. We cannot say what it may lead to."

"Indeed I have nothing more to tell. Once or twice it seemed to me that he was on the point of telling me something. He spoke one evening of the importance of the secret, and I have some recollection that he said that no doubt foreign spies would pay a great deal to have it."

My friend's face grew graver still.

"Anything else?"

"He said that we were slack about such matters—that it would be easy for a traitor to get the plans."

"Was it only recently that he made such remarks?"

"Yes, quite recently."

"Now tell us of that last evening."

"We were to go to the theatre. The fog was so thick that a cab was useless. We walked, and our way took us close to the office. Suddenly he darted away into the fog."

"Without a word?"

"He gave an exclamation; that was all. I waited but he never returned. Then I walked home. Next morning, after the office opened, they came to inquire. About twelve o'clock we heard the terrible news. Oh, Mr. Holmes, if you could only, only save his honour! It was so much to him."

Holmes shook his head sadly.

"Come, Watson," said he, "our ways lie elsewhere. Our next station must be the office from which the papers were taken. . . .

"It was black enough before against this young man, but our inquiries make it blacker," he remarked, as the cab lumbered off.

"His coming marriage gives a motive for the crime. He naturally wanted money. The idea was in his head, since he spoke about it. He nearly made the girl an accomplice in the treason by telling her his plans. It is all very bad."

"But surely, Holmes, character goes for something? Then, again, why should he leave the girl in the street and dart away to commit a felony?"

"Exactly! There are certainly objections. But it is a formidable case which they have to meet."

Mr. Sidney Johnson, the senior clerk, met us at the office, and received us with that respect which my companion's card always commanded. He was a thin, gruff, bespectacled man of middle age, his cheeks haggard, and his hands twitching from the nervous strain to which he had been subjected.

"It is bad, Mr. Holmes, very bad! Have you heard of the death of the chief?"

"We have just come from his house."

"The place is disorganized. The chief dead, Cadogan West dead, our papers stolen. And yet, when we closed our door on Monday evening we were as efficient an office as any in the Government service. Good God, it's dreadful to think of! That West, of all men, should have done such a thing!"

"You are sure of his guilt, then?"

"I can see no other way out of it. And yet I would have trusted him as I trust myself."

"At what hour was the office closed on Monday?"

"At five."

"Did you close it?"

"I am always the last man out."

"Where were the plans?"

"In that safe. I put them there myself."

"Is there no watchman to the building?"

"There is; but he has other departments to look after as well. He is an old soldier and a most trustworthy man. He saw nothing that evening. Of course, the fog was very thick."

"Suppose that Cadogan West wished to make his way into the building after hours; he would need three keys, would he not, before he could reach the papers?"

"Yes, he would. The key of the outer door, the key of the office, and the key of the safe."

"Only Sir James Walter and you had those keys?"

"I had no keys of the doors—only of the safe."

"Was Sir James a man who was orderly in his habits?"

"Yes, I think he was. I know that so far as those three keys are concerned he kept them on the same ring. I have often seen them there."

"And that ring went with him to London?"

"He said so."

"And your key never left your possession?"

"Never."

"Then West, if he is the culprit, must have had a duplicate. And yet none was found upon his body. One other point: if a clerk in this office desired to sell the plans, would it not be simpler to copy the plans for himself than to take the originals, as was actually done?"

"It would take considerable technical knowledge to copy the plans in an effective way."

"But I suppose either Sir James, or you, or West had that technical knowledge?"

"No doubt we had, but I beg you won't try to drag me into the matter, Mr. Holmes. What is the use of our speculating in this way when the original plans were actually found on West?"

"Well, it is certainly singular that he should run the risk of taking originals if he could safely have taken copies, which would have equally served his turn."

"Singular, no doubt—and yet he did so."

"Every inquiry in this case reveals something inexplicable. Now there are three papers still missing. They are, as I understand, the vital ones."

"Yes, that is so."

"Do you mean to say that anyone holding these three papers, and without the seven others, could construct a Bruce-Partington submarine?"

"I reported to that effect to the Admiralty. But today I have been over the drawings again, and I am not so sure of it. The double valves with the automatic self-adjusting slots are drawn in one of the papers which have been returned. Until the foreigners had invented that for themselves they could not make the boat. Of course, they might soon get over the difficulty."

"But the three missing drawings are the most important?"

"Undoubtedly."

"I think, with your permission, I will now take a stroll round the premises. I do not recall any other question which I desired to ask."

He examined the lock of the safe, the door of the room, and finally the iron shutters of the window. It was only when we were on the lawn outside that his interest was strongly excited. There was a laurel bush outside the window, and several of the branches bore signs of having been twisted or snapped. He examined them carefully with his lens, and then some dim and vague marks upon the earth beneath. Finally he asked the chief clerk to close the iron shutters, and he pointed out to me that they hardly met in the centre, and that it would be possible for anyone outside to see what was going on within the room.

"The indications are ruined by the three days' delay. They may mean something or nothing. Well, Watson, I do not think that Woolwich can help us further. It is a small crop which we have gathered. Let us see if we can do better in London."

Yet we added one more sheaf to our harvest before we left Woolwich Station. The clerk in the ticket office was able to say with confidence that he saw Cadogan West—whom he knew well by sight—upon the Monday night, and that he went to London by the 8:15 to London Bridge. He was alone, and took a single third-class ticket. The clerk was struck at the time by his excited and nervous manner. So shaky was he that he could hardly pick up his change, and the clerk had helped him with it. A reference to the time-table showed that the 8:15 was the first train which it was possible for West to take after he had left the lady about 7:30.

"Let us reconstruct, Watson," said Holmes, after half an hour of silence. "I am not aware that in all our joint researches we have ever had a case which was more difficult to get at. Every fresh advance which we make only reveals a fresh ridge beyond. And yet we have surely made some appreciable progress.

"The effect of our inquiries at Woolwich has in the main been against young Cadogan West; but the indications at the window would lend themselves to a more favourable hypothesis. Let us suppose, for example, that he had been approached by some foreign agent. It might have been done under such pledges as would have prevented him from speaking of it, and yet would have affected his thoughts in the direction indicated by his remarks to his fiancée. Very good. We will now suppose that as he went to the theatre with the young lady he suddenly, in the fog, caught a glimpse of this same agent going in the direction of the office. He was an impetuous man, quick in his decisions. Everything gave way to his duty. He followed the man, reached the window, saw the abstraction of the documents, and pursued the thief. In this way we get over the objection that no one would take originals when he could make copies. This outsider had to take originals. So far it holds together."

"What is the next step?"

"Then we come into difficulties. One would imagine that under such circumstances the first act of young Cadogan West would be to seize the villain and raise the alarm. Why did he not do so? Could it have been an official superior who took the papers? That would explain West's conduct. Or could the thief have given West the slip in the fog, and West started at once to London to head him off from his own rooms, presuming that he knew where the rooms were? The call must have been very pressing, since he left his girl standing in the fog, and made no effort to communicate with her. Our scent runs cold here, and there is a vast gap between either hypothesis and the laying of West's body, with seven papers in his pocket, on the roof of a Metropolitan train. My instinct now is to work from the other end. If Mycroft has given us the list of addresses we may be able to pick our man, and follow two tracks instead of one."

Surely enough, a note awaited us at Baker Street. A Government messenger had brought it post-haste. Holmes glanced at it and threw it over to me.

There are numerous small fry, but few who would handle so big an affair. The only men worth considering are Adolph Meyer, of 13, Great George Street, Westminster; Louis La Rothière, of Campden Mansions, Notting Hill; and Hugo Oberstein, 13, Caulfield Gardens, Kensington. The latter was known to be in town on Monday, and is now reported as having left. Glad to hear you have seen some light. The Cabinet awaits your final report with the utmost anxiety. Urgent representations have arrived from the very highest quarter. The whole force of the State is at your back, if you should need it.

MYCROFT

"I'm afraid," said Holmes, smiling, "that all the Queen's horses and all the Queen's men cannot avail in this matter." He had spread out his big map of London, and leaned eagerly over it. "Well, well," said he presently, with an exclamation of satisfaction, "things are turning a little in our direction at last. Why, Watson, I do honestly believe that we are going to pull it off after all." He slapped me on the shoulder with a sudden burst of hilarity. "I am going out now. It is only a reconnaissance. I will do nothing serious without my trusted comrade and biographer at my elbow. Do you stay here, and the odds are that you will see me again in an hour or two. If time hangs heavy get foolscap and a pen, and begin your narrative of how we saved the State."

I felt some reflection of his elation in my own mind, for I knew well that he would not depart so far from his usual austerity of demeanour unless there was good cause for exultation. All the long November evening I waited, filled with impatience for his return. At last, shortly after nine o'clock there arrived a messenger with a note:

Am dining at Goldini's Restaurant, Gloucester Road, Kensington. Please come at once and join me there. Bring with you a jemmy, a dark lantern, a chisel, and a revolver. S.H.

It was nice equipment for a respectable citizen to carry through the dim, fog-draped streets. I stowed them all discreetly away in my overcoat, and drove straight to the address given. There sat my friend at a little round table near the door of the garish Italian restaurant.

"Have you had something to eat? Then join me in a coffee and curaçao. Try one of the proprietor's cigars. They are less poisonous than one would expect. Have you the tools?"

"They are here, in my overcoat."

"Excellent. Let me give you a short sketch of what I have done, with some indication of what we are about to do. Now, it must be evident to you, Watson, that this young man's body was placed on the roof of the train. That was clear from the instant that I determined the fact that it was from the roof, and not from a carriage, that he had fallen."

"Could it not have been dropped from a bridge?"

"I should say it was impossible. If you examine the roofs you will find that they are slightly rounded, and there is no railing round them. Therefore, we can say for certain that young Cadogan West was placed on it."

"How could he be placed there?"

"That was the question which we had to answer. There is only one possible way. You are aware that the Underground runs clear of tunnels at some points in the West End. I had a vague memory that as I have travelled by it I have occasionally seen windows just above my head. Now, suppose that a train halted under such a window, would there be any difficulty in laying a body upon the roof?"

"It seems most improbable."

"We must fall back upon the old axiom that when all other contingencies fail, whatever remains, however improbable, must be the truth. Here all other contingencies have failed. When I found that the leading international agent, who had just left London, lived in a row of houses which abutted upon the Underground, I was so pleased that you were a little astonished at my sudden frivolity."

"Oh, that was it, was it?"

"Yes, that was it. Mr. Hugo Oberstein, of 13, Caulfield Gardens, had become my objective. I began my operations at Gloucester Road Station, where a very helpful official walked with me along the track, and allowed me to satisfy myself, not only that the back-stair windows of Caulfield Gardens open on the line, but the even more essential fact that, owing to the intersection of one of the larger railways, the Underground trains are frequently held motionless for some minutes at that very spot."

"Splendid, Holmes! You have got it!"

"So far—so far, Watson. We advance, but the goal is afar. Well, having seen the back of Caulfield Gardens, I visited the front and satisfied myself that the bird was indeed flown. It is a considerable house, unfurnished, so far as I could judge, in the upper rooms. Oberstein lived there with a single valet, who was probably a confederate entirely in his confidence. We must bear in mind that Oberstein has gone to the Continent to dispose of his booty, but not with any idea of flight; for he had no reason to fear a warrant, and the idea of an amateur domiciliary visit would certainly never occur to him. Yet that is precisely what we are about to make."

"Could we not get a warrant and legalise it?"

"Hardly on the evidence."

"What can we hope to do?"

"We cannot tell what correspondence may be there."

"I don't like it, Holmes."

"My dear fellow, you shall keep watch in the street. I'll do the criminal part. It's not a time to stick at trifles. Think of Mycroft's note, of the Admiralty, the Cabinet, the exalted person who waits for news. We are bound to go."

My answer was to rise from the table.

"You are right, Holmes. We are bound to go."

He sprang up and shook me by the hand.

"I knew you would not shrink at the last," said he, and for a moment I saw something in his eyes which was nearer to tenderness than I had ever seen. The next instant he was his masterful, practical self once more.

"It is nearly half a mile, but there is no hurry. Let us walk," said he. "Don't drop the instruments, I beg. Your arrest as a suspicious character would be a most unfortunate complication."

Caulfield Gardens was one of those lines of flat-faced, pillared, and porticoed houses which are so prominent a product of the middle Victorian epoch in the West End of London. Next door, there appeared to be a children's party, for the merry buzz of young voices and the clatter of a piano resounded through the night. The fog still hung about and screened us with its friendly shade. Holmes had lit his lantern and flashed it upon the massive door.

"This is a serious proposition," said he. "It is certainly bolted as well as locked. We would do better in the area. There is an excellent archway down yonder in case a too zealous policeman should intrude. Give me a hand, Watson, and I'll do the same for you."

A minute later we were both in the area. Hardly had we reached the dark shadows before the step of the policeman was heard in the fog above. As its soft rhythm died away, Holmes set to work upon the lower door. I saw him stoop and strain until with a sharp crash it flew open. We sprang through into the dark passage, closing the area door behind us. Holmes led the way up the curving, uncarpeted stair. His little fan of yellow light shone upon a low window.

"Here we are, Watson—this must be the one." He threw it open, and as he did so there was a low, harsh murmur, growing steadily into a loud roar as a train dashed past us in the darkness. Holmes swept his light along the window sill. It was thickly coated with soot from the passing engines, but the black surface was blurred and rubbed in places.

"You can see where they rested the body. Halloa, Watson! What is this? There can be no doubt that it is a blood mark." He was pointing to faint discolorations along the woodwork of the window. "Here it is on the stone of the stair also. The demonstration is complete. Let us stay here until a train stops."

We had not long to wait. The very next train roared from the tunnel as before, but slowed in the open, and then, with a creaking of brakes, pulled up immediately beneath us. It was not four feet from the window-ledge to the roof of the carriages. Holmes softly closed the window.

"So far we are justified," said he. "What do you think of it, Watson?"

"A masterpiece. You have never risen to a greater height."

"I cannot agree with you there. From the moment that I conceived the idea of the body being upon the roof, which surely was not a very abstruse one, all the rest was inevitable. If it were not for the grave interests involved the affair up to this point would be insignificant. Our difficulties are still before us. But perhaps we may find something here which may help us."

We had ascended the kitchen stair and entered the suite of rooms upon the first floor. One was a dining-room, severely furnished and containing nothing of interest. A second was a bedroom, which also drew blank. The remaining room appeared more promising, and my companion settled down to a systematic examination. It was littered with books and papers, and was evidently used as a study. Swiftly and methodically Holmes turned over the contents of drawer after drawer and cupboard after cupboard, but no gleam of success came to brighten his austere face. At the end of an hour he was no further than when he started.

"The cunning dog has covered his tracks," said he. "He has left nothing to incriminate him. His dangerous correspondence has been destroyed or removed. This is our last chance."

It was a small tin cash-box which stood upon the writing desk. Holmes prised it open with his chisel. Several rolls of paper were within, covered with figures and calculations, without any note to show to what they referred. The recurring words "Water pressure" and "Pressure to the square inch" suggested some possible relation to a submarine. Holmes tossed them all impatiently aside. There only remained an envelope with some small news-slips inside it. He shook them out on the table, and at once I saw by his eager face that his hopes had been raised.

"What's this, Watson? Eh? What's this? Record of a series of messages in the advertisements of a paper. *Daily Telegraph* agony column, by the print and paper. Right-hand top corner of a page. No dates—but messages arrange themselves. This must be the first:

" 'Hoped to hear sooner. Terms agreed to. Write fully to address given on card.—Pierrot.'

"Next comes: 'Too complex for description. Must have full report. Stuff awaits you when goods delivered.—Pierrot.'

"Then comes: 'Matter presses. Must withdraw offer unless contract completed. Make appointment by letter. Will confirm by advertisement.—Pierrot.'

"Finally: 'Monday night after nine. Two taps. Only ourselves. Do not be so suspicious. Payment in hard cash when goods delivered.—Pierrot.'

"A fairly complete record, Watson! If we could only get at the man at the other end!" He sat lost in thought, tapping his fingers on the table. Finally he sprang to his feet.

"Well, perhaps it won't be so difficult after all. There is nothing more to be done here, Watson. I think we might drive round to the offices of the *Daily Telegraph*, and so bring a good day's work to a conclusion."

Mycroft Holmes and Lestrade had come round by appointment after breakfast next day and Sherlock Holmes had recounted to them our proceedings of the day before. The professional shook his head over our confessed burglary.

"We can't do these things in the force, Mr. Holmes," said he. "No wonder you get results that are beyond us. But one of these days you'll go too far, and you'll find yourself and your friend in trouble."

"For England, home and beauty—eh, Watson? Martyrs on the altar of our country. But what do you think of it, Mycroft?"

"Excellent, Sherlock! Admirable! But what use will you make of it?"

Holmes picked up the *Daily Telegraph* which lay upon the table.

"Have you seen Pierrot's advertisement to-day?"

"What! Another one?"

"Yes, here it is: 'Tonight. Same hour. Same place. Two taps. Most vitally important. Your own safety at stake.—Pierrot.' "

"By George!" cried Lestrade. "If he answers that we've got him!"

"That was my idea when I put it in. I think if you could both make it convenient to come with us about eight o'clock to Caulfield Gardens we might possibly get a little nearer to a solution."

One of the most remarkable characteristics of Sherlock Holmes was his power of throwing his brain out of action and switching all his thoughts on to lighter things whenever he had convinced himself that he could no longer work to advantage. I remember that during the whole of that memorable day he lost himself in a monograph which he had undertaken upon the *Polyphonic Motets of Lassus*. For my own part I had none of this power of detachment, and the day, in consequence, appeared to be interminable. The great national importance of the issue, the suspense in high quarters, the direct nature of the experiment which we were trying—all combined to work upon my nerve. It was a relief to me when at last, after a light dinner, we set out upon our expedition. Lestrade and Mycroft met us by appointment at the outside of Gloucester Road Station. The area door of Oberstein's house had been left open the night before, and it was necessary for me, as Mycroft Holmes absolutely and indignantly declined to climb the railings, to pass in and open the hall door. By nine o'clock we were all seated in the study, waiting patiently for our man.

An hour passed and yet another. When eleven struck, the measured beat of the great church clock seemed to sound the dirge of our hopes. Lestrade and Mycroft were fidgeting in their seats and looking twice a minute at their watches. Holmes sat silent and composed, his eyelids half shut, but every sense on the alert. He raised his head with a sudden jerk.

"He is coming," said he.

There had been a furtive step past the door. Now it returned. We heard a shuffling sound outside, and then two sharp taps with the knocker. Holmes rose, motioning to us to remain seated. The gas in the hall was a mere point of light. He opened the outer door, and then as a dark figure slipped past him he closed and fastened it. "This way!" we heard him say, and a moment later our man stood before us. Holmes had followed him closely, and as the man turned with a cry of surprise and alarm he caught him by the collar and threw him back into the room. Before our prisoner had recovered his balance, the door was shut and Holmes standing with his back against it. The man glared round him, staggered, and fell senseless upon the floor. With the shock, his broad-brimmed hat flew from his head, his cravat slipped down from his lips, and there was the long light beard and the soft, handsome delicate feature of Colonel Valentine Walter.

"You can write me down an ass this time, Watson," said he. "This was not the bird that I was looking for."

"Who is he?" asked Mycroft eagerly.

"The younger brother of the late Sir James Walter, the head of the Submarine Department. Yes, yes; I see the fall of the cards. He is coming to. I think that you had best leave his examination to me."

We had carried the prostrate body to the sofa. Now our prisoner sat up, looked round him with a horror-stricken face, and passed his hand over his forehead, like one who cannot believe his own senses.

"What is this?" he asked. "I came here to visit Mr. Oberstein."

"Everything is known, Colonel Walter," said Holmes. "How an English gentleman could behave in such a manner is beyond my comprehension. But your whole correspondence and relations with Oberstein are within our knowledge. So also are the circumstances connected with the death of young Cadogan West. Let me advise you to gain at least the small credit for repentance and confession, since there are still some details which we can only learn from your lips."

The man groaned and sank his face in his hands. We waited, but he was silent.

"I can assure you," said Holmes, "that every essential is already known. We know that you were pressed for money; that you took an impress of the keys which your brother held; and that you entered into a correspondence with Oberstein, who answered your letters through the advertisement columns of the *Daily Telegraph*. We are aware that you went down to the office in the fog on Monday night, but that you were seen and followed by young Cadogan West, who had probably some previous reason to suspect you. He saw your theft, but could not give the alarm, as it was just possible that you were taking the papers to your brother in London. Leaving all his private concerns, like the good citizen that he was, he followed you closely in the fog, and kept at your heels until you reached this very house. There he intervened, and then it was, Colonel Walter, that to treason you added the more terrible crime of murder."

"I did not! I did not! Before God I swear that I did not!" cried our wretched prisoner.

"Tell us then how Cadogan West met his end before you laid him upon the roof of a railway carriage."

"I will. I swear to you that I will. I did the rest. I confess it. It was just as you say. A Stock Exchange debt had to be paid. I needed the money badly. Oberstein offered me five thousand. It was to save myself from ruin. But as to murder, I am as innocent as you."

"What happened then?"

"He had his suspicions before, and he followed me as you describe. I never knew it until I was at the very door. It was thick fog, and one could not see three yards. I had given two taps and Oberstein had come to the door. The young man rushed up and demanded to know what we were about to do with the papers. Oberstein had a short life-preserver.* He always carried it with him. As West forced his way after us into the house Oberstein struck him on the head. The blow was a fatal one. He was dead within five minutes. There he lay in the hall, and we were at our wits' end what to do. Then Oberstein had this idea about the trains which halted under his back window. But first he examined the papers which I had brought. He said that three of them were essential, and that he must keep them. 'You cannot keep them,' said I. 'There will be a dreadful row at Woolwich if they are not

* Bludgeon.

returned.' 'I must keep them,' said he, 'for they are so technical that it is impossible in the time to make copies,' 'Then they must all go back together to-night,' said I. He thought for a little, and then he cried out that he had it. 'Three I will keep,' said he. 'The others we will stuff into the pocket of this young man. When he is found the whole business will assuredly be put to his account.' I could see no other way out of it, so we did as he suggested. We waited half an hour at the window before a train stopped. It was so thick that nothing could be seen, and we had no difficulty in lowering West's body on to the train. That was the end of the matter so far as I was concerned."

"And your brother?"

"He said nothing, but he had caught me once with his keys, and I think that he suspected. I read in his eyes that he suspected. As you know, he never held up his head again."

There was silence in the room. It was broken by Mycroft Holmes.

"Can you not make reparation? It would ease your conscience, and possibly your punishment."

"What reparation can I make?"

"Where is Oberstein with the papers?"

"I do not know."

"Did he give you no address?"

"He said that letters to the Hotel de Louvre, Paris, would eventually reach him."

"Then reparation is still within your power," said Sherlock Holmes.

"I will do anything I can. I owe this fellow no particular good-will. He has been my ruin and my downfall."

"Here are paper and pen. Sit at this desk and write to my dictation. Direct the envelope to the address given. That is right. Now the letter:

"Dear Sir,—With regard to our transaction, you will no doubt have observed by now that one essential detail is missing. I have a tracing which will make it complete. This has involved me in extra trouble, however, and I must ask you for a further advance of five hundred pounds. I will not trust it to the post, nor will I take anything but gold or notes. I would come to you abroad, but it would excite remark if I left the country at present. Therefore I shall expect to meet you in the smoking-room of the Charing Cross Hotel at noon on Saturday. Remember that only English notes, or gold, will be taken."

"That will do very well. I shall be very much surprised if it does not fetch our man."

And it did! It is a matter of history—that secret history of a nation which is often so much more intimate and interesting than its public chronicles—that Oberstein, eager to complete the coup of his lifetime, came to the lure and was safely engulfed for fifteen years in a British prison. In his trunk were found the invaluable Bruce-Partington plans, which he had put up for auction in all the naval centres of Europe.

Colonel Walter died in prison towards the end of the second year of his sentence. As to Holmes, he returned refreshed to his monograph upon the *Polyphonic Motets of Lassus*, which has since been printed for private circulation, and is said by experts to be the last word upon the subject. Some weeks afterwards I learned incidentally that my friend spent a day at Windsor, whence he returned with a remarkably fine emerald tie-pin. When I asked him if he had bought it, he answered that it was a present from a certain gracious lady in whose interests he had once been fortunate enough to carry out a small commission. He said no more; but I fancy that I could guess at that lady's august name, and I have little doubt that the emerald pin will for ever recall to my friend's memory the adventure of the Bruce-Partington plans.

ERSKINE CHILDERS

▼

2 The Intruders

The Riddle of the Sands, *published in 1903, is a curious book which stands alone in the roster of espionage literature. Primarily it is a marvelous yarn about yachting in small craft in the dangerous waters of the Frisian Islands off the North German coast. If you like to read about sailing, this is certainly your book. Erskine Childers was himself a yachtsman of great skill who had explored the waters he writes of. But Childers had a serious purpose in writing the book. He was convinced that the British Navy at the turn of the century was about to lose its dominance of the seas to the Germans and that one of its weaknesses was its lack of a fleet of small maneuverable naval vessels which could roam close to the coasts of Europe. Another was its lack of nautical knowledge of those coasts.*

To bring home his point, Childers sends his amateur yachtsman, Davies, alone on a private lark into the Frisian Islands, innocent of any purpose but the sport of exploring the area. While he is sailing among the islands, Davies encounters a German named Dollmann with a powerful yacht who one day suggests Davies follow him in order to reach harbor in a storm. But for Davies' excellent seamanship he would have been lost. Once he reaches land, Davies wires for his friend Carruthers in London to join him. His reasons are given in the excerpt.

In the second half of the book, the two yachtsmen spy on Dollmann and his German naval friends and in the end discover that "the riddle of the sands" is the construction of secret canals in the mainland behind the Frisian Islands in which a fleet of seagoing barges will later be concealed, to be used one day in the invasion of England.

FROM *The Riddle of the Sands.*

Childers himself led an adventurous life. He used his private yacht to run guns to Ireland for the Irish Republican Army and was finally caught and executed by a firing squad.

What about Dollmann?" I asked.

"Of course," said Davies, "what about him? I didn't get at much that night. It was all so sudden. The only thing I could have sworn to from the first was that he had purposely left me in the lurch that day. I pieced out the rest in the next few days. It was just a week after I ran ashore that I wired to you. You see, I had come to the conclusion that that chap was a spy."

In the end it came out quite quietly and suddenly, and left me in profound amazement. "I wired to you—that chap was a spy." It was the close association of these two ideas that hit me hardest at the moment. For a second I was back in the dreary splendour of the London club-room, spelling out that crabbed scrawl from Davies, and fastidiously criticising its proposal in the light of a holiday. Holiday! What was to be its issue? Chilling and opaque as the fog that filtered through the skylight there flooded my imagination a mist of doubt and fear.

"A spy!" I repeated blankly. "What do you mean? Why did you wire to me? A spy of what—of whom?"

"I'll tell you how I worked it out," said Davies. "I don't think 'spy' is the right word; but I mean something pretty bad. He purposely put me ashore. I don't think I'm suspicious by nature, but I know something about boats and the sea. I know he could have kept close to me if he had chosen. I can see now that it was a hundred to one in favour of my striking on a bad place outside, where I should have gone to pieces in three minutes."

"And how did Dollmann go?" I asked.

"It's as clear as possible," Davies answered. "He doubled back into the northern channel when he had misled me enough."

I tried with my landsman's fancy to conjure up that perilous scene. As to the truth of the affair, the chart and Davies's version were easy enough to follow, but I felt only half convinced. The "spy," as Davies strangely called his pilot, might have honestly mistaken the course himself, outstripped his convoy inadvertently, and escaped disaster as narrowly as he did. I suggested this on the spur of the moment, but Davies was impatient.

"Wait till you hear the whole thing," he said. "I must go back to when I first met him. I told you that on that first evening he began by being as rude as a bear and as cold as stone, and then became suddenly friendly. I can see now that in the talk that followed he was pumping me hard. . . . I was tremendously keen about my voyage, and I thought the chap was a good sportsman, even if he was a bit dark about the ducks. I talked quite freely—at least, as freely as I could with my bad German—about my last fortnight's sailing; how I had been smelling out all the channels in and out of the islands, how interested I had been in the whole business, puzzling out the effect of the winds on the tides, the set of the currents, and so on. I talked about my difficulties, too; the changes in the buoys, the prehistoric rottenness of the English charts. He drew me out as much as he could, and in the light of what followed I can see the point of scores of his questions.

"The next day and the next I saw a good deal of him, and the same thing went on. And then there were my plans for the future. My idea was, as I told you, to go on exploring the German coast just as I had the Dutch. His idea—heavens, how plainly I see it now—was to choke me off, get me to clear out altogether from that part of the coast. That was why he cracked up the Baltic as a cruising-ground and shooting-ground. And that was why he broached and stuck to that plan of sailing in company direct to the Elbe. It was to see me clear."

"He improved on that."

"Yes, but after that, it's guess-work. I mean that I can't tell when he first decided to go one better and drown me. He couldn't count for certain on bad weather, though he held my nose to it when it came. But, granted that he wanted to get rid of me altogether, he got a magnificent chance on that trip to the Elbe lightship. I expect it struck him suddenly, and he acted on the impulse. Left to myself I was all right; but the short cut was a grand idea of his. Everything was in its favour—wind, sea, sand, tide. He thinks I'm dead. . . ."

The incongruity of the whole business was striking me. Why should anyone want to kill Davies, and why should Davies, the soul of modesty and simplicity, imagine that anyone wanted to kill him? He must have cogent reasons, for he was the last man to give way to a morbid fancy.

"Go on," I said. "What was his motive? A German finds an Englishman exploring a bit of German coast, determines to stop him, and even to get rid of him. It looks so far as if you were thought to be the spy."

Davies winced. "But he's not a German," he said, hotly. "He's an Englishman."

"An Englishman?"

"Yes, I'm sure of it. Not that I've much to go on. He professed to know very little English, and never spoke it, except a word or two now and then to help me out of a sentence; and as to his German, he seemed to me to speak it like a native; but, of course, I'm no judge." Davies sighed. "That's where I wanted someone like you. You would have spotted him at once, if he wasn't German. I go more by a—what do you call it?—a—"

"General impression," I suggested.

"Yes, that's what I mean. It was something in his looks and manner; you know how different we are from foreigners. And it wasn't only himself, it was the way he talked—I mean about cruising and the sea, especially. It's true he let me do most of the talking; but, all the same—how can I explain it? I felt we understood one another, in a way that two foreigners wouldn't. He pretended to think me a bit crazy for coming so far in a small boat, but I could swear he knew as much about the game as I did; for lots of little questions he asked had the right ring in them. Mind you, all this is an after-thought. I should never have bothered about it—I'm not cut out for a Sherlock Holmes— if it hadn't been for what followed."

"It's rather vague," I said. "Have you no more definite reason for thinking him English?"

"There were one or two things rather more definite," said Davies, slowly. "You know when he hove to and hailed me, proposing the short cut, I told you roughly what he said. I forget the exact words, but 'abschneiden' came in—'durch Watten' and 'abschneiden' (they call the banks 'watts,' you know); they were simple words, and he shouted them loud, so as to carry through the wind. I understood what he meant, but, as I told you, I hesitated before consenting. I suppose he thought I didn't understand, for just as he was drawing ahead again he pointed to the suth'ard, and then shouted through his hands as a trumpet 'Verstehen Sie?' Short cut through Sands. Follow me!'—the last two sentences in downright English. I can hear those words now, and I'll swear they were in his native tongue. Of course I thought nothing of it at the time. I was quite aware that he knew a few English words, though he had always mispronounced them; an easy trick when your hearer suspects nothing. But I needn't say that just then I was observant of trifles. I don't pretend to be able to unravel a plot and steer a small boat before a heavy sea at the same moment."

"And if he was piloting you into the next world he could afford to commit himself before you parted!"

"I'm convinced," he said, "that he's an Englishman in German service. He must be in German service, for he had evidently been in

those waters a long time, and knew every inch of them; of course, it's a
very lonely part of the world, but he has a house on Norderney Island;
and he, and all about him, must be well known to a certain number of
people. One of his friends I happened to meet; what do you think he
was? A naval officer. It was on the afternoon of the third day, and we
were having coffee on the deck of the *Medusa*, and talking about next
day's trip, when a little launch came buzzing up from seaward, drew
alongside, and this chap I'm speaking of came on board, shook hands
with Dollmann, and stared hard at me. Dollmann introduced us,
calling him Commander von Brüning, in command of the torpedo
gunboat *Blitz*. He pointed towards Norderney, and I saw her—a low,
grey rat of a vessel—anchored in the Roads about two miles away. It
turned out that she was doing the work of fishery guardship on that
part of the coast.

"I must say I took to him at once. He looked a real good sort, and
a splendid officer, too—just the sort of chap I should have liked to be.
You know I always wanted—but that's an old story, and can wait. I
had some talk with him, and we got on capitally as far as we went, but
that wasn't far, for I left pretty soon, guessing that they wanted to be
alone."

"Were they alone then?" I asked, innocently.

"Oh, Fräulein Dollmann was there, of course," explained Davies,
feeling for his armour again.

"Did he seem to know them well?" I pursued, inconsequently.

"Oh, yes, very well."

Scenting a faint clue, I felt the need of feminine weapons for my
sensitive antagonist. But the opportunity passed.

"That was the last I saw of him," he said. "We sailed, as I told you,
at daybreak next morning. Now, have you got any idea what I'm
driving at?"

"A rough idea," I answered. "Go ahead."

Davies sat up to the table, unrolled the chart with a vigorous
sweep of his two hands, and took up his parable with new zest.

"I start with two certainties," he said. "One is that I was 'moved on'
from that coast, because I was too inquisitive. The other is that Dollmann is at some devil's work there which is worth finding out. About
this coast," resumed Davies. "In the event of war it seems to me that
every inch of it would be important, sand and all. Take the big estuaries first, which, of course, might be attacked or blockaded by an
enemy. At first sight you would say that their main channels were the
only things that mattered. Now, in time of peace there's no secrecy
about the navigation of these. They're buoyed and lighted like streets,

open to the whole world, and taking an immense traffic; well charted, too, as millions of pounds in commerce depend on them. But now look at the sands they run through, intersected, as I showed you, by threads of channels, tidal for the most part, and probably only known to smacks and shallow coasters. . . .

"It strikes me that in a war a lot might depend on these, both in defence and attack, for there's plenty of water in them at the right tide for patrol-boats and small torpedo craft, though I can see they take a lot of knowing. Now, say we were at war with Germany—both sides could use them as lines between the three estuaries; and to take our own case, a small torpedo-boat (not a destroyer, mind you) could on a dark night cut clean through from the Jade to the Elbe and play the deuce with the shipping there. But the trouble is that I doubt if there's a soul in our fleet who knows those channels. We haven't coasters there; and, as to yachts, it's a most unlikely game for an English yacht to play at; but it does happen that I have a fancy for that sort of thing and would have explored those channels in the ordinary course." I began to see his drift.

"Now for the islands. I was rather stumped there at first, I grant, because, though there are lashings of sand behind them, and the same sort of intersecting channels, yet there seems nothing important to guard or attack.

"Why shouldn't a stranger ramble as he pleases through them? Still Dollmann had his headquarters there, and I was sure that had some meaning. Then it struck me that the same point held good, for that strip of Frisian coast adjoins the estuaries, and would also form a splendid base for raiding midgets, which could travel unseen right through from the Ems to the Jade, and so to the Elbe, as by a covered way between a line of forts.

"Now here again it's an unknown land to us. Plenty of local galliots travel it, but strangers never, I should say. Perhaps at the most an occasional foreign yacht gropes in at one of the gaps between the islands for shelter from bad weather, and is precious lucky to get in safe. Once again, it was my fad to like such places, and Dollmann cleared me out. He's not a German, but he's in with Germans, and naval Germans too. He's established on that coast, and knows it by heart. And he tried to drown me. Now what do you think?" He gazed at me long and anxiously.

"There are two main points that I don't understand," I said. "First, you've never explained why an Englishman should be watching those waters and ejecting intruders; secondly, your theory doesn't supply sufficient motive. There may be much in what you say about the navigation of those channels, but it's not enough. You say he wanted to drown you—a big charge, requiring a big motive to support it. But I don't deny that you've got a strong case." Davies lighted up. "I'm willing to take a good deal for granted—until we find out more."

He jumped up, and did a thing I never saw him do before or since—bumped his head against the cabin roof.

"You mean that you'll come?" he exclaimed. "Why, I hadn't even asked you! Yes, I want to go back and clear up the whole thing. I know now that I want to; telling it all to you has been such an immense relief. And a lot depended on you, too, and that's why I've been feeling such an absolute hypocrite. I say, how can I apologise?"

"Don't worry about me; I've had a splendid time. And I'll come right enough; but I should like to know exactly what you—"

"No; but wait till I just make a clean breast of it—about you, I mean. You see, I came to the conclusion that I could do nothing alone; not that two are really necessary for managing the boat in the ordinary way, but for this sort of job you do want two; besides, I can't speak German properly, and I'm a dull chap all round. If my theory, as you call it, is right, it's a case for sharp wits, if ever there was one; so I thought of you. You're clever, and I knew you had lived in Germany and knew German, and I knew," he added, with a little awkwardness, "that you had done a good deal of yachting; but of course I ought to have told you what you were in for—roughing it in a small boat with no crew."

"Never mind! . . . What's your plan of action?"

"It's this," was the prompt reply: "to get back to the North Sea, via Kiel and the ship canal. Then there will be two objects: one, to work back to Norderney, where I left off before, exploring all those channels through the estuaries and islands; the other, to find Dollmann, discover what he's up to, and settle with him. The two things may overlap, we can't tell yet. I don't even know where he and his yacht are; but I'll be bound they're somewhere in those same waters, and probably back at Norderney."

"It's a delicate matter," I mused dubiously, "if your theory's correct. Spying on a spy—"

"It's not like that," said Davies, indignantly. "Anyone who likes can sail about there and explore those waters. I say, you don't really think it's like that, do you?"

"I don't think you're likely to do anything dishonourable," I hastened to explain. "I grant you that the sea's public property in your sense. I only mean that developments are possible, which you don't reckon on. There must be more to find out than the mere navigation of those channels, and if that's so, mightn't we come to be genuine spies ourselves?"

"And, after all, hang it!" exclaimed Davies, "if it comes to that, why shouldn't we? I look at it like this. The man's an Englishman, and if he's in with Germany he's a traitor to us, and we as Englishmen have a right to expose him. If we can't do it without spying we've a right to spy, at our own risk—"

"There's a stronger argument than that. He tried to take your life."

"I don't care a rap about that. I'm not such an ass as to thirst for revenge and all that, like some chap in a shilling shocker. But it makes me wild to think of that fellow masquerading as a German, and up to who knows what mischief—mischief enough to make him want to get rid of anyone. I'm keen about the sea, and I think they're apt to be a bit slack at home," he continued inconsequently. "Those Admiralty chaps want waking up."

MANNING COLES

▼

3 Guarding the Zeppelins

*Manning Coles is the nom de plume of a pair of English authors—
a lady, Adelaide Frances Manning, and a gentleman, Cyril Henry
Coles—who have been responsible ever since the early nineteen-
twenties for more than twenty spy novels and short stories.
Usually their scene is Germany and their hero the British Intelligence Service. They are probably the only authors who have kept
up a game of imaginary hare-and-hounds against the changing
German background of the last forty years or so: the Kaiser's
empire of World War I (Drink to Yesterday), the rise of Hitler's
Reich (Drink to Tomorrow), right up to the divided Germany of
the Iron Curtain epoch (No Entry). Through all these changes,
and in most of their books, they have kept a single, redoubtable,
ageless, and irrepressible character busy, a certain Tommy Hambledon, a schoolmaster who seems to be on permanent loan to the
British Secret Service.*

*The story goes that Coles, who himself went on British intelli-
gence missions behind the lines in Germany in World War I, sat
down one day to tell some stories about his experiences to Miss
Manning, who was an author and a neighbor of his in a small
village in Hampshire, and that their collaboration grew out of this
neighborly incident.*

In their first book, Drink to Yesterday, *from which our excerpt
is taken, Hambledon and a young Englishman, Bill Saunders, pose
in wartime Germany as two neutral Dutchmen, Hendrik Brandt
and his nephew Dirk Brandt, who favor the German side. Since,
disguised as neutrals, they are able to travel, even during wartime,
to countries such as England, they are soon recruited by the*

FROM *Drink to Yesterday.*

*German Intelligence Service in the person of a certain von Boden-
heim.*

*Among other innovations, the Manning Coles combination
managed to insert a wry British humor into all their tales, an
element for the most part missing from spy literature preceding
World War I, which generally tended to be sinister, mysterious,
and only unintentionally humorous.*

Much later that evening Bill rang up von Bodenheim to announce
his return with something to report, and was asked to go to the
house in the Blumenthalstrasse forthwith, so he went there and was
very cordially received.

"What I really wanted to tell you," said Dirk Brandt of the
German Intelligence, after various items of news had been told, "was
about an odd thing which happened on my last night in London. This
English officer whom I made friends with at the Southampton hotel I
was telling you about arranged to meet me for an evening together,
and we had quite a good time, dinner, show—the Coliseum to be
exact, there was a girl singing rather a good song called 'Not Yet'—
drinks at the bar, and finally a club he belonged to, which had an odd
name, the Clinging Codfish, of all things. It was a cheerful place."

"You seem to have enjoyed your trip," said von Bodenheim.
"Though I can think of pleasanter things than codfish to have clinging
to one. But I dare say the ultimate result would be much the
same—you'd wish you hadn't."

"I dare say," said Dirk laughing. "Can't say I've got that far yet.
Anyway, this fellow got pretty stewed as the evening went on, and he
talked. Oh, how he talked! I had his life history as time went on, but
that's not the point. There was another man in the club who rather
impressed me; he was drinking hard and quite reckless. He had a girl
with him, and just to impress her, I suppose, he ordered a half-dozen
new-laid eggs and shied them into the electric fan. The results came
back all over the adjacent diners, so, although they are fairly tolerant
towards the amusements of soldiers in London now, he wasn't popular, and they persuaded him to go away. Striking man to look at, too,
fine face, rather like a hawk. I said something to the effect that it was a
pity to see a splendid-looking chap like that make such an exhibition of
himself, and my friend said that perhaps I'd let myself go a bit if I had
his job in prospect."

"Did you hear what it was?"

"Yes, he was going to burn the Zeppelins at Ahlhorn."

"What?" cried von Bodenheim, in a tone of voice that brought his soldier servant hurrying out of the back premises. "What was his name? (It is all right, Hans, I do not require anything.) What regiment did he belong to?"

"I did my best to find out his name and regiment, but my man was not so drunk as all that, so all I could do was to memorize his face; I should know him again anywhere. I didn't recognize his badges."

"Can you describe him?"

"I don't know that I'm much good at describing people," said Dirk, with a frown of concentration. "He had fair hair, a hooked nose, and a prominent chin. Rather a red face, but that may have been due to the evening. Tallish—no, not very tall, but considerably taller than I am, for example; five foot eight or ten. The most outstanding thing about his appearance was his air of being somebody, if you know what I mean. You couldn't help noticing him."

"Even if he wasn't throwing new-laid eggs into an electric fan, I suppose," said von Bodenheim sarcastically. "You mean he had personality, an attribute which he could shed in a moment. Otherwise he was tallish, with fair hair and prominent features. It is a description of about a quarter of the British and German armies."

"I'm sorry," said Dirk, quite crestfallen. "I can't think of anything—"

"It is I who should apologize. You come to me with a most remarkable piece of intelligence, and all I do is to snub you because you cannot give a detailed description of him. My dear boy, please forgive me, it was unpardonable. My only excuse is that the news is so desperately important—more so than you have any idea."

"Indeed, sir?"

"You have done extraordinarily well and rendered a great service to my—our—country."

"Thank you," said Dirk in a tone of some emotion.

"There is only one thing to be done and you are the only man to do it."

"And that is?"

"You must go to Ahlhorn and keep a look-out for the man yourself."

Hendrik Brandt demurred as strongly as he dared to having his nephew taken away from him when he had only just returned to the office, but was imperiously overridden by von Bodenheim in person. So young Dirk Brandt was provided with a special pass which enabled him to go anywhere and do almost anything, and orders had been sent in advance to the commanding officer of the troops guarding the airship sheds to supply Dirk with whatever comfort and assistance he might need; in fact, broadly speaking, to do what the boy told him. Bill was shown the orders.

"Oh, it's almost too good to be true," said Hambledon. "Either there's a catch in it somewhere or you're too lucky to be human, and if I were you I would sacrifice something to the gods. Throw the youngest Miss Bluehm into the Rhine."

"Why Marie Bluehm?"

"I thought you were rather fond of her."

"She's a fine girl, that's all; she plays the piano rather well. I'm not smitten."

"Glad to hear it; on our job we can't afford these distractions. By the way, wasn't there a girl at home?"

"There was," said Bill, who had such a rooted disinclination to bring Diane into even the remotest contact with the job that he would not mention her to Hambledon if he could help it; at least, not here in Cologne. "But why mustn't we talk to girls occasionally?"

"Oh, talk to 'em occasionally, by all means, but don't for pity's sake marry any of 'em."

"Why not?"

"Consider the life of an Intelligence man's wife. Either he tells her what his job is, or else he doesn't. If he does, she will never know another peaceful moment as long as she lives, because there's no end to our war—that is, if she cares for him. If she doesn't, she may talk, and then he'd have to shoot her. Suppose he doesn't tell her. He says instead that he is an insurance agent, or a traveller in pig food, or an inspector of nuisances, which last is nearer the truth than most of us get in this life. He tells her he's going to Bristol to see a man about a drain, but you can bet your boots that some dear school-friend of hers will write and tell her that he was seen last Wednesday strolling along the promenade at Felixstowe with a dazzling blonde, after which he will spend the next twenty years of his life giving lucid and convincing explanations, and she won't believe any of 'em. No, we don't marry on our job, Bill. Pass the beer, lecturing is dry work. That's what's the matter with schoolmastering, too many lectures and not enough beer."

"Talking about schoolmasters, I've got to see Reck tonight."

"To collect the needful, of course. It's convenient having a chemist who'll get the stuff for you. When do you start?"

"At eight tomorrow morning."

Bill packed his shabby suitcase and departed for Ahlhorn in state and a staff car with a soldier driver, which had been placed at his disposal. It was only a hundred and fifty miles, but the tires were bad and the roads worse, and it was not till late in the evening that they arrived. The *Landsturm* officer commanding the small garrison was a portly Bavarian major of mature years, who was puzzled and pained at having to take orders from an insignificant civilian, and a Dutchman at that, and inclined to think it all too ridiculous for words.

"The country is going to the dogs," he said. "In my young days we'd have thrown a cordon of sentries round the place with instructions to shoot at sight anything approaching, from a rabbit upwards. All this stopping people and asking 'em questions, a lot of damned nonsense in my opinion, how d'you know they're speaking the truth? All this rubbish about English spies! In my opinion if the English spies are as clever as some people make out, they'll know better than to take on such a wild-goose chase. What? A total stranger to walk in here, set fire to the Zeppelins, and then quietly walk out again? Damned nonsense! I don't believe in your English spy, how do I know you aren't going to fire the balloons yourself? I don't know you, do I?"

This was nearly too much for even Bill's command of countenance, but he managed to assume an expression of pained surprise and to convey how unexpected it was to find an old and trusted officer in the army of His Imperial Majesty flouting the commands of authority.

"I don't flout them, sir; who says I flout 'em? I receive orders and those orders are obeyed, but that doesn't mean I'm going to sing a psalm about them. Well, it's your responsibility now, young man, not mine. If the Zeppelins are burned now, I wouldn't be in your shoes. Damned nonsense."

Dirk Brandt stayed at a hotel in Ahlhorn and drove the car the three or four miles to the airship station every day. At the times when the shifts went in, and at all times when anyone was admitted through the guarded gates, he was there to see that the sentries performed thoroughly their task of checking the passes carried by anyone, however unimportant, who sought to enter that sacred enclosure. He became intensely irksome to the management and the workmen because his inspection of passes and search for matches and other forbidden articles was so thorough as to delay considerably the entry of the shifts to their work. On three occasions he found splendid-looking men with fair hair and aquiline features and had them hauled into the guard-room for examination, but each time they proved to be perfectly honest Germans on their lawful occasions. As he explained to a sizzling works manager, it was not that he had forgotten what the man looked like—on the contrary, that ill-omened face was indelibly carved on the most retentive tablets of his memory—but that there would be a lot of difference in the appearance of a British company officer at a smart night club and a possibly grubby and inadequately shaved workman in blue overalls, and one must make sure. He, unworthy though he was of so great an honour, was personally responsible to the All-Highest in this matter, and he would fulfill his duties at whatever inconvenience to himself and others.

Von Bodenheim would have been pleased if he could have heard him, but even Dirk's magic pass barely saved him from personal violence upon one occasion when he detached a high-born and appropriately dignified Austrian officer from a party which was making a personally conducted tour of the sheds. Dirk kept him locked up all through the lunch hour and finally had him stripped to the skin to see if his pronounced figure was real, and examined his hair with a magnifying-glass to see if it had been bleached. The officer was, of course, released with profuse apologies, but Dirk hoped the Austrian would remember that curious and undignified things happened to haughty men who stuck monocles in their eyes, glared at unoffending strangers, and asked audibly: "Who is that funny snub-nosed little squirt?"

At times when there were no entrants to detain Dirk at the gates, he would wander about the vast echoing sheds, high as cathedrals, where if a man dropped a spanner on the concrete floors the sound rang like the last trump. He formed the habit of making a final tour of the buildings the last thing every night, walking through every passage and every compartment in each of the airships and even climbing the ladders to the platforms at the top. He noticed with an interest he did not display that there was no protection provided against attacks from above and that even the guns could only be trained on a level and downwards; evidently the stories of the exceptional climbing capabilities and high ceiling of these new Zeppelins were true. They saw no reason to expect attack from above.

He moved about on these tours at a rapid pace, alert, purposeful, and determined, and the perspiring elderly *Landsturm* privates who were detailed by their distrustful commander to follow him everywhere soon became content to wait downstairs, as it were, till he returned from his too athletic excursions. And every day the Zeppelins were more nearly completed.

One day he took the commandant aside and told him that he had been officially informed that a man had been detected passing the Dutch frontier near Rhede. Though fired on by the frontier guards, he had evaded them, and was now somewhere in Arenburg, doubtless making his way towards Ahlhorn. He was described as a tall man with fair hair.

"God bless my soul," said the agitated commandant, "you don't mean to tell me this ridiculous story is true?"

"Of course it's true," said Dirk Brandt, justly indignant. "What do you suppose I walk miles every night climbing all over these infernal flying cathedrals of yours for? To keep my figure down?"

"I don't see what more we can do," said the major, disregarding in his distress this delicate but unkind allusion to his own form.

"We will have every single soul who is not absolutely indispensable out of these sheds as early as possible every night. The few who remain will be all men who are known to us and to each other personally. Your men will form a close cordon at a distance from the sheds so as to obviate the danger of someone dodging past them into cover, and they will shoot at sight."

"Good. That is sense at last."

"I myself will make an extra careful inspection every night, and after I leave, no one is to be admitted under any pretext whatever."

"It shall be done."

"We will foil him yet, Herr Commandant."

"Has he wings?" asked the commandant, becoming almost lyrical with excitement. "Can he change himself into a bird or a rabbit? No. He cannot enter."

"Splendid," said Dirk approvingly.

The Zeppelin crews had arrived and taken over, and only a few workmen remained making last-minute adjustments. The envelope compartments were fully inflated with hydrogen, which, in spite of all precautions, leaked out slowly but continuously and accumulated in the wide barrel roofs, so the enormous ventilators placed in the roofs for the purpose were frequently opened to allow the gas to escape, but it always accumulated again. Now the huge tanks were being filled with gasoline and the racks with bombs; soon everything would be ready.

Dirk Brandt gave the commandant, whom he had encountered buying socks in Ahlhorn, a lift back to the airship station.

"It is not long to wait now," said the major. "Another two or three days and your spy will be too late; the airships will go out when this moon is full."

"I am glad," said young Brandt simply. "The responsibility is great and I am too young for it. I wish they would catch the man."

"It is true you are very young," said the German kindly, "but no one can say you are not conscientious. Himmel, you brood over those airships like an old hen."

"I want them to grow up big strong birds and lay nice eggs," said Dirk—a remark which amused the simple soul of the commandant.

"I have known eggs to burst with a loud report and scatter their contents abroad," he said, shaking with laughter like a well-moulded jelly, "but I would not call them nice eggs. No, not nice at all."

They looked ahead of them across the treeless fields to where the great sheds stood up like slag-heaps against the sky.

"But what a blaze if they should go!" continued the German. "In this flat country the fire would be seen for fifty miles. Do be careful!"

"I am sorry," said Dirk, who was driving. "The tires are smooth and this pavement is greasy. That ditch seems to draw the car like a magnet."

"She is tired, poor thing, and wishes to rest perhaps," said the Herr Commandant with a yawn. "I shall sleep sounder myself when the airships have gone to wake up England."

Brandt went his rounds that night with particular thoroughness, leaving unobtrusive little packets here and there, since his *Landsturm* companion made no attempt to follow him along narrow passages and up steep spidery ladders inside the envelopes of the Zeppelins and right out on to the top. Dirk's orders had been obeyed; the great hangars were silent under the glare of the huge lamps which were kept burning all night, and only a faint whispering echo running up the walls now and then told of the movements of a belated workman busy on some final urgency.

He left the place, taking care that the commandant saw him go, and had returned to his hotel, eaten his supper, and was preparing for bed in the dark with his eyes on the uncurtained window when a brilliant tongue of flame shot into the sky, to be followed by another, and another. Dirk rushed downstairs, convincingly half-clad, to be met by the landlord.

"I should not go out, Herr Brandt," he said. "It is the accursed English aeroplanes, they have bombed the sheds. My son assures me that he saw them distinctly."

"I must go," said Dirk distractedly. "It is my duty."

"At least resume your trousers before you go out, gracious sir," urged the proprietor, and Brandt, with a look of horror at his own attire, uttered a strangled cry and rushed upstairs again. Here, strangely enough, he seemed in no particular hurry about clothing himself once more in the garments of decorum. He opened the window to listen to the roar of the fire just in time to see the first roof fall in and the flames shoot up hundreds of feet into the sky.

" 'Phosphorus and fish-hooks,' " quoted Bill Saunders. "My giddy, sainted aunt, what a bonfire!"

He dressed himself and went out to get the car, expecting to find the streets full of staring people, but to his surprise there was no one

about, though lighted windows and moving shadows on blinds showed
that the town was wakeful and uneasy. He drove as fast as possible
along the slippery road till at a point about a mile from the sheds he
was stopped by a sentry, to whom Dirk showed his pass.

"I beg pardon, I did not recognize you," said the man. "Nevertheless, it will not be safe to take the car any nearer, for who knows that
the whole countryside may not burn with such a start? Thank Heaven
there is snow on the ground."

"Help me to back the car into this gateway," said Dirk, "and I will
go on on foot. Heaven help us, it looks as though even the sky was in
flames. I suppose there will be fire-engines along soon, I must not
block the roads."

"I expect there will," said the sentry, helping him to turn his front
wheels, "though I think it would be just as useful if everyone gathered
round and spat at it. Still, it is always a relief to one's feelings to feel
one is at least trying to do something."

"How true!" said Dirk, and sprinted up the road.

The heat increased as he went on till before he reached the entrance gates it became unbearable, so he pulled up and joined one of
many groups of men who, with arms flung up to shield their faces,
were watching in grim silence the destruction of months of their
devoted labour. The noise of the fire was so loud that no man could
hear himself speak. Every few moments there was an additional roar
as more of the great bombs exploded, and the circle of men backed
away as the flame of the blazing hydrogen became more than their
eyes could bear. The whole scene appeared to be dissolving in
unquenchable fire, and even Bill Saunders's natural exultation of spirit
was overawed by such an appalling success.

"Good God," he muttered, "this is really awful." He approached a
Landsturm private who was standing near, touched his arm to attract
his attention, and yelled in his ear: "Where's the commandant?"

The man pointed away to the left where a number of soldiers were
running about like ants and apparently trying to make something
work. Dirk Brandt went to the spot and found the commandant
supervising the employment of a primitive kind of pump which might
have been effective in putting out a burning cottage, but was mere
waste of energy in the face of such a disaster. When Dirk came up to
him he threw up his hands in a gesture of despair and signed to the
men to abandon the attempt. Dirk took his arm and drew him away
behind one of the numerous temporary buildings which surrounded
the actual sheds, and which afforded some shelter from the intolerable
heat and glare.

"It cannot be true," shouted the commandant. "He cannot have got through. It is impossible. Not a ghost can have passed through my line of sentries, and yet—"

"It is coincidence," yelled Dirk in an attempt to be consoling. "It is an accident; some spark caused by a dropped tool, some workman stupid enough to try and smoke."

"If one did, it was the last thing he ever did."

"Did any of the men who were inside escape?"

"Some from the farther sheds, yes, I saw them running like hares. Not from the end where the fire started."

Dirk shivered, and the old soldier, who had eventually come to like him, saw it and patted his arm.

"It is not your fault," he said, "you must not blame yourself. You could not have done more, could you?"

Dirk looked upwards where the incredible flames, high in the air, seemed to be licking the stars.

"No, I don't think I could," he said slowly.

▼

4 A Defector Who Didn't Make It

Peter Cheyney, whose real name was Harold Brust, wrote a whole series of thrillers, mysteries, and spy stories with titles featuring the word "dark"—Dark Dance, Dark Wanton—in case there was any doubt about how sinister were the tales he had to tell. In this one, Dark Duet, which appeared in the midst of World War II, he created a likable pair of assassins, Kane and Guelvada, the dark duet of the title, whose job was to hunt down German spies in England and elsewhere and kill them without benefit of trial or other legal process. While this is not the way British counter-espionage handled this particular problem, it makes for some exciting action in Cheyney's story, especially when the Germans turn their counter-counterspies on the pair. It is that side of the show we see in the excerpt which follows. The Nazi espionage apparatus is operating against England from a base in neutral Ireland, where the scene is laid. As a matter of historical fact, the Germans did use Ireland in both World Wars as an espionage center.

What is interesting in Cheyney's episode, however, is not the conflict of British and German spies but the situation which develops within the German camp itself. While some of the antics of the German team might seem somewhat old hat to the sophisticated reader of today, it is well to remember that Cheyney wrote this piece at a time when not much was really known about the Nazi intelligence organization.

Seitzen got up. Both he and Hiltsch, standing by the side of the doorway, said: "Heil Hitler!"

Hildebrand came into the room. He sat down by the table. He put

---

FROM *Dark Duet.*

his hand inside his coat and produced a large gold cigarette case. He opened it, laid it on the table, indicated it with a long finger. His attitude was easy, pleasant, and amiable.

"Sit down," he said, "and smoke."

The two men sat down at the table, Hiltsch opposite Hildebrand, Seitzen on his right. Hildebrand looked at them—first at Hiltsch— then at Seitzen. He said:

"I have come over here because I think you need to re-organise a little. Don't you think you do?" His voice was incisive, metallic, but not unpleasant. Only his eyes were unpleasant. They were very hard.

Hiltsch said: "You ought to know it's getting very difficult to work over here. The damned English get more cautious every day, and the Irish are a sick headache. They're being very neutral. During the last twelve weeks it has been awfully difficult to get anybody out at all."

Hildebrand nodded. He said to Seitzen: "What do you think?"

Seitzen said: "It's not easy. I agree with Hiltsch. But still I think we've done fairly well, don't you?"

Hildebrand looked at him. He smiled. He said:

"Do you?"

There was a silence. Hiltsch said: "Look, why not get it over with? There is some trouble, isn't there?"

Hildebrand nodded.

"Oh, yes," he said. "There's some trouble, and there's going to be some more trouble in a minute. There's going to be some trouble for you." He spat the words out of his mouth. His eyes were mere slits.

Hiltsch looked at the table. He found it difficult to look at Hildebrand. Seitzen's right hand fumbled with a loose thread in the cloth of his trousers.

Hildebrand went on: "I can stand most things, but I don't like being a joke. There are two other people who do not like being jokes either. One is called Heydrich and the other is Himmler. I have been on the mat. Having been there, I'm putting you there. Understand this: I don't want talk—I don't want excuses. I want action."

Hiltsch put out his hand to take a cigarette from the gold case. He lit it. He said: "What's the trouble about?"

Hildebrand said: "The trouble is about Kane."

Hiltsch nodded.

"I thought so," he said. "Kane and Guelvada?"

Hildebrand shrugged.

"Guelvada does not matter," he said. "Guelvada is merely an opportunist with an over-developed sense of the dramatic. Take Kane away and Guelvada would help to cut his own throat in six weeks. Guelvada by himself is nothing. The trouble is Kane."

Hiltsch said: "I gathered that. But exactly how? What's Kane been doing?"

Hildebrand raised his eyebrows.

"What has he been doing?" he said. "You ask me that? What in the name of God are you and Seitzen here for? You mean what hasn't he been doing?" He leaned forward over the table. "For your information, gentlemen," he said, "during the last nine months no less than twenty-seven of our most important agents in different parts of the world have been liquidated. Sixteen of them, including Helda Marques, operated from your group. Most of them have been liquidated after they have been jockeyed into a position in which they could be removed. There are a lot of other things, too numerous to be mentioned, apart from that. Well, you're nearest to them. You have ample opportunities for getting at them. We think it's time you did something about it."

Hiltsch said: "I don't think you understand how difficult the position is for us, Karl. We are in the dark. I agree with you that most of our people who have been liquidated have come from this group. Well . . . what do you expect? As you say, we're nearest, and so we do the most work. The fact that our people were killed doesn't help us. And, believe me, nearly all of them—including Helda Marques—were killed. Not one of them was taken by the English and shot officially. After Helda was killed, and we found out how it was done and who did it, I sent two of our smartest people over with instructions to worry about nothing but that cursed pair. They were arrested and shot. Since then we have had no news. And I can't work unless I have information."

Hildebrand said: "It's your business to have information. It's your business to keep your contact lines open. . . ."

"God Almighty!" snarled Hiltsch. "Keep my contact lines open. . . . I like that. For God's sake! Listen, Karl, do you think these bloody English are fools? You may think they are. I don't. England is about the easiest country in the world for an agent to go into, and the goddamned hardest to get out of. One might even think that they encouraged people to come in just to get themselves picked up and shot. And look at our Army people. Look at the lunatic things they do. They send half-trained soldiers, who can speak English, with little radio sets and attaché cases, and packets of English banknotes. My God! The last one was picked up on a railway station trying to read the time table. He had four hundred pounds in notes, a radio set, a pistol, and a sausage. I've been awake for nights on end trying to work out what he had the sausage for. I suppose it was in case he got hungry in the night. . . . But what do you think the sausage was? It was a sausage that is only made in Leipzig. . . . If the fool had been successful and got somewhere, and some Englishmen had looked in his attaché case and seen that sausage the game would have been up. Even an Englishman would have known by the smell that the sausage came from Germany. . . . Can't you see how difficult all this amateur business on the part of the Army branch makes things for us?"

Hildebrand said: "It is your business to overcome difficulties. You must try something new."

Hiltsch said: "Listen, Karl, it's all very well talking like that. We've tried everything."

Seitzen broke in: "We've got a very good man on the job now," he said. "Hillmer—one of our best men."

Hildebrand nodded. One side of his mouth was twisted up in a cynical smile. "So?" he said. "You have a good man on the job— Hillmer! Tell me about Hillmer."

Seitzen said: "Kane is in London. We learned that. I sent Hillmer out of here three weeks ago. He won't come back here unless he has done what he set out to do." He put his hands flat on the table in front of him. His little eyes bespoke a certain self-satisfaction.

"So!" repeated Hildebrand. "We are to rely on Hillmer? I wonder would it interest you two gentlemen to know that five days ago the unfortunate Hillmer had an accident? Perhaps you will remember it was a foggy night. He managed to fall over a railway siding near Euston in the fog. A train ran over him. . . ." He paused for a moment. "That makes twenty-eight," he said. "Thus exits Hillmer."

He got up, walked towards the window, kicked petulantly against the leg of the chair.

"I can imagine the accursed Guelvada—for I'll bet it was he— standing at the top of that railway embankment waiting for the train to go over your clever agent Hillmer. The Hillmer type makes me sick. . . ."

Hiltsch tilted his chair backwards. His eyes were focused on the middle of Hildebrand's back. They looked nasty, those eyes, thought Seitzen. He wondered if Hiltsch hated Hildebrand as much as he did. Hiltsch said: "Look, Karl, I know you're not satisfied. Neither are we. All right. Now you tell me something. . . . If you were me what would you do?"

Hildebrand turned abruptly; began to laugh. When he laughed he drew his lips back over his teeth. He looked rather like a snarling dog. He said:

"I'm going to tell you what you are going to do. I think it is time that you and this fellow here stirred your lazy stumps. I'm giving you a direct order. You get out of here. Go over to England and get Kane. If you don't I'm going to recall you both." He took a cigarette from the case on the table. "You know what that means?" he said.

Hiltsch said: "That's all right. But you still haven't answered my question. I wonder if you realise the difficulties of going after people like Kane and Guelvada."

"Why should there be extreme difficulties about Kane and Guelvada any more than anyone else?" asked Hildebrand.

Hiltsch got up. He put his hands in his pockets; began to walk about the room. Seitzen watched Hiltsch and Hildebrand in turn. His eyes went from one to the other. After a moment Hiltsch said: "They've got an odd way of working. They don't do anything that's conventional. They don't use any of the old systems."

"My God!" said Hildebrand. "Are you telling me that the British are beginning to use imagination?"

Hiltsch said: "Karl, I've never had any delusions about the British. Once they take the gloves off—once they forget to play cricket—to be English gentlemen—they are the toughest things on earth." He sighed. "The trouble with Kane is he doesn't play cricket."

Hildebrand said: "So much the easier." He drew on his cigarette. "Possibly," he went on, "you have heard of Achilles who had a weak spot? Well, this Kane will have one. No man is perfect. Every man leaves himself open in some place. Usually with a man it's a woman."

Seitzen said: "Exactly. That's always been a theory of mine. But here is a case in which it doesn't work. As far as Kane is concerned there is no woman."

Hildebrand turned towards Seitzen. His glance was almost vicious in its intensity. He said:

"Seitzen, you're a damned fool. You are one of those fools who is never right. I think if the English were to cut your throat or push you in front of a train in a fog, or do something else to you, I'd be positively relieved. In any event," he said, "if they don't do it, I shall, sooner or later."

Hiltsch said: "You suggested something just now. You suggested that . . ."

"That there was a woman," said Hildebrand. "There is. She is an actress in London. Kane sees her. He's fond of her. I don't know very much about her; whether she's working for him; whether she's merely his mistress. I don't know . . . but there's something."

Hiltsch stopped walking. He said:

"Now you've got something, Karl. I told you a man like Kane by himself is very difficult, but if he's fond of this woman maybe we can get at him through her." He turned to Seitzen. "You remember what we did in that other thing," he said, "through that blond woman . . . ?"

Hildebrand interrupted.

"Do we have to discuss things that are redundant?" he said. "Let us concentrate on this business. . . . The woman's name is Valetta Fallon."

He came back to the table and sat down.

"I'm coming back here in three weeks," he went on. "I want to know that this matter has been dealt with. If it has not been dealt with, it would be better if I did not see either of you again. It would be better if the English got you. Unless you get results. And if I do see you, I shall recall you, and, by God, things will go hard with you in Germany. You understand?"

"Perfectly," said Hiltsch.

Hildebrand shut the gold cigarette case with a snap.

"Very well," he said. "I look forward to seeing you in three weeks' time—to hear good news. Good evening, gentlemen."

He went out. They heard the car start outside. Seitzen said: "I wonder why we stand for this sort of thing."

Hiltsch began to laugh.

"That's the joke," he said. "You tell me what we can do about it. We're like people who have pushed a cart down a hill and jumped into it just as it gets going. We start it, but we can't stop it. We're caught up in something. We've got to go on. Our only hope is that the cart will one day arrive on the road at the bottom of the hill and stop of its own volition, so that we can get out."

Seitzen sighed again. "This is going to be tough," he said.

Hiltsch shrugged.

"I don't know," he said. "You've been lucky and so have I. I've been in a dozen things when I never expected to get out, but I've got out. This Kane has been lucky too. But no man's luck lasts for ever."

Seitzen said: "That's an idea. Perhaps we're going to be his bad luck."

Hiltsch said: "We've got to be his bad luck. Hildebrand's made it pretty clear, hasn't he? If Heydrich's interested in this business, you can bet your shirt on one thing. It's Kane or us, and I hope it's not going to be us." He took out his cigarette case, lit a cigarette.

Seitzen said: "I wish that damned rain would stop. That pattering outside is driving me crazy."

Hiltsch looked at him. He was grinning. He said:

"For a man who's supposed to be a first-class operative with a Gestapo training, you've got an odd set of nerves. Be careful they don't go back on you."

Seitzen said: "I'm not certain that they're not going back on me. And what about you? You don't feel as good as you did eighteen months ago, do you? You felt pretty good when you were leading that Standarte in Bremen. That was all right. That was really honest-to-goodness straight fighting. It's pretty easy to cut people's throats when you're top dog, but this is a different business. I tell you quite frankly the idea of going into England now, when those cursed British are getting so hot on everything, doesn't appeal to me. Does it to you?"

Hiltsch shrugged his shoulders.

"Candidly, no!" he said. "But what do we do? We're between the devil and the deep sea. The deep sea is the British and the devil is Hildebrand. If we're recalled, we'll be for it. They'll probably send us to the Russian front. They'll freeze some of that fat off you, Seitzen. . . ." He heaved a semi-humorous sigh. "I am afraid there's no way out for us," he said. "We've just got to go on, unless . . ."

Seitzen said softly: "Unless what . . . ?"

Hiltsch drew on his cigarette. He opened his mouth and exhaled a large volume of smoke.

"There is one way out," he said. "But you and I are good Party members. We wouldn't even consider it."

Seitzen said: "I can't consider anything unless I know what it is. What is it?"

Hiltsch drew on his cigarette again. There was a pause; then: "If we went to England and sold out to the British," he said, "we'd be all right." He laughed. "My God, would we give them some information!"

Seitzen said: "Yes . . . and when they'd got it, they'd probably shoot us."

"No," said Hiltsch, "they wouldn't do that. They'd keep us on ice. They'd want to refer to us about all sorts of things. They'd stick us into a gaol somewhere; keep us till the end of the war, using us as reference books from time to time. At the end of the war, if we'd behaved ourselves and told them what they wanted, they'd let us go. They do things like that."

Seitzen said: "It's an idea. . . . But you wouldn't consider a thing like that, would you?"

Hiltsch said: "I don't know. Why shouldn't I consider a thing like that? If we go on as we're going, we're going to be for it anyway. I don't fancy this Kane business. Somebody's going to get us—either the British or, if we fail, Hildebrand. In any event we haven't a long time to go. This way at least we'd be certain of going on living. . . . That is, if you want to go on living?"

Seitzen said: "Naturally I like life." He looked at Hiltsch for a long time; then he said: "Are you serious about this, Hiltsch?"

Hiltsch nodded. "I am if you are," he said. "We've got to make up our minds quickly. Shall we do it?"

"By God . . ." said Seitzen, "let's do it. Let's throw our hands in. I'm sick of being treated like a dog by that—"

"So am I," said Hiltsch. "Well, this is where we get even with him."

Seitzen grinned a little ruefully. "Well, if we do it," he said, "I hope the English win. It would be funny if the Führer took London and got us after all, wouldn't it?"

"Don't kid yourself. The English will win all right," said Hiltsch. "They always do. It's a habit. We've started to lose already. Look at this Russian business. . . ."

Seitzen said: "Give me a cigarette, Hiltsch." His fingers were trembling a little as he took the cigarette. "How are we going to do this?" he said.

"That's easy," said Hiltsch. "We shall pretend to work in the usual way. Hildebrand will expect that. In two or three days' time you'll get out of here and go to England. We shall use the usual process. We shall do that in case Karl is still hanging about here to see how soon we get working. You get there; you go to Liverpool to the usual place. I shall join you two or three days afterwards, coming by the other route. The rest's easy. We go to London. We walk into Scotland Yard; we say, 'Good morning, we're two German Secret Service agents who have been operating a group from Eire for the last nine months. We wish to give ourselves up!' "

He threw his cigarette stub into the fire.

"Of course," he went on, "they won't believe us at first. They'll think we're mad. But we shall be able to prove what we say. Once they realise just how much we know, and of what use we can be, we shall be safe enough." He laughed. "I shall only ask one favour of them. When I'm safely in prison," said Hiltsch, "I shall ask permission to send a rude telegram, through Sweden, to Karl. He will be very annoyed."

Seitzen said seriously: "He will be mad with rage if we talk. The whole of the organisation that he's built up here, in France, in Holland, and in England, will be broken down. If he ever gets his hands on us he'd kill us by inches."

Hiltsch shook his head. "No," he said, "he'd do it by quarter inches. . . . But don't worry. He'll never get us."

Seitzen nodded. He got up from the chair. He said:

"Then it's agreed." He put out his hand. Hiltsch took it.

"It's agreed, Seitzen," he said. "You and I have always worked together. Whatever we may have done, we've never let each other down. We will see this thing through together. We will be two people who will continue to live."

"That suits me," said Seitzen. "Well . . . I'm going to bed."

Hiltsch nodded.

"I shall take a walk," he said, "rain or no rain. I need exercise, and I have some thinking to do. You will leave here, say the day after tomorrow, and I shall be with you three or four days after that. Be ready for that."

"All right," said Seitzen. "Goodnight."

He went out. Hiltsch heard him walking up the stairs.

After a little while Hiltsch went into the hallway. He put on a raincoat and a soft hat. He opened the door and regarded the wet blackness without. The air smelt of rain. He opened his nostrils appreciatively.

He was thinking about Seitzen and the arrangements they had just concluded. Life was damned funny, thought Hiltsch.

He walked down the wet earth pathway on to the dirt road. The mud squelched beneath his well-polished shoes.

He thought, regretfully, that he should have changed them before he came out.

He walked along the road that led towards the village. On the way he began to think about the old days in Munich and Bremen. The brave old days when National Socialism was a word to conjure with and to be a Party member meant something. Hiltsch wondered if those days would ever come again. He thought not. Nothing ever happened twice. One had an experience and that was the end of it. Life was like a love affair. It was all right when things were good, but it was no use trying to resuscitate anything. You couldn't—even if you wanted to. Especially friendships with men and *affaires* with women. When they were dead they were dead, and that was that.

He stopped to light a cigarette, shielding the flame of his lighter with his cupped hand. The hand was strong, well-shaped—a practical hand. But then Hiltsch was a practical man—definitely practical. If you wanted to work for Karl Hildebrand and succeed, you had to be practical and a dozen other things too. . . .

He turned off the road and took the pathway that ran, through the plantation, behind the house. He experienced a certain feeling of satisfaction in pushing through the wet tree branches, in feeling the heavy drops of rain fall on his face.

Now he was behind the house and near it. He moved quietly and easily, treading carefully. As he came round the far side of the house he looked up towards Seitzen's window, noted that no crack of light showed through the tear in the dark curtain.

He flicked away his cigarette stub, moved towards the garage—a shed on the right of the house. He unlocked and opened the doors deftly in the darkness, got into the car, started it up, backed slowly out. As he turned on to the dirt road he looked up again at Seitzen's window. He shrugged his shoulders. Seitzen would be asleep. Nerves or no nerves, the fat Württemberger slept like a pig immediately his head touched the pillow.

Hiltsch drove slowly down the dirt road until he came to the intersection. He swung right, switched on his parking lights, headed for Dublin. He put his foot down hard on the accelerator.

He began to sing softly to himself—a Nazi marching song—one of the songs they used to sing in the good old days with the twenty-fourth Standarte in Bremen.

Hildebrand looked up and smiled as Hiltsch came into the room. He was wearing a black velvet dressing-gown with dark blue cords. He looked distinguished. He fitted into the tastefully-furnished background of the room with its rows of bookshelves.

He said: "I did not expect to see you so soon, Rupprecht. Your drive into Dublin must have been uncomfortable."

Hiltsch helped himself to a cigarette from the silver box on the table. He lit it with satisfaction. His face, in the flame of the lighter, was poised and equable.

He said: "I like sometimes to be uncomfortable, Karl. When one is uncomfortable it means that one appreciates the next comfort that arrives. I am a sensualist. I specialise in sensations."

Hildebrand laughed.

"You are a damned old Nazi trooper, Rupprecht," he said. "But I like you." He got up, stood in front of the glowing fire. "Well," he went on, "why are you here? Something has happened? Something good? You look almost pleased with yourself."

Hiltsch dropped into the big brown leather armchair.

"It is as I thought," he said. "Seitzen is rotten. He has had enough. He is prepared to sell out. He desires to go on living. He agreed with me that we had not much chance of continuing to live going on as we were. He agreed that we were between the devil and the deep sea—that is between you and the English." He laughed.

Hildebrand said: "So . . . ! Well, you always thought that Seitzen would crack. Anyhow you will allow that I gave you a good opening tonight."

Hiltsch nodded. "I thought you were working up for me to try

Seitzen out," he said. "I got to work on him immediately you had gone. He fell for it."

Hildebrand's face was serious.

"You know, Rupprecht," he said, "there is too much cracking on the part of our operatives. I have had several cases. Sometimes they have been good Nazis but unable to stand the strain. They have shot themselves or drowned themselves. But nobody—to my knowledge—at least, no real Party member, has ever thought of selling out to the enemy—except Seitzen."

"He didn't think of it, I did," said Hiltsch with a grin.

The other shrugged. "He liked the idea," he said. "It is the same thing." He lit a cigarette. "And now . . . ?"

Hiltsch said: "I shall do it on my own. I shall leave the day after tomorrow. I shall go to Liverpool and work from there. I gather you have a contact for me in London?"

"Yes?" smiled Hildebrand. "And how did you gather that? It was clever of you."

"It wasn't," said Hiltsch. "You had to find out about that woman of Kane's from somewhere. It isn't easy to get that sort of stuff."

"You are right," said Hildebrand. "It is not easy. Yes, Rupprecht. . . . I have two contacts for you. Two very good people. The very best people. I assure you they are not Seitzens. And then I am going to give you another one to take with you. . . ."

Hiltsch grunted: "I don't want another one. I don't want any of your goddamned novices pushed on to me for training. I am not a training school. Besides they are always so stupid. They bungle."

Hildebrand held up his hand.

"Not this one," he said, "I assure you. This one is good. Very good. He has been brought up in the right way. Direct into the Jugend, then a year in the Labour Front—in the field and on administration, then a year with the Party. Then a little toughening process." He smiled evilly. "You know . . . six months in the concentration camp at Haltz being nice to Jews, and another six months under me in the Investigation Room at Columbia House. He is amazing."

He drew on his cigarette with pleasure.

"After that a period of diplomatic training and languages," he went on. "He speaks five. He speaks languages nearly as well as you or I. And he is calm. I have seen him kill a man with a rubber truncheon as casually as one kills a fly. Also . . . and this is important . . . the women love him. He looks like that too . . . even if he isn't like it."

Hiltsch looked up.

"So!" he said. "He isn't like it, hey?"

Hildebrand said: "No . . . he doesn't like women—much. I think that's a good thing."

Hiltsch grunted.

He said, "My God . . . ! He must be marvellous. You'd better not let the Führer see him. He might be jealous. When can I see this paragon?"

"You can see him now," said Hildebrand. He walked to the other side of the fireplace and pressed a bell. Then he stood in front of the fire, looking towards the door.

Hiltsch screwed round in his chair as the door opened. A young man came into the room. An amazing young man. He was five feet ten inches in height, and he moved with a controlled grace that indicated perfect training. He was slim. When he walked he put his feet on the ground like a cat.

His face was long and oval. His complexion perfect. His skin was as beautiful as a woman's; yet there was nothing effeminate in his appearance. He was blond, and the wave in his hair, receding and fading out over the nape of his neck, gave him the appearance of a film star above the eyes.

His eyes were blue—rather light blue. When Hiltsch saw the eyes he knew the boy was a killer.

He felt for his cigarette case.

Hildebrand said: "Rupprecht, this is Kurt Nielek. He will work with you. Kurt . . . this is Rupprecht Hiltsch, once leader of the twenty-fourth Bremen Standarte—one of our most trusted people."

Nielek raised his right arm from the elbow. He said:

"Heil Hitler!"

Hiltsch said: "Heil Hitler!" They shook hands.

Hildebrand watched them. He said:

"You two will be good together. Your enthusiasm and energy, Kurt, tempered with the sage experience, caution, and knowledge, of Rupprecht. . . ."

He walked over to the oak cupboard let into the bookshelves by the door, opened it, took out a bottle and three glasses. "This champagne came from Soissons," he said. "I had sixty dozen. The owner had no further use for it—after we'd finished with him. Let us drink."

The wine frothed into the glasses.

Hiltsch and Nielek faced each other. They said "Sieg Heil!" They drank.

It was raining hard. The rain beat down on the top of the car, and the tires made a continuous splashing noise. As they went on, the road became worse. The automobile bumped and the springs protested.

Once or twice, over bad holes in the road, Hiltsch, who was a first-class driver, had trouble in keeping the wheel steady. Nielek said softly: "This Seitzen, he is, I suppose, the gross type—the type that runs to seed quickly—that becomes tired?"

Hiltsch shrugged his shoulders in the darkness. He was thinking that during the whole time of the journey back Nielek had never moved. He had sat quite still in the passenger seat beside Hiltsch, his hands folded in front of him, his legs stretched and relaxed. Excellent control, thought Hiltsch, perfect relaxation, the result of good physical training and condition. He wondered if Nielek's mind was as flexible and fit as his body.

"Seitzen is the result of circumstances," said Hiltsch. "Circumstances and women—the wrong sort of women—and beer—especially beer. It is almost impossible to drink great quantities of beer—as he does—and remain mentally alert. His brain is soaked in Pilsner and every other sort. Also his women are inclined to be gross and beefy—which is enervating. Also he is a sadist. But the fact that he has a brain that delights in certain twists, and therefore occasionally stirs itself, does not overcome his other disabilities."

He took his cigarette out of his mouth and peered through the windscreen. They were on the dirt road now, and it was very dark. . . .

Nielek nodded. "Hildebrand doesn't like him?" he asked.

Hiltsch grunted. "Hildebrand doesn't like or dislike anybody," he said. "He's damned efficient and he wants results. He's done well . . . damned well. Naturally, he wants keen people working under him. Enthusiastic people. He knows that if people don't have some sort of enthusiasm for the type of work we do they're no good to anyone."

"He thinks a lot of you," said Nielek. "He says the nicest things about you."

"Why shouldn't he?" said Hiltsch. "I've taken some goddamn chances since I've been working with him and he knows it."

"You like taking chances, don't you?" said Nielek.

"No . . . not particularly." Hiltsch threw his cigarette stub out of the half-opened window. "But this type of work fascinates me. It's like gambling. You're wondering all the time just how long you're going to get away with it. Another thing is that it's worth while in one way. You take big chances, of course, but so does a fellow fighting in the Army. Look at the time the men on the Russian front are having, for instance. But when we've won this war—as we shall do this year—those of us who get through will be in line for big jobs. We shall be sitting pretty on our backsides in the occupied countries. We shall be safe. We shall have the pick of everything."

The dirt road narrowed. Hiltsch slowed down. He drove very carefully. Presently they came to the cross roads.

"The cottage is a few hundred yards away," said Hiltsch. "We'll put the car up. Seitzen is asleep. He sleeps like a pig. We'll have a drink—I have some good hock—and I want to change my shoes. They're a little wet. After that we'll go and talk to Seitzen."

Hiltsch made up the fire. He put on the pieces of coal deftly and without noise. He had taken off his shoes and was wearing a pair of felt slippers lined with dark fur. A woman in Potsdam had made them for him. Every time Hiltsch put on the slippers he remembered the woman. She was big and blond and she had very blue eyes. She liked to eat and drink and more than anything else she liked Hiltsch. . . .

The fire began to burn brightly. Hiltsch went to the sideboard, took out a slender bottle of hock and two glasses. He poured out the golden wine and handed a glass to Nielek.

Nielek was standing on one side of the fire. He took the glass in his right hand. They said "Sieg Heill" and drank.

Nielek said: "This wine is good. There is no wine like hock. I seldom drink, but when I do I drink hock. It tastes clean."

"All our German drinks are good," said Hiltsch. He refilled the glasses. "And our food and everything else. The British are the only other people who eat and drink really well. The rest of the world eats trash and drinks wine that tastes like vinegar."

He put his empty glass down on the table. He said to Nielek:

"Are you ready for our friend?"

"Quite," said Nielek. Hiltsch noticed that he was entirely relaxed. His lips were relaxed and his shoulders and body. His eyes did not alter. They were light blue and hard. Their colour seemed metallic.

Hiltsch led the way out of the room and across the hallway. He went up the stairs that curved round and met the short passage at the top. He stopped at the second door, opened it, flicked on the electric light. He stood to one side of the door so that Nielek could enter. Facing the door was the bed. Seitzen was asleep in it. His bulk seemed greater under the bedclothes. Hiltsch thought again that Seitzen slept like a Württemberg pig—which was what he was.

Nielek stood just inside the door, which he had closed behind him. His hands hung straight down by his sides. He was looking at Seitzen. On his face was an expression of faint disgust.

Hiltsch said abruptly: "Wake up, Seitzen. I want to talk to you." He walked to the side of the bed and shook Seitzen's shoulder.

Seitzen awoke. He opened his eyes and looked vaguely round the room. Then he ran his tongue over his lips. After a moment he focused his gaze on the figure of Nielek. He frowned. Then he rubbed his eyes with the backs of his hands and slowly sat up in bed. He sat up, his hands clasped on the coverlet before him, looking first at Hiltsch and then at Nielek.

He said: "What the devil is all this about, Hiltsch? What has happened?" He yawned.

Hiltsch said: "Nothing of importance. Wipe the sleep out of your eyes and listen." His voice was hard.

Seitzen looked at him for a moment. Then:

"Well . . . I'm listening. What is this? And who is this?" He indicated Nielek.

Hiltsch said: "This is SS Group Leader Kurt Nielek. Together we constitute a Special Court Martial under the power conferred upon us by Herr Reichsführer Himmler through Special Section Director Karl Hildebrand."

Seitzen said: "For God's sake . . . !"

"You are accused and found guilty of the crime of treachery against the Führer and the Reich. You are found guilty of traitorous intent to the Party. You are found guilty of treachery against the Special Section. Under power conferred upon me by Special Section Director Karl Hildebrand I sentence you to death."

Seitzen looked at Hiltsch with wide eyes. Hiltsch took out his cigarette case and selected a cigarette. Nielek put his hand inside the breast of his double-breasted jacket.

Seitzen said in a croaking voice: "This is some joke, Hiltsch. You would not do a thing . . ."

Hiltsch said: "Get out of bed." His voice was almost disinterested.

There was a pistol in Nielek's hand. It was a short-barrel Mauser automatic with a flat wooden butt, taking eight cartridges—the special weapon, fitted with a two-inch silencer, light, compact and of high velocity, designed by Heydrich and supplied to all Secret Service operatives. It hung straight down by Nielek's side in fingers that were perfectly flexed.

Seitzen did not move. Nielek said in a soft voice:

"It would be better to do this somewhere else. One might make quite a mess in here."

"Precisely," said Hiltsch. "The bathroom is next door. Get out of bed, Seitzen."

v. The Mysterious East

In the East, spying is a way of life, a key to survival, one of the oldest of the professions, and a necessary instrument in governing. Among the earliest treatises on spying is one written in Sanskrit and another in Chinese. There is even evidence that the Pharaohs had an efficient secret-police system.

In the standard modern novel about spying under Oriental skies, we usually follow the adventures of a Western agent through the steaming bazaars and the new luxury hotels. It was rare, until recently, that we were ever taken any farther into the East than Istanbul, because this is just about as far as the author was willing to go in his search for material. And one thing is certain. You cannot write about the East if you haven't been there. Now the mobility of jet-set agents makes it as likely that our American or British hero can confront his Soviet counterpart in Bangkok as in Paris. James Bond in Tokyo. Hugh North in Zanzibar. Peter Ward in Calcutta.

But these fellows are, of course, merely travelers—Western adventurers in the East. No Westerner, to the best of my knowledge, has risked trying to write a story which is really about the East itself. It would not be easy to do. Yet some of the great dramas of our time have taken place there, beginning with the Chinese conquest of Tibet and the escape of the Dalai Lama and his retinue into India.

RUDYARD KIPLING

▲

1 A Message to Umballa

Kipling's Kim, *set in the British India of the eighteen-eighties, opens with the arrival of an aged Tibetan lama in Lahore on a pilgrimage to find the River of the Arrow.* Kim, *an orphan son of a deceased Irish soldier, who lives by his wits like a native beggar boy in the back alleys of Lahore, apprentices himself to the lama as his* chela *(disciple) and offers to take him to Benares, where he may find his river to be the Ganges. The night before leaving for Benares, Kim and the old lama go to the caravan of an Afghan horse trader, Mahbub Ali, for whom Kim does occasional favors, such as watching and following people, and from whom he hopes to cadge a meal and a night's lodging for himself and the lama. And with this Kim's career with the "Indian Survey Department" unexpectedly begins. The book is in great part a tale of Kim's long-term training as a future agent of British intelligence in India ("the Great Game," as Kipling calls it), a training closely inter-woven with Kim's experiences at the side of the lama.*

In Kim, *the five kings whose revolt the British intend to put down have kingdoms in the old North-West Frontier on the Afghanistan border and in what is present-day Kashmir. The "sympathetic Northern Power" which fomented the uprising of the confederated kings is Russia, whose southernmost reaches, as a look at a map will show, border on Kashmir and Afghanistan. Russia at the time also had territorial interests in Northern India. In the long climactic episode in the latter part of the novel, Kim and the lama go up into the mountains of the North to track two Russian agents, who under cover of a hunting expedition are doing a military reconnaissance of the passes and the terrain on the approaches to the Punjab.*

FROM *Kim.*

We go to Benares," said the lama, as soon as he understood the drift of Mahbub Ali's questions. "The boy and I. I go to seek for a certain River."

"May be—but the boy?"

"He is my disciple. He was sent, I think, to guide me to that River. Sitting under a gun was I when he came suddenly. Such things have befallen the fortunate to whom guidance was allowed. But I remember now, he said he was of this world—a Hindu."

"And his name?"

"That I did not ask. Is he not my disciple?"

"His country—his race—his village? Mussalman—Sikh—Hindu—Jain—low caste or high?"

"Why should I ask? There is neither high nor low in the Middle Way. If he is my chela—does—will—can any one take him from me? For, look you, without him I shall not find my River." He wagged his head solemnly.

"None shall take him from thee. Go, sit among my Baltis," said Mahbub Ali, and the lama drifted off, soothed by the promise.

"Is he not quite mad?" said Kim, coming forward to the light again. "Why should I lie to thee, Hajji?"

Mahbub puffed his hookah in silence. Then he began, almost whispering: "Umballa is on the road to Benares—if indeed ye two go there."

"Tck! Tck! I tell thee he does not know how to lie—as we two know."

"And if thou wilt carry a message for me as far as Umballa, I will give thee money. It concerns a horse—a white stallion which I have sold to an officer upon the last time I returned from the Passes. But then—stand nearer and hold up hands as begging—the pedigree of the white stallion was not fully established, and that officer, who is now at Umballa, bade me make it clear." (Mahbub here described the horse and the appearance of the officer.) "So the message to that officer will be: 'The pedigree of the white stallion is fully established.' By this will he know that thou comest from me. He will then say "What proof hast thou?" and thou wilt answer: 'Mahbub Ali has given me the proof.'"

"And all for the sake of a white stallion," said Kim, with a giggle, his eyes aflame.

"That pedigree I will give thee now—in my own fashion—and some hard words as well." A shadow passed behind Kim, and a feeding camel. Mahbub Ali raised his voice.

"Allah! Art thou the only beggar in the city? Thy mother is dead. Thy father is dead. So is it with all of them. Well, well—" he turned as feeling on the floor beside him and tossed a flap of soft, greasy Mussalman bread to the boy. "Go and lie down among my horse-boys for tonight—thou and the lama. To-morrow I may give thee service."

Kim slunk away, his teeth in the bread, and, as he expected, he found a small wad of folded tissue-paper wrapped in oil-skin, with three silver rupees—enormous largesse. He smiled and thrust money and paper into his leather amulet-case. The lama, sumptuously fed by Mahbub's Baltis, was already asleep in a corner of one of the stalls. Kim lay down beside him and laughed. He knew he had rendered a service to Mahbub Ali, and not for one little minute did he believe the tale of the stallion's pedigree.

But Kim did not suspect that Mahbub Ali, known as one of the best horse-dealers in the Punjab, a wealthy and enterprising trader, whose caravans penetrated far and far into the Back of Beyond, was registered in one of the locked books of the Indian Survey Department as C.25.1B. Twice or thrice yearly C.25 would send in a little story, badly told but most interesting, and generally—it was checked by the statements of R.17 and M.4—quite true. It concerned all manner of out-of-the-way mountain principalities, explorers of nationalities other than English, and the gun-trade—was, in brief, a small portion of that vast mass of "information received" on which the Indian Government acts. But, recently, five confederated Kings, who had no business to confederate, had been informed by a kindly Northern Power that there was a leakage of news from their territories into British India. So those Kings' prime ministers were seriously annoyed and took steps, after the Oriental fashion. They suspected, among many others, the bullying red-bearded horse-dealer whose caravans ploughed through their fastnesses belly deep in snow. At least, his caravan that season had been ambushed and shot at twice on the way down, when Mahbub's men accounted for three strange ruffians who might, or might not, have been hired for the job. Therefore Mahbub had avoided halting at the insalubrious city of Peshawur, and had come through without stop to Lahore, where, knowing his country-people, he anticipated curious developments.

And there was that on Mahbub Ali which he did not wish to keep an hour longer than was necessary—a wad of closely folded tissue-paper, wrapped in oil-skin—an impersonal, unaddressed statement, with five microscopic pinholes in one corner, that most scandalously betrayed the five confederated Kings, the sympathetic Northern Power, a Hindu banker in Peshawur, a firm of gun-makers in Belgium,

and an important, semi-independent Mohammedan ruler to the south.
This last was R.17's work, which Mahbub had picked up beyond the
Dora Pass and was carrying in for R.17, who, owing to circumstances
over which he had no control, could not leave his post of observation.
Dynamite was milky and innocuous beside that report of C.25; and
even an Oriental, with an Oriental's views of the value of time, could
see that the sooner it was in the proper hands the better. Mahbub had
no particular desire to die by violence, because two or three family
blood-feuds across the border hung unfinished on his hands, and when
these scores were cleared he intended to settle down as a more or less
virtuous citizen. He had never passed the serai gate since his arrival
two days ago, but had been ostentatious in sending telegrams to
Bombay, where he banked some of his money; to Delhi, where a sub-
partner of his own clan was selling horses to the agent of a Rajputana
state; and to Umballa, where an Englishman was excitedly demanding
the pedigree of a white stallion. The public letter-writer, who knew
English, composed excellent telegrams, such as—"Creighton, Laurel
Bank, Umballa.—Horse is Arabian as already advised. Sorrowful de-
layed-pedigree which am translating." And later to the same address:
"Much sorrowful delay. Will forward pedigree." To this sub-partner at
Delhi he wired: "Lutuf Ullah.—Have wired two thousand rupees your
credit Luchman Narain's bank." This was entirely in the way of trade,
but every one of those telegrams was discussed and re-discussed, by
parties who conceived themselves to be interested, before they went
over to the railway station in charge of a foolish Balti, who allowed all
sorts of people to read them on the road.

When, in Mahbub's own picturesque language, he had muddied
the wells of inquiry with the stick of precaution, Kim had dropped on
him, sent from heaven; and, being as prompt as he was unscrupulous,
Mahbub Ali, used to taking all sorts of gusty chances, pressed him into
service on the spot.

A wandering lama with a low-caste boy-servant might attract a
moment's interest as they wandered about India, the land of pilgrims;
but no one would suspect them or, what was more to the point, rob.

He called for a new light-ball to his hookah, and considered the
case. If the worst came to the worst, and the boy came to harm, the
paper would incriminate nobody. And he would go up to Umballa
leisurely and—at a certain risk of exciting fresh suspicion—repeat his
tale by word of mouth to the people concerned.

But R.17's report was the kernel of the whole affair, and it would
be distinctly inconvenient if that failed to come to hand. However,
God was great, and Mahbub Ali felt he had done all he could for the

time being. Kim was the one soul in the world who had never told him a lie. That would have been a fatal blot on Kim's character if Mahbub had not known that to others, for his own ends or Mahbub's business, Kim could lie like an Oriental.

Then Mahbub Ali rolled across the serai to the Gate of the Harpies who paint their eyes and trap the stranger, and was at some pains to call on the one girl who, he had reason to believe, was a particular friend of a smooth-faced Kashmiri pundit who had waylaid his simple Balti in the matter of the telegrams. It was an utterly foolish thing to do; because they fell to drinking perfumed brandy against the Law of the Prophet, and Mahbub grew wonderfully drunk, and the gates of his mouth were loosened, and he pursued the Flower of Delight with the feet of intoxication till he fell flat among the cushions, where the Flower of Delight, aided by a smooth-faced Kashmiri pundit, searched him from head to foot most thoroughly.

About the same hour Kim heard soft feet in Mahbub's deserted stall. The horse-trader, curiously enough, had left his door unlocked, and his men were busy celebrating their return to India with a whole sheep of Mahbub's bounty. A sleek young gentleman from Delhi, armed with a bunch of keys which the Flower had unshackled from the senseless one's belt, went through every single box, bundle, mat, and saddle-bag in Mahbub's possession even more systematically than the Flower and the pundit were searching the owner.

"And I think," said the Flower scornfully an hour later, one rounded elbow on the snoring carcase, "that he is no more than a pig of an Afghan horse-dealer, with no thought except women and horses. Moreover, he may have sent it away by now—if ever there were such a thing."

"Nay—in a matter touching Five Kings it would be next his black heart," said the pundit. "Was there nothing?"

The Delhi man laughed and resettled his turban as he entered. "I searched between the soles of his slippers as the Flower searched his clothes. This is not the man but another. I leave little unseen."

"They did not say he was the very man," said the pundit thoughtfully. "They said, 'Look if he be the man, since our councils are troubled.'"

"That North country is full of horse-dealers as an old coat of lice. There is Sikandar Khan, Nur Ali Beg, and Farrukh Shah—all heads of Kafilas—who deal there," said the Flower.

"They have not yet come in," said the pundit. "Thou must ensnare them later."

"Phew!" said the Flower with deep disgust, rolling Mahbub's head from her lap. "I earn my money. Farrukh Shah is a bear, Ali Beg a swashbuckler, and old Sikandar Khan—yaie! Go! I sleep now. This swine will not stir till dawn."

When Mahbub woke, the Flower talked to him severely on the sin of drunkenness. Asiatics do not wink when they have out-manoeuvred an enemy, but as Mahbub Ali cleared his throat, tightened his belt, and staggered forth under the early morning stars, he came very near to it.

"What a colt's trick," said he to himself. "As if every girl in Peshawur did not use it! But 'twas prettily done. Now God He knows how many more there be upon the road who have orders to test me—perhaps with the knife. So it stands that the boy must go to Umballa—and by rail—for the writing is something urgent. I abide here, following the Flower and drinking wine as an Afghan coper should."

He halted at the stall next but one to his own. His men lay there heavy with sleep. There was no sign of Kim or the lama.

"Up!" He stirred a sleeper. "Whither went those who lay here last even—the lama and the boy? Is aught missing?"

"Nay," grunted the man; "the old madman rose at second cock-crow saying he would go to Benares, and the young one led him away."

"The curse of Allah on all unbelievers," said Mahbub heartily, and climbed into his own stall, growling in his beard.

But it was Kim who had wakened the lama—Kim with one eye laid against a knot-hole in the planking, who had seen the Delhi man's search through the boxes. This was no common thief that turned over letters, bills, and saddles—no mere burglar who ran a little knife side-ways into the soles of Mahbub's slippers, or picked the seams of the saddle-bags so deftly. At first Kim had been minded to give the alarm—the long-drawn "cho-or—choor!" (thief! thief!) that sets the serai ablaze of nights; but he looked more carefully, and, hand on amulet, drew his own conclusions.

"It must be the pedigree of that made-up horse-lie," said he, "the thing that I carry to Umballa. Better that we go now. Those who search bags with knives may presently search bellies with knives. Surely there is a woman behind this. Hai! Hai!" in a whisper to the light-sleeping old man. "Come, it is time—time to go to Benares."

The lama rose obediently, and they passed out of the serai like shadows.

They entered the fort-like railway station, black in the end of night; the electrics sizzling over the goods yard where they handle the heavy Northern grain-traffic.

"This is the work of devils!" said the lama, recoiling from the hollow echoing darkness, the glimmer of rails between the masonry platforms, and the maze of girders above. He stood in a gigantic stone hall paved, it seemed, with the sheeted dead—third-class passengers who had taken their tickets overnight and were sleeping in the waiting-rooms. All hours of the twenty-four are alike to Orientals, and their passenger traffic is regulated accordingly.

"This is where the fire-carriages come. One stands behind that hole"—Kim pointed to the ticket-office—"who will give thee a paper to take thee to Umballa."

"But we go to Benares," he replied petulantly.

"All one. Benares then. Quick: she comes!"

"Take thou the purse."

The lama, not so well used to trains as he had pretended, started as the 3.25 A.M. southbound roared in. The sleepers sprang to life, and the station filled with clamour and shoutings, cries of water and sweet-meat vendors, shouts of native policemen, and shrill yells of women gathering up their baskets, their families, and their husbands.

"It is the train—only the te-rain. It will come here. Wait!" Amazed at the lama's immense simplicity (he had handed him a small bag full of rupees), Kim asked and paid for a ticket to Umballa. A sleepy clerk grunted and flung out a ticket to the next station, just six miles distant.

"Nay," said Kim, scanning it with a grin. "This may serve for farmers, but I live in the city of Lahore. It was cleverly done, babu. Now give the ticket to Umballa."

The babu scowled and dealt the proper ticket.

"Now another to Amritzar," said Kim, who had no notion of spending Mahbub Ali's money on anything so crude as a paid ride to Umballa. "The price is so much. The small money in return is just so much. I know the ways of the te-rain. . . . Never did yogi need chela as thou dost," he went on merrily to the bewildered lama. "They would have flung thee out at Mian Mir but for me. This way! Come." He returned the money, keeping only one anna in each rupee of the price of the Umballa ticket as his commission—the immemorial commission of Asia.

The lama jibbed at the open door of a crowded third-class carriage. "Were it not better to walk?" said he weakly.

A burly Sikh artisan thrust forth his bearded head. "Is he afraid? Do not be afraid. I remember the time when I was afraid of the te-rain. Enter! This thing is the work of the Government."

(Kim and the lama arrive in Umballa.)

Kim was anxious only to get the lama under shelter for the night, that he might seek Mahbub Ali's Englishman and deliver himself of the white stallion's pedigree.

"Now," said he, when the lama had come to an anchor in the inner courtyard of a decent Hindu house behind the cantonments, "I go away for a while—to—to buy us victual in the bazar. Do not stray abroad till I return."

"Thou wilt return? Thou wilt surely return?" The old man caught at his wrist. "And thou wilt return in this very same shape? Is it too late to look to-night for the River?"

"Too late and too dark. Be comforted. Think how far thou art on the road—an hundred kos from Lahore already."

"Yea—and farther from my monastery. Alas! It is a great and terrible world."

Kim stole out and away, as unremarkable a figure as ever carried his own and a few score thousand other folk's fate slung round his neck. Mahbub Ali's directions left him little doubt of the house in which his Englishman lived; and a groom, bringing a dog-cart home from the Club, made him quite sure. It remained only to identify his man, and Kim slipped through the garden hedge and hid in a clump of plumed grass close to the veranda. The house blazed with lights, and servants moved about tables dressed with flowers, glass, and silver. Presently forth came an Englishman, dressed in black and white, humming a tune. It was too dark to see his face, so Kim, beggar-wise, tried an old experiment.

"Protector of the Poor!"

The man backed towards the voice.

"Mahbub Ali says—"

"Hah! What says Mahbub Ali?" He made no attempt to look for the speaker, and that showed Kim that he knew.

"The pedigree of the white stallion is fully established."

"What proof is there?" The Englishman switched at the rose-hedge in the side of the drive.

"Mahbub Ali has given me this proof." Kim flipped the wad of folded paper into the air, and it fell on the path beside the man, who put his foot on it as a gardener came round the corner. When the servant passed he picked it up, dropped a rupee—Kim could hear the clink—and strode into the house, never turning round. Swiftly Kim took up the money; but, for all his training, he was Irish enough by birth to reckon silver the least part of any game. What he desired was the visible effect of action; so, instead of slinking away, he lay close in the grass and wormed nearer to the house.

He saw—Indian bungalows are open through and through—the Englishman return to a small dressing-room, in a corner of the veranda, that was half-office, littered with papers and despatch-boxes, and sit down to study Mahbub Ali's message. His face, by the full ray of the kerosene lamp, changed and darkened, and Kim, used as every beggar must be to watching countenances, took good note.

"Will! Will, dear!" called a woman's voice. "You ought to be in the drawing-room. They'll be here in a minute."

The man still read intently.

"Will!" said the voice, five minutes later. "He's come. I can hear the troopers in the drive."

The man dashed out bareheaded as a big landau with four native troopers behind it halted at the veranda, and a tall, black-haired man, erect as an arrow, swung out, preceded by a young officer who laughed pleasantly.

Flat on his belly lay Kim, almost touching the high wheels. His man and the black stranger exchanged two sentences.

"Certainly, sir," said the young officer promptly. "Everything waits while a horse is concerned."

"We shan't be more than twenty minutes," said Kim's man. "You can do the honours—keep 'em amused, and all that."

"Tell one of the troopers to wait," said the tall man, and they both passed into the dressing-room together as the landau rolled away. Kim saw their heads bent over Mahbub Ali's message, and heard the voices—one low and deferential, the other sharp and decisive.

"It isn't a question of weeks. It is a question of days—hours almost," said the elder. "I'd been expecting it for some time, but this"—he tapped Mahbub Ali's paper—"clenches it. Grogan's dining here tonight, isn't he?"

"Yes, sir, and Macklin too."

"Very good. I'll speak to them myself. That matter will be referred to the Council, of course, but this is a case where one is justified in assuming that we take action at once. Warn the Pindi and Peshawur brigades. It will disorganise all the summer reliefs, but we can't help that. This comes of not smashing them thoroughly the first time. Eight thousand should be enough."

"What about artillery, sir?"

"I must consult Macklin."

"Then it means war?"

"No. Punishment. When a man is bound by the action of his predecessor—"

"But C.25 may have lied."

"He bears out the other's information. Practically, they showed their hand six months back. But Devenish would have it there was a chance of peace. Of course they used it to make themselves stronger. Send off those telegrams at once—the new code, not the old—mine and Wharton's. I don't think we need keep the ladies waiting any longer. We can settle the rest over the cigars. I thought it was coming. It's punishment—not war."

As the trooper cantered off, Kim crawled round to the back of the house, where, going on his Lahore experiences, he judged there would be food—and information. The kitchen was crowded with excited scullions, one of whom kicked him.

"Aie," said Kim, feigning tears. "I came only to wash dishes in return for a bellyful."

"All Umballa is on the same errand. Get hence. They go in now with the soup. Think you that we who serve Creighton Sahib need strange scullions to help us through a big dinner?"

"It is a very big dinner," said Kim, looking at the plates.

"Small wonder. The guest of honour is none other than the Jang-i-Lat Sahib" (the Commander-in-Chief).

"Ho!" said Kim, with the correct guttural note of wonder. He had learned what he wanted, and when the scullion turned he was gone.

"And all that trouble," said he to himself, thinking as usual in Hindustanee, "for a horse's pedigree! Mahbub Ali should have come to me to learn a little lying. Every time before that I have borne a message, it concerned a woman. Now it is men. Better. The tall man said that they will loose a great army to punish some one—somewhere—the news goes to Pindi and Peshawur. There are also guns. Would I had crept nearer. It is big news!"

LAWRENCE DURRELL

▼

2 I.A.

I hope I will not unduly startle some readers by choosing for an anthology of spy stories passages from Lawrence Durrell's much-praised prose masterpiece, The Alexandria Quartet. *The fact is that in this exotic concoction of poetry, psychology, and the romance of the Near East one of the major elements holding the work together is the story of the Coptic conspiracy, first thought to be directed against the Egyptians but later discovered to be directed against the British in Palestine. Even if this were not so, Durrell's mordant depiction of the British intelligence officer in the Cairo Embassy, Brigadier Maskelyne, would have to find a place in this volume along with Conrad's description of Mr. Vladimir.*

The excerpt which follows is from a letter which Pursewarden, a senior official at the British Embassy in Cairo (and a novelist as well), writes to his old acquaintance David Mountolive, who has just been named Ambassador to Cairo. As a younger man, Mountolive had been previously posted to Cairo, and he is acquainted with the wealthy Coptic family, the Hosnanis, of whom Pursewarden writes. The purpose of Pursewarden's letter is to brief Mountolive before he arrives on the scene concerning a conflict in the Embassy between Pursewarden and the intelligence officer Maskelyne. Pursewarden, who screens the intelligence reports, has "suspended" a paper of Maskelyne's about the clandestine activities of the Hosnanis, because he does not regard it as reliable. When it is later discovered that the Hosnanis are in even deeper than Maskelyne first reported, Pursewarden commits suicide. The period in which the story takes place is shortly before World War II.

FROM *Mountolive.*

When Durrell writes of embassies and their personnel and their intrigues, he knows whereof he speaks, since he himself served during World War II in the British Embassy in Cairo as a press officer and after the war in the Embassy in Belgrade as press attaché.

Maskelyne reaches his office at eight having bought his day-late copy of the *Daily Telegraph*. I have never seen him read anything else. He sits at his huge desk, consumed with a slow dark contempt for the venality of the human beings around him, perhaps the human race as a whole; imperturbably he examines and assorts their differing corruptions, their maladies, and outlines them upon marble minute-paper which he always signs with his little silver pen in a small awkward fly's handwriting. The current of his loathing flows through his veins slowly, heavily, like the Nile at flood. Well, you can see what a *numéro* he is. He lives purely in the military imagination for he never sees or meets the subjects of most of his papers; the information he collates comes in from suborned clerks, or discontented valets, or pent-up servants. It does not much matter. He prides himself on his readings of it, his I.A. (intelligence appreciation), just like an astrologer working upon charts belonging to unseen, unknown subjects. He is judicial, proud as the Caliph, unswerving. I admire him very much. Honestly I do.

Maskelyne has set up two marks between which (as between degree signs on a calibrated thermometer) the temperatures of his approval and disapproval are allowed to move, expressed in the phrases: "A good show for the Raj" and "Not such a good show for the Raj." He is too single-minded of course, ever to be able to imagine a really Bad Show for the Bloody Raj. Such a man seems unable to see the world around him on open sights; but then his profession and the need for reserve make him a complete recluse, make him inexperienced in the ways of the world upon which he sits in judgment. . . . Well, I am tempted to go on and frame the portrait of our spy-catcher, but I will desist. Read my next novel but four, it should also include a sketch of Telford, who is Maskelyne's Number Two—a large blotchy ingratiating civilian with ill-fitting dentures who manages to call one "old fruit" a hundred times a second between nervous guffaws. His worship of the cold snaky soldier is marvelous to behold. "Yes, Brigadier," "No, Brigadier," falling over a chair in his haste to serve; you would say he was completely in love with his boss. Maskelyne sits and watches his confusion coldly, his brown chin, cleft by a dark dimple, jutting like an arrow. Or he will lean back in his swivel chair and tap softly on the door of the huge safe behind him with the faintly satisfied air of a gourmet patting his paunch as he says, "You don't believe me? I have it all in here, all in here." Those files, you think, watching this superlative, all-comprehending gesture, must contain material enough to indict the world! Perhaps they do.

Well, this is what happened: one day I found a characteristic document from Maskelyne on my desk headed *Nessim Hosnani,* and subtitled *A Conspiracy Among the Copts* which alarmed me somewhat. According to the paper, our Nessim was busy working up a large and complicated plot against the Egyptian Royal House. Most of the data were rather questionable I thought, knowing Nessim, but the whole paper put me in a quandary for it carried the bland recommendation that the details should be transmitted by the Embassy to the Egyptian Ministry of Foreign Affairs! I can hear you draw your breath sharply. Even supposing this were true, such a course would put Nessim's life in the greatest danger. Have I explained that one of the major characteristics of Egyptian nationalism is the gradually growing envy and hate of the "foreigners"—the half-million or so of non-Moslems here? And that the moment full Egyptian sovereignty was declared the Moslems started in to bully and expropriate them? The brains of Egypt, as you know, is its foreign community. The capital which flowed into the land while it was safe under our suzerainty, is now at the mercy of the paunchy pashas. The Armenians, Greeks, Copts, Jews—they are all feeling the sharpening edge of this hate; many are wisely leaving, but most cannot. These huge capital investments in cotton, etc., cannot be abandoned overnight. The foreign communities are living from prayer to prayer and from bribe to bribe. They are trying to save their industries, their lifework from the gradual encroachment of the pashas. We have literally thrown them to the lions!

Well, I read and reread this document, as I say, in a state of considerable anxiety. I knew that if I gave it to Errol he would run bleating with it to the King. So I went into action myself to test the weak points in it—mercifully it was not one of Maskelyne's best papers—and succeeded in throwing doubt upon many of his contentions. But what infuriated him was that I actually *suspended* the paper—I had to in order to keep it out of Chancery's hands! My sense of duty was sorely strained, but then there was no alternative; what would those silly young schoolboys next door have done? If Nessim was really guilty of the sort of plot Maskelyne envisaged, well and good; one could deal with him later according to his lights. But . . .

you know Nessim. I felt that I owed it to him to be sure before passing such a paper upward.

But of course Maskelyne was furious, though he had the grace not to show it. We sat in his office with the conversational temperature well below zero and still falling while he showed me his accumulated evidence and his agents' reports. For the most part they were not as solid as I had feared. "I have this man Selim suborned," Maskelyne kept croaking, "and I'm convinced his own secretary can't be wrong about it. There is this small secret society with the regular meetings—Selim has to wait with the car and drive them home. Then there is this curious cryptogram which goes out all over the Middle East from Balthazar's clinic, and then the visits to arms manufacturers in Sweden and Germany. . . ." I tell you, my brain was swimming! I could see all our friends neatly laid out on a slab by the Egyptian Secret Police, being measured for shrouds.

I must say too, that *circumstantially* the inferences which Maskelyne drew appeared to hold water. It all looked rather sinister; but luckily a few of the basic points would not yield to analysis—things like the so-called cipher which friend Balthazar shot out once every two months to chosen recipients in the big towns of the Middle East. Maskelyne was still trying to follow these up. But the data were far from complete and I stressed this as strongly as I could, much to the discomfort of Telford, though Maskelyne is too cool a bird of prey to be easily discountenanced. Nevertheless I got him to agree to pend the paper until something more substantial was forthcoming to broaden the basis of the doctrine. He hated me but he swallowed it, and so I felt that I had gained at least a temporary respite. The problem was what to do next—how to use the time to advantage? I was of course convinced that Nessim was innocent of these grotesque charges. But I could not, I admit, supply explanations as convincing as those of Maskelyne. What, I could not help wondering, were they really up to? If I was to deflate Maskelyne, I must find out for myself. Very annoying, and indeed professionally improper—but *que faire?* Little Ludwig must turn himself into a private investigator, a Sexton Blake, in order to do the job! But where to begin?

Maskelyne's only direct lead on Nessim was through the suborned secretary, Selim; through him he had accumulated quite a lot of interesting though not intrinsically alarming data about the Hosnani holdings in various fields—the land bank, shipping line, ginning mills, and so on. The rest was largely gossip and rumor, some of it damaging, but none of it more than circumstantial. But piled up in a heap it did make our gentle Nessim sound somewhat sinister. I felt that I must take it all apart somehow. . . .

All these factors were tumbling over and over in my mind as I drove up to Alexandria, having secured myself a long duty weekend which even the good Errol found unexceptionable. I never dreamed then, that within a year you might find yourself engaged by these mysteries. I only knew that I wanted, if possible, to demolish the Maskelyne thesis and stay the Chancery's hand in the matter of Nessim. But apart from this I was somewhat at a loss. I am no spy, after all; was I to creep about Alexandria dressed in a pudding-basin wig with concealed earphones, trying to clear the name of our friend? Nor could I very well present myself to Nessim and, clearing my throat, say nonchalantly, "Now about this spy net you've got here. . . ."

The next morning I was up betimes though I had decided on nothing, was still bedeviled in mind about the whole issue. However, I thought I could at least visit Nessim in his office as I had so often done, to pass the time of day and cadge a coffee. Whispering up in the huge glass lift, so like a Byzantine sarcophagus, I felt confused. I had prepared no conversation for the event. The clerks and typists were all delighted and showed me straight through into the great domed room where he sat. . . . Now here is the curious thing. He not only seemed to be expecting me, but to have divined my reasons for calling! He seemed delighted, relieved and full of an impish sort of serenity. "I've been waiting months," he said with dancing eyes, "wondering when you were finally going to come and beard me, to ask me questions. At last! What a relief!" Everything melted between us after this and I felt I could take him on open sights. Nothing could exceed the warmth and candor of his answers. They carried immediate conviction with me.

The so-called secret society, he told me, was a student lodge of the Cabala devoted to the customary mumbo jumbo of parlor mysticism. God knows, this is the capital of superstition. Even Clea has her horoscope cast afresh every morning. Sects abound. Was there anything odd in Balthazar running such a small band of would-be hermetics—a study group? As for the cryptogram it was a sort of mystical calculus—the old *boustrophedon* no less—with the help of which the lodge masters all over the Middle East could keep in touch. Surely no more mysterious than a stock report or a polite exchange between mathematicians working on the same problem? Nessim drew one for me and explained roughly how it was used. He added that all this could be effectively checked by consulting Darley who had taken to visiting these meetings with Justine to suck up hermetical lore. *He* would be able to say just how subversive they were! So far so good. "But I can't disguise from you," he went on, "the existence of another movement, purely political, with which I am directly concerned. This is purely Coptic and is designed simply to rally the Copts—not to revolt against anyone (how could we?) but simply to band themselves together; to strengthen religious and political ties in order that the community can find its way back to a place in the sun. Now that Egypt is free from the Copt-hating British, we feel freer to seek high offices for our people, to get some Members of Parliament elected and so on. There is nothing in all this which should make an intelligent Moslem tremble. We seek nothing illegitimate or harmful; simply our rightful place in our own land as the most intelligent and able community in Egypt."

There was a good deal more about the back history of the Coptic community and its grievances—I won't bore you with it as you probably know it all. But he spoke it all with a tender shy fury which interested me as being so out of keeping with the placid Nessim we both knew. Later, when I met the mother, I understood; she is the driving force behind this particular minority dream, or so I believe. Nessim went on, "Nor need France and Britain fear anything from us. We love them both. Such modern culture as we have is modeled on both. We ask for no aid, no money. We think of ourselves as Egyptian patriots, but knowing how stupid and backward the Arab National element is, and how fanatical, we do not think it can be long before there are violent differences between the Egyptians and yourselves. They are already flirting with Hitler. In the case of a war . . . who can tell? The Middle East is slipping out of the grasp of England and France day by day. We minorities see ourselves in peril as the process goes on. Our only hope is that there is some respite, like a war, which will enable you to come back and retake the lost ground. Otherwise, we will be expropriated, enslaved. But we still place our faith in you both. Now, from this point of view, a compact and extremely rich little group of Coptic bankers and businessmen could exercise an influence out of all proportion to its numbers. *We are your fifth column in Egypt, fellow Christians.* In another year or two, when the movement is perfected, we could bring immediate pressure to bear on the economic and industrial life of the country—if it served to push through a policy which you felt to be necessary. That is why I have been dying to tell you about us, for England should see in us a bridgehead to the East, a friendly enclave in an area which daily becomes more hostile, to you." He lay back, quite exhausted, but smiling.

"But of course I realize," he said, "that this concerns you as an official. Please treat the matter as a secret, for friendship's sake. The Egyptians would welcome any chance to expropriate us Copts—confiscate the millions which we control: perhaps even kill some of us. They must not know about us. That is why we meet secretly, have been building up the movement so slowly, with such circumspection. There must be no slips, you see." . . .

So I rode back happily to Cairo to rearrange the chessboard accordingly. I went to see Maskelyne and tell him the good news. To my surprise he turned absolutely white with rage, the corners of his nose pinched in, his ears moving back about an inch like a greyhound. His voice and eyes remained the same. "Do you mean to tell me that you have tried to supplement a secret intelligence paper by consulting the subject of it? It goes against every elementary rule of intelligence. And how can you believe a word of so obvious a cover story? I have never heard of such a thing. You deliberately suspend a War Office paper, throw my fact-finding organization into disrepute, pretend we don't know our jobs, etc. . . ." You can gather the rest of the tirade. I began to get angry. He repeated dryly, "I have been doing this for fifteen years. I tell you it smells of arms, of subversion. You won't believe my I.A. and I think yours is ridiculous. Why not pass the paper to the *Egyptians* and let them find out for themselves?" Of course I could not afford to do this, and he knew it. He next said that he had asked the War Office to protest in London and was writing to Errol to ask for "redress." All this, of course, was to be expected. But then I tackled him upon another vector. "Look here," I said. "I have seen all your sources. They are all Arabs and as such unworthy of confidence. How about a gentleman's agreement? There is no hurry—we can investigate the Hosnanis at leisure—but how about choosing a new set of sources—English sources? If the interpretations still match, I promise you I'll resign and make a full recantation. Otherwise I shall fight this thing right through."

(After Mountolive arrives in Cairo he has a talk with Maskelyne. Among other things he tells him that he is to be transferred to Jerusalem.)

A silence fell. Maskelyne studied the ash of his cigar while the faintest trace of a smile hovered at the edges of his mouth.

"So Pursewarden wins," he said quietly. "Well, well!"

Mountolive was both surprised and insulted by his smile, though in truth it seemed entirely without malice.

"Pursewarden," he said quietly, "has been reprimanded for suppressing a War Office paper; on the other hand, I happen to know the subject of the paper rather well and I agree that you should supplement it more fully before asking us to take action."

"We are trying, as a matter of fact; Telford is putting down a grid about this Hosnani man—but some of the candidates put forward by Pursewarden seem to be rather . . . well, prejudicial, to put it mildly. However, Telford is trying to humor him by engaging them. But . . . well, there's one who sells information to the Press, and one who is at present consoling the Hosnani lady. Then there's another, Scobie, who spends his time dressed as a woman walking about the harbor at Alexandria—it would be a charity to suppose him in quest of police information. Altogether, I shall be quite glad to confide the net to Telford and tackle something a bit more serious. What people!"

"As I don't know the circumstances yet," said Mountolive quietly, "I can't comment. But I shall look into it."

"I'll give you an example," said Maskelyne, "of their general efficiency. Last week Telford detailed this policeman called Scobie to do a routine job. When the Syrians want to be clever, they don't use a diplomatic courier; they confide their pouch to a lady, the vice-consul's niece, who takes it down to Cairo by train. We wanted to see the contents of one particular pouch—details of arms shipments, we thought. Gave Scobie some doped chocolates—with the doped one clearly marked. His job was to send the lady to sleep for a couple of hours and walk off with her pouch. Do you know what happened? He was found doped in the train when it got to Cairo and couldn't be wakened for nearly twenty-four hours. We had to put him into the American hospital. Apparently as he sat down in the lady's compartment, the train gave a sudden jolt and all the chocolates turned over in their wrappers. The one we had so carefully marked was now upside down; he could not remember which it was. In his panic, he ate it himself. Now I ask you. . . ." Maskelyne's humorless eye flashed as he retailed this story. "Such people are not to be trusted," he added, acidly.

JAMES LEASOR

▼

3 Far from Home

The greater part of this action-packed spy story takes place in that same area where Kim and his lama have their final adventures, in the northernmost reaches of what is today West Pakistan, where Chinese and Russian Turkestan converge on the fringes of Kashmir. Mr. Leasor gives us a fascinating description of the area and its natives.

Dr. Jason Love has been invited by his old wartime buddy, the Nawab of Shahnagar, to pay him a visit in the remote principality which he governs just up under the Himalayas across the border from China. The Nawab wants Jason to try to do something for his young son, who has been partially blinded by a mysterious beam of light which one day flashed down from the mountain fastnesses above Shahnagar. The Nawab is being blackmailed to the tune of two million pounds by an organization known as the International Committee for the Preservation of Big Game. If he doesn't pay up, the organization threatens to blind the boy in both eyes. In the excerpt, we join the invulnerable Dr. Love en route to Shahnagar. Before this, violent episodes, obviously perpetrated by the blackmailers, have already taken place, including an attempt to blow up Dr. Love.

Anyone who has kept up with the advances of modern technology soon guesses what the source of the blinding light is. The geography of the situation readily suggests who is the evil party behind the blackmail. This is the first spy story I have read in which this particular party is the villain, though there may be others. I wanted to represent it in this collection for that reason in addition to its merits as a well-constructed, well-written, and exciting book.

FROM *Spylight.*

199

One further word of explanation. Leasor, like his predecessors Le Queux and Fleming, likes gadgets. Before leaving England on this trip, Dr. Love was given a few gadgets for emergencies by a friend in MI-6. One of these was a belt lined with powerfully magnetized metal. This causes the gun of the carpet merchant to be deflected.

Excuse me, sahib," another voice said softly.

Love glanced over his shoulder, surprised that anyone could have crept up on him so silently. A man with a pocked face, pitted with holes, and narrow, almost slanting eyes, was standing barely a yard behind him. He wore the familiar black astrakhan cap and tweed sports jacket, with the rolled-gold watch chain in his lapel buttonhole, grey shirt outside his baggy trousers, but he was not a Pakistani. From Tibet, perhaps, or the Chinese border near Assam?

Love glanced down at the man's feet, his canvas shoes would explain his quietness. He leaned on a bicycle as though he were tired and had pushed it for a long way. Over the crossbar were folded a number of handwoven carpets in russet, blue, red. All the prodigal colours of autumn were heaped on that bar.

"You are Dr. Love, sahib?"

"How did you know?"

The man smiled.

"All the best carpets," he went on, not answering his question. "Just for you, doctor sahib. Every one hand coloured. All from Chinese Turkestan."

That would explain his face; yet it seemed a long way to bring carpets across the hills of Hunza, then down to Gilgit, on to Rawalpindi, simply to make a few rupees profit. However, that was his concern; Love had no shares in his company.

"I'm sorry," Love said firmly, "but I'm travelling by air. They'd be too heavy. Perhaps, on the way back."

How the devil had this character found his name? From the hotel office?

"Please, sahib," the man pleaded. "It costs you nothing just to look."

"You're wrong," said Love, shaking his head. "Even a look can prove expensive."

He went into the room. The man followed him, wheeling his bicycle in over the haircord carpet; the ticking of the free wheel suddenly reminded Love of the ticking in the boot of his Cord. He did not like the memory.

"You got a lucky face, sahib," the man persisted. "I give you special price. Just to look, not to buy. I'm not asking you for money. Just to look."

"I've told you," said Love sharply. "I don't want the carpets. You're wasting your time."

The man stood watching Love in silence, his eyes downcast, almost masked by heavy, tortoise lids. Even so, Love caught the bright flicker of naked hate beneath them, sudden to rise, as swiftly concealed. Distant danger bells rang in his mind; he glanced down briefly at the carpets over the crossbar.

The man's hand moved like a brown, wrinkled snake. There was a flash of blued metal and the snout of an Army Smith and Wesson .38 was an inch from Love's stomach.

"What the hell is this?" asked Love. "You can't get away with robbery here."

"Get your hands up. Higher."

Love had hoped to keep his elbows close to his sides, so that, if the chance came, he could swing to the left, deflect the revolver, and bring up his right knee into the carpet-seller's groin, the first two fingers of his right hand into his eyes. How often had he demonstrated this sequence to the judo class at the British Legion meetings in the local Hall at Bishop's Combe; but the carpet-seller might have been in his class. He clearly knew this basic defence.

"Hold your hands straight up, you English filth," he said, kicking the door shut behind him. "You may have ruled the world years ago, but you mean nothing now."

He spat on the carpet to show how little the English meant.

"What do you want then?" Love asked. "Money?"

"I want to know who you are, and why you're going to see the Nawab of Shahnagar."

"How do you know I am?"

"Don't give me that shit. We do know."

"We?"

Love batted the dialogue to and fro, hoping someone would come into the room; maybe a bearer to see about his clothes, a bheestie with some hot water. He moved forward half a pace towards the carpet-seller.

"Don't get any ideas, doctor. No one can help you. Only yourself. Now talk."

Love moved forward another half pace. The man jabbed the revolver muzzle into his stomach. It jolted against the heavy metal buckle of his belt. Suddenly the barrel whipped to the right, away from Love. In that splintered second, before the carpet-seller could take a second aim, Love's knee came up. The man doubled forward like a hinge closing. Both Love's fists, locked together, came down on the bridge of his nose. The carpet-seller collapsed untidily on the floor; his bicycle with its carpets fell on top of him. Love picked up his revolver, broke it to check that it was loaded, slipped it into his pocket. One down and two to play; a mark for MacGillivray's gadget after all.

"Now," he said, "you talk for a change. Who sent you?"

The man pushed the bicycle away, and sat up shakily, his back against the wall. Blood began to drip from his left nostril; he did nothing to stop it, said nothing.

"Well, if you won't talk, I'll have to call the police. Maybe they'll make you change your mind."

The man shook his head.

"No, please," he said faintly. "Not the police. I'll talk—if you'll let me have a cigarette."

Love nodded, watching him, his right hand around the comforting butt of the revolver in his pocket.

The carpet-seller pulled out a packet of Lion cigarettes, offered it to Love with a trembling hand.

"No," said Love. "Not for me."

Sweat glistened on the man's face; the smell of fear and failure was sharp in the room. He pulled out a cigarette, put it in his mouth, felt in his pocket as though for a match.

"Now," said Love. "For the second time, who sent you here?"

The carpet-seller swallowed awkwardly, as though he had difficulty in speech.

"I'm here," he began slowly, "because . . . because . . . I came to see you. . . ." He swallowed again, his face grimaced with distaste, and then he began to chew desperately, grinding the cheap tobacco in his cigarette to shreds. Love watched, not realizing the significance of this until a thin rope of stained saliva drooled from the man's mouth. His speech slurred, the words running together like a record played too fast. Arteries stood out in his neck, his whole body shuddered, and the carpet-seller fell across his cycle, face down against the oily chain.

Love pulled the sodden, shredded, still unlit cigarette from his mouth; he sniffed the sweet apricot smell of cyanide. He picked up the opened cigarette packet from the gritty carpet, broke the filter of another cigarette; the same deadly scent. He rolled the carpet-seller over on to his back, felt his pulse automatically, although he knew there would be none. The man was dead.

Love stood up, lit a Gitane, wondering what he should do. In any normal circumstances, his duty would be plain; but these were violently abnormal happenings. Here he was, several thousand miles from home, with one possible, one certain attempt on his life. But what did they think he knew that could endanger them? And who were they?

As Love stood looking at the dead carpet-seller, around whose bloody face the flies were already buzzing hungrily, he remembered the good advice of Sir Thomas Browne: "Quarrel not rashly with Adversaries not yet understood."

How powerful must these unknown people be if a man would try to kill him, first with a gun, then with the offer of a poisoned cigarette, and when he failed, take his own life rather than admit his failure? He was beginning a complicated nightmare.

He had possibly only minutes before someone else would come to the door—a bearer, a pedlar with other rugs, shawls, carvings, tourist bric-a-brac to try and sell. If he told Mr. Fernandez he had been threatened with a gun, the admission would only lead to delays, enquiries, statements. It would be safer to conceal his knowledge, simply to say that the man had suffered a seizure. As a doctor, his word would be accepted at least long enough to let him reach Shahnagar and try to accomplish what he had come so far to do.

He made up his mind quickly, wiped the cigarette packet with his handkerchief to remove any fingerprints and then replaced it carefully in the man's pocket. He tore off the corner of one of the pages of the *Civil and Military Gazette* that lined the top drawer in the chest, wrapped it round the damp cigarette butt and put that in his own pocket. The bathroom had no flush where he could lose this, only an ancient china pot in a wooden stand. He would have to get rid of the butt later.

Love then took a pair of rubber surgical gloves from his medical bag, and emptied the dead man's pockets. He carried no means of identification, no money, only a book of matches, a piece of string, an imitation tortoise-shell comb with four teeth missing. Love went into the bathroom, poured some water from the ewer into an enamel mug, spread a towel on the carpet-seller's chest and washed out his mouth as best he could to clear away the more obvious traces of cyanide. He'd have to risk there being an autopsy, but from his memories of the East he didn't think that it was a very serious risk.

He took the man's revolver out of his pocket, wiped it to remove his fingerprints, slipped it into his zipped shaving bag in his suitcase, glanced around the room to make sure he had forgotten nothing. Then he went to the door, shouted: "Bearer! *Idhar ao, jaldi!* Come quickly!"

The bearer had been cleaning a pair of shoes; he arrived wearing a brown brogue on his left hand like a claw.

"This man has died suddenly," Love told him. "Get Mr. Fernandez from the office. Quickly!"

The Anglo-Indian with the steel-rimmed glasses came running.

"What has happened, sir?" he asked, his face contorted with concern in case it should mean trouble for him.

"This carpet wallah's had a seizure," Love told him. "He's dead."

"Dead?"

Mr. Fernandez echoed the word in disbelief, as though this was the first time he had ever heard it. A black crow flew in through the open fanlight, hopeful for a few crumbs, screeched in terror and frustration when it found people, flew right out again.

"Dead," Mr. Fernandez repeated. His eyes, as bright and sharp as those of the bird, flickered around the room, missing nothing, finding nothing. How he hated the English with their pale skins, their assurance; and yet it was only by the cruelest chance that he was as he was. His father had been Portuguese, from Gôa; his mother, so everyone had said, was three-quarters European. How strong must that last dark quarter of pigmentation have been to colour him like this, to put him perpetually between two worlds, belonging to neither, and as he imagined, despised secretly by both. He bent down and looked into the face of the carpet-seller, already glazed with the patina of death.

"He's Bahadur," he said at last, as though the discovery was important.

"You know him?"

"Oh, yes, sir. He's done many years in gaol. Even in the British time."

"Well, he's starting his longest sentence," said Love.

"I'll call the police," said the man. "It will only be a formality for you, sir. He's well known around here, this fellow."

"Any dependents?"

"None here. He's part Chinese. I don't think he's any relations anywhere." He padded away to his office.

The police inspector was a cheerful man in his middle forties, wearing the ribbon of the Burma star. Four policemen in starched K.D. bush shirts and shorts covered the body with a blanket, carried it into the back of the Morris ambulance, while the inspector wrote down what details Love gave him.

"Quite a villain, doctor," he said at last. "We've known him a long time, as I think Mr. Fernandez told you. Robbery with violence. Been threatening with a gun recently, too."

"I'll be in Gilgit for a couple of days, if you want me," Love told him. "Then I'll be here on my way home."

They shook hands. Love watched the ambulance crawl away down the drive in low gear; then he locked his door, drew the curtains across the glass panes, opened his suitcase, took out Bahadur's revolver. On the barrel was stamped the broad arrow of the War Department and the date, 1943.

He wondered where Bahadur had been then, to whom it had originally been issued; it was strange to think that it might even have been his own.

He broke it, squinted through the barrel. The rifling was clean; so at least it hadn't been fired recently. Love slipped back the six shells, rolled a shirt around the revolver, put it in his shaving bag. Then he locked his suitcase and lay back on his bed, hands clasped behind his head, thinking. He didn't like his thoughts. Who could have been the "we" Bahadur had mentioned? Someone involved with the International Committee for the Preservation of Big Game, whoever they might be? Was it likely that they were really trying to be rid of him before he could reach the Nawab—or were the accident to his Cord and this hold-up completely unrelated? Either way, he felt marked, watched; he liked the feeling no more than he liked his other thoughts. He swung his feet down to the floor, walked across to the hotel office.

"Is there anything you want, sir?" asked Mr. Fernandez, anxious to please as ever.

"Information," said Love, and put a folded ten-rupee note on the desk under a paperweight. "Did this man Bahadur ask you whether I was in the hotel?"

Mr. Fernandez hung his head; the glass top on his desk reflected the gold caps on his teeth. At last he nodded.

"Yes, sir. He asked for you specially. The way he spoke I thought you wanted him to call. Did I do wrong in telling him, sir?"

"No. I just wondered. Now tell me something else. How many hotels are there in 'Pindi like this—small ones?"

"Maybe ten like ours, sir. Then there's Flashman's, of course."

"Right. Leave Flashman's out of it, as they're fully booked. You ring these others and find out whether Bahadur had been to see them this morning, asking for me. O.K.?"

"O.K., sir." Mr. Fernandez nodded. His dark brown hand, dry and scaly as a turkey's claw, folded over the note.

Half an hour later he was knocking on Love's door.

"I have found the information," he said as he came inside. "He'd been to six of these hotels, sir. This was the seventh. All times asking for you."

"Thank you," said Love.

He lay back on the bed and lit another Gitane. So Bahadur had been sent to find him and to kill him; if he had hoped for the slightest doubt before, he had none now. Thus the sooner he was on his way, the less chance anyone else would have to succeed where Bahadur had failed. His best chance was to try the airport direct on the off chance of a seat being free, and be out of Rawalpindi as soon as possible. He was still alive and unhurt, but he felt no elation. This was not final victory. He merely lived to die another day.

The airport number was engaged. When he rang ten minutes later, a voice explained that the number was out of order. He telephoned for the third time.

"They are not just now taking messages," another voice informed him. "It is a rest day," and rang off. He remembered telephones in the East; they did not seem to have changed greatly. He must drive out to the airport and try his luck in person.

He paid his bill, hired a bedding roll with brass padlocks on its strap buckles, folded some clothes inside it, pushed Bahadur's revolver in the inside pocket of his jacket, and left his suitcase as a deposit against his return. Then he hired a taxi and drove through the mid-day heat of empty streets and clouds of dust that the wind blew listlessly across open compounds and the squares.

The waiting room at Chaklala was crowded when he arrived; men dozed on benches around the walls; women wore black, like nuns, with eye-holes cut in the cloth. Children with bare feet and running noses played at their mothers' knees; flies buzzed busily and hopefully around their tiered, aluminium cans of food. Love called over their heads at the harassed clerk: "Any hope of a seat to Gilgit?"

The man looked up from his sheaves of passenger lists. "There's just one seat that has been cancelled. The plane is on the runway now. Please let me see your ticket."

A coolie led Love out to a silver Fokker Friendship that glittered in the afternoon sunshine. Inside, the fuselage was green, with the words "EMERGENCY FREIGHT DROP," "SIGNAL ALERT" stencilled in white on one wall. Love's bedding roll and several drums of ghee were lashed to the floor under a net in the centre of the aircraft. The scent of apricots that had been the cargo brought in from Gilgit hung sweetly on the air. The only other passengers were a group of soldiers in grey mazri shirts and khaki shorts; they all sat on leather tip-up seats in the tail of the plane.

The pilot ran up his engines against the brakes; the smell of the fruit, the metallic-flavoured breeze from the ventilator made Love remember wartime flights in Burma, when everyone sat on the floor, backs against the cold-headed rivets on the walls.

When they were airborne, he opened his eyes and looked out of the oval window. They were flying above the Gilgit river. Mountains soared up on either side; behind them stood mile after mile of even higher, snow-tipped peaks, as remote and unreal as the painted backcloth of a stage. Flecks of foam whitened the jade-green river where it ran over hidden rocks.

They passed another plane on its way back to 'Pindi, like a silver minnow in the sky; the pilots joked with each other over their radios. Love dozed until they began to lose altitude. Ahead a mountain brooded over a grey runway, as craggy and uncompromising as Gibraltar. The safety belt warning lit up, and for a moment Love thought they would actually hit the wrinkled rocks; then the pilot veered sharply away, and landed smoothly.

They stopped outside a flowerbed built around a stone building. Over this, a model airplane with a huge rudder moved like a weathercock, its propeller spinning as a crude windspeed indicator. Twenty or thirty locals in flat woollen hats and baggy trousers and sweaters loafed around a pyramid of petrol tins and Army equipment. Someone wheeled out a set of aluminium steps; Love climbed down into the fading afternoon sunshine.

So this was Gilgit. It might have been almost any wartime airfield; even the jeep on the perimeter was the right vintage. As he waited while his bedding roll was being unloaded, a man in sports jacket and sambur-skin shoes strolled up to the pilot. His skin was the colour of polished oak; he wore a military moustache and the look of a soldier in mufti.

"Anything for me?" he asked in English. "Regional Tourist Officer."

"Oh, yes. A package. Perhaps you'd sign for it?"

The pilot handed down a large foolscap envelope covered with red, official-looking seals; on the front was printed in block letters: "REGIONAL TOURIST OFFICER—GILGIT. TO BE COLLECTED PERSONALLY."

The man turned to Love.

"I'm the Tourist Officer. You're booked in at the Rest House?"

"I'm not booked in anywhere," said Love.

"Come with me," said the man. "We've no hotels, you know. Only the Rest House. I'll fix you up. Your name, please?"

"Dr. Jason Love."

They climbed into his jeep. The road ahead was powdered with dust; Love had forgotten about the dust; now he remembered. On either side, water trickled in deep irrigation ditches; cottonwood trees lent circles of shade to little boys playing their own brand of polo with round stones and peeled sticks.

Gilgit, the centre of a vast area known as the Gilgit Agency, which stretched to the borders of Russia, India, and China, was virtually only a single street, lined with silver-barked chinar trees that threw shadows across the open-fronted shops. Outside the headquarters of the Gilgit Scouts Regiment two old cannons pointed fiercely at the road; a couple of hundred yards further on, a wooden archway stretched across a gate. Love saw a sign in English: "GOVERNMENT REST HOUSE."

They drove in, round the dusty lawn; blue and yellow flowers flamed in a centre bed. The driver stopped outside a single-storeyed, L-shaped building with a verandah. To one side, a cow was tethered to a tree; a goat made water at the end of a rope; men gathered fallen twigs for firewood.

There was some coming and going and banging of wire mosquito screens across doors by a babu in sports coat and baggy flannels, who resented being prized off his bed in the middle of sleep, and then Love was given a room. It had green walls, wooden rafters, a stone floor covered by blue and red carpets. In the hearth stood a crude stove made out of a five-gallon oil drum with a hole cut in its front. The air felt chill, as though the dying warmth of the sun had not penetrated the thick walls; Love shivered.

"You are a tourist?" asked the Government Tourist Officer.

"Yes. I'm going to Shahnagar."

"Then I wish you a pleasant journey. You'll need to see the Political Agent here before you go. It's only a courtesy. You have a pass already, I expect?"

"Yes."

"Then my driver will take you to his bungalow, and bring you back. Perhaps you could drop me off on the way?"

"Delighted. It's most kind of you. What's my best way of getting to Shahnagar? I didn't get your name, by the way."

"That's because I didn't give it you, doctor. Let me introduce myself, Ismail Beg. At your service."

They shook hands gravely.

"You'll have to hire a jeep. I know several drivers in Gilgit who'll take you. I'll send one along. You may have to bargain, of course."

"Of course," said Love. "I know that. I was here years ago."

"In the war?"

"Yes," said Love. "Why?"

"Nothing. I was also in the old British-run Indian Army for a time. A lieutenant in the Baluchis. I was captured in the Andaman Islands. You British abandoned us to the Japs. But then, all that belongs to the past. Like so much else."

Just for a moment, Ismail Beg's eyes grew cold with the memory: the little ships sailing away from Port Blair over the strangely dark sea (the local name of the penal settlement was Kala Pani, meaning black water). Beyond the reefs and the breakwaters the sharks turned and dived and turned again. The prisoners in the gaol shouted a lunatic chorus to the gloom of imminent surrender. Often since that dreadful day, Ismail Beg had awoke sweating in the night at the memory. But not now; not any longer.

"I'm sorry," said Love. "Well, these days, we've no one left to abandon."

"Quite so," said Ismail Beg briskly. "That is the way of history. Imperialist empires rise and fall. Only the people they have ruled go on. And one day—who knows? Now, if you please, we should go before it is dark."

Love slipped the key of his room into his pocket and climbed into the jeep. They set off through the narrow main street; goats stood tethered to posts and trouserless children played in the dust. Ismail Beg spoke to his driver. The jeep slowed and stopped.

"I get off here. My man will wait for you at the P.A.'s bungalow and take you back to the Rest House. Good-bye, doctor. A pleasant stay. And if I can help you in any way, please let me know."

It was only when he had disappeared into a shop doorway that Love remembered he had given him no address.

For a moment after the jeep had puttered away through the crowds, dodging the running, clucking chickens, Ismail Beg stood looking after it. He wanted to make sure that Love was not returning, that he did not glance back.

Then he walked up a narrow alleyway between two shops. Their wooden floors were raised to keep the leather bags, the bales of cloth, out of the mud in the rainy season; underneath, dogs slept curled up, and goats rooted optimistically amid rubbish. The shopkeepers squatted among their wares, legs crossed like tailors, smoking, watching him.

Above one shop was a red-and-yellow sign, "THE GILGIT TRAVEL AGENCY." Ismail Beg went up the steps. Inside, the floor smelled of new concrete, still rough and dusty. The walls were bright with posters: a Basque girl looked at a Tyrolean castle; a Beefeater stood, pike in hand, outside the Tower of London.

Two barefooted chaprassis wearing faded khaki shirts and

trousers leaned against the counter, watching Ismail Beg without interest, simply because they had nothing else to do. They had no shares in the firm, it was of no concern to them who came or went. An olive-skinned man with an unhealthy face and dark-ringed eyes looked up from a desk behind the counter.

When he saw the Tourist Officer, he pressed a button and spoke rapidly into an intercom. Then he banged a handbell. The nearest chaprassi led Ismail Beg through a back door, into an inner office, came back, leaned against the counter.

The office was plainly furnished with a brown Turkestan carpet, three chairs, a desk, a row of filing cabinets along the far wall. The air felt too sweet, almost like a sickroom, heavy with scent from a bowl of red frangipani on the desk. In the far corner, a man stood filing his nails, and then blowing away the parings. Because he was of barely middle height, he appeared even fatter than he was, a gross swollen bladder of flesh in a lightweight brown suit, creased at the buttons, dark stains of sweat under the armpits. His neck was so thick and short that his head merged into his body like the head of a tortoise. His face was completely hairless, his brown Chinese eyes as empty of emotion as peeled and slanted almonds.

Ismail Beg stood respectfully at attention as the door shut silently behind him. How often had he stood like this, facing the C.O. of the Baluchis half a lifetime ago, yet with one inestimable difference—he feared Mr. Chin as he had never feared the colonel.

Mr. Chin knew this, and enjoyed the knowledge. He let Ismail Beg stand for a full minute before he nodded to him. Then he turned on a pocket transistor radio that stood on the desk. He always did this as a routine precaution when conferring with underlings. It confused anyone who might wish to eavesdrop, and also demonstrated to an inferior that he was of little consequence. Even in a classless China, face remained important.

The wail of Indian music, convoluted and tortured as a basket of shaken snakes, filled the room. Mr. Chin blew on his nails for the last time, put away his file and sat down behind his desk.

"Well?" he asked briefly.

"This, sir."

He handed to Mr. Chin the sealed brown envelope that the pilot of the Gilgit airplane had given to him: Mr. Chin picked up a silver paper knife, slit the package open. Inside was a single piece of plain board and nothing else. He tossed it into the wastepaper basket. Ismail Beg watched him, wondering what this signified.

"No strangers on the plane?" asked Mr. Chin casually.

"Yes, sir. An Englishman?"

"Ah, yes. What's his name?"

"Dr. Jason Love."

"Ah," said Mr. Chin pleasantly. "Well, I have news for you. And you'll have news for him."

He paused. The plain piece of cardboard was a simple yet unbreakable code from a colleague in Rawalpindi. Blank, and with nothing to give away, no message to crack, it told him that the attempt on this English stranger's life had failed. Action was for him to take.

VI. *Interlude Between the Wars*

The most serious spying going on from 1919 to 1939 remained unknown to the writers of the period, as it was unknown
to the public, if not also to the police of the countries in which
it was happening. This was the activity fostered by the burgeoning secret police of Soviet Russia, who were just beginning
to feel their strength and to branch out into Western Europe
and indeed into the Western Hemisphere. As I say, no one knew
it, and you could hardly expect the fiction writers to be clair-
voyant. I have, however, included here two pieces about Soviet
espionage and "political action" in the between-war period,
written later, one by a man who knew it from the inside, Arthur
Koestler, and one by Vladimir Nabokov, who didn't but doesn't
seem to have suffered from this lack.

In the Koestler piece, the organization which confronts us
is the Comintern, the central bureau in Moscow for the control
and guidance of Communist Parties outside Soviet Russia; in
Nabokov's it is the GPU, precursor of today's KGB, an organization which has changed its name many times because of its evil
reputation, but never changed its actual business as a secret
political police both inside and outside Russia.

The Ambler excerpt is an example of a genre of spy story
which was an innovation of the period between the wars, after
the craze for old-style German spies had died down and we had
not yet faced up to the realities of Nazism, Fascism, and Com-

213

munism. The milieu is international with a strong dash of the Balkans and the Near East. The actors move in that dimly lighted half-world where espionage, smuggling, drug traffic, and fancy criminal doings all more or less overlap and merge.

VLADIMIR NABOKOV

▼

1 The Assistant Producer

In this excerpt from a short story, Vladimir Nabokov takes us into the confused world of the White Russian émigrés in Paris and Berlin in the nineteen-twenties, a world he knew well because he and his family belonged to it. Nabokov's father, a liberal politician under the Czar, but not liberal enough to want to stay to enjoy the new dispensation under Lenin, was himself murdered in 1922 by an émigré of the monarchist faction at a public meeting in Berlin. The assassin had actually meant to murder another man, also a liberal, who was with the elder Nabokov at the time, but the wrong man was killed in the scuffle.

It would be hopeless in a brief space to try to describe the atmosphere of these émigré colonies. Nabokov gives some of the special flavor in his story but rather obliquely. After the Russian Revolution, the Czarist military exiles in Western Europe created numberless anti-Soviet societies and factions which naturally fought among themselves and within which prominent ex-generals and admirals of Czarist days fought for position. The aim of these societies was to foment a counterrevolution in Russia, though there was in reality little they could do but perform rather fruitless spying on the homeland and try to entangle the governments of Western Europe in their political projects.

Nevertheless, the struggling and suspicious Soviet Union found reason to fear these single-minded expatriates enough to place spies within their formations and to suborn their leaders where possible. In the Paris of the nineteen-twenties, there were frequent murders and kidnapings of the exiles, many never fully explained.

FROM *Nabokov's Dozen.*

Nabokov is not especially explicit. His story is kept in the shadows. He is interested in the unreal atmosphere in which the episode takes place and in the odor of corruption that clings to the displaced person. His General Golubkov, aided by his unscrupulous wife, is not only anxious to become president of the White Warriors Union for the glory of it; he has sold out secretly to the Soviets and possibly to the Germans, and one or both of these backers is happy to see him as chief because they will be able to watch and control the organization through him. It is their helping hands we see come out of the doorway to fetch General Fedchenko to his doom.

General Golubkov and his wife already formed one team, one song, one cipher. Quite naturally he became an efficient member of the W.W. (White Warriors Union), traveling about, organizing military courses for Russian boys, arranging relief concerts, unearthing barracks for the destitute, settling local disputes, and doing all this in a most unobtrusive manner. I suppose it was useful in some ways, that W.W.

There was also another type of person connected with the W.W. I am thinking of those adventurous souls who helped the cause by crossing the frontier through some snow-muffled fir forest, to potter about their native land in the various disguises worked out, oddly enough, by the social revolutionaries of yore, and quietly bring back to the little café in Paris called "Esh-Bubliki," or to the little *Kneipe* in Berlin that had no special name, the kind of useful trifles which spies are supposed to bring back to their employers. Some of those men had become abstrusely entangled with the spying departments of other nations and would give an amusing jump if you came from behind and tapped them on the shoulder. A few went a-scouting for the fun of the thing. One or two perhaps really believed that in some mystical way they were preparing the resurrection of a sacred, if somewhat musty, past. . . .

Golubkov was not only a very versatile spy (a triple agent to be exact); he was also an exceedingly ambitious little fellow. Why the vision of presiding over an organization that was but a sunset behind a cemetery happened to be so dear to him is a conundrum only for those who have no hobbies or passions. He wanted it very badly—that is all. What is less intelligible is the faith he had in being able to safeguard his puny existence in the crush between the formidable parties whose dangerous money and dangerous help he received. I want all your attention now, for it would be a pity to miss the subtleties of the situation.

The Soviets could not be much disturbed by the highly improbable prospect of a phantom White Army ever being able to resume war operations against their consolidated bulk; but they could be very much irritated by the fact that scraps of information about forts and factories, gathered by elusive W. W. meddlers, were automatically falling into grateful German hands. The Germans were little interested in the recondite color variations of émigré politics, but what did annoy them was the blunt patriotism of a W.W. president every now and then obstructing on ethical grounds the smooth flow of friendly collaboration.

Thus, General Golubkov was a godsend. The Soviets firmly expected that under his rule all W.W. spies would be well known to them—and shrewdly supplied with false information for eager German consumption. The Germans were equally sure that through him they would be guaranteed a good cropping of their own absolutely trustworthy agents distributed among the usual W.W. ones. Neither side had any illusions concerning Golubkov's loyalty, but each assumed that it would turn to its own profit the fluctuations of double-crossing. The dreams of simple Russian folk, hard-working families in remote parts of the Russian diaspora, plying their humble but honest trades, as they would in Saratov or Tver, bearing fragile children and naïvely believing that the W.W. was a kind of King Arthur's Round Table that stood for all that had been, and would be, sweet and decent and strong in fairy-tale Russia—these dreams may well strike the film pruners as an excrescence upon the main theme.

When the W.W. was founded, General Golubkov's candidacy (purely theoretical, of course, for nobody expected the leader to die) was very far down the list—not because his legendary gallantry was insufficiently appreciated by his fellow officers, but because he happened to be the youngest general in the army. Toward the time of the next president's election Golubkov had already disclosed such tremendous capacities as an organizer that he felt he could safely cross out quite a few intermediate names in the list, incidentally sparing the lives of their bearers. After the second general had been removed, many of the W.W. members were convinced that General Fedchenko, the next candidate, would surrender in favor of the younger and more efficient man the rights that his age, reputation and academic distinction entitled him to enjoy. The old gentleman, however, though doubtful of the enjoyment, thought it cowardly to avoid a job that had cost two men their lives. So Golubkov set his teeth and started to dig again.

Physically he lacked attraction. There was nothing of your popular Russian general about him, nothing of that good, burly, popeyed, thick-necked sort. He was lean, frail, with sharp features, a clipped mustache, and the kind of haircut that is called by Russians "hedgehog"; short, wiry, upright, and compact. There was a thin silver bracelet round his hairy wrist, and he offered you neat homemade Russian cigarettes or English prune-flavored "Kapstens," as he pronounced it, snugly arranged in an old roomy cigarette case of black leather that had accompanied him through the presumable smoke of numberless battles. He was extremely polite and extremely inconspicuous.

One day, late in the afternoon, General Golubkov escorted his wife to her dressmaker, sat there for a while reading the *Paris-Soir*, and then was sent back to fetch one of the dresses she wanted loosened and had forgotten to bring. At suitable intervals she gave a passable imitation of telephoning home and volubly directing his search. The dressmaker, an Armenian lady, and a seamstress, little Princess Tumanov, were much entertained in the adjacent room by the variety of her rustic oaths. This threadbare alibi was intended to provide a man whom none would ever dream of suspecting with a routine account of his movements when people would want to know who had seen General Fedchenko last. After enough imaginary wardrobes had been ransacked Golubkov was seen to return with the dress (which long ago, of course, had been placed in the car). He went on reading his paper while his wife kept trying things on.

The thirty-five minutes or so during which he was gone proved quite a comfortable margin. About the time she started fooling with that dead telephone, he had already picked up the General [Fedchenko] at an unfrequented corner and was driving him to an imaginary appointment the circumstances of which had been so framed in advance as to make its secrecy natural and its attendance a duty. A few minutes later he pulled up and they both got out. "This is not the right street," said General Fedchenko. "No," said General Golubkov, "but it is a convenient one to park my car on. I should not like to leave it right in front of the café. We shall take a short cut through that lane. It is only two minutes' walk." "Good, let us walk," said the old man and cleared his throat.

In that particular quarter of Paris the streets are called after various philosophers, and the lane they were following had been named by some well-read city father Rue Pierre Labime. It gently steered you past a dark church and some scaffolding into a vague region of shuttered private houses standing somewhat aloof within their own grounds behind iron railings on which moribund maple leaves would pause in their flight between bare branch and wet pavement. Along the left side of that lane there was a long wall with crossword puzzles of brick showing here and there through its rough grayness; and in that wall there was at one spot a little green door.

As they approached it, General Golubkov produced his battle-scarred cigarette case and presently stopped to light up. General Fedchenko, a courteous non-smoker, stopped too. There was a gusty wind ruffling the dusk, and the first match went out. "I still think—" said General Fedchenko in reference to some petty business they had been discussing lately, "I still think," he said (to say something as he stood near that little green door), "that if Father Fedor insists on paying for all those lodgings out of his own funds, the least we can do is to supply the fuel." The second match went out too. The back of a passer-by hazily receding in the distance at last disappeared. General Golubkov cursed the wind at the top of his voice, and as this was the all-clear signal the green door opened and three pairs of hands with incredible speed and skill whisked the old man out of sight. The door slammed. General Golubkov lighted his cigarette and briskly walked back the way he had come.

The old man was never seen again. The quiet foreigners who had rented a certain quiet house for one quiet month had been innocent Dutchmen or Danes. It was but an optical trick. There is no green door, but only a gray one, which no human strength can burst open. I have vainly searched through admirable encyclopedias: there is no philosopher called Pierre Labime.

But I have seen the toad in her eyes. We have a saying in Russian: *vsevo dvoe i est; smert' da sovest'*—which may be rendered thus: "There are only two things that really exist—one's death and one's conscience." The lovely thing about humanity is that at times one may be unaware of doing right, but one is always aware of doing wrong. A very horrible criminal, whose wife had been even a worse one, once told me in the days when I was a priest that what had troubled him all through was the inner shame of being stopped by a still deeper shame from discussing with her the puzzle: whether perhaps in her heart of hearts she despised him or whether she secretly wondered if perhaps in his heart of hearts he despised her. And that is why I know perfectly well the kind of face General Golubkov and his wife had when the two were at last alone.

Not for very long, however. About 10 P.M. General L., the W.W. Secretary, was informed by General R. that Mrs. Fedchenko was extremely worried by her husband's unaccountable absence. Only then did General L. remember that about lunch time the President had told him in a rather casual way (but that was the old gentleman's manner) that he had some business in town in the late afternoon and that if he was not back by 8 P.M. would General L. please read a note left in the middle drawer of the President's desk. The two generals now rushed to the office, stopped short, rushed back for the keys General L. had forgotten, rushed again, and finally found the note. It read: "An odd feeling obsesses me of which later I may be ashamed. I have an appointment at 5:30 P.M. in a café 45 Rue Descartes. I am to meet an informer from the other side. I suspect a trap. The whole thing has been arranged by General Golubkov, who is taking me there in his car."

We shall skip what General L. said and what General R. replied—but apparently they were slow thinkers and proceeded to lose some more time in a muddled telephone talk with an indignant café owner. It was almost midnight when the Slavska [General Golubkov's wife], clad in a flowery dressing gown and trying to look very sleepy, let them in. She was unwilling to disturb her husband, who, she said, was already asleep. She wanted to know what it was all about and had perhaps something happened to General Fedchenko. "He has vanished," said honest General L. The Slavska said, "Akh!" and crashed in a dead swoon, almost wrecking the parlor in the process. The stage had not lost quite so much as most of her admirers thought.

Somehow or other the two generals managed not to impart to General Golubkov anything about the little note, so that when he accompanied them to the W.W. headquarters he was under the impression that they really wanted to discuss with him whether to ring up the police at once or first go for advice to eighty-eight-year-old Admiral Gromoboyev, who for some obscure reason was considered the Solomon of the W.W.

"What does this mean?" said General L. handing the fatal note to Golubkov. "Peruse it, please."

Golubkov perused—and knew at once that all was lost. We shall not bend over the abyss of his feelings. He handed the note back with a shrug of his thin shoulders.

"If this has been really written by the General," he said, "and I must admit it looks very similar to his hand, then all I can say is that somebody has been impersonating me. However, I have grounds to believe that Admiral Gromoboyev will be able to exonerate me. I suggest we go there at once."

"Yes," said General L., "we had better go now, although it is very late."

General Golubkov swished himself into his raincoat and went out first. General R. helped General L. to retrieve his muffler. It had half slipped down from one of those vestibule chairs which are doomed to accommodate things, not people. General L. sighed and put on his old felt hat, using both hands for this gentle action. He moved to the door. "One moment, General," said General R. in a low voice. "I want to ask you something. As one officer to another, are you absolutely sure that . . . well, that General Golubkov is speaking the truth?"

"That's what we shall find out," answered General L., who was one of those people who believe that so long as a sentence is a sentence it is bound to mean something.

They delicately touched each other's elbows in the doorway. Finally the slightly older man accepted the privilege and made a jaunty exit. Then they both paused on the landing, for the staircase struck them as being very still. "General!" cried General L. in a downward direction. Then they looked at each other. Then hurriedly, clumsily, they stomped down the ugly steps, and emerged, and stopped under a black drizzle, and looked this way and that, and then at each other again.

She was arrested early on the following morning. Never once during the inquest did she depart from her attitude of grief-stricken innocence. The French police displayed a queer listlessness in dealing with possible clews, as if it assumed that the disappearance of Russian generals was a kind of curious local custom, an Oriental phenomenon, a dissolving process which perhaps ought not to occur but which could not be prevented. One had, however, the impression that the Sûreté knew more about the working of that vanishing trick than diplomatic wisdom found fit to discuss. Newspapers abroad treated the whole matter in a good-natured but bantering and slightly bored manner. On the whole, "*L'Affaire Slavska*" did not make good headlines—Russian émigrés were decidedly out of focus. By an amusing coincidence both a German press agency and a Soviet one laconically stated that a pair of White Russian generals in Paris had absconded with the White Army funds.

The trial was strangely inconclusive and muddled, witnesses did not shine, and the final conviction of the Slavska on a charge of kidnaping was debatable on legal grounds. Irrelevant trifles kept obscuring the main issue. The wrong people remembered the right things and vice versa. General L. and General R. had a dreadful time at the hands of a sadistic barrister. A Parisian clochard, one of those colorful ripe-nosed unshaven beings (an easy part, that) who keep all their earthly belongings in their voluminous pockets and wrap their feet in layers of bursting newspapers when the last sock is gone and are seen comfortably seated, with widespread legs and a bottle of wine against the crumbling wall of some building that has never been completed, gave a lurid account of having observed from a certain vantage point an old man being roughly handled. Two Russian women, one of whom had been treated some time before for acute hysteria, said they saw on the day of the crime General Golubkov and General Fedchenko driving in the former's car. A Russian violinist while sitting in the diner of a German train—but it is useless to retell of those lame rumors.

ARTHUR KOESTLER

▼

2 Betrayal

The selection I have chosen from Arthur Koestler's famous Darkness at Noon *does not bear directly on the central substance of the
book, which, as the reader may recall, concerns the interrogation
and brainwashing of an imaginary Soviet political figure, N. S.
Rubashov, during the Stalinist purges of the late nineteen-thirties.
In an early part of the book, after he has first been imprisoned and
is awaiting interrogation, Rubashov reminisces—goes over his
accounts, so to speak—with particular emphasis on certain memories which trouble his conscience. In most of these instances, the
Party, in the person of Rubashov, has thrown its servants to the
wolves. It is one of these memories of Rubashov's which follows. It
is a remarkable and disturbing vignette, depicting a situation
which has long since been forgotten among all the other overwhelming and massive tragedies of World War II and of the
period which followed it.*

*It is not strictly a spy story except that the situation of a
clandestine worker of the Communist Party in a country in which
the Party is outlawed and doomed is very much the same as that
of a spy in enemy territory. There is one difference, however—the
latter can hope that if he evades capture and reaches safety his
employers will reward him; he can also be fairly certain that they
will not betray him.*

The picture gallery of a town in southern Germany on a Monday
afternoon. There was not a soul in the place, save for Rubashov and
the young man whom he had come to meet; their conversation took

FROM *Darkness at Noon.*

place on a round plush sofa in the middle of an empty room, the walls of which were hung with tons of heavy female flesh by the Flemish masters. It was in the year 1933, during the first months of terror, shortly before Rubashov's arrest. The movement had been defeated, its members were outlawed and hunted and beaten to death. The Party was no longer a political organization; it was nothing but a thousand-armed and thousand-headed mass of bleeding flesh. As a man's hair and nails continue to grow after his death, so movement still occurred in individual cells, muscles and limbs of the dead Party. All over the country existed small groups of people who had survived the catastrophe and continued to conspire underground. They met in cellars, woods, railway stations, museums and sport clubs. They continuously changed their sleeping quarters, also their names and their habits. They knew each other only by their Christian names and did not ask for each other's addresses. Each gave his life into the other's hands, and neither trusted the other an inch. They printed pamphlets in which they tried to convince themselves and others that they were still alive. They stole at night through narrow suburban streets and wrote on the walls the old slogans, to prove that they were still alive. They climbed at dawn on factory chimneys and hoisted the old flag, to prove that they were still alive. Only a few people ever saw the pamphlets and they threw them away quickly, for they shuddered at the message of the dead; the slogans on the walls were gone by cock's crow and the flags were pulled down from the chimneys; but they always appeared again. For all over the country there were small groups of people who called themselves "dead men on holiday," and who devoted their lives to proving that they still possessed life.

They had no communication with each other; the nerve fibres of the Party were torn and each group stood for itself. But, gradually, they started to put out feelers again. Respectable commercial travellers came from abroad, with false passports and with double-bottomed trunks; they were the Couriers. Usually they were caught, tortured and beheaded; others took their place. The Party remained dead, it could neither move nor breathe, but its hair and nails continued to grow; the leaders abroad sent galvanizing currents through its rigid body, which caused spasmodic jerks in the limbs.

. . . Rubashov . . . went on doing his six and a half steps up and down; he found himself again on the round plush sofa in the picture gallery, which smelled of dust and floor polish. He had driven straight from the station to the appointed meeting place and had arrived a few minutes too soon. He was fairly sure that he had not been observed.

His suit-case, which contained samples of a Dutch firm's latest novelties in dentists' equipment, lay in the cloakroom. He sat on the round plush sofa, looking through his pince-nez at the masses of flabby flesh on the walls and waited.

The young man, who was known by the name of Richard, and was at this time leader of the Party group in this town, came a few minutes too late. He had never seen Rubashov and Rubashov had never seen him, either. He had already gone through two empty galleries when he saw Rubashov on the round sofa. On Rubashov's knee lay a book: Goethe's *Faust* in Reclam's Universal Edition. The young man noticed the book, gave a hurried look round and sat down beside Rubashov. He was rather shy and sat on the edge of the sofa, about two feet away from Rubashov, his cap on his knees. He was a locksmith by trade and wore a black Sunday suit; he knew that a man in overalls would be conspicuous in a museum.

"Well?" he said. "You must please excuse my being late."

"Good," said Rubashov. "Let us first go through your people. Have you got a list?"

The young man called Richard shook his head. "I don't carry lists," he said. "I've got it all in my head—addresses and all."

"Good," said Rubashov. "But what if they get you?"

"As for that," said Richard, "I have given a list to Anny. Anny is my wife, you know."

He stopped and swallowed and his Adam's apple moved up and down; then for the first time he looked Rubashov full in the face. Rubashov saw that he had inflamed eyes; the slightly prominent eyeballs were covered by a net of red veins; his chin and cheeks were stubbly over the black collar of the Sunday suit. "Anny was arrested last night, you know," he said and looked at Rubashov; and Rubashov read in his eyes the dull, childish hope that he, the Courier of the Central Committee, would work a miracle and help him.

"Really?" said Rubashov and rubbed his pince-nez on his sleeve. "So the police have got the whole list."

"No," said Richard, "for my sister-in-law was in the flat when they came to fetch her, you know, and she managed to pass it to her. It is quite safe with my sister-in-law, you know; she is married to a police constable, but she is with us."

"Good," said Rubashov. "Where were you when your wife was arrested?"

"This is how it was," said Richard. "I haven't slept in my flat for three months, you know. I have a pal who is a cinema operator; I can go to him, and when the performance is over I can sleep in his cabin.

One gets in straight from the street by the fire escape. And cinema for nothing . . ." He paused and swallowed. "Anny was always given free tickets by my pal, you know, and when it was dark she would look up to the projecting room. She couldn't see me, but sometimes I could see her face quite well when there was a lot of light on the screen. . . ."

He stopped. Just opposite him hung a "Last Judgment": curly-headed cherubs with rotund behinds flying up into a thunderstorm, blowing trumpets. To Richard's left hung a pen drawing by a German master; Rubashov could only see a part of it—the rest was hidden by the plush back of the sofa and by Richard's head; the Madonna's thin hands, curved upwards, hollowed to the shape of a bowl, and a bit of empty sky covered with horizontal pen-lines. More was not to be seen as, while speaking, Richard's head persisted immovably in the same position on his slightly bowed, reddish neck.

"Really?" said Rubashov. "How old is your wife?"

"She is seventeen," said Richard.

"Really? And how old are you?"

"Nineteen," said Richard.

"Any children?" asked Rubashov and stretched his head out a little, but he could not see more of the drawing.

"The first one is on the way," said Richard. He sat motionlessly, as if cast in lead.

There was an interval and then Rubashov let him recite the list of the Party's members. It consisted of about thirty names. He asked a few questions and wrote down several addresses in his order book for the Dutch firm's dental instruments. He wrote them in the spaces he had left in a long list of local dentists and respectable citizens copied out of the telephone directory. When they had finished, Richard said:

"Now I would like to give you a short report on our work, comrade."

"Good," said Rubashov. "I'm listening."

Richard made his report. He sat slightly bent forward—a couple of feet away from Rubashov, on the narrow plush sofa, his big red hands on the knees of his Sunday suit; he did not change his position once while speaking. He spoke of the flags on the chimney stacks, the inscriptions on the walls and the pamphlets which were left in the factory latrines, stiffly and matter-of-factly as a book-keeper. Opposite him the trumpet-blowing angels flew into the thunderstorm, at the back of his head an invisible Virgin Mary stretched out her thin hands; from all around the walls colossal breasts, thighs and hips stared at them.

Breasts fitting to champagne glasses came into Rubashov's head.

He stood still on the third black tile from the cell-window, to hear whether No. 402 was still tapping. There was no sound. Rubashov went to the spy-hole and looked over to No. 407, who had stretched out his hands for the bread. He saw the grey steel door of cell 407 with the small black judas. Electric light was burning in the corridor as always; it was bleak and silent; one could hardly believe that human beings lived behind those doors.

While the young man called Richard was giving his report, Rubashov did not interrupt him. Of the thirty men and women whom Richard had grouped together after the catastrophe, only seventeen remained. Two, a factory hand and his girl, had thrown themselves out of the window when they came to fetch them. One had deserted—had left the town, vanished. Two were suspected of being spies for the police, but this was not certain. Three had left the Party as a protest against the policy of the Central Committee; two of them had founded a new oppositional group, the third had joined the Moderates. Five had been arrested last night, among them Anny; it was known that at least two of these five were no longer alive. So there remained seventeen, who continued to distribute pamphlets and scribble on walls.

Richard told him all this in minute detail, so that Rubashov should understand all the personal connections and causes which were particularly important; he did not know that the Central Committee had their own man in the group, who had long ago given Rubashov most of the facts. He did not know either that this man was his pal, the cinema operator, in whose cabin he slept; neither that this person had been for a long time on intimate terms with his wife Anny, arrested last night. None of this did Richard know; but Rubashov knew it. The movement lay in ruins, but its Intelligence and Control Department still functioned; it was perhaps the only part of it which did function, and at that time Rubashov stood at the head of it. The bull-necked young man in the Sunday suit did not know that either; he only knew that Anny had been taken away and that one had to go on distributing pamphlets and scribbling on walls; and that Rubashov, who was a comrade from the Central Committee of the Party, was to be trusted like a father; but that one must not show this feeling nor betray any weakness. For he who was soft and sentimental was no good for the task and had to be pushed aside—pushed out of the movement, into solitude and the outer darkness.

Outside in the corridor steps were approaching. Rubashov went to the door, took his pince-nez off and put his eye to the judas. Two officials with leather revolver-belts were conducting a young peasant along the corridor; behind them came the old warder with the bunch of keys. The peasant had a swollen eye and dry blood on his upper lip; as he passed he wiped his sleeve over his bleeding nose; his face was flat and expressionless. Further down the corridor, outside Rubashov's range, a cell door was unlocked and slammed. Then the officials and the warder came back alone.

Rubashov walked up and down in his cell. He saw himself, sitting on the round plush sofa next to Richard; he heard again the silence which had fallen when the boy had finished his report. Richard did not move; sat with his hands on his knees and waited. He sat as one who had confessed and was waiting for the father-confessor's sentence. For a long while Rubashov said nothing. Then he said:

"Good. Is that all?"

The boy nodded; his Adam's apple moved up and down.

"Several things are not clear in your report," said Rubashov. "You spoke repeatedly of the leaflets and pamphlets which you made yourselves. They are known to us and their content was criticized sharply. There are several phrases which the Party cannot accept."

Richard looked at him frightenedly: he reddened. Rubashov saw the skin over his cheek-bones becoming hot and the net of red veins in his inflamed eyes become denser.

"On the other hand," continued Rubashov, "we have repeatedly sent you our printed material for distribution amongst which was the special small-size edition of the official Party organ. You received these consignments."

Richard nodded. The heat did not leave his face.

"But you did not distribute our material; it is not even mentioned in your report. Instead, you circulated the material made by your-selves—without the control or approval of the Party."

"B-but we had to," Richard brought out with a great effort. Rubashov looked at him attentively through his pince-nez; he had not noticed before that the boy stammered. "Curious," he thought, "this is the third case in a fortnight. We have a surprising number of defectives in the Party. Either it is because of the circumstances under which we work—or the movement itself promotes a selection of defectives. . . ."

"You m-must understand, c-comrade," said Richard in growing distress. "The t-tone of your propaganda material was wrong, b-because—"

"Speak quietly," said Rubashov suddenly in a sharp tone, "and don't turn your head to the door."

A tall young man in the uniform of the black bodyguard of the regime had entered the room with his girl. The girl was a buxom

blonde; he held her round her broad hip, her arm lay on his shoulder.
They paid no attention to Rubashov and his companion and stopped
in front of the trumpeting angels, with their backs to the sofa.

"Go on talking," said Rubashov in a calm, low voice and automatically took his cigarette case out of his pocket. Then he remembered
that one may not smoke in museums and put the case back. The boy
sat as if paralysed by an electric shock, and stared at the two. "Go on
talking," said Rubashov quietly. "Did you stammer as a child? Answer
and don't look over there."

"S-sometimes," Richard managed to bring out with a great effort.

The couple moved along the row of pictures. They stopped in
front of a nude of a very fat woman, who lay on a satin couch and
looked at the spectator. The man murmured something presumably
funny, for the girl giggled and glanced fleetingly at the two figures on
the sofa. They moved on a bit, to a still-life of dead pheasants and
fruit.

"Sh-shouldn't we go?" asked Richard.

"No," said Rubashov. He was afraid that when they stood up the
boy in his agitation would behave conspicuously. "They will soon go.
We have our backs to the light; they cannot see us clearly. Breathe
slowly and deeply several times. It helps."

The girl went on giggling and the pair moved slowly towards the
way out. In passing, they both turned their heads towards Rubashov
and Richard. They were just about to leave the room, when the girl
pointed with her finger at the pen drawing of the Pietà; they stopped
to look at it. "Is it very di-disturbing when I s-stammer?" asked
Richard in a low voice, staring down at the floor.

"One must control oneself," said Rubashov shortly. He could not
now let any feeling of intimacy creep into the conversation.

"It will b-be b-better in a minute," said Richard, and his Adam's
apple moved convulsively up and down. "Anny always laughed at me
about it, you kn-now."

As long as the couple remained in the room, Rubashov could not
steer the conversation. The back of the man in uniform nailed him
down next to Richard. The common danger helped the boy over his
shyness; he even slid a bit closer to Rubashov.

"She was fond of me all the s-same," he continued, whispering in
another, quieter kind of agitation. "I n-never knew quite how to take
her. She did not want to have the child, b-but she could not get rid of
it. P-perhaps they won't do anything to her as she is p-pregnant. You c-
can see it quite clearly, you know. Do you think that they beat pregnant women, t-too?"

With his chin, he indicated the young man in uniform. In the same instant the young man suddenly turned his head towards Richard. For a second they looked at each other. The young man in uniform said something to the girl in a low voice; she too turned her head. Rubashov again grasped his cigarette case, but this time let it go while still in his pocket. The girl said something and pulled the young man away with her. The pair of them left the gallery slowly, the man rather hesitatingly. One heard the girl giggling again outside and their footsteps receding.

Richard turned his head and followed them with his eyes. As he moved, Rubashov gained a better view of the drawing; he could now see the Virgin's thin arms up to the elbow. They were meagre, little girl's arms, raised weightlessly towards the invisible shaft of the cross.

Rubashov looked at his watch. The boy moved a bit further away from him on the sofa.

"We must come to a conclusion," said Rubashov. "If I understand you rightly, you said that you purposely did not distribute our material because you did not agree with its contents. But neither did we agree with the contents of your leaflets. You will understand, comrade, that certain consequences must come of that."

Richard turned his reddened eyes towards him. Then he lowered his head. "You know yourself that the material you sent was full of nonsense," he said in a flat voice. He had suddenly stopped stammering.

"Of that I know nothing," said Rubashov drily.

"You wrote as if nothing had happened," said Richard in the same tired voice. "They beat the Party to shambles, and you just wrote phrases about our unbroken will to victory—the same kind of lies as the communiqués in the Great War. Whoever we showed it to would just spit. You must know all that yourself."

Rubashov looked at the boy, who now sat leaning forward, elbows on his knees, his chin on his red fists. He answered drily:

"For the second time you ascribe to me an opinion which I do not hold. I must ask you to stop doing so."

Richard looked at him unbelievingly out of his inflamed eyes. Rubashov went on.

"The Party is going through a severe trial. Other revolutionary parties have been through even more difficult ones. The decisive factor is our unbroken will. Whoever now goes soft and weak does not belong in our ranks. Whoever spreads an atmosphere of panic plays into our enemy's hands. What his motives are in doing so does not make any difference. By his attitude he becomes a danger to our movement, and will be treated accordingly."

Richard still sat with his chin in his hands, his face turned to Rubashov.

"So I am a danger to the movement," he said. "I play into the enemy's hands. Probably I am paid for doing so. And Anny, too. . . ."

"In your pamphlets," continued Rubashov in the same dry tone of voice, "of which you admit to be the author, there frequently appear phrases such as this: that we have suffered a defeat, that a catastrophe has befallen the Party, and that we must start afresh and change our policy fundamentally. That is defeatism. It is demoralizing and it lames the Party's fighting spirit."

"I only know," said Richard, "that one must tell people the truth, as they know it already, in any case. It is ridiculous to pretend to them."

"The last congress of the Party," Rubashov went on, "stated in a resolution that the Party has not suffered a defeat and has merely carried out a strategic retreat; and that there is no reason whatever for changing its previous policy."

"But that's rubbish," said Richard.

"If you go on in this style," said Rubashov, "I am afraid we will have to break off the conversation."

Richard was silent for a while. The room began to darken, the contours of the angels and women on the walls became still softer and more nebulous.

"I am sorry," said Richard. "I mean, the Party leadership is mistaken. You talk of a 'strategic retreat' while half of our people are killed, and those which are left are so pleased to be still alive that they go over to the other side in shoals. These hair-splitting resolutions which you people outside fabricate are not understood here. . . ."

Richard's features began to become hazy in the growing dusk. He paused, then added:

"I suppose Anny also made a 'strategic retreat' last night. Please, you must understand. Here we are all living in the jungle. . . ."

Rubashov waited to see whether he still had anything to say, but Richard said nothing. Dusk was falling rapidly now. Rubashov took his pince-nez off and rubbed it on his sleeve.

"The Party can never be mistaken," said Rubashov. "You and I can make a mistake. Not the Party. The Party, comrade, is more than you and I and a thousand others like you and I. The Party is the embodiment of the revolutionary idea in history. History knows no scruples and no hesitation. Inert and unerring she flows towards her goal. At every bend in her course she leaves the mud which she carries and the corpses of the drowned. History knows her way. She makes no mistakes. He who has not absolute faith in History does not belong in the Party's ranks."

Richard said nothing; head on his fists, he kept his immovable face turned to Rubashov. As he remained silent, Rubashov went on:

"You have prevented the distribution of our material; you have suppressed the Party's voice. You have distributed pamphlets in which every word was harmful and false. You wrote: 'The remains of the revolutionary movement must be gathered together and all powers hostile to tyranny must unite; we must stop our old internal struggles and start the common fight afresh.' That is wrong. The Party must not join the Moderates. It is they who in all good faith have countless times betrayed the movement, and they will do it again next time, and the time after next. He who compromises with them buries the revolution. You wrote: 'When the house is on fire, all must help to quench it; if we go on quarrelling about doctrines, we will all be burnt to ashes.' That is wrong. We fight against the fire with water; the others do with oil. Therefore we must first decide which is the right method, water or oil, before uniting the fire-brigades. One cannot conduct politics that way. It is impossible to form a policy with passion and despair. The Party's course is sharply defined, like a narrow path in the mountains. The slightest false step, right or left, takes one down the precipice. The air is thin; he who becomes dizzy is lost."

Dusk had now progressed so far that Rubashov could no longer see the hands on the drawing. A bell rang twice, shrill and penetratingly; in a quarter of an hour the museum would be closed. Rubashov looked at his watch; he still had the decisive word to say, then it would be over. Richard sat motionless next to him, elbows on knees.

"Yes, to that I have no answer," he said finally, and again his voice was flat and very tired. "What you say is doubtless true. And what you said about that mountain path is very fine. But all I know is that we are beaten. Those who are still left desert us. Perhaps, because it is too cold up on our mountain path. The others—they have music and bright banners and they all sit round a nice warm fire. Perhaps that is why they have won. And why we are breaking our necks."

Rubashov listened in silence. He wanted to hear whether the young man had any more to say, before he himself pronounced the decisive sentence. Whatever Richard said, it could not now change that sentence in any way; but yet he waited.

Richard's heavy form was more and more obscured by the dusk. He had moved still further away on the round sofa; he sat with bent shoulders and his face nearly buried in his hands. Rubashov sat straight up on the sofa and waited. He felt a slight drawing pain in his upper jaw; probably the defective eye-tooth. After a while he heard Richard's voice:

"What will happen to me now?"

Rubashov felt for the aching tooth with his tongue. He felt the need to touch it with his finger before pronouncing the decisive word, but forbade himself. He said quietly:

"I have to inform you, in accordance with the Central Committee's decision, that you are no longer a member of the Party, Richard."

Richard did not stir. Again Rubashov waited for a while, before standing up. Richard remained sitting. He merely lifted his head, looked up at him and asked:

"Is that what you came here for?"

"Chiefly," said Rubashov. He wanted to go, but still stood there in front of Richard and waited.

"What will now become of me?" asked Richard. Rubashov said nothing. After a while, Richard said:

"Now I suppose I cannot live at my friend's cabin either?"

After a short hesitation Rubashov said:

"Better not."

He was at once annoyed with himself for having said it, and he was not certain whether Richard had understood the meaning of the phrase. He looked down on the seated figure:

"It will be better for us to leave the building separately. Good-bye."

Richard straightened himself, but remained sitting. In the twilight Rubashov could only guess the expression of the inflamed, slightly prominent eyes; yet it was just this blurred image of the clumsy, seated figure which stamped itself in his memory for ever.

He left the room and crossed the next one, which was equally empty and dark. His steps creaked on the parquet floor. Only when he had reached the way out did he remember that he had forgotten to look at the picture of the Pietà: now he would only know the detail of the folded hands and part of the thin arms, up to the elbow.

On the steps which led down from the entrance he stopped. His tooth was hurting him a bit more; it was cold outside. He wrapped the faded grey woollen scarf more tightly round his neck. The street lamps were already lit in the big quiet square in front of the gallery; at this hour there were few people about; a narrow tram ringing its bell clanged up the elm-bordered avenue. He wondered whether he would find a taxi here.

On the bottom step Richard caught him up, panting breathlessly. Rubashov went straight on, neither hastening nor slacking his pace and without turning his head. Richard was half a head bigger than he and much broader, but he held his shoulders hunched, making himself small beside Rubashov and shortening his steps. After a few paces he said:

"Was that meant to be a warning, when I asked you if I could go on living with my friend and you said 'Better not'?"

Rubashov saw a taxi with bright lights coming up the avenue. He stopped on the curb and waited for it to come closer. Richard was standing beside him. "I have no more to say to you, Richard," Rubashov said, and hailed the taxi.

"Comrade, b-but you couldn't d-denounce me, comrade. . . ." said Richard. The taxi slowed down, it was no more than twenty paces from them. Richard stood hunched in front of Rubashov; he had caught the sleeve of Rubashov's overcoat and was talking straight down into his face; Rubashov felt his breath and a slight dampness sprayed on to his forehead.

"I am not an enemy of the Party," said Richard. "You c–can't throw me to the wolves, c-comrade. . . ."

The taxi stopped at the curb; the driver must certainly have heard the last word. Rubashov calculated rapidly that it was no use sending Richard away; there was a policeman posted a hundred yards further up. The driver, a little old man in a leather jacket, looked at them expressionlessly.

"To the station," said Rubashov and got in. The taxi driver reached back with his right arm and slammed the door behind him. Richard stood on the edge of the pavement, cap in hand; his Adam's apple moved rapidly up and down. The taxi started; it drove off towards the policeman; it passed the policeman. Rubashov preferred not to look back, but he knew that Richard was still standing on the edge of the pavement, staring at the taxi's red rear-light.

ERIC AMBLER

▼

3 Belgrade, 1926

Eric Ambler himself originally excerpted this story for separate publication from his novel A Coffin for Dimitrios *and gave it its title. In England this novel was called* A Mask for Dimitrios, *and you may recall that it is a book James Bond packs in his bag when he leaves on his mission to Istanbul at the beginning of* From Russia with Love. *The* Dimitrios *novel also gets under way in Istanbul, and Bond may have wanted to soak up some of the atmosphere from Ambler.*

The larger part of Belgrade, 1926 *is devoted to a carefully devised and executed entrapment. In actual practice, an intelligence service would probably not go to such great lengths to recruit an agent. I tremble to think of the endless evenings spent in the boring company of two such unattractive people as Mr. and Mrs. Bulic. But then, in 1926, everybody had a lot more time.*

In the novel, Ambler's hero, the English writer Latimer, is shown the corpse of the recently defunct Dimitrios by the chief of the secret police in Istanbul, is intrigued by the mystery of the man's death and life, and sets about tracking it down. He talks to a series of people who were entangled with Dimitrios at various times, and, as frequently happens to people who dig too deeply, eventually learns more than is healthy for him. Belgrade, 1926 *finds him about midway in his researches.*

Men have learned to distrust their imaginations. It is, therefore, strange to them when they chance to discover that a world conceived in the imagination, outside experience, does exist in fact. The after-

---

FROM A *Coffin for Dimitrios.*

235

noon which Latimer spent at the Villa Acacias, listening to Wlady-slaw Grodek, he recalls as, in that sense, one of the strangest of his life. In a letter to the Greek, Marukakis, which he began that evening, while the whole thing was still fresh in his mind, he placed it on record.

Geneva,
Saturday.

MY DEAR MARUKAKIS,

I remember that I promised to write to you to let you know if I discovered anything more about Dimitrios. I wonder if you will be as surprised as I am that I have actually done so. Discovered something, I mean; for I intended to write to you in any case to thank you again for the help you gave me in Sofia.

When I left you there, I was bound, you may remember, for Belgrade. Why, then, am I writing from Geneva?

I was afraid that you would ask that question.

My dear fellow, I wish that I knew the whole answer. I know part of it. The man who employed Dimitrios in Belgrade in nineteen twenty-six, lives just outside Geneva. I can even explain how I got into touch with him. I was introduced. But just why I was introduced and just what the man who introduced us hopes to get out of it I cannot imagine. I shall, I hope, discover those things eventually. Meanwhile, let me say that if you find this mystery irritating, I find it no less so.

Did you ever believe in the existence of the "master" spy? Until to-day I most certainly did not. Now I do. The reason for this is that I have spent the greater part of today talking to one.

He is a tall, broad-shouldered man of about sixty, with thinning grey hair still tinged with the original straw colour. He has a clear complexion, bright blue eyes and steady hands—obviously, a man with few vices who has taken good care of himself. He lives in an expensive lakeside villa with two servants and a chauffeur for the Rolls. No wife in evidence. He looks like a man quietly enjoying the well-earned fruits of a blameless and worthy career. He professes to be engaged, for recreational purposes, in writing a life of St. Stephen. His nationality, I understand, was originally Polish. I may not tell you his name, so I shall call him, in the best spy-story tradition, "G."

G. was a "master" spy (he has retired now, of course) in the same sense that the printer my publisher uses is a "master" printer. He was an employer of spy labour. His work was mainly (though not entirely) administrative in character.

Now I know that a lot of nonsense is talked and written about spies and espionage, but let me try to put the question to you as G. put it to me.

He began by quoting Napoleon as saying that in war the basic element of all successful strategy was surprise.

G. is, I should say, a confirmed Napoleon-quoter. No doubt Napoleon did say that or something like it. I am quite sure he wasn't the first military leader to do so. Alexander, Caesar, Genghis Khan and Frederick of Prussia all had the same idea. In nineteen eighteen Foch thought of it, too. But to return to G.

G. says that "the experiences of the 1914–18 conflict" showed that in a future war (that sounds so beautifully distant, doesn't it?) the mobility and striking power of modern armies and navies and the existence of air forces would render the element of surprise more important than ever; so important, in fact, that it was possible that the people who got in with a surprise attack first might win the war. It was more than ever necessary to guard against surprise, to guard against it, moreover, before the war had started.

Now, there are roughly twenty-seven independent states in Europe. Each has an army and an air force and most have some sort of navy as well. For its own security, each of those armies, air forces and navies must know what each corresponding force in each of the other twenty-six countries is doing—what its strength is, what its efficiency is, what secret preparations it is making. That means spies—armies of them.

In nineteen twenty-six, G. was employed by Italy; and in the spring of that year he set up house in Belgrade.

Relations between Yugoslavia and Italy were strained at the time. The Italian seizure of Fiume was still as fresh in Yugoslav minds as the bombardment of Corfu; there were rumours, too (not unfounded as it was learned later in the year), that Mussolini contemplated occupying Albania.

Italy, on her side, was suspicious of Yugoslavia. Fiume was held under Yugoslav guns. A Yugoslav Albania alongside the Straits of Otranto was an unthinkable proposition. An independent Albania was tolerable only as long as it was under a predominantly Italian influence. It might be desirable to make certain of things. But the Yugoslavs might put up a fight. Reports from Italian agents in Belgrade indicated that in the event of war Yugoslavia intended to protect her seaboard by bottling herself up in the Adriatic with minefields lain just north of the Straits of Otranto.

I don't know much about these things, but apparently one does not have to lay a couple of hundred miles' worth of mines to make a two-hundred-miles-wide corridor of sea impassable. One just lays one or two small fields without letting one's enemy know just where. It is necessary, then, for them to find out the positions of those minefields.

That, then, was G.'s job in Belgrade. Italian agents found out about the minefields. G., the expert spy, was commissioned to do the real work of discovering where they were to be laid, without—a most important point this—without letting the Yugoslavs find out that he had done so. If they did find out, of course, they would promptly change the positions.

In that last part of his task G. failed. The reason for his failure was Dimitrios.

It has always seemed to me that a spy's job must be an extraordinarily difficult one. What I mean is this. If I were sent to Belgrade by the British Government with orders to get hold of the details of a secret mine-laying project for the Straits of Otranto, I should not even know where to start. Supposing I knew, as G. knew, that the details were recorded by means of markings on a navigational chart of the Straits. Very well. How many copies of the chart are kept? I would not know. Where are they kept? I would not know. I might reasonably suppose that at least one copy would be kept somewhere in the Ministry of Marine; but the Ministry of Marine is a large place. Moreover, the chart will almost certainly be under lock and key. And even if, as seems unlikely, I were able to find in which room it is kept and how to get to it, how would I set about obtaining a copy of it without letting the Yugoslavs know that I had done so?

When I tell you that within a month of his arrival in Belgrade, G. had not only found out where a copy of the chart was kept, but had also made up his mind how he was going to copy that copy without the Yugoslavs knowing, you will see that he is entitled to describe himself as competent.

How did he do it? What ingenious manoeuvre, what subtle trick made it possible? I shall try to break the news gently.

Posing as a German, the representative of an optical instrument-maker in Dresden, he struck up an acquaintance with a clerk in the Submarine Defence Department (which dealt with submarine nets, booms, mine-laying and mine-sweeping) of the Ministry of Marine!

Pitiful, wasn't it! The amazing thing is that he himself regards it as a very astute move. His sense of humour is quite paralysed. When I asked him if he ever read spy stories, he said that he did not, as they always seemed to him very naïve. But there is worse to come.

He struck up this acquaintance by going to the Ministry and asking the door-keeper to direct him to the Department of Supply, a perfectly normal request for an outsider to make. Having got past the door-keeper, he stopped someone in a corridor, said that he had been directed to the Submarine Defence Department and had got lost and asked to be redirected. Having got to the S.D. Department, he marched in and asked if it was the Department of Supply. They said that it was not, and out he went. He was in there not more than a minute, but in that time he had cast a quick eye over the personnel of the department, or, at all events, those of them he could see. He marked down three. That evening he waited outside the Ministry until the first of them came out. This man he followed home. Having found out his name and as much as he could about him, he repeated the process on succeeding evenings with the other two. Then he made his choice. It fell on a man named Bulic.

Now, G.'s actual methods may have lacked subtlety; but there was considerable subtlety in the way he employed them. He himself is quite oblivious of any distinction here. He is not the first successful man to misunderstand the reasons for his own success.

G.'s first piece of subtlety lay in his choice of Bulic as a tool.

Bulic was a disagreeable, conceited man of between forty and fifty, older than most of his fellow clerks and disliked by them. His wife was ten years younger than he, dissatisfied and pretty. He suffered from catarrh. He was in the habit of going to a café for a drink when he left the Ministry for the day, and it was in this café that G. made his acquaintance by the simple process of asking him for a match, offering him a cigar and, finally, buying him a drink.

You may imagine that a clerk in a government department dealing with highly confidential matters would naturally tend to be suspicious of café acquaintances who tried to pump him about his work. G. was ready to deal with those suspicions long before they had entered Bulic's head.

The acquaintance ripened. G. would be in the café every evening when Bulic entered. They would carry on a desultory conversation. G., as a stranger to Belgrade, would ask Bulic's advice about this and that. He would pay for Bulic's drinks. He let Bulic condescend to him. Sometimes they would play a game of chess. Bulic would win. At other times they would play four-pack bezique with other frequenters of the café. Then, one evening, G. told Bulic a story.

He had been told by a mutual acquaintance, he said, that he, Bulic, held an important post in the Ministry of Marine.

For Bulic the "mutual acquaintance" could have been one of several men with whom they played cards and exchanged opinions and who were vaguely aware that he worked in the Ministry. He frowned and opened his mouth. He was probably about to enter a mock-modest qualification of the adjective "important." But G. swept on. As chief salesman for a highly respectable firm of optical instrument-makers, he was deputed to obtain an order due to be placed by the Ministry of Marine for binoculars. He had submitted his quotation and had hopes of securing the order but, as Bulic would know, there was nothing like a friend at court in these affairs. If, therefore, the good and influential Bulic would bring pressure to bear to see that the Dresden company secured the order, Bulic would be in pocket to the tune of twenty thousand dinar.

Consider that proposition from Bulic's point of view. Here was he, an insignificant clerk, being flattered by the representative of a great German company and promised twenty thousand dinar for doing precisely nothing. As the quotation had already been submitted, there was nothing to be done there. It would stand its chance with the other quotations. If the Dresden company secured the order he would be twenty thousand dinar in pocket without having compromised himself in any way. If they lost it he would lose nothing except the respect of this stupid and misinformed German.

G. admits that Bulic did make a half-hearted effort to be honest. He mumbled something about his not being sure that his influence could help. This, G. chose to treat as an attempt to increase the bribe. Bulic protested that no such thought had been in his mind. He was lost. Within five minutes he had agreed.

In the days that followed, Bulic and G. became close friends. G. ran no risk. Bulic could not know that no quotation had been submitted by the Dresden company as all quotations received by the Department of Supply were confidential until the order was placed. If he were inquisitive enough to make inquiries, he would find, as G. had found by previous reference to the *Official Gazette,* that quotations for binoculars had actually been asked for by the Department of Supply.

G. now got to work.

Bulic, remember, had to play the part assigned to him by G., the part of influential official. G., furthermore, began to make himself very amiable by entertaining Bulic and the pretty but stupid Madame Bulic at expensive restaurants and night clubs. The pair responded like thirsty plants to rain. Could Bulic be cautious when, having had the best part of a bottle of sweet champagne, he found himself involved in an argument about Italy's overwhelming naval strength and her threat to Yugoslavia's seaboard? It was unlikely. He was a little drunk. His wife was present. For the first time in his dreary life, his judgment was being treated with the deference due to it. Besides, he had his part to play. It would not do to seem to be ignorant of what was going on behind the scenes. He began to brag. He himself had seen the very plans that in operation would immobilize Italy's fleet in the Adriatic. Naturally, he had to be discreet, but . . .

By the end of that evening G. knew that Bulic had access to a copy of the chart. He had also made up his mind that Bulic was going to get that copy for him.

He made his plans carefully. Then he looked round for a suitable man to carry them out. He needed a go-between. He found Dimitrios.

Just how G. came to hear of Dimitrios is not clear. I fancy that he was anxious not to compromise any of his old associates. One can conceive that his reticence might be understandable. Anyway, Dimitrios was recommended to him. I asked in what business the recommender was engaged; but G. became vague. It was so very long ago. But he remembered the verbal testimonial which accompanied the recommendation.

Dimitrios Talat was a Greek-speaking Turk with an "effective" passport and a reputation for being "useful" and at the same time discreet. He was also said to have had experience in "financial work of a confidential nature."

If one did not happen to know just what he was useful for and the nature of the financial work he had done, one might have supposed that the man under discussion was some sort of accountant. But there is, it seems, a jargon in these affairs. G. understood it and decided that Dimitrios was the man for the job in hand.

Dimitrios arrived in Belgrade five days later and presented himself at G.'s house just off the Knez Miletina.

G. remembers the occasion very well. Dimitrios, he says, was a man of medium height who might have been almost any age between thirty-five and fifty—he was actually thirty-seven. He was smartly dressed and . . . But I had better quote G.'s own words:

"He was chic in an expensive way, and his hair was becoming grey at the sides of his head. He had a sleek, satisfied, confident air and something about the eyes that I recognized immediately. The man was a pimp. I can always recognize it. Do not ask me how. I have a woman's instinct for these things."

So there you have it. Dimitrios had prospered. Had there been any more Madame Prevezas?* We shall never know. At all events, G. detected the pimp in Dimitrios and was not displeased. A pimp, he reasoned, could be relied upon not to fool about with women to the detriment of the business in hand. Also Dimitrios was of pleasing address. I think that I had better quote G. again:

---

* A woman whom Latimer had consulted about Dimitrios in an earlier episode.

"He could wear his clothes gracefully. Also he looked intelligent. I was pleased by this because I did not care to employ riff-raff from the gutters. Sometimes it was necessary but I never liked it. They did not always understand my curious temperament."

G., you see, was fussy.

Dimitrios had not wasted his time. He could now speak both German and French with reasonable accuracy. He said:

"I came as soon as I received your letter. I was busy in Bucharest but I was glad to get your letter as I had heard of you."

G. explained carefully and with circumspection (it did not do to give too much away to a prospective employee) what he wanted done. Dimitrios listened unemotionally. When G. had finished, he asked how much he was to be paid.

"Thirty thousand dinar," said G.

"Fifty thousand," said Dimitrios, "and I would prefer to have it in Swiss francs."

They compromised on forty thousand to be paid in Swiss francs. Dimitrios smiled and shrugged his agreement.

It was the man's eyes when he smiled, says G., that first made him distrust his new employee.

I found that odd. Could it be that there was honour among scoundrels, that G., being the man he was and knowing (up to a point) the sort of man Dimitrios was, would yet need a smile to awaken distrust? Incredible. But there was no doubt that he remembered those eyes very vividly. Preveza remembered them, too, didn't she? "Brown, anxious eyes that made you think of a doctor's eyes when he is doing something to you that hurts." That was it, wasn't it? My theory is that it was not until Dimitrios smiled that G. realized the quality of the man whose services he had bought. "He had the appearance of being tame but when you looked into his brown eyes you saw that he had none of the feelings that make ordinary men soft, that he was always dangerous." Preveza again. Did G. sense the same thing? He may not have explained it to himself in that way—he is not the sort of man to set much store by feelings—but I think he may have wondered if he had made a mistake in employing Dimitrios. Their two minds were not so very dissimilar and that sort of wolf prefers to hunt alone. At all events, G. decided to keep a wary eye on Dimitrios.

Meanwhile, Bulic was finding life more pleasant than it had ever been before. He was being entertained at rich places. His wife, warmed by unfamiliar luxury, no longer looked at him with contempt and distaste in her eyes. With the money they saved on the meals provided by the stupid German she could drink her favourite cognac;

and when she drank she became friendly and agreeable. In a week's time, moreover, he might become the possessor of twenty thousand dinar. There was a chance. He felt very well, he said one night, and added that cheap food was bad for his catarrh. That was the nearest he came to forgetting to play his part.

The order for the binoculars was given to a Czech firm. The *Official Gazette*, in which the fact was announced, was published at noon. At one minute past noon, G. had a copy and was on his way to an engraver on whose bench lay a half-finished copper die. By six o'clock he was waiting opposite the entrance to the Ministry. Soon after six, Bulic appeared. He had seen the *Official Gazette*. A copy was under his arm. His dejection was visible from where G. stood. G. began to follow him.

Ordinarily, Bulic would have crossed the road before many minutes had passed, to get to his café. To–night he hesitated and then walked straight on. He was not anxious to meet the man from Dresden.

G. turned down a side street and hailed a taxi. Within two minutes his taxi had made a detour and was approaching Bulic. Suddenly, he signalled to the driver to stop, bounded out on to the pavement and embraced Bulic delightedly. Before the bewildered clerk could protest, he was bundled into the taxi and G. was pouring congratulations and thanks into his ear and pressing a cheque for twenty thousand dinar into his hand.

"But I thought you'd lost the order," mumbles Bulic at last.

G. laughs as if at a huge joke. "Lost it!" And then he "understands." "Of course! I forgot to tell you. The quotation was submitted through a Czech subsidiary of ours. Look, does this explain it?" He thrusts one of the newly printed cards into Bulic's hand. "I don't use this card often. Most people know that these Czechs are owned by our company in Dresden." He brushes the matter aside. "But we must have a drink immediately. Driver!"

That night they celebrated. His first bewilderment over, Bulic took full advantage of the situation. He became drunk. He began to brag of the potency of his influence in the Ministry until even G., who had every reason for satisfaction, was hard put to it to remain civil.

But towards the end of the evening, he drew Bulic aside. Estimates, he said, had been invited for rangefinders. Could he, Bulic, assist? Of course he could. And now Bulic became cunning. Now that the value of his co-operation had been established, he had a right to expect something on account.

G. had not anticipated this, but, secretly amused, he agreed at once. Bulic received another cheque; this time it was for ten thousand dinar. The understanding was that he should be paid a further ten thousand when the order was placed with G.'s "employers."

Bulic was now wealthier than ever before. He had thirty thousand dinar. Two evenings later, in the supper room of a fashionable hotel, G. introduced him to a Freiherr von Kiessling. The Freiherr von Kiessling's other name was, needless to say, Dimitrios.

"You would have thought," says G., "that he had been living in such places all his life. For all I know, he may have been doing so. His manner was perfect. When I introduced Bulic as an important official in the Ministry of Marine, he condescended magnificently. With Madame Bulic he was superb. He might have been greeting a princess. But I saw the way his fingers moved across the palm of her hand as he bent to kiss the back of it."

Dimitrios had displayed himself in the supper room before G. had affected to claim acquaintance with him in order to give G. time to prepare the ground. The "Freiherr," G. told the Bulics after he had drawn their attention to Dimitrios, was a very important man. Something of a mystery, perhaps; but a very important factor in international big business. He was enormously rich and was believed to control as many as twenty-seven companies. He might be a useful man to know.

The Bulics were enchanted to be presented to him. When the "Freiherr" agreed to drink a glass of champagne at their table, they felt themselves honoured indeed. In their halting German they strove to make themselves agreeable. This, Bulic must have felt, was what he had been waiting for all his life: at last he was in touch with the people who counted, the real people, the people who made men and broke them, the people who might make him. Perhaps he saw himself a director of one of the "Freiherr"'s companies, with a fine house and others dependent on him, loyal servants who would respect him as a man as well as a master. When, the next morning, he went to his stool in the Ministry, there must have been joy in his heart, joy made all the sweeter by the faint misgivings, the slight prickings of conscience which could so easily be stilled. After all, G. had received his money's worth. He, Bulic, had nothing to lose. Besides, you never knew what might come of it all. Men had taken stranger paths to fortune.

The "Freiherr" had been good enough to say that he would have supper with Herr G. and his two charming friends two evenings later.

I questioned G. about this. Would it not have been better to have struck while the iron was hot? Two days gave the Bulics time to think. "Precisely," was G.'s reply; "time to think of the good things to come, to prepare themselves for the feast, to dream." He became preternaturally solemn at the thought and then, grinning, suddenly quoted Goethe at me. *"Ach! warum, ihr Götter, ist unendlich, alles, alles, endlich unser Glück nur?"* G., you see, lays claim to a sense of humour.

That supper was the critical moment for him. Dimitrios got to work on Madame. It was such a pleasure to meet such pleasant people as Madame—and, of course, her husband. She—and her husband, naturally—must certainly come and stay with him in Bavaria next month. He preferred it to his Paris house and Cannes was sometimes chilly in the spring. Madame would enjoy Bavaria; and so, no doubt, would her husband. That was, if he could tear himself away from the Ministry.

Crude, simple stuff, no doubt; but the Bulics were crude, simple people. Madame lapped it up with her sweet champagne while Bulic became sulky. Then the great moment arrived.

The flower girl stopped by the table with her tray of orchids. Dimitrios turned round and, selecting the largest and most expensive bloom, handed it with a little flourish to Madame Bulic with a request that she accept it as a token of his esteem. Madame would accept it. Dimitrios drew out his wallet to pay. The next moment a thick wad of thousand-dinar notes fell from his breast pocket on to the table.

With a word of apology Dimitrios put the money back in his pocket. G., taking his cue, remarked that it was rather a lot of money to carry in one's pocket and asked if the "Freiherr" always carried as much. No, he did not. He had won the money at Alesandro's earlier in the evening and had forgotten to leave it upstairs in his room. Did Madame know Alessandro's? She did not. Both the Bulics were silent as the "Freiherr" talked on: they had never see so much money before. In the "Freiherr"'s opinion Alessandro's was the most reliable gambling place in Belgrade. It was your own luck not the croupier's skill that mattered at Alessandro's. Personally he was having a run of luck that evening—this with velvety eyes on Madame—and had won a little more than usual. He hesitated at that point. And then: "As you have never been in the place, I should be delighted if you would accompany me as my guests later."

Of course, they went; and, of course, they were expected and preparations had been made. Dimitrios had arranged everything. No roulette—it is difficult to cheat a man at roulette—but there was trente et quarante. The minimum stake was two hundred and fifty dinar.

They had drinks and watched the play for a time. Then G. decided that he would play a little. They watched him win twice. Then the

"Freiherr" asked Madame if she would like to play. She looked at her husband. He said, apologetically, that he had very little money with him. But Dimitrios was ready for that. No trouble at all, Herr Bulic! He personally was well known to Alessandro. Any friend of his could be accommodated. If he should happen to lose a few dinar, Alessandro would take a cheque or a note.

The farce went on. Alessandro was summoned and introduced. The situation was explained to him. He raised protesting hands. Any friend of the "Freiherr" need not even ask such a thing. Besides, he had not yet played. Time to talk of such things if he had a little bad luck.

G. thinks that if Dimitrios had allowed the two to talk to one another for even a moment, they would not have played. Two hundred and fifty dinar was the minimum stake, and not even the possession of thirty thousand could overcome their consciousness of the value in terms of food and rent of two hundred and fifty. But Dimitrios did not give them a chance to exchange misgivings. Instead, as they were waiting at the table behind G.'s chair, he murmured to Bulic that if he, Bulic, had time, he, the "Freiherr," would like to talk business with him over luncheon one day that week.

It was beautifully timed. It could, I feel, have meant only one thing to Bulic: "My dear Bulic, there really is no need for you to concern yourself over a paltry few hundred dinar. I am interested in you, and that means that your fortune is made. Please do not disappoint me by showing yourself less important than you seem now."

Madame Bulic began to play.

Her first two hundred and fifty she lost on couleur. The second won on inverse. Then, Dimitrios, advising greater caution, suggested that she play a cheval. There was a refait and then a second refait. Ultimately she lost again.

At the end of an hour the five thousand dinar's worth of chips she had been given had gone. Dimitrios, sympathizing with her for her "bad luck," pushed across some five-hundred-dinar chips from a pile in front of him and begged that she would play with them "for luck."

The tortured Bulic may have had the idea that these were a gift, for he made only the faintest sound of protest. That they had not been a gift he was presently to discover. Madame Bulic, thoroughly miserable now and becoming a little untidy, played on. She won a little; she lost more. At half past two Bulic signed a promissory note to Alessandro for twelve thousand dinar. G. bought them a drink.

It is easy to picture the scene between the Bulics when at last they were alone—the recriminations, the tears, the interminable arguments

—only too easy. Yet, bad as things were, the gloom was not unrelieved; for Bulic was to lunch the following day with the "Freiherr." And they were to talk business.

They did talk business. Dimitrios had been told to be encouraging. No doubt he was. Hints of big deals afoot, of opportunities for making fabulous sums for those who were in the know, talk of castles in Bavaria—it would all be there. Bulic had only to listen and let his heart beat faster. What did twelve thousand dinar matter? You had to think in millions.

All the same, it was Dimitrios who raised the subject of his guest's debt to Alessandro. He supposed that Bulic would be going along that very night to settle it. He personally would be playing again. One could not, after all, win so much without giving Alessandro a chance to lose some more. Supposing that they went along together—just the two of them. Women were bad gamblers.

When they met that night Bulic had nearly thirty-five thousand dinar in his pocket. He must have added his savings to G.'s thirty thousand. When Dimitrios reported to G.—in the early hours of the following morning—he said that Bulic had, in spite of Alessandro's protests, insisted on redeeming his promissory note before he started to play. "I pay my debts," he told Dimitrios proudly. The balance of the money he spent, with a flourish, on five-hundred-dinar chips. Tonight he was going to make a killing. He refused a drink. He meant to keep a cool head.

G. grinned at this and perhaps he was wise to do so. Pity is sometimes too uncomfortable; and I do find Bulic pitiable. You may say that he was a weak fool. So he was. But Providence is never quite as calculating as were G. and Dimitrios. It may bludgeon away at a man, but it never feels between his ribs with a knife. Bulic had no chance. They understood him and used their understanding with devilish skill. With the cards as neatly stacked against me as they were against him, I should perhaps be no less weak, no less foolish. It is a comfort to me to believe that the occasion is unlikely to arise.

Inevitably he lost. He began to play with just over forty chips. It took him two hours of winning and losing to get rid of them. Then, quite calmly, he took another twenty on credit. He said that his luck must change. The poor wretch did not even suspect that he might be being cheated. Why should he suspect? The "Freiherr" was losing even more than he was. He doubled his stakes and survived for forty minutes. He borrowed again and lost again. He had lost thirty-eight thousand dinar more than he had in the world when, white and sweating, he decided to stop.

After that it was plain sailing for Dimitrios. The following night Bulic returned. They let him win thirty thousand back. The third night he lost another fourteen thousand. On the fourth night, when he was about twenty-five thousand in debt, Alessandro asked for his money. Bulic promised to redeem his notes within a week. The first person to whom he went for help was G.

G. was sympathetic. Twenty-five thousand was a lot of money, wasn't it? Of course, any money he used in connection with orders received was his employers', and he was not empowered to do what he liked with it. But he himself could spare two hundred and fifty for a few days if it were any help. He would have liked to do more, but . . . Bulic took the two hundred and fifty.

With it G. gave him a word of advice. The "Freiherr" was the man to get him out of his difficulty. He never lent money—with him it was a question of principle, he believed—but he had a reputation for helping his friends by putting them in the way of earning quite substantial sums. Why not have a talk with him?

The "talk" between Bulic and Dimitrios took place after a dinner for which Bulic paid and in the "Freiherr"'s hotel sitting-room. G. was out of sight in the adjoining bedroom.

When Bulic at last got to the point, he asked about Alessandro. Would he insist on his money? What would happen if he were not paid?

Dimitrios affected surprise. There was no question, he hoped, of Alessandro's not being paid. After all, it was on his personal recommendation that Alessandro had given credit in the first place. He would not like there to be any unpleasantness. What sort of unpleasantness? Well, Alessandro held the promissory notes and could take the matter to the police. He hoped sincerely that that would not happen.

Bulic was hoping so, too. Now, he had everything to lose, including his post at the Ministry. It might even come out that he had taken money from G. That might even mean prison. Would they believe that he had done nothing in return for those thirty thousand dinar? It was madness to expect them to do so. His only chance was to get the money from the "Freiherr"—somehow.

To his pleas for a loan Dimitrios shook his head. No. That would simply make matters worse, for then he would owe the money to a friend instead of to an enemy; besides, it was a matter of principle with him. At the same time, he wanted to help. There was just one way; but would Herr Bulic feel disposed to take it? That was the question. He scarcely liked to mention the matter; but, since Herr

Bulic pressed him, he knew of certain persons who were interested in obtaining some information from the Ministry of Marine that could not be obtained through the usual channels. They could probably be persuaded to pay as much as fifty thousand dinar for this information if they could rely upon its being accurate.

G. said that he attributed quite a lot of the success of his plan (he deems it successful in the same way that a surgeon deems an operation successful when the patient leaves the operating theatre alive) to his careful use of figures. Every sum from the original twenty thousand dinar to the amounts of the successive debts to Alessandro (who was an Italian agent) and the final amount offered by Dimitrios was carefully calculated with an eye to its psychological value. That final fifty thousand, for example. Its appeal to Bulic was two-fold. It would pay off his debt and still leave him with nearly as much as he had had before he met the "Freiherr." To the incentive of fear they added that of greed.

But Bulic did not give in immediately. When he heard exactly what the information was, he became frightened and angry. The anger was dealt with very efficiently by Dimitrios. If Bulic had begun to entertain doubts about the bona fides of the "Freiherr" those doubts were now made certainties; for when he shouted "dirty spy," the "Freiherr"'s easy charm deserted him. Bulic was kicked in the abdomen and then, as he bent forward retching, in the face. Gasping for breath and with pain and bleeding at the mouth, he was flung into a chair while Dimitrios explained coldly that the only risk he ran was in not doing as he was told.

His instructions were simple. Bulic was to get a copy of the chart and bring it to the hotel when he left the Ministry the following evening. An hour later the chart would be returned to him to replace in the morning. That was all. He would be paid when he brought the chart. He was warned of the consequences to himself if he should decide to go to the authorities with his story, reminded of the fifty thousand that awaited him and dismissed.

He duly returned the following night with the chart folded in four under his coat. Dimitrios took the chart in to G. and returned to keep watch on Bulic while it was photographed and the negative developed. Apparently Bulic had nothing to say. When G. had finished he took the money and the chart from Dimitrios and went without a word.

G. says that in the bedroom at that moment, when he heard the door close behind Bulic and as he held the negative up to the light, he was feeling very pleased with himself. Expenses had been low; there had been no wasted effort; there had been no tiresome delays; everybody, even Bulic, had done well out of the business. It only remained to hope that Bulic would restore the chart safely. There was really no reason why he should not do so. A very satisfactory affair from every point of view.

And then Dimitrios came into the room.

It was at that moment that G. realized that he had made one mistake.

"My wages," said Dimitrios, and held out his hand.

G. met his employee's eyes and nodded. He needed a gun and he had not got one. "We'll go to my house now," he said and started towards the door.

Dimitrios shook his head deliberately. "My wages are in your pocket."

"Not your wages. Only mine."

Dimitrios produced a revolver. A smile played about his lips. "What I want is in your pocket, mein Herr. Put your hands behind your head."

G. obeyed. Dimitrios walked towards him. G., looking steadily into those brown anxious eyes, saw that he was in danger. Two feet in front of him Dimitrios stopped. "Please be careful, mein Herr."

The smile disappeared. Dimitrios stepped forward suddenly and, jamming his revolver into G.'s stomach, snatched the negative from G.'s pocket with his free hand. Then, as suddenly, he stood back. "You may go," he said.

G. went. Dimitrios, in turn, had made his mistake.

All that night men, hastily recruited from the criminal cafés, scoured Belgrade for Dimitrios. But Dimitrios had disappeared. G. never saw him again.

What happened to the negative? Let me give you G.'s own words:

"When the morning came and my men had failed to find him, I knew what I must do. I felt very bitter. After all my careful work it was most disappointing. But there was nothing else for it. I had known for a week that Dimitrios had got into touch with a French agent. The negative would be in that agent's hands by now. I really had no choice. A friend of mine in the German Embassy was able to oblige me. The Germans were anxious to please Belgrade at the time. What more natural than that they should pass on an item of information interesting to the Yugoslav government?"

"Do you mean," I said, "that you deliberately arranged for the Yugoslav authorities to be informed of the removal of the chart and of the fact that it had been photographed?"

"Unfortunately, it was the only thing I could do. You see, I had to render the chart worthless. It was really very foolish of Dimitrios to let me go; but he was inexperienced. He probably thought that I would blackmail Bulic into bringing the chart out again. But I realized that I would not be paid much for bringing in information already in the possession of the French. Besides, my reputation would have suffered. I was very bitter about the whole affair. The only amusing aspect of it was that the French had paid over to Dimitrios half the agreed price for the chart before they discovered that the information on it had been rendered obsolete by my little *démarche*."

"What about Bulic?"

G. pulled a face. "Yes, I was sorry about that. I always have felt a certain responsibility towards those who work for me. He was arrested almost at once. There was no doubt as to which of the Ministry copies had been used. They were kept rolled in metal cylinders. Bulic had folded this one to bring it out of the Ministry. It was the only one with creases in it. His finger-prints did the rest. Very wisely he told the authorities all he knew about Dimitrios. As a result they sent him to prison for life instead of shooting him. I quite expected him to implicate me, but he did not. I was a little surprised. After all it was I who introduced him to Dimitrios. I wondered at the time whether it was because he was unwilling to face an additional charge of accepting bribes or because he felt grateful to me for lending him that two hundred and fifty dinar. Probably he did not connect me with the business of the chart at all. In any case, I was pleased. I still had work to do in Belgrade, and being wanted by the police, even under another name, might have complicated my life. I have never been able to bring myself to wear disguises."

I asked him one more question. Here is his answer:

"Oh, yes, I obtained the new charts as soon as they had been made. In quite a different way, of course. With so much of my money invested in the enterprise I could not return empty-handed. It is always the same: for one reason or another there are always these delays, these wastages of effort and money. You may say that I was careless in my handling of Dimitrios. That would be unjust. It was a small error of judgment on my part, that is all. I counted on his being like all the other fools in the world, on his being too greedy; I thought he would wait until he had had from me the forty thousand dinar due to him before he tried to take the photograph as well. He took me by surprise. That error of judgment cost me a lot of money."

"It cost Bulic his liberty." I am afraid I said it a trifle stuffily, for he frowned.

"My dear Monsieur Latimer," he retorted, "Bulic was a traitor and he was rewarded according to his deserts. One cannot sentimentalize over him. In war there are always casualties. Bulic was very lucky. I would certainly have used him again, and he might ultimately have been shot. As it was, he went to prison. For all I know he is still in prison. I do not wish to seem callous, but I must say that he is better off there. His liberty? Rubbish! He had none to lose. As for his wife, I have no doubt that she has done better for herself. She always gave me the impression of wanting to do so. I do not blame her. He was an objectionable man. I seem to remember that he tended to dribble as he ate. What is more, he was a nuisance. You would have thought, would you not, that on leaving Dimitrios that evening he would have gone there and then to Alessandro to pay his debt? He did not do so. When he was arrested late the following day he still had the fifty thousand dinar in his pocket. More waste. It is at times like those, my friend, that one needs one's sense of humour."

Well, my dear Marukakis, that is all. It is, I think, more than enough. For me, wandering among the ghosts of old lies, there is comfort in the thought that you might write to me and tell me that all this was worth finding out. You might. For myself, I begin to wonder. It is such a poor story, isn't it? There is no hero, no heroine; only villains and fools.

We shall, I hope, meet again very soon. *Croyez en mes meilleurs souvenirs.*

CHARLES LATIMER

VII. *Spit and Image*

It would be interesting to count up how many hundreds of times the device of accidental physical resemblance has been used as the mainspring of a spy plot and to note what different changes can be rung on it. Dickens, of course, uses it in *A Tale of Two Cities* where the coincidental likeness of Sydney Carton and Charles Darnay enables the one man to go to the guillotine in place of the other. John Buchan uses it in *The Thirty-nine Steps* when a German villain manages to gain access to a top-level secret meeting of British Cabinet members by impersonating the First Sea Lord. The advent of plastic surgery has widened the possibilities (and supported the credibility of the scheme). In a recent American spy novel, *The Man in the Mirror*, by Frederick Ayer, Jr., the author went for high stakes and based a full-length thriller on the idea that the Soviets, with the aid of a little plastic surgery, could substitute an agent for the Security Adviser to the President of the United States and succeed by this in penetrating the highest secret councils.

In the excerpts which follow there is no resort to plastic surgery. We are asked to believe that nature sometimes turns out two models which are twins and that an astute intelligence service discovers this and makes use of it. All you have to do is accept that possibility and we are on our way. Merely in passing and with no intention of spoiling the fun, I would say that no intelligence service, to the best of my knowledge, has ever based any serious long-range operation on such an arrangement, although the use of doubles to impersonate well-known public figures has been standard practice, particularly in wartime, in order to safeguard their persons.

▼

1 A Problem of Identity

I would give The Great Impersonation, *by E. Phillips Oppenheim, the prize for cleverness among all novels about espionage, and that includes all of them written since he wrote this one in 1920. As the title explains, we are asked to accept as the basis for the whole plot the physical substitution of one person for another, an arrangement which in Oppenheim's hands keeps us up in the air through a hundred risky episodes until the final revelation in the last chapter all but floors us. You must only believe that the dissolute English nobleman Sir Everard Dominey, who is going to rack and ruin in darkest Africa, is the spit and image of the German Major General Baron Leopold von Ragastein, governor of a German colony in Africa, who was educated in England and speaks English so well that he can pass for a native.*

The period is that just preceding the outbreak of World War I. Knowing that in case of war the German espionage network in England will eventually come to grief, the German Intelligence Service, under the direct command of the Kaiser himself, conceives the plan of secretly doing away with Dominey in Africa and sending Ragastein to England to impersonate him. If Ragastein succeeds in becoming accepted as Dominey, the Germans will have an agent in the highest circles in Britain who can safely ride out the war.

There are numerous complications and difficulties. Dominey has a wife, Rosamund, suffering from mental illness. She must accept Ragastein as her husband, Dominey. Ragastein has a mistress, the Hungarian Princess Stephanie Eiderstrom. She happens to be in England and must be brought in on the secret that

---

FROM *The Great Impersonation.*

Ragastein has taken on Dominey's identity. The other people who know the secret are the German Ambassador Prince Terniloff and Mr. Seaman, a member of the German Secret Service who is assigned as an aide to Ragastein for this operation. To avoid too much confusion, Ragastein is referred to as Dominey throughout the major part of the novel, since this is the person he has become.

The long excerpt which follows is from the dead center of the story at a time when Ragastein has succeeded almost completely in assuming the role of Dominey except to Dominey's wife, Rosamund, who finds him such an improvement over the alcoholic and unreliable husband she knew before that she does not believe he can have changed so. The scene is a shooting party at Dominey's estate, where all the persons I have mentioned and a number of others are present, including a mysterious stranger, Ludwig Miller, whose secret message to Ragastein, alias Dominey, begins to upset the applecart. All the threads of the story are drawn together here. While we see Rosamund, the wife, suspecting that Dominey is not Dominey, we also see Stephanie suspecting that Ragastein is not Ragastein. With this one hint Oppenheim points to the main secret which he keeps until the end. After giving it to us, he covers his tracks. Perhaps I should add that the playboy, Eddy Pelham, is really an officer of British Intelligence and is responsible for the disappearance of Mr. Ludwig Miller.

There was nothing in the least alarming about the appearance of Mr. Ludwig Miller. He had been exceedingly well entertained in the butler's private sitting-room and had the air of having done full justice to the hospitality which had been offered him. He rose to his feet at Dominey's entrance and stood at attention. But for some slight indications of military training, he would have passed anywhere as a highly respectable retired tradesman.

"Sir Everard Dominey?" he enquired.

Dominey nodded assent. "That is my name. Have I seen you before?"

The man shook his head. "I am a cousin of Doctor Schmidt. I arrived in the Colony from Rhodesia, after your Excellency had left."

"And how is the doctor?"

"My cousin is, as always, busy but in excellent health," was the reply. "He sends his respectful compliments and his good wishes. Also this letter."

With a little flourish the man produced an envelope inscribed:

To Sir Everard Dominey, Baronet,
    Dominey Hall,
       In the County of Norfolk,
         England.

Dominey broke the seal just as Seaman entered.

"A messenger here from Doctor Schmidt, an acquaintance of mine in East Africa," he announced. "Mr. Seaman came home from South Africa with me," he explained to his visitor.

The two men looked steadily into each other's eyes. Dominey watched them, fascinated. Neither betrayed himself by even the fall of an eyelid. Yet Dominey, his perceptive powers at their very keenest in this moment which instinct told him was one of crisis, felt the unspoken, unbetokened recognition which passed between them. Some commonplace remark was uttered and responded to. Dominey read the few lines which seemed to take him back for a moment to another world:

HONOURED AND HONOURABLE SIR,

I send you my heartiest and most respectful greeting. Of the progress of all matters here you will learn from another source.

I recommend to your notice and kindness my cousin, the bearer of this letter—Mr. Ludwig Miller. He will lay before you certain circumstances of which it is advisable for you to have knowledge. You may speak freely with him. He is in all respects to be trusted.

[Signed] KARL SCHMIDT.

"Your cousin is a little mysterious," Dominey remarked, as he passed the letter to Seaman. "Come, what about these circumstances?"

Ludwig Miller looked around the little room and then at Seaman. Dominey affected to misunderstand his hesitation.

"Our friend here knows everything," he declared. "You can speak to him as to myself."

The man began as one who has a story to tell.

"My errand here is to warn you," he said, "that the Englishman whom you left for dead at Big Bend, on the banks of the Blue River, has been heard of in another part of Africa."

Dominey shook his head incredulously. "I hope you have not come all this way to tell me that! The man was dead."

"My cousin himself," Miller continued, "was hard to convince. The man left his encampment with whisky enough to kill him, thirst enough to drink it all, and no food."

"So I found him," Dominey assented, "deserted by his boys and raving. To silence him forever was a child's task."

"The task, however, was unperformed," the other persisted. "From three places in the Colony he has been heard of, struggling to make his way to the coast."

"Does he call himself by his own name?" Dominey asked.

"He does not," Miller admitted. "My cousin, however, desired me to point out to you the fact that in any case he would probably be shy of doing so. He is behaving in an absurd manner; he is in a very weakly state; and without a doubt he is to some degree insane. Nevertheless, the fact remains that he is in the Colony, or was three months ago, and that if he succeeds in reaching the coast you may at any time be surprised by a visit from him here. I am sent to warn you in order that you may take what steps may be necessary and not be placed at a disadvantage if he should appear."

"This is queer news you have brought us, Miller," Seaman said thoughtfully.

"It is news which greatly disturbed Doctor Schmidt," the man replied. "He has had the natives up one after the other for cross-examination. Nothing can shake their story."

"If we believed it," Seaman continued, "this other European, if he had business in this direction, might walk in here at any moment."

"It was to warn you of that possibility that I am here."

"How much do you know personally," Seaman asked, "of the existent circumstances?"

The man shook his head vaguely.

"I know nothing," he admitted. "I went out to East Africa some years ago, and I have been a trader in Mozambique in a small way. I supplied outfits for officers and hospitals and sportsmen. Now and then I have to return to Europe to buy fresh stock. Doctor Schmidt knew that, and he came to see me just before I sailed. He first thought of writing a very long letter. Afterwards he changed his mind. He wrote only those few lines I brought, but he told me those other things."

"You have remembered all that he told you?" Dominey asked.

"I can think of nothing else," was the reply, after a moment's pause. "The whole affair has been a great worry to Doctor Schmidt. There are things connected with it which he has never understood, things connected with it which he has always found mysterious."

"Hence your presence here, Johann Wolff, eh?" Seaman asked, in an altered tone.

The visitor's expression remained unchanged except for the faint surprise which shone out of his blue eyes.

"Johann Wolff," he repeated. "That is not my name. I am Ludwig Miller, and I know nothing of this matter beyond what I have told you. I am just a messenger."

"Once in Vienna and twice in Cracow, my friend, we have met," Seaman reminded him softly but very insistently.

The other shook his head gently. "A mistake. I have been in Vienna once, many years ago, but Cracow never."

"You have no idea with whom you are talking?"

"Herr Seaman was the name, I understood."

"It is a very good name," Seaman scoffed. "Look here and think."

He undid his coat and waistcoat and displayed a plain vest of chamois leather. Attached to the left-hand side of it was a bronze decoration, with lettering and a number. Miller stared at it blankly and shook his head.

"Information Department, Bureau Twelve, password—'The Day is coming,'" Seaman continued, dropping his voice.

His listener shook his head and smiled with the puzzled ignorance of a child.

"The gentleman mistakes me for some one else," he replied. "I know nothing of these things."

Seaman sat and studied this obstinate visitor for several minutes without speaking, his finger tips pressed together, his eyebrows gently contracted. His vis-à-vis endured this scrutiny without flinching, calm, phlegmatic, the very prototype of the bourgeois German of the tradesman class.

"Do you propose," Dominey enquired, "to stay in these parts long?"

"One or two days—a week, perhaps," was the indifferent answer. "I have a cousin in Norwich who makes toys. I love the English country. I spend my holiday here, perhaps."

"Just so," Seaman muttered grimly. "The English country under a foot of snow! So you have nothing more to say to me, Johann Wolff?"

"I have executed my mission to his Excellency," was the apologetic reply. "I am sorry to have caused displeasure to you, Herr Seaman."

The latter rose to his feet. Dominey had already turned towards the door.

"You will spend the night here, of course, Mr. Miller?" he invited. "I dare say Mr. Seaman would like to have another talk with you in the morning."

"I shall gladly spend the night here, your Excellency," was the polite reply. "I do not think that I have anything to say, however, which would interest your friend."

"You are making a great mistake, Wolff," Seaman declared angrily.

"I am your superior in the Service, and your attitude towards me is indefensible."

"If the gentleman would only believe," the culprit begged, "that he is mistaking me for some one else!"

There was trouble in Seaman's face as the two men made their way to the front of the house and trouble in his tone as he answered his companion's query.

"What do you think of that fellow and his visit?"

"I do not know yet what to think, but there is a great deal that I know," Seaman replied gravely. "The man is a spy, a favourite in the Wilhelmstrasse and only made use of on important occasions. His name is Wolff—Johann Wolff."

"And this story of his?"

"You ought to be the best judge of that."

"I am," Dominey assented confidently. "Without the shadow of a doubt I threw the body of the man I killed into the Blue River and watched it sink."

"Then the story is a fake," Seaman decided. "For some reason or other we have come under the suspicion of our own secret service."

Seaman, as they emerged into the hall, was summoned imperiously to her side by the Princess Eiderstrom. Dominey disappeared for a moment and returned presently, having discarded some of his soaked shooting garments. He was followed by his valet, bearing a note upon a silver tray.

"From the person in Mr. Parkins' room—to Mr. Seaman, sir," the man announced in a low tone.

Dominey took it from the salver with a little nod. Then he turned to where the youngest and most frivolous of his guests was in the act of rising from the tea table.

"A game of pills, Eddy," he proposed. "They tell me that pool is one of your great accomplishments."

"I'm pretty useful," the young man confessed, with a satisfied chuckle. "Give you a black at snooker, what?"

Dominey took his arm and led him into the billiard-room.

"You will give me nothing, young fellow," he replied. "Set them up, and I will show you how I made a living for two months at Johannesburg!"

The evening at Dominey Hall was practically a repetition of the previous one, with a different set of guests from the outer world. After dinner, Dominey was absent for a few minutes and returned with Rosamund upon his arm. She received the congratulations of her neighbours charmingly, and a little court soon gathered around her. Doctor Harrison, who had been dining, remained upon its outskirts, listening to her light-hearted and at times almost brilliant chatter with grave and watchful interest. Dominey, satisfied that she was being entertained, obeyed Terniloff's gestured behest and strolled with him to a distant corner of the hall.

"Let me now, my dear host," the Prince began, with some eagerness in his tone, "continue and, I trust, conclude the conversation to which all that I said this morning was merely the prelude."

"I am entirely at your service," murmured his host.

"I have tried to make you understand that from my own point of view—and I am in a position to know something—the fear of war between this country and our own has passed. England is willing to make all reasonable sacrifices to ensure peace. She wants peace, she intends peace, therefore there will be peace. Therefore, I maintain, my young friend, it is better for you to disappear at once from this false position."

"I am scarcely my own master," Dominey replied. "You yourself must know that. I am here as a servant under orders."

"Join your protest with mine," the Prince suggested. "I will make a report directly I get back to London. To my mind, the matter is urgent. If anything should lead to the discovery of your false position in this country, the friendship between us which has become a real pleasure to me must seriously undermine my own position."

Dominey had risen to his feet and was standing on the hearthrug, in front of a fire of blazing logs. The Ambassador was sitting with crossed legs in a comfortable easy-chair, smoking one of the long, thin cigars which were his particular fancy.

"Your Excellency," Dominey said, "there is just one fallacy in all that you have said."

"A fallacy?"

"You have come to the absolute conclusion," Dominey continued, "that because England wants peace there will be peace. I am of Seaman's mind. I believe in the ultimate power of the military party of Germany. I believe that in time they will thrust their will upon the Kaiser, if he is not at the present moment secretly in league with them. Therefore, I believe that there will be war."

"If I shared that belief with you, my friend," the Ambassador said quietly, "I should consider my position here one of dishonour. My mandate is for peace, and my charge is from the Kaiser's lips."

Stephanie, with the air of one a little weary of the conversation, broke away from a distant group and came towards them. Her beautiful eyes seemed tired, she moved listlessly, and she even spoke with less than her usual assurance.

"Am I disturbing a serious conversation?" she asked. "Send me away if I am."

"His Excellency and I," Dominey observed, "have reached a cul-de-sac in our argument,—the blank wall of good-natured but fundamental disagreement."

"Then I shall claim you for a while," Stephanie declared, taking Dominey's arm. "Lady Dominey has attracted all the men to her circle, and I am lonely."

The Prince bowed.

"I deny the cul-de-sac," he said, "but I yield our host! I shall seek my opponent at billiards."

He turned away and Stephanie sank into his vacant place.

"So you and my cousin," she remarked, as she made room for Dominey to sit by her side, "have come to a disagreement."

"Not an unfriendly one," her host assured her.

"That I am sure of. Maurice seems, indeed, to have taken a wonderful liking to you. I cannot remember that you ever met before, except for that day or two in Saxony?"

"That is so. The first time I exchanged any intimate conversation with the Prince was in London. I have the utmost respect and regard for him, but I cannot help feeling that the pleasant intimacy to which he has admitted me is to a large extent owing to the desire of our friends in Berlin. So far as I am concerned, I have never met any one, of any nation, whose character I admire more."

"Maurice lives his life loftily. He is one of the few great aristocrats I have met who carries his nobility of birth into his simplest thought and action. There is just one thing," she added, "which would break his heart."

"And that?"

"The subject upon which you two disagree—a war between Germany and this country."

"The Prince is an idealist," Dominey said. "Sometimes I wonder why he was sent here, why they did not send some one of a more intriguing character."

She shrugged her shoulders.

"You agree with that great Frenchman," she observed, "that no ambassador can remain a gentleman—politically."

"Well, I have never been a diplomat, so I cannot say," Dominey replied.

"You have many qualifications, I should think," she observed cuttingly.

"Such as?"

"You are absolutely callous, absolutely without heart or sympathy where your work is concerned."

"I do not admit it," he protested.

"I go back to London tomorrow," she continued, "a very miserable and unhappy woman. I take with me the letter which should have brought me happiness. The love for which I have sacrificed my life has failed me. Not even the whip of a royal command, not even all that I have to offer, can give me even five seconds of happiness."

"All that I have pleaded for," Dominey reminded her earnestly, "is delay."

"And what delay do you think," she asked, with a sudden note of passion in her tone, "would the Leopold von Ragastein of six years ago have pleaded for? Delay! He found the words then which would have melted an ice-berg. He found words the memory of which comes to me sometimes in the night and which mock me. He had no country then save the paradise where lovers walk, no ruler but a queen, and I was she. And now—"

Dominey felt a strange pang of distress. She saw the unusual softening in his face, and her eyes lit up.

"Just for a moment," she broke off, "you were like Leopold. As a rule, you know, you are not like him. I think that you left him somewhere in Africa and came home in his likeness."

"Believe that for a little time," Dominey begged earnestly.

"What if it were true?" she asked abruptly. "There are times when I do not recognize you. There are words Leopold used to use which I have never heard from your lips. Is not West Africa the sorcerer's paradise? Perhaps you are an impostor, and the man I love is there still, in trouble—perhaps ill. You play the part of Everard Dominey like a very king of actors. Perhaps before you came here you played the part of Leopold. You are not my Leopold. Love cannot die as you would have me believe."

"Now," he said coolly, "you are coming round to my way of thinking. I have been assuring you, from the very first moment we met at the Carlton, that I was not your Leopold—that I was Everard Dominey."

"I shall put you to the test," she exclaimed suddenly, rising to her feet. "Your arm if you please."

She led him across the hall to where little groups of people were gossiping, playing bridge, and Seaman, the centre of a little group of gullible amateur speculators, was lecturing on mines. They stopped to say a word or two here and there, but Stephanie's fingers never left her companion's arm. They passed down a corridor hung with a collection of wonderful sporting prints in which she affected some interest, into a small gallery which led into the ballroom. Here they were alone. She laid her hands upon his shoulders and looked up into his eyes. Her lips drew nearer to his.

"Kiss me—upon the lips, Leopold," she ordered.

"There is no Leopold here," he replied; "you yourself have said it."

She came a little nearer. "Upon the lips," she whispered.

He held her, stooped down, and their lips met. Then she stood apart from him. Her eyes were for a moment closed, her hands were extended as though to prevent any chance of his approaching her again.

"Now I know the truth," she muttered.

Dominey found an opportunity to draw Seaman away from his little group of investment-seeking friends.

"My friend," he said, "trouble grows."

"Anything more from Schmidt's supposed emissary?" Seaman asked quickly.

"No. I am going to keep away from him this evening, and I advise you to do the same. The trouble is with the Princess."

"With the Princess," declared Seaman, "I think you have blundered. I quite appreciate your general principles of behaving internally and externally as though you were the person whom you pretend to be. It is the very essence of all successful espionage. But you should know when to make exceptions. I see grave objections myself to your obeying the Kaiser's behest. On the other hand, I see no objection whatever to your treating the Princess in a more human manner, to your visiting her in London, and giving her more ardent proofs of your continued affection."

"If I once begin—"

"Look here," Seaman interrupted, "the Princess is a woman of the world. She knows what she is doing, and there is a definite tie between you. I tell you frankly that I could not bear to see you playing the idiot for a moment with Lady Dominey, but with the Princess, scruples don't enter into the question at all. You should by no means make an enemy of her."

"Well, I have done it," Dominey acknowledged. "She has gone off to bed now, and she is leaving early tomorrow morning. She thinks I have borrowed some West African magic, that I have left her lover's soul out there and come home in his body."

"Well, if she does," Seaman declared, "you are out of your trouble."

"Am I!" Dominey replied gloomily. "First of all, she may do a lot of mischief before she goes. And then, supposing by any thousand-to-one chance the story of this cousin of Schmidt's should be true, and she should find Dominey out there, still alive? The Princess is not of German birth, you know. She cares nothing for Germany's future. As a matter of fact, I think, like a great many Hungarians, she prefers England. They say that an Englishman has as many lives as a cat. Supposing that chap Dominey did come to life again and she brings him home? You say yourself that you do not mean to make much use of me until after the war has started. In the parlance of this country of idioms, that will rather upset the apple cart, will it not?"

"Has the Princess a suite of rooms here?" Seaman enquired.

"Over in the west wing. Good idea! You go and see what you can do with her. She will not think of going to bed at this time of night."

Seaman nodded.

"Leave it to me," he directed. "You go out and play the host."

Dominey played the host first and then the husband. Rosamund welcomed him with a little cry of pleasure.

"I have been enjoying myself so much, Everard!" she exclaimed. "Everybody has been so kind, and Mr. Mangan has taught me a new Patience."

"And now, I think," Doctor Harrison intervened a little gruffly, "it's time to knock off for the evening."

She turned very sweetly to Everard.

"Will you take me upstairs?" she begged. "I have been hoping so much that you would come before Doctor Harrison sent me off."

"I should have been very disappointed if I had been too late," Dominey assured her. "Now say good night to everybody."

"Why, you talk to me as though I were a child," she laughed. "Well, goodbye, everybody, then. You see, my stern husband is taking me off. When are you coming to see me, Doctor Harrison?"

"Nothing to see you for," was the gruff reply. "You are as well as any woman here."

"Just a little unsympathetic, isn't he?" she complained to Dominey. "Please take me through the hall, so that I can say goodbye to every one else. Is the Princess Eiderstrom there?"

"I am afraid that she has gone to bed," Dominey answered, as they passed out of the room. "She said something about a headache."

"She is very beautiful," Rosamund said wistfully. "I wished she looked as though she liked me a little more. Is she very fond of you, Everard?"

"I think that I am rather in her bad books just at present," Dominey confessed.

"I wonder! I am very observant, and I have seen her looking at you sometimes— Of course," Rosamund went on, "as I am not really your wife and you are not really my husband, it is very stupid of me to feel jealous, isn't it, Everard?"

"Not a bit," he answered. "If I am not your husband, I will not be anybody else's."

"I love you to say that," she admitted, with a little sigh, "but it seems wrong somewhere. Look how cross the Duchess looks! Some one must have played the wrong card."

Rosamund's farewells were not easily made; Terniloff especially seemed reluctant to let her go. She excused herself gracefully, however, promising to sit up a little later the next evening. Dominey led the way upstairs, curiously gratified at her lingering progress. He took her to the door of her room and looked in. The nurse was sitting in an easy-chair, reading, and the maid was sewing in the background.

"Well, you look very comfortable here," he declared cheerfully. "Pray do not move, nurse."

Rosamund held his hands, as though reluctant to let him go. Then she drew his face down and kissed him.

"Yes," she said a little plaintively, "it's very comfortable.— Everard?"

"Yes, dear?"

She drew his head down and whispered in his ear.

"May I come in and say good night for two minutes?"

He smiled—a wonderfully kind smile—but shook his head.

"Not tonight, dear," he replied. "The Prince loves to sit up late, and I shall be downstairs with him. Besides, that bully of a doctor of yours insists upon ten hours' sleep."

She sighed like a disappointed child.

"Very well." She paused for a moment to listen. "Wasn't that a car?" she asked.

"Some of our guests going early, I dare say," he replied, as he turned away.

Seaman did not at once start on his mission to the Princess. He made his way instead to the servants' quarters and knocked at the door of the butler's sitting-room. There was no reply. He tried the handle in vain. The door was locked. A tall, grave-faced man in sombre black came out from an adjoining apartment.

"You are looking for the person who arrived this evening from abroad, sir?" he enquired.

"I am," Seaman replied. "Has he locked himself in?"

"He has left the Hall, sir!"

"Left!" Seaman repeated. "Do you mean gone away for good?"

"Apparently, sir. I do not understand his language myself, but I believe he considered his reception here, for some reason or other, unfavourable. He took advantage of the car which went down to the station for the evening papers and caught the last train."

Seaman was silent for a moment. The news was a shock to him.

"What is your position here?" he asked his informant.

"My name is Reynolds, sir," was the respectful reply. "I am Mr. Pelham's servant."

"Can you tell me why, if this man has left, the door here is locked?"

"Mr. Parkins locked it before he went out, sir. He accompanied— Mr. Miller, I think his name was—to the station."

Seaman had the air of a man not wholly satisfied.

"Is it usual to lock up a sitting-room in this fashion?" he asked.

"Mr. Parkins always does it, sir. The cabinets of cigars are kept there, also the wine-cellar key and the key of the plate chest. None of the other servants use the room except at Mr. Parkins' invitation."

"I understand," Seaman said, as he turned away. "Much obliged for your information, Reynolds. I will speak to Mr. Parkins later."

"I will let him know that you desire to see him, sir."

"Good night, Reynolds!"

"Good night, sir!"

Seaman passed back again to the crowded hall and billiard-room, exchanged a few remarks here and there, and made his way up the southern flight of stairs towards the west wing. Stephanie consented without hesitation to receive him. She was seated in front of the fire, reading a novel, in a boudoir opening out of her bedroom.

"Princess," Seaman declared, with a low bow, "we are in despair at your desertion."

She put down her book.

"I have been insulted in this house," she said. "Tomorrow I leave it."

Seaman shook his head reproachfully.

"Your Highness," he continued, "believe me, I do not wish to presume upon my position. I am only a German tradesman, admitted to circles like these for reasons connected solely with the welfare of my country. Yet I know much, as it happens, of the truth of this matter, the matter which is causing you distress. I beg you to reconsider your decision. Our friend here is, I think, needlessly hard upon himself. So much greater will be his reward when the end comes. So much the greater will be the rapture with which he will throw himself on his knees before you."

"Has he sent you to reason with me?"

"Not directly. I am to a certain extent, however, his major-domo in this enterprise. I brought him from Africa. I have watched over him from the start. Two brains are better than one. I try to show him where to avoid mistakes, I try to point out the paths of danger and of safety."

"I should imagine Sir Everard finds you useful," she remarked calmly.

"I hope he does."

"It has doubtless occurred to you," she continued, "that our friend has accommodated himself wonderfully to English life and customs?"

"You must remember that he was educated here. Nevertheless, his aptitude has been marvellous."

"One might almost call it supernatural," she agreed. "Tell me, Mr. Seaman, you seem to have been completely successful in the installation of our friend here as Sir Everard. What is going to be his real value to you? What work will he do?"

"We are keeping him for the big things. You have seen our gracious master lately?" he added hesitatingly.

"I know what is at the back of your mind," she replied. "Yes! Before the summer is over I am to pack up my trunks and fly. I understand."

"It is when that time comes," Seaman said impressively, "that we expect Sir Everard Dominey, the typical English country gentleman, of whose loyalty there has never been a word of doubt, to be of use to us. Most of our present helpers will be under suspicion. The authorised staff of our secret service can only work underneath. You can see for yourself the advantage we gain in having a confidential correspondent who can day by day reflect the changing psychology of the British mind in all its phases. We have quite enough of the other sort of help arranged for. Plans of ships, aerodromes and harbours, sailings of convoys, calling up of soldiers—all these are the A.B.C. of the secret service profession. We shall never ask our friend here for a single fact, but, from his town house in Berkeley Square, the host of Cabinet Ministers, of soldiers, of the best brains of the country, our fingers will never leave the pulse of Britain's day-by-day life."

Stephanie threw herself back in her easy-chair and clasped her hands behind her head.

"These things you are expecting from our present host?"

"We are, and we expect to get them. I have watched him day by day. My confidence in him has grown."

Stephanie was silent. She sat looking into the fire. Seaman, keenly observant as always, realised the change in her, yet found something of mystery in her new detachment of manner.

"Your Highness," he urged, "I am not here to speak on behalf of

the man who at heart is, I know, your lover. He will plead his own
cause when the time comes. But I am here to plead for patience, I am
here to implore you to take no rash step, to do nothing which might
imperil in any way his position here. I stand outside the gates of the
world which your sex can make into a paradise. I am no judge of the
things that happen here. But in your heart I feel there is bitterness,
because the man for whom you care has chosen to place his country
first. I implore your patience, Princess. I implore you to believe what I
know so well—that it is the sternest sense of duty only which is the
foundation of Leopold von Ragastein's obdurate attitude."

"What are you afraid that I shall do?" she asked curiously.

"I am afraid of nothing—directly."

"Indirectly, then? Answer me, please."

"I am afraid," he admitted frankly, "that in some corner of the
world, if not in this country, you might whisper a word, a scoffing or
an angry sentence, which would make people wonder what grudge
you had against a simple Norfolk baronet. I would not like that word
spoken in the presence of any one who knew your history and realised
the rather amazing likeness between Sir Everard Dominey and Baron
Leopold von Ragastein."

"I see," Stephanie murmured, a faint smile parting her lips. "Well,
Mr. Seaman, I do not think that you need have many fears. What I
shall carry away with me in my heart is not for you or any man to
know. In a few days I shall leave this country."

"You are going back to Berlin—to Hungary?"

She shook her head, beckoned her maid to open the door, and held
out her hand in token of dismissal.

"I am going to take a sea voyage," she announced. "I shall go to
Africa."

The morrow was a day of mild surprises. Eddy Pelham's empty
place was the first to attract notice, towards the end of breakfast
time.

"Where's the pink and white immaculate?" the Right Honourable
gentleman asked. "I miss my morning wonder as to how he tied his
tie."

"Gone," Dominey replied, looking round from the sideboard.

"Gone?" every one repeated.

"I should think such a thing has never happened to him before,"
Dominey observed. "He was wanted in town."

"Fancy any one wanting Eddy for any serious purpose!" Caroline
murmured.

"Fancy any one wanting him badly enough to drag him out of bed in the middle of the night with a telephone call and send him up to town by the breakfast train from Norwich!" their host continued. "I thought we had started a new ghost when he came into my room in a purple dressing-gown and broke the news."

"Who wanted him?" the Duke enquired. "His tailor?"

There was a little ripple of good-humoured laughter.

"Does Eddy do anything for a living?" Caroline asked, yawning.

"Mr. Pelham is a director of the Chelsea Motor Works," Mangan told them. "He received a small legacy last year, and his favourite taxicab man was the first to know about it."

"You're not suggesting," she exclaimed, "that it is business of that sort which has taken Eddy away!"

"I should think it most improbable," Mangan confessed. "As a matter of fact, he asked me the other day if I knew where their premises were."

"We shall miss him," she acknowledged. "It was quite one of the events of the day to see his costume after shooting."

"His bridge was reasonably good," the Duke commented.

"He shot rather well the last two days," Mangan remarked.

"And he told me confidentially," Caroline concluded, "that he was going to wear brown today. Now I think Eddy would have looked nice in brown."

The missing young man's requiem was finished by the arrival of the local morning papers. A few moments later Dominey rose and left the room. Seaman, who had been unusually silent, followed him.

"My friend," he confided, "I do not know whether you have heard, but there was another curious disappearance from the Hall last night."

"Whose?" Dominey asked, pausing in the act of selecting a cigarette.

"Our friend Miller, or Wolff—Doctor Schmidt's emissary," Seaman announced, "has disappeared."

"Disappeared?" Dominey repeated. "I suppose he is having a prowl round somewhere."

"I have left it to you to make more careful enquiries," Seaman replied. "All I can tell you is that I made up my mind last night to interview him once more and try to fathom his very mysterious behaviour. I found the door of your butler's sitting-room locked, and a very civil fellow—Mr. Pelham's valet he turned out to be—told me that he had left in the car which went for the evening papers."

"I will go and make some enquiries," Dominey decided, after a moment's puzzled consideration.

"If you please," Seaman acquiesced. "The affair disconcerts me because I do not understand it. When there is a thing which I do not understand, I am uncomfortable."

Dominey vanished into the nether regions, spent half an hour with Rosamund, and saw nothing of his disturbed guest again until they were walking to the first wood. They had a moment together after Dominey had pointed out the stands.

"Well?" Seaman enquired.

"Our friend," Dominey announced, "apparently made up his mind to go quite suddenly. A bed was arranged for him—or rather it is always there—in a small apartment opening out of the butler's room, on the ground floor. He said nothing about leaving until he saw Parkins preparing to go down to the station with the chauffeur. Then he insisted upon accompanying him, and when he found there was a train to Norwich he simply bade them both good night. He left no message whatever for either you or me."

Seaman was thoughtful.

"There is no doubt," he said, "that his departure was indicative of a certain distrust in us. He came to find out something, and I suppose he found it out. I envy you your composure, my friend. We live on the brink of a volcano, and you shoot pheasants."

"We will try a partridge for a change," Dominey observed, swinging round as a single Frenchman with a dull whiz crossed the hedge behind them and fell a little distance away, a crumpled heap of feathers. "Neat, I think?" he added, turning to his companion.

"Marvellous!" Seaman replied, with faint sarcasm, "I envy your nerve."

"I cannot take this matter very seriously," Dominey acknowledged. "The fellow seemed to me quite harmless."

"My anxieties have also been aroused in another direction," Seaman confided.

"Any other trouble looming?" Dominey asked.

"You will find yourself minus another guest when you return this afternoon."

"The Princess?"

"The Princess," Seaman assented. "I did my best with her last night, but I found her in a most peculiar frame of mind. We are to be relieved of any anxiety concerning her for some time, however. She has decided to take a sea voyage."

"Where to?"

"Africa!"

Dominey paused in the act of inserting a cartridge into his gun. He turned slowly around and looked into his companion's face.

"Why the mischief is she going out there?" he asked.

"I can no more tell you that," Seaman replied, "than why Johann Wolff was sent over here to spy upon our perfect work. I am most unhappy, my friend. The things which I understand, however threatening they are, I do not fear. Things which I do not understand oppress me."

Dominey laughed quietly.

"Come," he said, "there is nothing here which seriously threatens our position. The Princess is angry, but she is not likely to give us away. This man Wolff could make no adverse report about either of us. We are doing our job and doing it well. Let our clear consciences console us."

"That is well," Seaman replied, "but I feel uneasy. I must not stay here any longer. Too intimate an association between you and me is unwise."

"Well, I think I can be trusted," Dominey observed, "even if I am to be left alone."

"In every respect except as regards the Princess," Seaman admitted, "your deportment has been most discreet."

"Except as regards the Princess," Dominey repeated irritably. "Really, my friend, I cannot understand your point of view in this matter. You could not expect me to mix up a secret honeymoon with my present commitments!"

"There might surely have been some middle way?" Seaman persisted. "You show so much tact in other matters."

"You do not know the Princess," Dominey muttered. . . .

The next morning saw the breaking-up of Dominey's carefully arranged shooting party. The Prince took his host's arm and led him to one side for a few moments, as the cars were being loaded up. His first few words were of formal thanks. He spoke then more intimately.

"Von Ragastein," he said, "I desire to refer back for a moment to our conversation the other day."

Dominey shook his head and glanced behind.

"I know only one name here, Prince."

"Dominey, then. I will confess that you play and carry the part through perfectly. I have known English gentlemen all my life, and you have the trick of the thing. But listen. I have already told you of my disapproval of this scheme in which you are the central figure."

"It is understood," Dominey assented.

"That," the Prince continued, "is a personal matter. What I am now going to say to you is official. I had despatches from Berlin last night. They concern you."

Dominey seemed to stiffen a little.

"Well?"

"I am given to understand," the Ambassador continued, "that you practically exist only in the event of that catastrophe which I, for one, cannot foresee. I am assured that if your exposure should take place at any time, your personation will be regarded as a private enterprise, and there is nothing whatever to connect you with any political work."

"Up to the present that is absolutely so," Dominey agreed.

"I am further advised to look upon you as my unnamed and unsuspected successor here, in the event of war. For that reason I am begged to inaugurate terms of intimacy with you, to treat you with the utmost confidence, and if the black end should come, to leave in your hands all such unfulfilled work as can be continued in secrecy and silence. I perhaps express myself in a somewhat confused manner."

"I understand perfectly," Dominey replied. "The authorities have changed their first ideas as to my presence here. They want to keep every shadow of suspicion away from me, so that in the event of war I shall have an absolutely unique position, an unsuspected yet fervently patriotic German, living hand in glove with the upper classes of English Society. One can well imagine that there would be work for me."

"Our understanding is mutual," Terniloff declared. "What I have to say to you, therefore, is that I hope you will soon follow us to London and give me the opportunity of offering you the constant hospitality of Carlton House Gardens."

"You are very kind, Prince," Dominey said. "My instructions are, as soon as I have consolidated my position here—an event which I fancy I may consider attained—to establish myself in London and to wait orders. I trust that amongst other things you will then permit me to examine the memoirs you spoke of the other day."

"Naturally, and with the utmost pleasure," the Ambassador assented. "They are a faithful record of my interviews and negotiations with certain Ministers here, and they reflect a desire and intention for peace which will, I think, amaze you.—I venture now upon a somewhat delicate question," he continued, changing the subject of their conversation abruptly, as they turned back along the terrace. "Lady Dominey will accompany you?"

"Of that I am not sure," Dominey replied thoughtfully. "I have noticed, Prince, if I may be allowed to say so, your chivalrous regard for that lady. You will permit me to assure you that in the peculiar position in which I am placed I shall never forget that she is the wife of Everard Dominey."

Terniloff shook hands heartily.

"I wanted to hear that from you," he admitted. "You I felt instinctively were different, but there are many men of our race who are willing enough to sacrifice a woman without the slightest scruple, either for their passions or their policy. I find Lady Dominey charming."

"She will never lack a protector in me," Dominey declared.

There were more farewells and, soon after, the little procession of cars drove off. Rosamund herself was on the terrace, bidding all her guests farewell. She clung to Dominey's arm when at last they turned back into the empty hall.

"What dear people they were, Everard!" she exclaimed. "I only wish that I had seen more of them. The Duchess was perfectly charming to me, and I never knew any one with such delightful manners as Prince Terniloff. Are you going to miss them very much, dear?"

"Not a bit," he answered. "I think I shall take a gun now and stroll down the meadows and across the rough ground. Will you come with me, or will you put on one of your pretty gowns and entertain me downstairs at luncheon? It is a very long time since we had a meal alone together."

She shook her head a little sadly.

"We never have had," she answered. "You know that, Everard, and, alas! I know it. But we are going on pretending, aren't we?"

He raised her fingers to his lips and kissed them.

"You shall pretend all that you like, dear Rosamund," he promised, "and I will be the shadow of your desires. No!— No tears!" he added quickly, as she turned away. "Remember there is nothing but happiness for you now. Whoever I am or am not, that is my one aim in life."

She clutched at his hand passionately, and suddenly, as though finding it insufficient, twined her arms around his neck and kissed him.

"Let me come with you," she begged. "I can't bear to let you go. I'll be very quiet. Will you wait ten minutes for me?"

"Of course," he answered.

He strolled down towards the gun room, stood by the fire for a moment, and then wandered out into the courtyard, where Middleton and a couple of beaters were waiting for him with the dogs. He had scarcely taken a step towards them, however, when he stopped short. To his amazement Seaman was there, standing a little on one side, with his eyes fixed upon the windows of the servants' quarters.

"Hullo, my friend!" he exclaimed. "Why, I thought you went by the early train from Thursford Station?"

"Missed it by two minutes," Seaman replied with a glance towards the beaters. "I knew all the cars were full for the eleven o'clock, so I thought I'd wait till the afternoon."

"And where have you been to for the last few hours, then?"

Seaman had reached his side now and was out of earshot of the others.

"Trying to solve the mystery of Johann Wolff's sudden departure last night. Come and walk down the avenue with me a little way."

"A very short distance, then. I am expecting Lady Dominey."

They passed through the thin iron gates and paced along one of the back entrances to the Hall.

"Do not think me indiscreet," Seaman began. "I returned without the knowledge of any one, and I kept out of the way until they had all gone. It is what I told you before. Things which I do not understand depress me, and behold! I have found proof this morning of a further significance in Wolff's sudden departure."

"Proceed," Dominey begged.

"I learned this morning, entirely by accident, that Mr. Pelham's servant was either mistaken or wilfully deceived me. Wolff did not accompany your butler to the station."

"And how did you find that out?" Dominey demanded.

"It is immaterial! What is material is that there is a sort of conspiracy amongst the servants here to conceal the manner of his leaving. Do not interrupt me, I beg! Early this morning there was a fresh fall of snow which has now disappeared. Outside the window of the room which I found locked were the marks of footsteps and the tracks of a small car."

"And what do you gather from all this?" Dominey asked.

"I gather that Wolff must have had friends in the neighbourhood," Seaman replied, "or else—"

"Well?"

"My last supposition sounds absurd," Seaman confessed, "but the whole matter is so incomprehensible that I was going to say—or else he was forcibly removed."

Dominey laughed softly.

"Wolff would scarcely have been an easy man to abduct, would he," he remarked, "even if we could hit upon any plausible reason for such a thing! As a matter of fact, Seaman," he concluded, turning on his heel a little abruptly as he saw Rosamund standing in the avenue, "I cannot bring myself to treat this Johann Wolff business seriously. Granted that the man was a spy, well, let him get on with it. We are doing our job here in the most perfect and praiseworthy fashion. We neither of us have the ghost of a secret to hide from his employers."

"In a sense that is true," Seaman admitted.

"Well, then, cheer up," Dominey enjoined. "Take a little walk with us, and we will see whether Parkins cannot find us a bottle of that old Burgundy for lunch. How does that sound, eh?"

"It you will excuse me from taking the walk," Seaman begged, "I would like to remain here until your return."

"You are more likely to do harm," Dominey reminded him, "and set the servants talking, if you show too much interest in this man's disappearance."

"I shall be careful," Seaman promised, "but there are certain things which I cannot help. I work always from instinct, and my instinct is never wrong. I will ask no more questions of your servants, but I know that there is something mysterious about the sudden departure of Johann Wolff."

Dominey and Rosamund returned about one o'clock to find only a note from Seaman, which the former tore open as his companion stood warming her feet in front of the fire. There were only a few lines:

I am following an idea. It takes me to London. Let us meet there within a few days.

S.

"Has he really gone?" Rosamund asked.

"Back to London."

She laughed happily. "Then we shall lunch *à deux* after all! Delightful! I have my wish!"

There was a sudden glow in Dominey's face, a glow which was instantly suppressed.

"Shall I ever have mine?" he asked, with a queer little break in his voice.

HELEN MacINNES

▼

2 A Confusion of Celts

The beauty of Helen MacInnes's use of the ancient and obviously attractive game of impersonation, her particular innovation, is that while the physical resemblance causes no problems, the inner differences between the spy and the man whose person he assumes do. One instance of this, which works out in the spy's favor, is contained in the present excerpt.

Assignment in Brittany was one of the earliest spy novels about World War II, published in 1942 before the war was even half over. It was one of the first novels to make use of what was at the time a new technique both for attack and for sending spies on their way, the parachute drop. The action takes place not long after the fall of France when the British were expecting a German invasion of the British Isles. Much that seemed highly original in the book at the time no longer seems so because of the subsequent use of similar material once the infiltration of agents by air had become almost commonplace.

Before writing this book, Helen MacInnes had made her debut with Above Suspicion, which immediately established her reputation as a natural master of the thriller. Since then she has produced several more novels, all with different European settings. Her favorite gambit is to place some more or less innocent Englishman or American (not a trained agent, as in the present excerpt) in the path of sinister and mysterious doings and to take it from there. By this means she has—very wisely, I think—avoided cluttering her books with a lot of unauthentic claptrap about contemporary intelligence services and methods, which is what puts off the reader who has any acquaintance at all with the real business.

FROM *Assignment in Brittany.*

Hearne waited until the pounding of his blood had stopped. Then, gathering the parachute once more in his arms, he dragged it further into the wood. He moved quietly and capably, like a man who had so often imagined this moment that his movements were almost mechanical. When the undergrowth was thick enough to please him, he halted and eyed the ground round the bush he had chosen. He went to work with his clasp knife, cutting the turf into neat squares, stacking them methodically at his side. The loam under them he scooped out with his hands. It took time, but in the end he was satisfied. He had packed the parachute into the hole he had scraped, thrusting it tightly down under the thin straggling roots of the bush. On top of the parachute lay his flying suit and helmet, and over them all spread the thick rich soil and the sods, fitted together as neatly as the bulging earth would allow. He had worked lying uncomfortably flat on his stomach. Now he crawled out from the thickness of the bush to find some twigs and leaves and, with luck, some stones. These he scattered over the . parachute's grave, covering the gaping cuts between the sods. After two such journeys, he had finished. The evidence was well buried.

He looked at the unfamiliar watch on his wrist. Three hours ago he had joked with the redhaired pilot over a last cup of hot chocolate. Three hours ago he had stood on English earth. Three hours ago he had been Martin Hearne with twenty-seven years of his own life behind him. Now he was Bertrand Corlay, with twenty-six years of another man's life reduced to headings and subheadings in his memory. He looked down at the faded uniform which had been Corlay's, felt once more for the papers in the inside pocket.

"All set?" the gunner had asked.

Well, that would be the last time he would listen to English for some weeks. All set. . . . He patted the pocket of the tunic with his earth-stained hand and smiled grimly. From now on, he would not only have to speak, but think, in French.

He moved slowly westwards along the wood, keeping parallel to the open stretch of fields, so that he would not wander too far into the maze of trees. He still moved carefully and quietly, but he was less worried. He had plenty of time, now that he had got rid of the parachute and flying suit. Once he got far enough away from where he had buried them, he would find some place to lie hidden until night came again. Fourteen hours ahead of him for thought; for sleep, if he felt safe enough. Yes, there was plenty of time, and plenty to think about.

He would review all the details he had learned by heart, all the movements and expressions he had memorized. Nothing which he had discovered in the past three weeks must be neglected.

At last he found his hiding place under a small, unimportant-looking tree, with a tangle of bramble bushes behind him and a screen of bracken in front. When he lay stretched out under the tall curling fronds of the fern, he felt safe. Barring accidents, such as a rabbit-hunting farmer and his dog, there would be little chance of anyone stumbling across him. And a farmer wouldn't be surprised to find a disheveled poilu waiting for the daylight to fade. There were many of them, this summer of 1940.

It was cold and damp, but the discomfort sharpened his mind. He thought of Corlay in his white hospital bed in England, and smiled wryly as he felt the heavy dew soak efficiently through his clothes, as he watched the black bugs clinging to the underleaves of the bracken. Well, if Corlay's hipbone hadn't been shattered on the way out of Dunkirk, he might have been doing this job himself. And if Matthews hadn't been examining a boatload of French and Belgian wounded after it had arrived at Folkestone; if he hadn't seen the unconscious Corlay, believed he was Hearne, and then notified Military Intelligence that one of their men had just got back in an uncomfortably original way, then this scheme would never have been born in Matthews' fertile brain. That was like Matthews. He must have mulled it all over in his mind for a couple of days, and out of his sardonic amusement had grown the germ of an idea.

"Well, I'm damned," he would say. "Well, I'm damned." And then he'd begin to think of a use for such an extraordinary likeness, especially when he learned more about the Frenchman and where he came from. That was like Matthews. He never wasted an opportunity. Two days after he had seen Corlay, he had not only the idea shaping nicely, but also the go-ahead signal from his own department.

Strange bird, Matthews, thought Hearne, and rolled over on his side to ease a hipbone. He took some deep breaths, tautening his muscles to warm himself. His clothes would dry when the sun really got into this glade. He'd be warm enough then. Strange bird, Matthews; he sort of sensed things coming. He'd cook up some plan, keep it simmering until the right moment arrived, and then dish it up piping hot. The right moment in this case had been a week before the French-German armistice. It was then that he sent for Hearne.

"Glad you got back in time," he had begun, and smiled quietly. Hearne knew that smile. He waited, wondering what was coming this time.

"How would you like to spend a summer in France?"

That meant he was going to spend a summer in France. He allowed himself one objection—not that Matthews would show that he had ever noticed it.

"But I've just come back from there." Thirty-six hours ago, Hearne added under his breath.

"Brittany, this time." Matthews gave his imitation of a benevolent Santa Claus. "That should interest you, Hearne."

It did, in spite of the fact that for the last month he hadn't slept in a clean bed, or seen anything which might be remotely called a bathroom. Hearne saw his leave and the quiet comfort of his flat evaporating as quickly as August rain on a hot London pavement.

"When do I go?" he asked. Brittany . . . well, that was something.

"In about two or three weeks. That is, if things go the way they are shaping. Looks bad, at the moment. If there's a separate armistice, then we shall use you, because every Frenchman who can get back to his home will then make a beeline for it. A lot of them won't get back; and there will be some with the guts to fight on. But you are to be one of the Frenchmen who do get back, and stay there."

"Home?" Hearne was incredulous. Home meant relatives, and complications. He had never tackled anything so domestic as that.

And then Matthews explained about Corlay.

"Here's all the official knowledge about him," he ended, pushing a folder across his desk to Hearne. "All checked and amplified by a French Intelligence chap—Fournier, he's called—who will be one of those who fight on, so there's no danger of the wrong people learning about our interest in Corlay. You'll find that Fournier has done a pretty good job. He included a detailed map and description of the district. St. Deodat is the name of the village. Know it?"

Hearne shook his head. He had no idea where it was. He searched his memory in annoyance. Hell, he thought, Brittany is supposed to be my pidgin.

"North or South Brittany?" he asked at last.

"North. Just southwest of the town of Dol. Within walking distance of the railway line from Rennes to St. Malo. Near enough Dinan to admire the canal. Close enough to the main north road from Rennes." Matthews was speaking slowly, underlining the importance of the towns with the inflection of his voice. "And also," he added, "not so very far from Mont St. Michel, and our old friends Duclos and Plehec, if you must send us news about your health."

Hearne smothered a smile. Matthews was at his old trick again of coating the pill lavishly with sugar. He liked to make his assignments sound like a Cook's tour.

"Duclos is still there?" Hearne asked.

"Yes, and very useful he will be from now on. I am rather afraid his archeological researches are going to be disturbed. Then, for emergency use only, you will find another friend outside St. Malo. Fournier guarantees him. You'd better talk to him about this man of his before you leave."

Hearne nodded. "And I've to take moonlight strolls around the railway line and road and canal?" he asked.

There was almost a smile on Matthews' face. "You are being sent to this farm so that, within a patch of about two hundred square miles, you can find information which will fit neatly into the reports which we hope to get from all the other patches of two hundred square miles. Then, when all the pieces of the crossword puzzle are fitted together, we will have a working idea of German intentions. Now, here are the particular pieces of information which we need. First, we want to know if North Brittany is being fortified and garrisoned for defense; or is it being prepared as a base for an attack on the British Isles? If so, then just in what way are the Germans preparing to attack? If airfields are being constructed then they are aiming for our southern ports and our shipping lanes. If huge masses of troops and boats are being prepared, then our southwest flank is in danger." Matthews stabbed at the map on the desk in front of him. "The Devon Coast, the Bristol Channel, Southern Ireland. Brittany is just the right position to try for these places. So look for airfields, troop movements, types of supplies being sent by road and rail and canal, new construction works, underground dumps, gun installations. You may not see much sense in what you observe, but your report will fit neatly into the other reports we'll receive. When we fit them together, they will make a pretty pattern. So don't even let the little things escape you. Work at night. I think you'll find plenty of material for your usual precise reports. Anything you pick up will probably be useful."

There was a note in Matthews' voice which raised Hearne's eyes from the map to the older man's face. Anything you pick up . . . Was that inflection on the *you* intended? If it were, then that was high praise.

Matthews was speaking again. "I don't think you'll find this a difficult job." Again, there was that hint of emphasis on the *you*. "I think," he was saying, "I think we can depend on you only to follow your instructions, and not to suffer from any attacks of misplaced brilliance."

Hearne's elation faded, and then he saw the gleam in Matthews' eye, and the repressed smile. He breathed again. So Matthews wasn't displeased over his last attack of "misplaced brilliance," after all. Hearne suddenly thought, Perhaps he's giving me this job just because I find it hard to be orthodox in my methods. Perhaps he isn't so much against them as he always pretends to be.

Matthews seemed to guess Hearne's thoughts. "Seriously," he said, "you did a good job at Bordeaux. But I'd like you to restrain yourself on this trip. No good getting lost to us." And then, as if he felt he had been too expansive, he added, "Not after all the trouble I've had in training you."

"Yes, sir," Hearne said.

Matthews' voice was matter-of-fact once more. "I suggest you memorize the contents of that folder. You'll find all the necessary data in it, including observations on Corlay by one of his officers and by a man who had known him as a student. After you've got all that information memorized, you can start on Corlay himself. You'll visit him each day in hospital, for two or three weeks. He can talk now. Find out everything you can to fill in the gaps. Study his voice, his expressions, all that sort of thing."

"What if he won't talk? The Bretons can be very reticent, you know."

"I think he will. There is a certain amount of questioning which all strangers in Britain must go through at this time. We've never had so many aliens dumped so unexpectedly on our shores, and at rather a dangerous moment for us, too. There are rumors, even among the wounded, of what's now called the Fifth Column. Fournier has seen Corlay, and dropped him that hint. He will talk, just to identify himself."

"Well, that sounds more hopeful. . . . You say he looks like me?"

"Looks? My dear Hearne, he's the dead spit of you. If he could mislead me, you can mislead anyone who knows him."

"But his mother and father?"

"Father killed in 1917. Mother bedridden. You'll find it all in that folder. I investigated that sort of thing before I called you in. Now, if there had been a wife . . ." Matthews smiled, and shook his head slowly. When he spoke again, his voice was crisp and businesslike. "I think you're in luck this time, Hearne. You'll learn more about your Celtic peoples in a month at St. Deodat than you did that year at Rennes University." There was the sugar coating being spread on again. "What made you interested in the Bretons, anyway? Was it because you are a Cornishman, yourself?"

Hearne nodded. "That, and the fact that I like them, and that my father spent all his time in between his sermons writing about the early British saints. A lot of them ended up in Brittany, you know."

"Deodat being one? Well, that makes one of these nice coincidences."

"I can't think of any Deodat except Saint Augustine's son," Hearne said with a smile.

"Saint Augustine?" Matthews looked startled. "Didn't know he was married."

"He wasn't," Hearne said, enjoying the shocked look on Matthews' face. He added, "That was probably during Augustine's 'O God, make me pure, but not yet' period." For a strong Scots Presbyterian, Matthews was reacting in a very High Church manner. Hearne grinned amiably.

"Well, I'll be damned," said Matthews. "Well, I'll be—"

"That's about all, then?" Hearne asked tactfully.

"Yes," said Matthews. "Yes. I'll see you again before you leave."

"How do I go?"

It was Matthews' turn to smile. "Just drop in," he said.

The sun had come out, and with it a swarm of flies, fat black flies, inquisitive, persistent. But, at least, Hearne was beginning to feel dry and warm. He took the map out of his pocket to verify his position again. It was a detailed French map of Brittany, with well-worn creases, stains and a jagged tear over the Atlantic corner for good measure. If he were questioned, he was to say that this map had been given him at Brest, after he had arrived there by fishing boat from Dunkirk. Better allow himself a slight case of shell shock to account for the period between Dunkirk and the armistice. Shell shock might be useful later: it could explain any strangeness, any lapse of memory. So, with this map, he had found his way home to the North of Brittany. The food in his pocket could be explained away, too . . . friendly peasantry department. Could be explained away. He smiled grimly at the phrase. He would just have to take especial care tonight in his short journey to St. Deodat, and then no explanations would be necessary to any curious patrol.

He examined the map for the last time. He must be able to remember the details of the district to the north and west of this wood, to reach the toy railway which trailed the main road from Rennes to St. Malo. It would guide him part of the way. The rest would depend on his knowledge of these thin and thick red lines and winding black ones. He had looked at them so often in the past few days that they were etched on his memory as well as on this map. At last he admitted that he could do no more, that he must depend now on a combination of intelligence and intuition. There would be no moon tonight, but if the sky stayed clear the stars would be enough. Failing them, it would have to be by guess and by God.

He settled himself more comfortably in his bracken bed. The sweet smell of fern and grass, the warmth of the sun, the increasing hum of the innumerable insects, drowsed him pleasantly. He felt himself slipping into light sleep. Tomorrow, he was thinking, tomorrow Bertrand Corlay would be home.

(Hearne has established himself as Bertrand Corlay in the Corlay household without difficulty. After a visit to the house by the German occupation authorities during which it turns out that the real Corlay was in the good books of the Germans, a fact Hearne had not previously known, he begins to sense that Corlay's invalid mother may have seen through his masquerade. He decides to find out if she has.)

He said to Madame Corlay, "I'd like to talk a little with you, if I may." He drew a chair towards the old woman, again sitting erectly with her hands clasped on the walking stick. The knuckles no longer showed white.

"Yes?"

"First of all, when did you guess?" That could apply to either Corlay's "powerful friends" or to himself. If she really knew about him, that was . . . He might have jumped too quickly to conclusions in this last half hour. He would soon learn, anyway.

She returned his look calmly. Her voice was gentle. "About you?"

He now knew, anyway. He smiled halfheartedly. Damn, he was thinking, you couldn't have been so good after all.

"I wish you hadn't broken my glasses," Madame Corlay said with some asperity, and narrowed her eyes as she looked at his face. "Yes, as far as I can see, the likeness is remarkable. Are you Breton, too?"

"I am a Celt," admitted Hearne truthfully.

"Yes, you look like Bertrand: you even talk and move like him. At first, I thought you were my son. And then the little things were different."

"What?"

"Albertine talks with me a good deal. You see, we've been a long time together. She came to this farm when she was a girl, and she has stayed here ever since, except for two visits to Rennes when I needed her. One was when Bertrand was born: the other was when I was very ill. She was waiting here to welcome me when I came back after my uncle's death. So, you see, we talk a good deal."

Hearne smothered his impatience. "Yes?"

"Although I sit up here, I know what's going on downstairs. When Albertine told me how much easier it was to live with you nowadays, I thought that perhaps war had made you gentler, more sympathetic. Suffering can do that to men. You didn't grumble about the food, you didn't grumble about Albertine going to Mass, you didn't grumble at having to eat in the kitchen. Apart from the time when you lost your temper with Albertine in your bedroom—when I first saw you—you did seem changed by the war. I was beginning to hope that perhaps some good comes of war even in little things, that perhaps you had stopped being so self-centered and opinionated. Then you offered to work in the fields, you helped the American and even admitted, at that time, that clothes for him would be a difficult problem as he was so tall. Taller than you. Bertrand would never have admitted that. Then you went down to the village to find Henri. And today, Bertrand would have gone down to welcome the Germans himself. He might even have offered them wine. He would certainly have not risked hiding the American."

"That's incredible," burst out Hearne, and then lowered his voice. "Why?"

"I don't know why. All I know is that he would have. He never thought of anyone except himself since he was a small boy. You see, that's how I guessed. You had the one quality which Bertrand lacked. Even Anne, when she came to see me that evening you went to find Henri, even she thought the war had changed and improved you. I found in you, and Anne did too, just what I always had looked for in my son."

Hearne's eyes were fixed on his hands. He cleared his throat, but he didn't speak. Whatever was coming was going to embarrass him. He knew that from Madame Corlay's voice.

"And that was," continued Madame Corlay, "just ordinary human kindness. That was something Bertrand couldn't even understand."

VIII. *Deception*

While deception is one of the more intriguing aspects of intelligence work, it is rarely the subject of spy fiction. The general idea is to mislead the enemy concerning one's intentions as to the place, timing, and size of a forthcoming attack. Where the deception is of the kind which can be accomplished by arranging for a single piece of false information to fall into the hands of the enemy, as in the excerpts which follow, a compact story can be told. But it is unlikely, for example, that anyone could create a novel around the kind of deception operations which preceded the Normandy invasion of 1944. They consisted of hundreds of carefully interlocked feints and diversionary probes, as well as the planting of false information through every available channel, the whole complex undertaking having the sole purpose of making the Germans think that we would land in the Pas de Calais area rather than on the Normandy coast.

There is still another kind of deception which no novel I know of has yet treated. This is the kind quite current during peacetime which often has a primarily political aim and is best called by what it is, forgery. Trumped-up official documents or letters ostensibly written by persons in high authority are fobbed off on an unsuspecting public in newspapers and magazines chiefly with the intent of embarrassing another government. Such operations are, in Soviet Russia and its satellites, entrusted to the intelligence services, although in a case which has recently come

287

to light, that of the famous "Zinoviev letter," it appears that a group of White Russian exiles in Berlin forged the document which helped to cause the downfall of Ramsay MacDonald's Labour government in the British general elections of 1924. This was achieved by the newspaper publication of an authentic-looking letter on official Soviet stationery, purportedly signed by the Comintern chief Zinoviev, directing the British Communist Party to engage in a program of subverting the armed forces of Great Britain. It created a Red scare in certain British circles, sufficiently upsetting to turn them against the Labour Party because of its more tolerant attitude toward the Russia of that day.

I have included Mark Twain's delightful little tale in this section because it is about a rather wayward category of deception. The false information is not passed to the enemy in order to win the battle and not for gain—but from some other motive. Within any intelligence service, more time than most people realize is spent separating valid information from false information invented and offered by fakers and cranks.

1 The Trojan Horse

*The famous episode of the Trojan horse from Book II of Virgil's
Aeneid ranks as an intelligence operation not simply because of
the concealment of Greek warriors in the hollow wooden horse,
but because of the whole stratagem by which the Greeks induce
the Trojans to open their gates and haul the horse inside the
city.*

*The Greeks have to find a way to dispel the suspicions of the
Trojans and to mislead them as to their true intentions. This they
accomplish by two distinct moves. First of all, their fleet sails
away, giving the impression that the siege of Troy has been
abandoned. In actuality, the fleet is concealed in a nearby harbor
waiting to return when the signal is given. Secondly, the Greeks
send an agent to the Trojans, a certain Sinon, who poses as a
defector who has run away from the Greeks because he has been
mistreated. Since he tells a convincing story about the causes of his
disaffection and is ostensibly seeking refuge with the Trojans, they
open their arms to him and, more important, believe the intelligence he brings about the Greeks' abandonment of the siege and
about the harmless religious purpose of the wooden horse. This
double-barreled deception succeeds in disarming the Trojans with
the well-known result.*

*Ancient history is full of deceptions of this kind. The wooden
horse is undoubtedly a poetic invention, but the ruses of appearing
to leave the scene of battle and of sending an ostensibly dis-
gruntled turncoat to feed the enemy false information are not.*

Broken in war, set back by fate, the leaders
Of the Greek host, as years went by, contrived,
With Pallas' help, a horse as big as a mountain.

FROM *The Aeneid.*

289

They wove its sides with planks of fir, pretending
This was an offering for their safe return,
At least, so rumor had it. But inside
They packed, in secret, into the hollow sides
The fittest warriors; the belly's cavern,
Huge as it was, was filled with men in armor.
There is an island, Tenedos, well-known,
Rich in the days of Priam; now it is only
A bay, and not too good an anchorage
For any ship to trust. They sailed there, hid
On the deserted shore. We thought they had gone,
Bound for Mycenae, and Troy was very happy,
Shaking off grief, throwing the gates wide open.
It was a pleasure, for a change, to go
See the Greek camp, station and shore abandoned;
Why, this was where Achilles camped, his minions,
The Dolopes, were here; and the fleet just yonder,
And that was the plain where we used to meet in battle.
Some of us stared in wonder at the horse,
Astounded by its vastness. . . .

Some others, knowing better,
Suspicious of Greek plotting, said to throw it
Into the sea, to burn it up with fire,
To cut it open, see what there was inside it.
The wavering crowd could not make up its mind. . . .

Meanwhile, some Trojan shepherds, pulling and hauling,
Had a young fellow, with his hands behind him,
Tied up, and they were dragging him to Priam.
He had let himself be taken so, on purpose,
To open Troy to the Greeks, a stranger, ready
For death or shifty cunning, a cool intriguer,
Let come what may. They crowd around to see him.
Take turns in making fun of him, that captive.
Listen, and learn Greek trickiness; learn all
Their crimes from one.
He stopped in the middle, frightened and defenceless,
Looked at the Trojan ranks,—"What land, what waters,
Can take me now?" he cried. "There is nothing, nothing
Left for me any more, no place with the Greeks,
And here are the Trojans howling for my blood!"

Our mood was changed. We pitied him, poor fellow,
Sobbing his heart out. We bade him tell his story,
His lineage, his news: what can he count on,
The captive that he is? His fear had gone
As he began: "O King, whatever happens,
I will tell the truth, tell all of it; to start with,
I own I am a Greek. Sinon is wretched,
Fortune has made him so, but she will never
Make him a liar." . . .

"The Greeks were tired of the long war; they often
Wanted to sail from Troy for home. Oh, would
That they had only done it! But a storm
Would cut them off, or the wrong wind terrify them.
Especially, just after the horse was finished,
With the joined planks of maple, all the heaven
Roared loud with storm-clouds. In suspense and terror
We sent Eurypylus to ask Apollo
What could be done; the oracle was gloomy,
Foreboding: 'Blood, O Greeks, and a slain virgin
Appeased the winds when first you came here; blood
Must pay for your return, a life be given,
An Argive life.' The word came to our ears
With terror in it, our blood ran cold in our veins,
For whom was fate preparing? Who would be
The victim of Apollo? Then Ulysses
Dragged Calchas into our midst, with a great uproar,
Trying his best to make the prophet tell us
What the gods wanted. And there were many then
Who told me what was coming, or kept silent
Because they saw, and all too well, the scheme
Ulysses had in mind. For ten days Calchas
Said nothing at all, hid in his tent, refusing
To have a word of his pronounce the sentence,
And all the time Ulysses kept on shouting,
Till Calchas broke, and doomed me to the altar.
And all assented; what each man had feared
In his own case, he bore with great composure
When turned another way.
The terrible day was almost on me; fillets
Were ready for my temples, the salted meal
Prepared, the altars standing. But I fled,

I tore myself away from death, I admit it,
I hid all night in sedge and muddy water
At the edge of the lake, hoping, forever hoping,
They might set sail. And now I hope no longer
To see my home, my parents, or my children,
Poor things, whom they will kill because I fled them,
Whom they will murder for my sacrilege.
But oh, by the gods above, by any power
That values truth, by any uncorrupted
Remnant of faith in all the world, have pity,
Have pity on a soul that bears such sorrow,
More than I ever deserved."
He had no need to ask us. Priam said,
Untie him, and we did so with a promise
To spare his life. Our king, with friendly words,
Addressed him, saying, "Whoever you are, forget
The Greeks, from now on. You are ours; but tell me
Why they have built this monstrous horse? Who made it,
Who thought of it? What is it, war-machine,
Religious offering?" And he, instructed
In every trick and artifice, made answer. . . .

(*Sinon explains that the horse is an offering to the gods.*)

We broke the walls, exposing
The city's battlements, and all were busy
Helping the work, with rollers underfoot
And ropes around the neck. It climbed our walls,
The deadly engine. Boys, unwedded girls
Sang alleluias round it, all rejoicing
To have a hand on the tow-rope. It came nearer,
Threatening, gliding, into the very city.
O motherland! O Ilium, home of gods,
O walls of Troy! Four times it stopped, four times
The sound of arms came from it, and we pressed on,
Unheedful, blind in madness, till we set it,
Ill-omened thing, on the citadel we worshipped.
And even when Cassandra gave us warning,
We never believed her; so a god had ordered.
That day, our last, poor wretches, we were happy,
Garlanding the temples of the gods

All through the town.
        And the sky turned, and darkness
Came from the ocean, the great shade covering earth
And heaven, and the trickery of the Greeks.
Sprawling along the walls, the Trojans slumbered,
Sleep holding their weary limbs, and the Greek armada,
From Tenedos, under the friendly silence
Of a still moon, came surely on. The flagship
Blazed at the masthead with a sudden signal,
And Sinon, guarded by the fates, the hostile
Will of the gods, swung loose the bolts; the Greeks
Came out of the wooden womb. The air received them
The happy captains, Sthenelus, Ulysses,
Thessandrus, Acamas, Achilles' son
Called Neoptolemus, Thoas, Machaon,
Epeos, who designed the thing,—they all
Came sliding down the rope, and Menelaus
Was with them in the storming of a city
Buried in sleep and wine. The watch was murdered,
The open doors welcome the rush of comrades,
They marshal the determined ranks for battle.

▼

2 A Belated Promotion

Of the many novels based on or inspired by actual intelligence operations, Duff Cooper's Operation Heartbreak *is one of the most unusual. The greater part of the book is not about the operation at all. In fact it doesn't get mentioned until the very last chapter (our excerpt) and then is disposed of in a very few pages.*

The operation behind Duff Cooper's story was dubbed "Mincemeat" by the British intelligence officers who prepared it in 1943, and it was described in detail in a book by Ewen Montagu called The Man Who Never Was, *published in 1954. This book was in turn made into a movie. I will not describe the operation here and spoil Duff Cooper's somewhat romanticized presentation of it except to say that it required a corpse—not just any corpse, but a fresh male corpse of a certain age and appearance. How the officers involved in "Mincemeat" actually went about procuring their corpse remains untold even in Montagu's book, and the identity and history of the person whose body was used is naturally a matter which will permanently remain unknown except to very few people.*

But it was precisely this hidden side of the whole affair which engaged Duff Cooper's imagination. In Operation Heartbreak *he has invented the life, from childhood to death, of the man whose corpse was used, one Willie Maryngton, for whom nothing ever quite pans out; who is, in short, a fine fellow, lovable, capable within certain limitations, but a failure by ordinary standards. He misses all the action in love and in war. His part in* Operation Heartbreak *is the culmination of this pathetic career. His moment of glory comes, but too late for him to appreciate it. He is promoted in death—a promotion he dearly wanted in life but never*

FROM *Operation Heartbreak.*

achieved—because it is felt that the corpse should wear the uniform of a major.

I have heard it said, although I cannot vouch for it, that British intelligence did not intend to make any public revelation of this operation after the war. Deception operations are usually kept about as secret as anything can be kept in the intelligence business. And the technique used in this one could conceivably have been used again (although I don't know in what situation). However, once Duff Cooper had let the cat out of the bag in the excerpt which follows, there was no point in maintaining further secrecy, and as a result Ewen Montagu was authorized to write his book, which gave the story in full. Or almost in full.

On that day Garnet went to have luncheon at the Service club to which he belonged. He was sad and weary, having sat up half the night. He was overwhelmed with work and felt that unless he relaxed for an hour and had a quiet meal instead of the glass of milk and sandwiches that he was accustomed to snatch at midday, he would become a casualty himself. That one of the first duties of a soldier was to take care of his own health was a maxim that he frequently impressed on others.

The large club dining-room was nearly full. In a corner he saw an old friend whom he had known in Panang. He was a Scotsman and now, so Garnet noticed, a brigadier. He sank into the seat opposite, and the two old soldiers began to exchange grievances. Having disposed of the climate, they proceeded to condemn the long hours during which men were expected to work on this side of the world. Garnet explained that this was the first occasion for many months that he had been able to lunch at the club and that he was only doing so today because he had felt on the verge of a breakdown.

"I was up half the night with a poor fellow who died early this morning, and when I got to the hospital there were a series of operations, so that I haven't even had time to certify his death."

"Do you have to nurse your patients as well as dose them?" asked the brigadier.

"No, but this was a dear friend, who had been living in my flat, Willie Maryngton. Did you ever know him?" Garnet mentioned his regiment.

"I think I met him in India—a nice fellow—very sad."

"Yes indeed, and I suppose I shall have to make all the funeral arrangements."

"Can't you leave that to his relations?"

"The extraordinary thing is that he hasn't got any. I've known him all my life. His father, who was killed in the last war, made my father his guardian. My father was killed, and Willie was brought up with us from the age of fourteen. He never had a single relation that he knew of."

The brigadier seemed interested and began to put questions. "You say he died this morning? And you have not certified his death? And he had neither kith nor kin?"

Garnet confirmed all these particulars, and the brigadier went on to make inquiries about Willie's activities during the war, about his age and rank, and ended by asking, "How many people have you informed of his death?"

"I telephoned to my sister this morning. We were both very fond of him. The nursing sister and the charwoman, who looks after my flat, are of course aware. But why all these questions? It's very kind of you to take so much interest, but I don't quite understand."

"I am going to ask one more. Did he make a will? If so, where is it? Who benefits by it, and who is the executor?"

"Yes, he made a will. I found it this morning. He left everything to his regimental benevolent fund and appointed as his executors the firm of lawyers who have always acted for him."

"Osborne," said the Scotsman, solemnly, "do you believe in Providence?"

"No," said Garnet.

"Well, I do. I was brought up so to believe, and I have never lost my faith. Providence is a great mystery, and I have seen many proofs of it in my life. I am going to make three requests of you. First, that you will not sign that certificate today. Second, that you will not mention Maryngton's death to another living soul. Third, that you will call on me at my office this afternoon."

Garnet protested that he had no time to spare.

"You will have the time you would have given to registering the death and making the funeral arrangements. You have known me for many years and you know that I do not use words lightly. I tell you that this is a matter of the very greatest importance."

His Scottish r's rolled impressively, and Garnet, although he felt that he was dreaming, agreed to do as he was asked. Five o'clock was the hour decided upon. The brigadier drew a blank visiting card from his pocket-book, and wrote upon it. "That is the address," he said.

Garnet raised his eyebrows as he read it. "Well," he said, "I should have thought that that was the last place you would have chosen for your office."

"That," replied the brigadier, "is precisely why I chose it."

They parted, and a few minutes later the brigadier was entering that ill-famed building outside which Willie had waited a few days before. He took a lift to the third floor, where he let himself into one of the two flats. A slovenly-looking man, sitting in the passage, sprang smartly to attention.

"Fergusson," said the brigadier, "a colonel R.A.M.C., in uniform, will be calling at five o'clock. Show him straight in. I don't wish to be disturbed while he is with me."

"Sir," replied Fergusson.

The brigadier went into his office, a small room with a large writing table, sat down, and rang the bell. Felicity appeared.

"I shall have a Colonel Osborne coming to see me about five," he said. "I don't wish any telephone calls put through while he is here, unless it is a matter of great importance."

"Colonel Osborne?" she repeated tentatively.

"Colonel Garnet Osborne, R.A.M.C."

"He is my brother."

"Is that so, Miss Osborne? Is that so? Another remarkable co-incidence. Do you believe in Providence, Miss Osborne?"

"I don't know. I've never thought about it."

"There are worse things to think about. Your brother is an old friend of mine. We were together in Malaya. Have you all the documents ready and in order for Operation Z?"

"Yes, sir."

"Have you not thought of any better name for it? Z is a daft sort of a name for an operation."

"I haven't thought of another."

"Well, just go on thinking. Thank you."

She left the room.

When Garnet arrived he was shown straight in to the brigadier, who greeted him with the question, "Did you know that your sister is my personal assistant?"

"My sister Felicity?" he asked in astonishment.

"She is Miss Osborne to me, but she tells me you are her brother, and I have no reason to doubt her veracity."

"Well, well! This is a strange day in my life," said Garnet.

"And you have not got to the end of it yet," replied the brigadier. "Sit down."

He then proceeded to confirm all the particulars concerning Willie with which Garnet had supplied him at luncheon. He had a paper in his hand on which he had recorded them. He went through them in order to be sure they were correct.

"Thank you," he concluded when he came to the end of his questions. "You have given me some information—and now you are going to receive some in return.

"The purpose of this department, in which you find yourself, Colonel Osborne, is to deceive the enemy. Our methods of deception are, at certain times, extremely elaborate. The more important the military operations under contemplation the more elaborate are our preparations to ensure, not so much that the enemy shall be ignorant of what we intend to do, but rather that he shall have good reason to believe that we intend to do something quite different. I need not impress upon you the importance of secrecy, but I would say to you what I say to all those who work with me, that there is only one way to keep a secret. There are not two ways. That way is not to whisper it to a living soul—neither to the wife of your bosom nor to the man you trust most upon earth. I know you for a loyal, trustworthy, and discreet soldier, but for a million pounds I would not tell you what I am about to tell you if I did not need your help.

"A military operation of immense magnitude is in course of preparation. That is a fact of which the enemy is probably aware. Its success must depend largely upon the enemy's ignorance of when and where it will be launched. Every security precaution has been taken to prevent that knowledge from reaching him. Those security precautions are not, I repeat, the business of this department. It is not our business to stop him getting correct information. It is our business to provide him, through sources which will carry conviction of their reliability, with information that is false.

"In a few days from now, Colonel Osborne, the dead body of a British officer will be washed ashore on the coast of a neutral country whose relations with the enemy are not quite so neutral as we might wish them to be. It will be found that he is carrying in a packet that is perfectly waterproof, which will be firmly strapped to his chest, under his jacket, documents of a highly confidential character—documents of such vital importance to the conduct of the war that no one will wonder that they should have been entrusted to a special mission and a special messenger. These documents, including a private letter from the Chief of the Imperial General Staff to the General Officer Commanding North Africa, although couched in the most, apparently, guarded language, will yet make perfectly plain to an intelligent reader exactly what the Allies are intending to do. You will appreciate the importance of such an operation; and you will also appreciate that its success or failure must depend entirely upon the convincing character of the evidence, that will prove the authenticity of these documents and will remove from the minds of those who are to study them any suspicion that a trick has been played upon them. The most important of all the links in that chain of evidence must be the dead body on which the documents are found.

"Now, Osborne, you are a medical man, and you must have discovered in your student days, when you were in need of material to work upon, what I have discovered only lately, the extraordinary importance that people attach to what becomes of the dead bodies of their distant relations. People who can ill afford it will travel from the north of Scotland to the south of England to assure themselves that the mortal remains of a distant cousin have been decently committed to the earth. You can hardly imagine the difficulty I have experienced. The old profession of body-snatching has no longer any practitioners, or I would have employed one. I have now secured the services of a gentleman in your line of business, a civilian, and our hopes rest upon what a pauper lunatic asylum may produce. But there must be difficulties. You may have heard, Osborne, that death is the great leveller, but even after death has done his damnedest there is apt to remain a very considerable difference between a pauper lunatic deceased from natural causes and a British officer, in the prime of life, fit to be entrusted with a most important mission."

"I see what you are getting at," interrupted Garnet. "You want me to agree to poor Maryngton's body being used for this purpose."

"Bide a while, bide a while," said the brigadier, who had not completed his thesis. "You will appreciate the cosmic importance of this operation, upon which the lives of thousands of men must depend and which may affect even the final issue of the war. This morning I was wrestling desperately with the problem of the pauper lunatic for whom an identity, a name, a background had to be created. Our enemies are extremely painstaking and thorough in their work. You may be quite certain that they have copies of the last published Army List, and I am sure that they have also easily available a complete register of all officers who have been killed since that publication, or whose names have appeared in the obituary columns. Their first action on being informed that the body of a dead British officer has been discovered will be to ascertain whether such a British officer was ever alive. If they fail to find the name of such an officer in the Army List their suspicions will be aroused, and those suspicions, once aroused, may easily lead them to the true solution of the mystery. We should be forced to give to our unknown one of those names that are shared by hundreds and should have to hope that, in despair of satisfying themselves as to the identity of the particular Major Smith or Brown in question, they would abandon the inquiry. But—I say again—we are dealing with a nation whose thoroughness in small matters of detail is unequalled, and it is my belief that within a few days the chief of their intelligence service would be informed that no officer of the name in question has ever served in the British Army. From that moment all the information contained in the documents, about which I told you, would be treated as information of doubtful value and of secondary importance. The result might well be that the whole operation would fail completely.

"While this grave problem is occupying my mind today, you sit yourself down before me and tell me of an officer who died this morning, whose death has not been registered, who has no relations, who was of an age and standing entirely suitable for such a mission, and over the disposal of whose dead body you have control. Call it the long arm of coincidence, whatever that may mean, if you desire, but to me Colonel Osborne"—the brigadier's voice grew hoarse with emotion—"it is the hand of Providence stretched out to aid His people in their dire need, and I ask you to give me your help, as God has given me His, in the fulfilment of my task."

He ceased, and both sat silent. After a while Garnet said, "What you are asking me to do is very extraordinary, and although I perfectly understand the terrible urgency, you must allow me to reflect." He paused, and then continued, "In the first place I should be acting quite illegally. I have no more right to conceal Maryngton's death than I have to dispose of his body."

"*Silent leges inter arma,*" replied the brigadier. "I will give you my personal guarantee, written if you wish it, that will cover you from any legal consequences."

They sat again in silence for two or three minutes. When Garnet next spoke it was to ask, "What should I actually have to do? And what am I going to say when Maryngton's friends, many of whom must have known that he was living with me, ask me what has become of him?"

The brigadier was obviously relieved. He felt now that the other's mind was moving in the right direction.

"What you have to do is to lay out by the side of Maryngton's body tonight his uniform, omitting no detail of it. Don't forget his cap or his belt, and above all make sure that the identity disc is there. Put on the table his watch, his cheque book and any small personal possessions that he always carried. At two A.M. some friends of mine will call upon you. There may be two of them, there may be three. You will show them which is Maryngton's room. Then you will go to bed and sleep soundly. You will, however, dream that Maryngton comes to you in the night and tells you that he is leaving England in the early morning. His mission is of a secret nature, and in case anything should go wrong he hands you his will, which you have already told me is in your possession. When you wake in the morning he will certainly have gone, and you will therefore believe your dream was a reality. It will probably be many days before you have to answer any inquiry. During those days you will repeat to yourself continually how he told you one night that he was leaving on a secret mission, how he gave you his will, and how he was gone on the following morning. You will come to believe this yourself, and it will be all that you know, all that you have to say to anyone who asks questions. One day you will read in the paper that Maryngton has died on active service. Then you will send his will to his lawyers; and that will be all."

Again Garnet sat in silence for several minutes.

"Does my sister know about this affair?" he asked.

"Miss Osborne is aware," said the brigadier, "that an operation of this nature is in preparation."

"I would rather," said Garnet, "that she did not know that it was— that we were making use of—damn it, respect for the dead bodies of those we love is a very profound instinct in human nature. Willie Maryngton has been like a brother to us all our lives. I am sure it would distress her horribly."

The brigadier looked grave and answered, "You may be sure that I have already given very careful consideration to this part of the problem. Besides ourselves there are three other people, so far as we are aware, who know that Maryngton died of pneumonia this morning. I have decided that the best method of securing the discretion of the nurse and the servant is to say no more to them on the subject. To neither of them will the case present any peculiar or interesting feature. To impose secrecy upon them would merely stimulate their curiosity. If either of them reads the announcement of his death, which is unlikely, the fact that it is described as having taken place on active service will be accepted as part of the incomprehensible vocabulary of Whitehall.

"Now your sister is another matter. I have the greatest confidence in her reliability, but I cannot expect even her to keep a secret if she doesn't know it is a secret. She may have told someone of Maryngton's death already. If not, she is almost sure to do so."

"She's a strange girl," said Garnet; "she keeps her friends in separate compartments, isolated cells as it were. Since my brother was killed she and Willie had no mutual friends. I think it unlikely that she has told anybody. But I can make sure, which I promise to do. What is more, I can pretend to her that my conduct has not been strictly professional in allowing a friend to die in my own flat without calling in a second opinion, and failing to inform the authorities within twenty-four hours. On that ground I can ask her not to mention the matter, and then we can safely count on her silence."

"I don't like it, Osborne," said the brigadier. "In affairs of this sort I like to have everything water-tight. The smallest leak may sink the ship—and what a ship it is! Think, man, the whole British Empire is on board!"

An ugly cloud of obstinacy crept into Garnet's eyes. "I'm sorry," he said. "The whole business is hateful to me, and I just can't bear to bring my sister into it. Between ourselves, I once suspected that she was in love with Maryngton. I even hoped that they might marry. Can you imagine telling a girl what it is that you are intending to do with the dead body of a man who might have been her husband? It is a kind of sacrilege."

The brigadier looked into Garnet's eyes, and he saw the obstinacy that lay there. He looked at his watch, and then he said, "I'll not tell her. You have my word for it."

Garnet sighed.

"In that case I suppose I must consent," he said. "I can see no good reason for not doing so—except sentiment, or perhaps sentimentality—and I have never considered myself to be ruled by either. In any case, service must come first. You have given me my instructions. They are simple enough. They shall be carried out. Have you anything further to ask of me?"

"Lay out the uniform," said the brigadier, "omitting no detail of it. Leave the small personal possessions on the table. Open the door when the bell rings. Dream as I told you, and believe that your dream is true."

They shook hands, and Garnet turned to go.

"One more detail," said the brigadier. "You have not by any chance got some spare major's badges among your equipment?"

"I doubt it," said Garnet.

"Very well. My friends will provide them. I have been thinking that the rank of captain is just one too low for an officer charged with such a very important mission. He appears as a captain in the last prewar Army List. If he had been employed on important work since then he would have become a major by now, so I intend to make him one. These small details can prove of vast importance in this sort of work."

"Oh dear," said Garnet, "that was the promotion he was so anxious to obtain. Poor Willie! It is a heartbreaking business."

"Ay," said the brigadier. "Operation Heartbreak would not be a bad name for it."

Felicity met Garnet in the passage. "Come into my room," she said, "I've got a cup of tea for you."

"It will be welcome," he answered. "I had a wretched night and I've been hard at it all day. Odd to find you here. You are, I must say, a very secretive girl."

"Now tell me all there is to tell about Willie. I felt that I couldn't bear to hear more this morning, when you told me he was dead, so I rang off in an abrupt and what must have appeared a callous way. But I can bear it now. Go on."

Garnet recounted the course of the short illness and explained that it was not uncommon for healthy men in middle age to be carried off suddenly by a sharp attack of pneumonia.

"But I do think," he went on, "that there was something else, another contributory cause, as it were, in Willie's case. I told you not long ago that I thought there was something wrong with him. In all illness, and especially in cases of this sort, the will of the patient plays a great part. There comes a moment when an effort is required. In this case that effort wasn't made. I am afraid that one of the reasons why Willie died was that he did not greatly wish to live."

"Ah!" Felicity gave a little cry, as though in sudden pain, but said no more.

After a pause Garnet went on to ask, "Do you happen to have mentioned his death to anyone you've seen today, Felicity?"

"No," she answered. "I haven't seen anyone, for one thing, and there isn't anyone to whom I talk about Willie, for another."

"Well, I had rather that you kept it to yourself," he said, and went on to tell her the story he had invented about his alleged lapse from professional rectitude.

"I promise not to breathe a word," she said, but she looked at him with curiosity, asking herself whether such conduct was really unprofessional and, if so, whether Garnet could have been guilty of it.

"How about the funeral?" she asked.

"Oh, it seems there are some distant cousins in Yorkshire. The lawyers have communicated with them. They want him to be buried up there. It appears his forebears came from that part of the country. I couldn't object."

"He always told me he hadn't any cousins anywhere, but I'm glad they've been discovered. I hate funerals, and he would never have expected me to go to Yorkshire to attend one among people whom I don't know."

Hers was not an inquisitive nature, but it seemed strange to her that cousins who had remained unknown throughout his life should assert themselves within a few hours of his death.

Having finished his tea, Garnet rose to go.

"Good-bye, dear old Garnet," she said. "Now that you have found out where I work you might come and see me sometimes. I can always give you tea."

"I should like to come," he replied. "I am very busy, but I feel lonely sometimes."

"I suppose everybody does."

"Yes, I suppose so."

He went, and a few minutes later the bell summoned her to the brigadier. She picked up her pad and pencil and went into his room.

"I had an interesting conversation with your brother," he said. "Did he tell you about it?"

"No."

"I told you that I met him in the Far East. We both know something about the pretty ways of the Japanese and we've been having a fine crack about them. Our government will never resort to bacteriological warfare, you know, but I think it's just the sort of trick the Japs might play on us. So I was thinking that we might get it whispered around that we had something up our sleeve in that line more terrible than anything they would imagine. That might make them think twice before they used it."

"It might, on the other hand, make them use it immediately so as to be sure of getting their blow in first."

"Ay, but I think they've held off poison gas so far because they suspect we've got a deadlier brew than they have. Your brother is very knowledgeable in the matter of oriental diseases."

Felicity wondered why he was telling her all this. She had studied the brigadier's methods, and she had noticed that when he volunteered information it was usually with a motive, and that the information itself was usually incorrect. Was he trying to deceive her, or had he perhaps some more subtle purpose?

"To change the subject," he went on, "to Operation Z, or Operation Heartbreak, as I'm thinking of calling it. I've received information from that doctor of whom I told you. He has to hand exactly what we were looking for. So the matter is now urgent. Time and tide—we depend on both of them, and neither will wait upon the other. There is not an hour to be lost. The admiralty are standing by. They await only the pressure of a button to go ahead. And I am about to press that button. You have the wallet and the papers. I should like to have another look at them."

As Felicity went to her room to fetch them it occurred to her that the news which had come to the brigadier from the doctor could not have been received that afternoon by telephone, for she had had control of all the calls that reached him and it was strange, if time were precious, that he should have wasted so much of it in discussing remote possibilities with Garnet, and should have attached so much importance to the conversation.

She returned with the carefully constructed waterproof wallet and a thin sheaf of papers. The brigadier slipped on a pair of gloves before he touched them. She smiled.

"You think, Miss Osborne, my precautions are a wee bit ridiculous. But it is always wiser to err on the side of prudence. I hope that in a few days these papers will be in the hands of a gentleman as prudent as I am, and better equipped. It may be that he will have them tested for fingerprints, and it may be that he has a photograph of my fingerprints on his writing table. We are dealing with a very thorough people, Miss Osborne, a very thorough people.

"So this is the letter from the C.I.G.S.,"* he went on, carefully taking it out of the envelope. He read it slowly and chuckled. "He must have enjoyed putting in that joke about the Secretary of State. It just gives the hallmark of authenticity. He has made a very good job of it indeed."

He laid the papers on the table in front of him and remained silent for three or four minutes, apparently lost in thought.

"A man setting out on a journey of this sort," he said at last, speaking very slowly, "would probably put into his wallet what was most precious and dear to him. A married man might put there the photographs of his wife and children. This is to be a single man." He paused again. "Do you think, Miss Osborne," he asked, "that you could draft a love letter?"

"I can try," she replied, impassively.

"Do that," he said. "Meanwhile I must get on to the Admiralty and see the young men in our Operations Branch, who have a full night before them."

She rose to go.

"Make sure that there's no 'G.R.' in the corner of the paper you write on, nor 'For the service of His Majesty's Government' in the watermark."

* Commander, Imperial General Staff.

"I will make sure," she said.

"And there is one more thing." He hesitated. "You must try to make the letter the kind a man would think worth keeping."

"I will try," she said, and left the room.

The brigadier continued to look at the door after she had shut it. He had the habit of observing people closely. Was he mistaken or had he detected a light of revelation in her eyes, a kind of exultation in her manner, the air of one who goes with confidence to the performance of a grateful task?

He had no time to waste on speculation. His evening was fully occupied. He first had a long interview with two young men, who were members of his staff but not regular attendants at the office. Then there were a number of telephone conversations with the Admiralty and with other government departments. When he looked at his watch he was surprised to see how late it was. He rang the bell and Felicity came in with a sheet of paper in her hand.

"I am sorry I have detained you so long," he said. "All our preparations are now complete. Have you drafted the letter that I suggested?"

She handed him the paper she was carrying and said nothing. He put on his gloves before taking it and held it up to the light, examining it with a magnifying glass, and then, seemingly satisfied with his inspection, adjusted his spectacles and began to read:

Darling, my darling, you are going away from me, and I have never told you how much I love you. How sad, how heartbreaking it would be if you had never known. But this will tell you, and this you must take with you on your dark mission. It brings you my passionate and deathless love. Forgive me all the disappointment that I caused you. Remember now only the hours that I lay in your arms. I cannot have known how much I loved you until I knew that you must go away. I have been weak and wanton, as I warned you once that I should always be, but I have been in my own odd way, believe me, oh, believe me, darling, I have been true. When we meet again you will understand everything, and perhaps we shall be happy at last.

When he had finished reading it he did not look up.

"This should be signed with a Christian name," he said.

"Have you any suggestions?" she asked. There was a faint note of bitterness in her voice.

"An unusual one is likely to be more convincing than a common one. Your brother told me yours this afternoon. Have you any objection to making use of it? People show by the way they sign their own names that they are accustomed to doing so. Handwriting experts might be able to tell the difference."

"I will sign it 'Felicity,' " she said.

"If the pen you have in your hand is the one with which you wrote the letter," he said, "you can sign it here," and he pointed to the chair on the other side of his table. She sat down and wrote and handed him back the letter. At the end of it she had written in her clear, bold hand "Felicity" and at the beginning "My Willie."

The brigadier made sure that the ink was dry and then he crumpled the letter between his two hands so that she thought he was going to throw it into the waste-paper basket. He smoothed it out again very carefully, saying as he did so, "This is a letter which a man would have read many times. It should bear signs of usage." Then, still looking down at the letter and still smoothing it, he said, "So you have guessed our secret. I gave your brother my word of honour that I would not tell you. I think I have kept my word."

"But why did he want me not to know?" she asked.

"He feared that it would cause you pain."

"He ought to have understood," she said, "that it is just what Willie would have wished more than anything in all the world."

Dawn had not broken, but was about to do so, when the submarine came to the surface. The crew were thankful to breathe the cool fresh air, and they were still more thankful to be rid of their cargo. The wrappings were removed, and the lieutenant stood to attention and saluted as they laid the body of the officer in uniform as gently as possible on the face of the waters. A light breeze was blowing shoreward, and the tide was running in the same direction. So Willie went to the war at last, the insignia of field rank on his shoulders, and a letter from his beloved lying close to his quiet heart.

Everything worked as had been intended. The neutral government behaved with the courtesy that is expected of neutral governments. After a certain delay, such as is inevitable in the movements of government departments, they informed the ambassador with regret that the body of a British officer, whose identity appeared to be established, had been washed up by the sea, and that he was bearing a waterproof packet which they had the honour to forward intact. They would be glad to make any arrangements for the funeral that His Excellency might desire. They did not think it necessary to mention that the packet in question had been already opened with infinite care, and that before being closed again with care as infinite, every document in it had been photographed, and that those photographs were now lying under the eyes of the enemy, where the false information that they contained powerfully contributed to the success of one of the greatest surprises ever achieved in military history.

SAMUEL L. CLEMENS

▼

3 A Curious Experience

In an earlier part of this story, we are told how young Robert Wicklow, a Northern sympathizer from the Deep South, joined a Union regiment stationed at New London as a drummer boy. The story is told in the first person by a major of the regiment.

Whether this tale is based on an actual happening, or is largely an invention which displays the author's well-known flair for exaggeration and elaborate spoofs, I do not know, but it certainly reflects a touchiness about spies in their midst which was prevalent among Union troops during the Civil War. And for good reason, because in a civil war, where language and custom and appearance do not immediately distinguish friend from foe as in other wars, the spy's job is immeasurably easier.

I do know that the author has very nicely put his finger on the psychology of fabrication. I have seen instances in intelligence work during and after World War II in which informants, under pressure and possessed of lively imaginations, have spun out incredible tales of enemy plots which had to be taken seriously, at least for the moment, since even the remote possibility that they might be true made it incumbent upon any responsible officer to investigate them. More often than not, it turned out that one was dealing with an addlebrained impostor or something more venal.

There was one young woman, I recall, who, when passed along the chain of command from post to post, claimed at each higher echelon that the people she had just previously talked to were in the pay of the enemy. This sort of thing can cause a great deal of turmoil and we sometimes wondered, after the air had been cleared, whether it was the enemy who had sent us these nut cases in order to waste our time and tie us in knots.

FROM *The American Claimant.*

308

Now comes Sergeant Rayburn, one morning, and says:

"That new boy acts mighty strange, sir."

"How?"

"Well, sir, he's all the time writin'."

"Writing? What does he write—letters?"

"I don't know, sir; but whenever he's off duty, he is always pokin' and nosin' around the fort, all by himself—blest if I think there's a hole or corner in it he hasn't been into—and every little while he outs with pencil and paper and scribbles somethin' down."

This gave me a most unpleasant sensation. I wanted to scoff at it, but it was not a time to scoff at anything that had the least suspicious tinge about it. Things were happening all around us in the North then that warned us to be always on the alert, and always suspecting. I recalled to mind the suggestive fact that this boy was from the South—the extreme South, Louisiana—and the thought was not of a reassuring nature, under the circumstances. Nevertheless, it cost me a pang to give the orders which I now gave to Rayburn. I felt like a father who plots to expose his own child to shame and injury. I told Rayburn to keep quiet, bide his time, and get me some of those writings whenever he could manage it without the boy's finding it out. And I charged him not to do anything which might let the boy discover that he was being watched. I also ordered that he allow the lad his usual liberties, but that he be followed at a distance when he went out into the town.

During the next two days Rayburn reported to me several times. No success. The boy was still writing, but he always pocketed his paper with a careless air whenever Rayburn appeared in the vicinity. He had gone twice to an old deserted stable in the town, remained a minute or two, and come out again. One could not pooh-pooh these things—they had an evil look. I was obliged to confess to myself that I was getting uneasy. I went into my private quarters and sent for my second in command—an officer of intelligence and judgment, son of General James Watson Webb. He was surprised and troubled. We had a long talk over the matter, and came to the conclusion that it would be worth while to institute a secret search. I determined to take charge of that myself. So I had myself called at two in the morning; and pretty soon after I was in the musicians' quarters, crawling along the floor on my stomach among the snorers. I reached my slumbering waif's bunk at last, without disturbing anybody, captured his clothes and kit, and crawled stealthily back again. When I got to my own quarters, I found Webb there, waiting and eager to know the result.

We made search immediately. The clothes were a disappointment. In the pockets we found blank paper and a pencil; nothing else, except a jackknife and such queer odds and ends and useless trifles as boys hoard and value. We turned to the kit hopefully. Nothing there but a rebuke for us!—a little Bible with this written on the fly-leaf: "Stranger, be kind to my boy, for his mother's sake."

I looked at Webb—he dropped his eyes; he looked at me—I dropped mine. Neither spoke. I put the book reverently back in its place. Presently Webb got up and went away, without remark. After a little I nerved myself up to my unpalatable job, and took the plunder back to where it belonged, crawling on my stomach as before. It seemed the peculiarly appropriate attitude for the business I was in.

I was most honestly glad when it was over and done with.

About noon next day Rayburn came, as usual, to report. I cut him short. I said:

"Let this nonsense be dropped. We are making a bugaboo out of a poor little cub who has got no more harm in him than a hymn-book."

The sergeant looked surprised, and said:

"Well, you know it was your orders, sir, and I've got some of the writin'."

"And what does it amount to? How did you get it?"

"I peeped through the keyhole, and see him writin'. So, when I judged he was about done, I made a sort of a little cough, and I see him crumple it up and throw it in the fire, and look all around to see if anybody was comin'. Then he settled back as comfortable and careless as anything. Then I comes in, and passes the time of day pleasantly, and sends him on an errand. He never looked uneasy, but went right along. It was a coal fire and new built; the writin' had gone over behind a chunk, out of sight; but I got it out; there it is; it ain't hardly scorched, you see."

I glanced at the paper and took in a sentence or two. Then I dismissed the sergeant and told him to send Webb to me. Here is the paper in full:

Fort Trumbull, the 8th

COLONEL

I was mistaken as to the caliber of the three guns I ended my list with. They are 18-pounders; all the rest of the armament is as I stated. The garrison remains as before reported, except that the two light infantry companies that were to be detached for service at the front are to stay here for the present—can't find out for how long, just now, but will soon. We are satisfied that, all things considered, matters had better be postponed un-

There it broke off—there is where Rayburn coughed and interrupted the writer. All my affection for the boy, all my respect for him and charity for his forlorn condition, withered in a moment under the blight of this revelation of cold-blooded baseness.

But never mind about that. Here was business—business that required profound and immediate attention, too. Webb and I turned the subject over and over, and examined it all around. Webb said:

"What a pity he was interrupted! Something is going to be postponed until—when? And what is the something? Possibly he would have mentioned it, the pious little reptile!"

"Yes," I said, "we have missed a trick. And who is 'we' in the letter? Is it conspirators inside the fort or outside?"

That "we" was uncomfortably suggestive. However, it was not worth while to be guessing around that, so we proceeded to matters more practical. In the first place, we decided to double the sentries and keep the strictest possible watch. Next, we thought of calling Wicklow in and making him divulge everything; but that did not seem wisest until other methods should fail. We must have some more of the writings; so we began to plan to that end. And now we had an idea: Wicklow never went to the post-office—perhaps the deserted stable was his post-office. We sent for my confidential clerk—a young German named Sterne, who was a sort of natural detective—and told him all about the case, and ordered him to go to work on it. Within the hour we got word that Wicklow was writing again. Shortly afterward word came that he had asked leave to go out into the town. He was detained awhile and meantime Sterne hurried off and concealed himself in the stable. By and by he saw Wicklow saunter in, look about him, then hide something under some rubbish in a corner, and take leisurely leave again. Sterne pounced upon the hidden article—a letter—and brought it to us. It had no superscription and no signature. It repeated what we had already read, and then went on to say:

We think it best to postpone till the two companies are gone. I mean the four inside think so; have not communicated with the others—afraid of attracting attention. I say four because we have lost two; they had hardly enlisted and got inside when they were shipped off to the front. It will be absolutely necessary to have two in their places. The two that went were the brothers from Thirty-Mile Point. I have something of the greatest importance to reveal, but must not trust it to this method of communication; will try the other.

"The little scoundrel!" said Webb; "who could have supposed he was a spy? However, never mind about that; let us add up our particulars, such as they are, and see how the case stands to date. First, we've got a rebel spy in our midst, whom we know; secondly, we've got three more in our midst whom we don't know; thirdly, these spies have been introduced among us through the simple and easy process of enlisting as soldiers in the Union army—and evidently two of them have got sold at it, and been shipped off to the front; fourthly, there are assistant spies 'outside'—number indefinite; fifthly, Wicklow has very important matter which he is afraid to communicate by the 'present method'—will 'try the other.' That is the case, as it now stands. Shall we collar Wicklow and make him confess? Or shall we catch the person who removes the letters from the stable and make him tell? Or shall we keep still and find out more?"

We decided upon the last course. We judged that we did not need to proceed to summary measures now, since it was evident that the conspirators were likely to wait till those two light infantry companies were out of the way. We fortified Sterne with pretty ample powers, and told him to use his best endeavors to find out Wicklow's "other method" of communication. We meant to play a bold game; and to this end we proposed to keep the spies in an unsuspecting state as long as possible. So we ordered Sterne to return to the stable immediately, and, if he found the coast clear, to conceal Wicklow's letter where it was before, and leave it there for the conspirators to get.

The night closed down without further event. It was cold and dark and sleety, with a raw wind blowing; still I turned out of my warm bed several times during the night, and went the rounds in person, to see that all was right and that every sentry was on the alert. I always found them wide awake and watchful; evidently whispers of mysterious dangers had been floating about, and the doubling of the guards had been a kind of indorsement of these rumors. Once, toward morning, I encountered Webb, breasting his way against the bitter wind, and learned then that he, also, had been the rounds several times to see that all was going right.

Next day's events hurried things up somewhat. Wicklow wrote another letter; Sterne preceded him to the stable and saw him deposit it; captured it as soon as Wicklow was out of the way, then slipped out and followed the little spy at a distance, with a detective in plain clothes at his own heels, for we thought it judicious to have the law's assistance handy in case of need. Wicklow went to the railway station, and waited around till the train from New York came in, then stood scanning the faces of the crowd as they poured out of the cars. Presently an aged gentleman, with green goggles and a cane, came limping along, stopped in Wicklow's neighborhood, and began to look about him expectantly. In an instant Wicklow darted forward, thrust an envelope into his hand, then glided away and disappeared in the throng. The next instant Sterne had snatched the letter; and as he hurried past the detective he said: "Follow the old gentleman—don't lose sight of him." Then Sterne scurried out with the crowd, and came straight to the fort.

We sat with closed doors, and instructed the guard outside to allow no interruption.

First we opened the letter captured at the stable. It read as follows:

HOLY ALLIANCE

Found, in the usual gun, commands from the Master, left there last night, which set aside the instructions heretofore received from the subordinate quarter. Have left in the gun the usual indication that the commands reached the proper hand—

Webb, interrupting: "Isn't the boy under constant surveillance now?"

I said yes; he had been under strict surveillance ever since the capturing of his former letter.

"Then how could he put anything into a gun, or take anything out of it, and not get caught?"

"Well," I said, "I don't like the look of that very well."

"I don't either," said Webb. "It simply means that there are conspirators among the very sentinels. Without their connivance in some way or other, the thing couldn't have been done."

I sent for Rayburn, and ordered him to examine the batteries and see what he could find. The reading of the letter was then resumed:

The new commands are peremptory, and require that the MMMM shall be FFFFF at 3 o'clock to-morrow morning. Two hundred will arrive, in small parties, by train and otherwise, from various directions, and will be at appointed place at right time. I will distribute the sign to-day. Success is apparently sure, though something must have got out, for the sentries have been doubled, and the chiefs went the rounds last night several times. W.W. comes from southerly to-day and will receive secret orders—by the other method. All six of you must be in 166 at sharp 2 A.M. You will find B.B. there, who will give you detailed instructions. Password same as last time, only revised—put first syllable last and last syllable first. Remember XXXX. Do not forget. Be of good heart; before the next sun rises you will be heroes; your fame will be permanent; you will have added a deathless page to history. Amen.

"Thunder and Mars," said Webb, "but we are getting into mighty hot quarters, as I look at it!"

I said there was no question but that things were beginning to wear a most serious aspect. Said I:

"A desperate enterprise is on foot, that is plain enough. To-night is the time set for it—that, also, is plain. The exact nature of the enterprise—I mean the manner of it—is hidden away under those blind bunches of M's and F's, but the end and aim, I judge, is the surprise and capture of the post. We must move quick and sharp now. I think nothing can be gained by continuing our clandestine policy as regards Wicklow. We must know, and as soon as possible, too, where '166' is located, so that we can make a descent upon the gang there at 2 A.M.; and doubtless the quickest way to get that information will be to force it out of that boy. But first of all, and before we make any important move, I must lay the facts before the War Department, and ask for plenary powers."

The despatch was prepared in cipher to go over the wires; I read it, approved it, and sent it along.

We presently finished discussing the letter which was under consideration, and then opened the one which had been snatched from the lame gentleman. It contained nothing but a couple of perfectly blank sheets of note-paper! It was a chilly check to our hot eagerness and expectancy. We felt as blank as the paper, for a moment, and twice as foolish. But it was for a moment only; for, of course, we immediately afterward thought of "sympathetic ink." We held the paper close to the fire and watched for the characters to come out, under the influence of the heat; but nothing appeared but some faint tracings, which we could make nothing of. We then called in the surgeon, and sent him off with orders to apply every test he was acquainted with till he got the right one, and report the contents of the letter to me the instant he brought them to the surface. This check was a confounded annoyance, and we naturally chafed under the delay; for we had fully expected to get out of that letter some of the most important secrets of the plot.

Now appeared Sergeant Rayburn, and drew from his pocket a piece of twine string about a foot long, with three knots tied in it, and held it up.

"I got it out of a gun on the waterfront," said he. "I took the tompions out of all the guns and examined close; this string was the only thing that was in any gun."

So this bit of string was Wicklow's "sign" to signify that the "Master"'s commands had not miscarried. I ordered that every sentinel who had served near that gun during the past twenty-four hours be put in confinement at once and separately, and not allowed to communicate with any one without my privity and consent.

A telegram now came from the Secretary of War. It read as follows:

SUSPEND HABEAS CORPUS. PUT TOWN UNDER MARTIAL LAW. MAKE NECESSARY ARRESTS. ACT WITH VIGOR AND PROMPTNESS. KEEP THE DEPARTMENT INFORMED.

We were now in shape to go to work. I sent out and had the lame gentleman quietly arrested and as quietly brought into the fort; I placed him under guard, and forbade speech to him or from him. He was inclined to bluster at first, but he soon dropped that.

Next came word that Wicklow had been seen to give something to a couple of our new recruits; and that, as soon as his back was turned, these had been seized and confined. Upon each was found a small bit of paper, bearing these words and signs in pencil:

EAGLE'S THIRD FLIGHT

REMEMBER XXXX

166

In accordance with instructions, I telegraphed to the Department, in cipher, the progress made, and also described the above ticket. We seemed to be in a strong enough position now to venture to throw off the mask as regarded Wicklow; so I sent for him. I also sent for and received back the letter written in sympathetic ink, the surgeon accompanying it with the information that thus far it had resisted his tests, but that there were others he could apply when I should be ready for him to do so.

Presently Wicklow entered. He had a somewhat worn and anxious look, but he was composed and easy, and if he suspected anything it did not appear in his face or manner. I allowed him to stand there a moment or two; then I said, pleasantly:

"My boy, why do you go to that old stable so much?"

He answered, with simple demeanor and without embarrassment:

"Well, I hardly know, sir; there isn't any particular reason, except that I like to be alone, and I amuse myself there."

"You amuse yourself there, do you?"

"Yes, sir," he replied, as innocently and simply as before.

"Is that all you do there?"

"Yes, sir," he said, looking up with childlike wonderment in his big, soft eyes.

"You are sure?"

"Yes, sir, sure."

After a pause I said:

"Wicklow, why do you write so much?"

"I? I do not write much, sir."

"You don't?"

"No, sir. Oh, if you mean scribbling, I do scribble some, for amusement."

"What do you do with your scribblings?"

"Nothing, sir—throw them away."

"Never send them to anybody?"

"No, sir."

I suddenly thrust before him the letter to the "Colonel." He started slightly, but immediately composed himself. A slight tinge spread itself over his cheek.

"How came you to send this piece of scribbling, then?"

"I nev—never meant any harm, sir!"

"Never meant any harm! You betray the armament and condition of the post, mean no harm by it?"

He hung his head and was silent.

"Come, speak up, and stop lying. Whom was this letter intended for?"

He showed signs of distress now; but quickly collected himself, and replied, in a tone of deep earnestness:

"I will tell you the truth, sir—the whole truth. The letter was never intended for anybody at all. I wrote it only to amuse myself. I see the error and foolishness of it now; but it is the only offense, sir, upon my honor."

"Ah, I am glad of that. It is dangerous to be writing such letters. I hope you are sure this is the only one you wrote?"

"Yes, sir, perfectly sure."

His hardihood was stupefying. He told that lie with as sincere a countenance as any creature ever wore. I waited a moment to soothe down my rising temper, and then said:

"Wicklow, jog your memory now, and see if you can help me with two or three little matters which I wish to inquire about."

"I will do my very best, sir."

"Then, to begin with—who is the 'Master'?"

It betrayed him into darting a startled glance at our faces, but that was all. He was serene again in a moment, and tranquilly answered:

"I do not know, sir."

"You do not know?"

"I do not know."

"You are sure you do not know?"

He tried hard to keep his eyes on mine, but the strain was too great; his chin sunk slowly toward his breast and he was silent; he stood there nervously fumbling with a button, an object to command one's pity, in spite of his base acts. Presently I broke the stillness with the question:

"Who are the 'Holy Alliance'?"

His body shook visibly, and he made a slight random gesture with his hands, which to me was like the appeal of a despairing creature for compassion. But he made no sound. He continued to stand with his face bent toward the ground. As we sat gazing at him, waiting for him to speak, we saw the big tears begin to roll down his cheeks. But he remained silent. After a little, I said:

"You must answer me, my boy, and you must tell me the truth. Who are the Holy Alliance?"

He wept on in silence. Presently I said, somewhat sharply: "Answer the question!"

He struggled to get command of his voice; and then, looking up appealingly, forced the words out between his sobs:

"Oh, have pity on me, sir! I cannot answer it, for I do not know."

"What!"

"Indeed, sir, I am telling the truth. I never have heard of the Holy Alliance till this moment. On my honor, sir, this is so."

"Good heavens! Look at this second letter of yours; there, do you see those words, 'Holy Alliance'? What do you say now?"

He gazed up into my face with the hurt look of one upon whom a great wrong had been wrought, then said, feelingly:

"This is some cruel joke, sir; and how could they play it upon me, who have tried all I could to do right, and have never done harm to anybody? Some one has counterfeited my hand; I never wrote a line of this; I have never seen this letter before!"

"Oh, you unspeakable liar! Here, what do you say to this?"—and I snatched the sympathetic-ink letter from my pocket and thrust it before his eyes.

His face turned white—as white as a dead person's. He wavered slightly in his tracks, and put his hand against the wall to steady himself. After a moment he asked, in so faint a voice that it was hardly audible:

"Have you—read it?"

Our faces must have answered the truth before my lips could get out a false "yes," for I distinctly saw the courage come back into that boy's eyes. I waited for him to say something, but he kept silent. So at last I said:

"Well, what have you to say as to the revelations in this letter?"

He answered, with perfect composure:

"Nothing, except that they are entirely harmless and innocent; they can hurt nobody."

I was in something of a corner now, as I couldn't disprove his assertion. I did not know exactly how to proceed. However, an idea came to my relief, and I said:

"You are sure you know nothing about the Master and the Holy Alliance, and did not write the letter which you say is a forgery?"

"Yes, sir—sure."

I slowly drew out the knotted twine string and held it up without speaking. He gazed at it indifferently, then looked at me inquiringly. My patience was sorely taxed. However, I kept my temper down, and said, in my usual voice:

"Wicklow, do you see this?"

"Yes, sir."

"What is it?"

"It seems to be a piece of string."

"Seems? It is a piece of string. Do you recognize it?"

"No, sir," he replied, as calmly as the words could be uttered.

His coolness was perfectly wonderful! I paused now for several seconds, in order that the silence might add impressiveness to what I was about to say; then I rose and laid my hand on his shoulder, and said, gravely:

"It will do you no good, poor boy, none in the world. This sign to the 'Master,' this knotted string, found in one of the guns on the waterfront—"

"Found in the gun! Oh, no, no, no! Do not say in the gun, but in a crack in the tompion!—it must have been in the crack!" and down he went on his knees and clasped his hands and lifted up a face that was pitiful to see, so ashy it was, and wild with terror.

"No, it was in the gun."

"Oh, something has gone wrong! My God, I am lost!" And he sprang up and darted this way and that, dodging the hands that were put out to catch him, and doing his best to escape from the place. But of course escape was impossible. Then he flung himself on his knees again, crying with all his might, and clasped me around the legs; and so he clung to me and begged and pleaded, saying, "Oh, have pity on me! Oh, be merciful to me! Protect me, save me. I will confess everything!"

It took us some time to quiet him down and modify his fright, and get him into something like a rational frame of mind. Then I began to question him, he answering humbly, with downcast eyes, and from time to time swabbing away his constantly flowing tears:

"So you are at heart a rebel?"

"Yes, sir."

"And a spy?"

"Yes, sir."

"And have been acting under distinct orders from outside?"

"Yes, sir."

"Willingly?"

"Yes, sir."

"Gladly, perhaps?"

"Yes, sir; it would do no good to deny it. The South is my country; my heart is Southern, and it is all in her cause."

"Then the tale you told me of your writings and the persecution of your family was made up for the occasion?"

"They—they told me to say it, sir."

"And you would betray and destroy those who pitied and sheltered you. Do you comprehend how base you are, you poor misguided thing?"

He replied with sobs only.

"Well, let that pass. To business. Who is the 'Colonel,' and where is he?"

He began to cry hard, and tried to beg off from answering. He said he would be killed if he told. I threatened to put him in the dark cell and lock him up if he did not come out with the information. At the same time I promised to protect him from all harm if he made a clean breast. For all answer, he closed his mouth firmly and put on a stubborn air which I could not bring him out of. At last I started with him; but a single glance into the dark cell converted him. He broke into a passion of weeping and supplicating, and declared he would tell everything.

So I brought him back, and he named the "Colonel," and described him particularly. Said he would be found at the principal hotel in the town, in citizen's dress. I had to threaten him again before he would describe and name the "Master." Said the Master would be found at No. 15 Bond Street, New York, passing under the name of R. F. Gaylord. I telegraphed name and description to the chief of police of the metropolis, and asked that Gaylord be arrested and held till I could send for him.

"Now," said I, "it seems that there are several of the conspirators 'outside,' presumably in New London. Name and describe them."

He named and described three men and two women—all stopping

at the principal hotel. I sent out quietly, and had them and the "Colonel" arrested and confined in the fort.

"Next, I want to know all about your three fellow-conspirators who are here in the fort."

He was about to dodge me with a falsehood, I thought; but I produced the mysterious bits of paper which had been found upon two of them, and this had a salutary effect upon him. I said we had possession of two of the men, and he must point out the third. This frightened him badly, and he cried out:

"Oh, please don't make me; he would kill me on the spot!"

I said that that was all nonsense; I would have somebody near by to protect him, and, besides, the men should be assembled without arms. I ordered all the raw recruits to be mustered, and then the poor, trembling little wretch went out and stepped along down the line, trying to look as indifferent as possible. Finally he spoke a single word to one of the men, and before he had gone five steps the man was under arrest.

As soon as Wicklow was with us again, I had those three men brought in. I made one of them stand forward, and said:

"Now, Wicklow, mind, not a shade's divergence from the exact truth. Who is this man, and what do you know about him?"

Being "in for it," he cast consequences aside, fastened his eyes on the man's face, and spoke straight along without hesitation—to the following effect:

"His real name is George Bristow. He is from New Orleans; was second mate of the coast-packet *Capitol* two years ago; is a desperate character, and has served two terms for manslaughter—one for killing a deck-hand named Hyde with a capstan-bar, and one for killing a roustabout for refusing to heave the lead, which is no part of a roustabout's business. He is a spy, and was sent here by the Colonel to act in that capacity. He was third mate of the *St. Nicholas* when she blew up in the neighborhood of Memphis, in '58, and came near being lynched for robbing the dead and wounded while they were being taken ashore in an empty wood-boat."

And so forth and so on—he gave the man's biography in full. When he had finished, I said to the man:

"What have you to say to this?"

"Barring your presence, sir, it is the infernalist lie that ever was spoke!"

I sent him back into confinement, and called the others forward in turn. Same result. The boy gave a detailed history of each, without ever hesitating for a word or a fact; but all I could get out of either rascal was the indignant assertion that it was all a lie. They would confess nothing. I returned them to captivity, and brought out the rest of my prisoners, one by one. Wicklow told all about them—what towns in the South they were from, and every detail of their connection with the conspiracy.

But they all denied his facts, and not one of them confessed a thing. The men raged, the women cried. According to their stories, they were all innocent people from out West, and loved the Union above all things in this world. I locked the gang up, in disgust, and fell to catechizing Wicklow once more.

"Where is No. 166, and who is B.B.?"

But there he was determined to draw the line. Neither coaxing nor threats had any effect upon him. Time was flying—it was necessary to institute sharp measures. So I tied him up a-tiptoe by the thumbs. As the pain increased, it wrung screams from him which were almost more than I could bear. But I held my ground, and pretty soon he shrieked out:

"Oh, please let me down, and I will tell!"

"No—you'll tell before I let you down."

Every instant was agony to him now, so out it came:

"No. 166, Eagle Hotel!"—naming a wretched tavern down by the water, a resort of common laborers, longshoremen, and less reputable folk.

So I released him, and then demanded to know the object of the conspiracy.

"To take the fort to-night," said he, doggedly and sobbing.

"Have I got all the chiefs of the conspiracy?"

"No. You've got all except those that are to meet at 166."

"What does 'Remember XXXX' mean?"

No reply.

"What is the password to No. 166?"

No reply.

"What do those bunches of letters mean—'FFFFF' and 'MMMM'? Answer! Or you will catch it again."

"I never will answer! I will die first. Now do what you please."

"Think what you are saying, Wicklow. Is it final?"

He answered steadily, and without a quiver in his voice:

"It is final. As sure as I love my wronged country and hate everything this Northern sun shines on, I will die before I will reveal those things."

I tied him up by the thumbs again. When the agony was full upon him it was heartbreaking to hear the poor thing's shrieks, but we got nothing else out of him. To every question he screamed the same reply: "I can die, and I will die; but I will never tell."

Well, we had to give it up. We were convinced that he certainly would die rather than confess. So we took him down, and imprisoned him under strict guard.

Then for some hours we busied ourselves with sending telegrams to the War Department, and with making preparations for a descent upon No. 166.

It was stirring times, that black and bitter night. Things had leaked out, and the whole garrison was on the alert. The sentinels were trebled, and nobody could move, outside or in, without being brought to a stand with a musket leveled at his head. However, Webb and I were less concerned now than we had previously been, because of the fact that the conspiracy must necessarily be in a pretty crippled condition, since so many of its principals were in our clutches.

I determined to be at No. 166 in good season, capture and gag B.B., and be on hand for the rest when they arrived. At about a quarter past one in the morning I crept out of the fortress with half a dozen stalwart and gamy U.S. regulars at my heels, and the boy Wicklow, with his hands tied behind him. I told him that we were going to No. 166, and that if I found he had lied again and was misleading us, he would have to show us the right place or suffer the consequences.

We approached the tavern stealthily and reconnoitered. A light was burning in the small barroom, the rest of the house was dark. I tried the front door; it yielded, and we softly entered, closing the door behind us. Then we removed our shoes, and I led the way to the barroom. The German landlord sat there, asleep in his chair. I woke him gently, and told him to take off his boots and precede us, warning him at the same time to utter no sound. He obeyed without a murmur, but evidently he was badly frightened. I ordered him to lead the way to 166. We ascended two or three flights of stairs as softly as a file of cats; and then, having arrived near the farther end of a long hall, we came to a door through the glazed transom of which we could discern the glow of a dim light from within. The landlord felt for me in the dark and whispered to me that that was 166. I tried the door—it was locked on the inside. I whispered an order to one of my biggest soldiers; we set our ample shoulders to the door, and with one heave we burst it from its hinges. I caught a half-glimpse of a figure in a bed—saw its head dart toward the candle; out went the light and we were in pitch darkness.

With one big bound I lit on that bed and pinned its occupant down with my knees. My prisoner struggled fiercely, but I got a grip on his throat with my left hand, and that was a good assistance to my knees in holding him down. Then straightway I snatched out my revolver, cocked it, and laid the cold barrel warningly against his cheek.

"Now somebody strike a light!" said I. "I've got him safe."

It was done. The flame of the match burst up. I looked at my captive, and, by George, it was a young woman!

I let go and got off the bed, feeling pretty sheepish. Everybody stared stupidly at his neighbor. Nobody had any wit or sense left, so sudden and overwhelming had been the surprise. The young woman began to cry, and covered her face with the sheet. The landlord said, meekly:

"My daughter, she has been doing something that is not right, *nicht wahr?*"

"Your daughter? Is she your daughter?"

"Oh, yes, she is my daughter. She is just to-night come home from Cincinnati a little bit sick."

"Confound it, that boy has lied again. This is not the right 166; this is not B.B. Now, Wicklow, you will find the correct 166 for us, or—hello! where is that boy?"

Gone, as sure as guns! And, what is more, we failed to find a trace of him. Here was an awful predicament. I cursed my stupidity in not tying him to one of the men; but it was of no use to bother about that now. What should I do in the present circumstances?—that was the question. That girl might be B.B., after all. I did not believe it, but still it would not answer to take unbelief for proof. So I finally put my men in a vacant room across the hall from 166, and told them to capture anybody and everybody that approached the girl's room, and to keep the landlord with them, and under strict watch, until further orders. Then I hurried back to the fort to see if all was right there yet.

Yes, all was right. And all remained right. I stayed up all night to make sure of that. Nothing happened. I was unspeakably glad to see the dawn come again, and be able to telegraph the Department that the Stars and Stripes still floated over Fort Trumbull.

An immense pressure was lifted from my breast. Still I did not relax vigilance, of course, nor effort, either; the case was too grave for that. I had up my prisoners, one by one, and harried them by the hour, trying to get them to confess, but it was a failure. They only gnashed their teeth and tore their hair, and revealed nothing.

About noon came tidings of my missing boy. He had been seen on the road, tramping westward, some eight miles out, at six in the morning. I started a cavalry lieutenant and a private on his track at once. They came in sight of him twenty miles out. He had climbed a fence and was wearily dragging himself across a slushy field toward a large old-fashioned mansion in the edge of a village. They rode through a bit of woods, made a detour, and closed upon the house from the opposite side; then dismounted and scurried into the kitchen. Nobody there. They slipped into the next room, which was also unoccupied; the door from that room into the front or sitting room was open. They were about to step through it when they heard a low voice; it was somebody praying. So they halted reverently, and the lieutenant put his head in and saw an old man and an old woman kneeling in a corner of that sitting-room. It was the old man that was praying, and just as he was finishing his prayer, the Wicklow boy opened the front door and stepped in. Both of those old people sprang at him and smothered him with embraces, shouting:

"Our boy! Our darling! God be praised. The lost is found! He that was dead is alive again!"

Well, sir, what do you think! That young imp was born and reared on that homestead, and had never been five miles away from it in all his life till the fortnight before he loafed into my quarters and gulled me with that maudlin yarn of his! It's as true as gospel. That old man was his father—a learned old retired clergyman; and that old lady was his mother.

Let me throw in a word or two of explanation concerning that boy and his performances. It turned out that he was a ravenous devourer of dime novels and sensation-story papers—therefore, dark mysteries and gaudy heroisms were just in his line. Then he had read newspaper reports of the stealthy goings and comings of rebel spies in our midst, and of their lurid purposes and their two or three startling achievements, till his imagination was all aflame on that subject. His constant comrade for some months had been a Yankee youth of much tongue and lively fancy, who had served for a couple of years as "mud clerk" (that is, subordinate purser) on certain of the packet-boats plying between New Orleans and points two or three hundred miles up the Mississippi—hence his easy facility in handling the names and other details pertaining to that region. Now I had spent two or three months in that part of the country before the war; and I knew just enough about it to be easily taken in by that boy, whereas a born Louisianian would probably have caught him tripping before he had talked fifteen minutes. Do you know the reason he said he would rather die than explain certain of his treasonable enigmas? Simply because he couldn't explain them!—they had no meaning; he had fired them out of his imagination without forethought or afterthought; and so, upon sudden call, he wasn't able to invent an explanation of them. For instance, he couldn't reveal what was hidden in the "sympathetic ink" letter, for the ample reason that there wasn't anything hidden in it; it was blank paper only. He hadn't put anything into a gun, and had never intended to—for his letters were all written to imaginary persons, and when he hid one in the stable he always removed the one he had put there the day before; so he was not acquainted with that knotted string, since he was seeing it for the first time when I showed it to him; but as soon as I had let him find out where it came from, he straightway adopted it, in his romantic fashion, and got some fine effects out of it. He invented "Mr. Gaylord"; there wasn't any 15 Bond Street, just then—it has been pulled down three months before. He invented the "Colonel"; he invented the glib histories of those unfortunates whom I captured and confronted him with; he invented "B.B."; he even invented No. 166, one may say, for he didn't know there was such a number in the Eagle Hotel until we went there. He stood ready to invent anybody or anything whenever it was wanted. If I called for "outside" spies, he promptly described strangers whom he had seen at the hotel, and whose names he had happened to hear. Ah, he lived in a gorgeous, mysterious, romantic world during those few stirring days, and I think it was real to him, and that he enjoyed it clear down to the bottom of his heart.

But he made trouble enough for us, and just no end of humiliation. You see, on account of him we had fifteen or twenty people under arrest and confinement in the fort, with sentinels before their doors. A lot of the captives were soldiers and such, and to them I didn't have to apologize; but the rest were first-class citizens, from all over the country, and no amount of apologies was sufficient to satisfy them. They just fumed and raged and made no end of trouble! And those two ladies—one was an Ohio Congressman's wife, the other a Western bishop's sister—well, the scorn and ridicule and angry tears they poured out on me made up a keepsake that was likely to make me remember them for a considerable time—and I shall. That old lame gentleman with the goggles was a college president from Philadelphia, who had come up to attend his nephew's funeral. He had never seen young Wicklow before, of course. Well, he not only missed the funeral, and got jailed as a rebel spy, but Wicklow had stood up there in my quarters and coldly described him as a counterfeiter, nigger-trader, horse-thief, and firebug from the most notorious rascal-nest in Galveston; and this was a thing which that poor old gentleman couldn't seem to get over at all.

And the War Department! But, oh, my soul, let's draw the curtain over that part!

IX. *Brainwashing*

While books like Koestler's *Darkness at Noon* and the reports of the great Soviet purge trials of the nineteen-thirties acquainted the public with the practice of obtaining false confessions for political purposes by relentless interrogation and torture, it was really not until after the Korean War that the term "brainwashing" came into use, denoting a means by which the content of a man's thought, his opinions, and his convictions could be changed. This was because the method had been used on large numbers of captured American soldiers who seemed on the surface, at least, to have succumbed to a process of indoctrination and intimidation while in captivity which succeeded in making them publicly repudiate the American cause in favor of the enemy's.

It was to be expected that this exercise would be attractive to the novelists in a day when psychology, especially in its more lurid aspects, has such wide appeal. Of course, the idea is not entirely new. There are plenty of grisly nineteenth-century tales in which the mad scientist or the criminal hypnotist gains control of another's mind and will, turns him into something which he previously was not, and gets him to perform acts which would otherwise be repugnant to him. The more recent version, instead of relying on hypnotism, is based on the Pavlovian psychology of conditioning, brought up to date as "reconditioning." The old responses have to be broken down and removed and new ones substituted for them. The excerpt from Deighton's *Ipcress File* makes use almost entirely of this idea. Deighton's brainwashed subject is conditioned to think differently in the future; his loyalties are reversed so that he will be willing to divulge information to the enemy without a qualm. Thus brainwashing serves the purposes of espionage. In Richard Condon's *Manchurian Candidate,* the conditioning consists of planting a group of "triggers" in the mind of a born killer, so that when the proper impulse reaches the subject he will respond with a reflex to murder. Combine this with a politically subversive purpose on the part of the brainwashers and you have an explosive tale.

LEN DEIGHTON

▼

1 A Little Piece of Hungary

*I don't think anyone has ever invented more complicated plots
than Len Deighton, or documented them so carefully with foot-
notes and appendixes that the tales, however wild, have a disturbing tone of authenticity about them. He has undoubtedly read
widely in the published literature about intelligence, and he makes
good use of it in his books. He was also at one time in British Air
Intelligence.*

*"IPCRESS" stands for "Induction of Psycho-Neuroses by Condi-
tioned Reflex with Stress." This extremely clever excerpt from* The
Ipcress File *shows what the method is. The treatment is only the
preliminary stage in the long brainwashing process—"the severing
of connections, a feeling of isolation and physical and mental
fatigue and uncertainty."*

*The narrator is an officer of British Military Intelligence who,
while investigating the defection of a brace of British scientists,
comes a little too close to the reasons behind it for the comfort of
the instigators. Inexplicably, he is framed while on a visit to a
Pacific atoll as a member of a British team of observers at an
American H-bomb experiment. He is accused of being an Iron
Curtain spy and is deported (while unconscious) to Hungary,
where, it is claimed, his mission began. At the beginning of our
excerpt he awakes from the long hypodermic sleep, during which
he was transported eastward.*

*Deighton never gives his hero a name, and he is also respon-
sible for another innovation. While the detectives and heroes of
crime fiction have frequently been ungrammatical lowlifes, the
heroes and agents of spy stories have not. Especially not in Britain.*

FROM *The Ipcress File.*

329

And especially not if they are members of the "Service." They usually wear the old-school tie and speak the King's English. Deighton's hero, possibly reflecting certain changes in the social and economic life of England in the last two decades, is proudly lower-class in origin and somewhat of a wisecracking punk, just barely tolerated by his superiors.

I came up to the surface very, very slowly; from the dark deeps I floated freely towards the dim-blue rippling surface of undrugged life.

I hurt, therefore I am.

I hugged close against the damp soil. By the light of a small window I was able to closely inspect the broken wristwatch upon which I was gently vomiting. It said 4.22. I shivered. From somewhere nearby I heard voices. No one was talking, merely groaning.

I gradually became sentient. I became aware of the heavy hot, humid air. My eyes focussed only with difficulty. I closed them. I slept. Sometimes the nights seemed as long as a week. Rough bowls of porridge-like stuff were put before me and if uneaten, removed. It was always the same man who came with the food. He had short blond hair. His features were flat with high cheekbones. He wore a light-grey two-piece track suit. One day I was sitting in the corner on the earth floor—there was no furniture—when I heard the bolts being drawn back. Kublai Khan entered, but without food. I'd never heard his voice before. His voice was hard and unattractive. He said, "Sky is blue, earth black." I looked at him for a minute or so. He said it again, "Sky is blue, earth black."

"So what?" I said.

He walked towards me and hit me with his open hand. It didn't need much to hurt me at that stage of my education. K.K. left the room and the bolts were closed and I was hungry. It took me two days to discover that I had to repeat the things K.K. said after him. It was simple enough. By the time I made that discovery I was weak from hunger and licked my food bowl avidly. The gruel was delicious and I never missed the spoon. Sometimes K.K. said, "Fire is red; cloud is white," or perhaps, "Sand is yellow; silk is soft." Sometimes his accent was so thick that it would be hours later when I had repeated the words over and over that I'd finally understand what we'd both been talking about. One day I said to him, "Suppose I buy you a Linguaphone course; do I get out of here?" For that I not only remained unfed by day, but that night he didn't bother to bring the paper-thin dirty blanket either. I'd learnt what colour the sky was by the ninth day. By then K.K. merely pointed and I reeled off all the junk I could remember. But I'd done it wrong. Somehow "Sky is red; silk is blue." K.K. shouted and hit me softly against the face. I had no food or blanket and shivered with the intense cold of the nighttime. From then on sometimes I got things right, sometimes wrong, according to the colour K.K. had decided everything was that day. Even with gruel every day I would have become weaker and weaker. I passed the "wisecrack stage," the "asking questions" stage, the "do you understand English?" stage. I was weak and exhausted, and on the day I got everything so correct that K.K. brought me a small piece of cold cooked meat, I sobbed for an hour without feeling sad—with pleasure, perhaps it was.

Every morning the door was opened and I handed out my slop pail; every night it came back again. I began to count the days. With my fingernails I incised a crude calendar in the soft wood of the door; behind it I was out of sight of the peephole. Some of the days were marked by means of a double stroke; these were the ones I heard the noises. They were generally loud enough to wake me, the noises, when they happened. They were human noises but difficult to describe as either groans or screams. They were somewhere between the two. Some days K.K. gave me a small slip of paper; typewritten on them there were orders such as: "The prisoner will sleep with arms above blankets." "The prisoner will not sleep in the daytime."

One day K.K. gave me a cigarette and lit it for me. As I sat back to puff at it he said, "Why do you smoke?" I said I didn't know and he went away; but the next day grass was sepia and I got beat about the head again.

After I had marked twenty-five days on my calendar K.K. brought me a slip that said, "The prisoner will receive a visitor for six minutes only." There was a lot of shouting in the corridor and K.K. let in a young Hungarian Army captain. He spoke reasonably good English. We stood facing each other until he said, "You requested a meeting with the Great Britain ambassador."

"I don't remember it," I said slowly.

K.K. pushed me in the chest with force that thudded me against the wall of my cell and left me breathless.

The captain continued, "I don't question. I say this. You ask." He was charming; he never once stopped smiling. "A secretary is without. He sees you now. I go. Six minutes only."

K.K. showed a man into my cell. He was so tall he beat his head against the doorjamb. He was embarrassed and awkward. He explained reluctantly that the decision wasn't his, that he was only the third under-secretary, and that sort of thing. He explained that there was no record of my being a British citizen, although he admitted that I sounded like an Englishman to him. He was so embarrassed and awkward that I almost believed that he was the British official he purported to be.

"You wouldn't think me impertinent, sir," I said, "if I asked you to give proof of identity?"

He looked madly embarrassed and said, "Not at all," a few times.

"I don't mean papers of identity, you understand, sir. Just something to show that you are in regular contact with the old country."

He looked at me blankly.

"Everyday things, sir, just so I can be sure."

He was keen to be helpful; he came back with the everyday things and a load of reasons why the Embassy could do nothing. His greatest anxiety was in case I should implicate Dalby's group, and he was always fishing for news of any statement I was going to make to the Hungarian police.

Doing this while maintaining that I wasn't a British subject was a strain even for old-school British diplomacy. "Don't get sent to a political prison," he kept saying. "They treat prisoners very badly."

"This isn't the Y.M.C.A.," I told him on one occasion. I began to wish he'd stop coming. I almost preferred K.K. At least I knew where I was with him.

Every day seemed hotter and more humid than the previous one, while the nights became more chilly.

Although K.K. knew enough English for everyday needs, that is, to feed me or punch me on the nose, I found I could get a cup of sweet black coffee from one of the guards when I learnt enough Hungarian to ask. He was an old man looking like a bit-player in a Ruritanian schmaltz opera. Sometimes he gave me a small piece of chewing tobacco.

Finally the tall British man came to see me for the last time. They went through the shouting and preliminaries, but this time it was only the Army captain who spoke. He told me that "Her Majesty's Government" under no circumstances can regard me as a British subject. "Therefore," he said, "the trial will proceed under Hungarian law." The man from the Embassy said how sorry he was.

"Trial?" I said, and K.K. smashed me against the wall again, so I kept quiet. The British man gave me a sorry-old-chap look with a flick of the eyes, put on his rolled-brim hat and disappeared.

K.K. had a rare flash of altruism and brought me a black coffee in a real porcelain cup. Surprise followed surprise, for when I sipped it, I discovered it had a shot of plum brandy in it. It had been a long day. I curled my feet as near to my head as possible and, curling my arms close, I went to sleep, thinking, "If I don't get out of here quickly you fellows are going to miss each other."

Some nights they left the light on all night, and on nights when I had got every single K.K. colour wrong they sent the old moustachioed guard in to keep me awake all night. He talked to me and, if K.K. was there, shouted at me not to lean against the wall. He talked about everything he knew, his family and his days in the Army, anything to keep me awake. I couldn't translate a word of it, but he was a simple man and easy to understand. He showed me the height of his four children, photos of all his family, and now and again made a flickering movement with his hand that meant I could lean against the wall and rest while he stood half in the corridor, listening for K.K.'s return.

Once every third day the Army captain returned, and although I may have misunderstood, I believe he told me that he was my defence counsel. On the first visit he read my indictment; it took about an hour. It was in Hungarian. He translated a few phrases like "enemy of the state," "high treason," "plotting for the illegal overthrow of peoples' democracies," and there were a few "imperialism"s and "capitalism"s thrown in for good measure.

There were thirty-four marks on my door now. By resting and sleeping in snatches I had put a few of my nerve endings together, but I was no Steve Reeves. The diet was keeping me pretty low physically and mentally. Each morning I got up feeling like the first few frames in a Horlick's strip. It was pretty obvious that if I didn't swim against the current there would be nothing left of the me I'd known and loved. There was no chance of a "Houdini" through the boltwork and a fighting retreat out of the main gates. It was to be a cool, calm, slow walk or I wouldn't be there. Thus did I reason on my thirty-fifth day of isolation and hunger.

The only person around who broke the rules was the old man. Everyone else had the door locked behind them; the old man stood halfway out of it to give me a few minutes' sleep. There was no alternative. I had no weapon but the door. I wanted to escape at night, so that meant I couldn't use the light flex. The slop pail was too heavy to be used adroitly. No, it was the door, which meant, I'm afraid, that the old man got it. That night I was all set to try. Pretending to rest, I leaned against the wall, lining the door up against my target. He didn't come close enough. I did nothing. When I finally went to bed I shivered until I went to sleep. It was a couple of nights later that the old man brought me a cigarette. I hit him with the door—the bolt mechanism swung against his head and he dropped unconscious to the floor. I dragged him inside the door; his breathing was irregular and his face very flushed. He was an old man. At the last minute my training almost failed. I almost couldn't hit him again as he lay there, the cigarette he'd brought me still in his hand.

I took his wooden HB pencil, relocked the door, and in his guard's jacket and cap and my dark prison trousers I softly descended the old dark wooden stairs. A light of low wattage glowed in the main hall, and from under a door to my right a slot of light and soft American music slid across to me. The main door was unguarded from inside, but I decided against touching it. Instead I took the pencil and I opened the door* of an unlit room to my right. It must have been three and a half minutes at least since I had left my cell, walked the couple of yards to the stairs and negotiated them without causing a creak.

I closed the door behind me. The moonlight showed me the filing cases and books that lined the room. I ran my fingers round the window frame and encountered the electric wire of the alarm. Then I stood on the desk to remove the electric bulb. There was a loud cracking noise—I had cracked a pencil underfoot. The soft music from the radio in the next room ceased suddenly. I held my breath, but there was only a whistle as the tuning control was turned. The exertion of stretching my hands above my head left me shaking and weak.

From my pocket I took the English sixpence that Anthony Eden's friend had given me and slipped it into the bulb socket before replacing the bulb. Still in the moonlight, I got slowly down from the desk. I groped around on the floor. I was lucky. There was a big two-kilowatt electric fire plugged into a wall point. The strong rosary that snaggle tooth had brought me as my second English "everyday thing" I wrapped tightly round and round the elements. There was no time for electrical legerdemain. It was the work of a minute to switch on the wall plug and the light switch. There was no emergency lighting system and the flash and bang were pretty good. I could hear people blundering into doors and clicking switches. The main power fuse seemed to have gone, and the window opened easily without bells or buzzers. I slipped through and closed it behind me, although I couldn't lock it.

I crouched down in the wet grass and I heard the front door open

* This method of opening a lock with a pencil has been withdrawn from the MS.

and saw a torch flash in the room I had just left. No one tried the window. I remained crouching. A car started up and I could hear two people speaking loudly quite close by, but the sound of the engine blotted out the words.

I walked without hurrying towards the rear of the house. I probably put too much reliance on my peaked cap. I fell into some soft earth and, backing out of it, grabbed at some thorny bushes. A dog barked, too close for comfort. I could see the rear wall now; it was about as high as I was. I ran a tentative finger along it, but there was no barbed wire or broken glass. I had both palms on it, but it required more strength than I had to pull myself up bodily. That damn dog barked again. I looked back at the prison building. Someone was in the conservatory now, with one of those powerful portable lights. They had only to swing it round the walls. Perhaps I should lie down flat in the grass, but when the big beam shot out I managed to get the side of one foot on the wall top. I flexed my leg muscles, and as the light skimmed the wall I rolled my empty belly over and fell down the far side. I knew I mustn't stay down, although it was very pleasant, breathing long grassy lungfuls of the wet night air. I felt soaked, hungry, free and frightened, but as I started to walk, I found myself entrapped in an intricate framework of slim wooden rods and wires that enmeshed head and limbs. The more I tried to free myself, the more tangled I was. A narrow slit of light ahead of me grew fatter to become a rectangle, and a man's silhouette was centred in it.

"Here! Is someone there?" he called, then as his eyes became accustomed to the darkness, "Here, get out of my bloody 'runners,' you silly——!"

I heard a clock strike ten P.M.

It would be easy now to pretend that I knew all the answers at that stage. Easy to pretend that I'd known they were holding me in a big house in London's Wood Green from the word go. But I didn't. I half guessed, but the conviction had oozed from my body day by day. As I languished, underfed and miserable, it became more and more difficult to think of anything outside of my little cell and K.K. In another ten days the theory that London was just over the garden wall would have been totally beyond my comprehension. That's why I'd escaped. It was then or never.

▼

2 The Trigger

The Manchurian Candidate is about an American hero of the Korean War, a Medal of Honor winner, Sergeant Raymond Shaw, who was captured along with his fellow soldiers and officers while out on patrol. He was then subjected to a Chinese brainwashing operation, the purpose of which was to implant in Shaw, whom the Chinese had spotted as a man with murder in his blood, certain psychological "triggers," to which he would at any future time automatically respond by carrying out whatever act was immediately suggested to him. The intention was that this act should be murder, political murder, but in the episode which follows, in which the trigger is accidentally discovered, a quite random act is committed by Shaw, simply because it happens to be the first thing he hears after the trigger has activated his built-in reflexes. Colonel Marco is one of the officers captured with Shaw and present with him when the American captives, after a concentrated dose of drugs, mass hypnotism, and brainwashing, were exhibited by the Chinese specialists to their Russian colleagues in order to show how men can be transformed into automatons. Marco vaguely remembers this scene in his nightmares—sufficiently, at any rate, to suspect what the Chinese have done to Shaw, and to take on the project for Army counterintelligence of looking for the key to Shaw's behavior, along with the FBI agent Lou Amjac and a host of specialists.

The first break in the long, long wait through dread, even though it was a totally incomprehensible break, came in May 1960. It hap-

FROM *The Manchurian Candidate.*

pened when Marco was late for a two o'clock date with Raymond at Hungarian Charlie's booze outlet, across the street from the flash shop.

It was a fairly well-known fact to practically anyone who did not lack batteries for his hearing aid that Hungarian Charlie was one of the more stridently loquacious publicans in that not unsilent business. Only one other boniface, who operated farther north on Fifty-first Street, had a bigger mouth. Charlie talked as though Sigmund Freud himself had given permission, nay, had urged him, to tell everyone everything that came into his head, and in bad grammar, yet. Ten minutes before Marco got to the saloon, with Raymond seated at bar centre staring at a glass of beer on a slow afternoon, Charlie had pinned a bookmaker at the entrance end of the bar, a man who would much rather have talked to his new friend, a young, dumpy blonde with a face like a bat's and the thirst of a burning oil field. Charlie was telling them, loud and strong, hearty and healthy, about his wife's repulsive elder brother who lived with them and about how he had followed Charlie all over the apartment all day Sunday telling him what to do with his life, which was a new development brought on by the fact that he had just inherited twenty-three hundred dollars from a deceased friend whom he had been engaged to marry for fourteen years, which was a generous thing for her to have done when it was seen from the perspective, Charlie said, that this bum had never given the broad so much as a box of talcum powder for Christmas, it having been his policy always to pick a fight with her immediately preceding gift-exchanging occasions.

"Lissen," Charlie yelled, "you inherit that kinda money and you naturally feel like you know alla answers and also it puts me in a position where I can't exactly kick him inna ankle, you know what I mean? So, wit' the new pernna view, I say tuh him, very patient, 'Why don't you pass the time by playing a liddul solitaire?' "

Raymond was on a bar stool twelve feet away from Charlie and had in no way been eavesdropping on the conversation, as that could have been judged suicidal. He rapped on the bar peremptorily with a half dollar. Charlie looked up, irritated. One lousy customer in the whole lousy joint and he has to be a point killer.

"What arreddy?" Charlie inquired.

"Give me a deck of cards," Raymond said. Charlie looked at the bookmaker, then rolled his eyes heavenward. He shrugged his shoulders like the tenor in *Tosca*, opened a drawer behind him, took out a blue bicycle deck, and slid it along the polished surface to Raymond.

Raymond took the deck from its box and began to shuffle smoothly

and absentmindedly, and Charlie went back to barbering the bookmaker and the young, dumpy blonde. Raymond was laying down the
second solitaire spread when Marco came in, ten minutes later. He
greeted Charlie as he passed him, ordering a beer, then stood at the
bar at Raymond's elbow. "I got held up in traffic," he said ritualis-
tically. "And so forth." Raymond didn't answer.

"Are you clear for dinner, Raymond?" Marco wasn't aware that
Raymond was ignoring him. "My girl insists that the time has come to
meet you, and no matter how I try to get out of it, that's the way it's
got to be. Besides, I am about to marry the little thing, ringside one
hundred and thirty-nine pounds, and we would like you to be the best
man."

The queen of diamonds showed at the twenty-third card turn.
Raymond scooped the cards together, ignoring Marco. Become aware
of the silence, Marco was studying Raymond. Raymond squared the
deck, put it face down on top of the bar, placed the queen of
diamonds face up on top of the stack, and stared at it in a detached
and preoccupied manner, unaware that Marco was there. Charlie put
the glass of beer in front of Marco at the rate of one hundred and
thirty-seven words a minute, decibel count well above the middle
register, then turned, walking back to the bookmaker and the broad to
punctuate his narrative by recalling the height of the repartee with his
brother-in-law: "Why don't you take a cab quick to Central Park and
jump inna lake, I says," and his voice belted it loud and strong as
though a sound engineer were riding gain on it. Raymond brushed
past Marco, walked rapidly past the bookmaker and the girl, and out
of the saloon.

"Hey! Hey, Raymond!" Marco yelled. "Where you going?" Raymond was gone. By the time Marco got to the street he saw Raymond
slamming the door of a cab. The taxi took off fast, disappearing around
the corner, going uptown.

Marco returned to the saloon. He sipped at his beer with growing
anxiety. The action of the game of solitaire nagged at him until he
placed it in the dreams. It was one of the factors in the dreams that he
had placed no meaning upon because he had come to regard the game
as an aberration that had wriggled into the fantasy. He had discussed
it because it had been there, but after one particularly bright young
doctor said that Raymond had undoubtedly been doing something
with his hands which had *looked* as though he were playing solitaire,
Marco had gradually allowed the presence of the game in the dream to
dim and fade. He now felt the conviction that something momentous
had just happened before his eyes but he did not know what it was.

"Hey, Charlie."

Business of rolling eyes heavenward, business of slow turn, exaggerating the forbearance of an extremely patient man.

"Yeah, arreddy."

"Does Mr. Shaw play solitaire in here much?"

"Whatta you mean—much?"

"Did he ever play solitaire in here before?"

"No."

"Give me another beer." Marco went to the telephone booth, digging for change. He called Lou Amjac.

Amjac sounded sourer than ever. "What the hell happened to you?"

"He rented a rowboat and he jumped in the lake."

"If you're kidding me, Lou—"

"I'm not kidding you!"

"I'll meet you there in ten minutes."

"Colonel Marco!"

"What?"

"Did it finally break?"

"I think so. I—yeah, I think so."

At first, Raymond flatly denied he had done such a thing but when the shock and embarrassment had worn off and he was forced to agree that his clothes were sopping wet, he was more nearly ready to admit that something which tended towards the unusual had happened. He, Amjac, and Marco sat in a squad room, at Marco's request. When Raymond seemed to have done with spluttering and expostulating, Marco spoke to him in a low, earnest voice, like a dog trainer, in a manner too direct to be evaded.

"We've been kidding each other for a long time, Raymond, and I put up with it because I had no other choice. You didn't believe me. You decided I was sick and that you had to go along with the gag to help me. Didn't you, Raymond?" Raymond stared at his sodden shoes. "Raymond! Am I right?"

"Yes."

"Now hear this. You stood beside me at Hungarian Charlie's and you didn't know I was there. You played a game of solitaire. Do you remember that?"

Raymond shook his head. Marco and Amjac exchanged glances.

"You took a cab to Central Park. You rented a rowboat. You rowed to the middle of the lake, then you jumped overboard. You have always been as stubborn as a dachshund, Raymond, but we can produce maybe thirty eye-witnesses who saw you go over the side, then walk to shore, so don't tell me again that you never did such a thing—and stop kidding yourself that they are not inside your head. We can't help you if you won't help us."

"But I don't *remember*," Raymond said. Something had happened to permit him to feel fear. Jocie was coming home. He might have something to lose. The creeping paralysis of fright was so new to him that his joints seemed to have rusted.

The capacious house in the Turtle Bay district jumped with activity that evening and it went on all through the night. A Board review agreed to accept the game of solitaire as Raymond's trigger; and once they had made the connection they were filled with admiration for the technician who had conceived of it. Three separate teams worked with Hungarian Charlie, the talker's talker, the bookmaker, and the young, dumpy blonde.

At first, the blonde refused to talk, as she had every reason to believe that she had been picked up on an utterly non-political charge. She said, "I refuse to answer on the grounds. It might intend to incriminate." They had to bring Marco in to bail her attitude out of that stubborn durance. She knew Marco from around Charlie's place and she liked the way he smelled so much that she was dizzy with the hope of co-operating with him. He held her hand for a short time and explained in a feeling voice that she had not been arrested and that she was co-operating mainly as a big favour to him, and who knew?—the whole thing could turn out to be pretty exciting. "I dig," she said, and everything was straightened out although she seemed purposely to misunderstand his solicitude by trying to climb into his lap as they discussed the various areas, but everybody was too busy to notice, and he was gone about two seconds after she had said, listen, she'd love to co-operate but why did they have to co-operate in different rooms?

The bookmaker was even more wary. He was a veritable model of shiftiness, which was heightened by the fact that he was carrying over twenty-nine thousand dollars' worth of action on the sixth race at Jamaica, so he couldn't possibly keep his mind on what these young men were talking to him about. They persuaded him to take a mild sedative, then a particularly sympathetic young fellow walked with him along the main corridor and, in a highly confidential manner, asked him to feel free to discuss what had him so disturbed. The bookmaker knew (1) that these were not the type police which booked gamblers, and (2) he had always responded to highly confidential, whispering treatment. He explained about his business worries, stating, for insurance, that a friend of his—not he himself—was carrying all that action. Amjac made a call and got the race result. It was Pepper Dog, Wendy's Own, and Italian Mae, in that order. Not one client had run in the money. The bookmaker was opened up like a hydrant.

Hungarian Charlie, natch, was with it from the word go.

Marco played through one hundred and twenty-five solitaire layouts until the technicians were sure, time after time and averaging off, where Raymond had stopped his play in Hungarian Charlie's saloon. They tested number systems as possible triggers, then they settled down to a symbol system and began to work with face cards because of the colours and their identification with human beings. They threw out the male face cards, kings and knaves, based on Raymond's psychiatric pattern. They started Marco working with the four queens. He discarded the queens of spades and clubs, right off. They stacked decks with different red queens at the twenty-third position, which fell as the fifth card on the fifth stack, and Marco dealt out solitaire strips. He made it the queen of diamonds, for sure. They kept him at it, but he connected the queen of diamonds with the face-up card on the squared deck on the bar; then all at once, as it is said to happen to saints and alcoholics, a voice he had heard in nightmares perhaps seven hundred times came to him. It was Yen Lo's voice saying: "The queen of diamonds, in so many ways reminiscent of Raymond's dearly loved and hated mother, is the second key that will clear his mechanism for any assignments." They had it made. Marco knew they had it made. Hungarian Charlie, the bookmaker, and the young, dumpy blonde filled in the background of minor confirmations.

The FBI called Cincinnati and arranged to have one dozen factory-sealed force packs flown to New York by Army plane. The cards reached the Turtle Bay house at 9:40 A.M. A force pack is an item usually made up for magic shops and novelty stores for party types who fan out cards before their helpless quarries saying, "Take a card, any card." Force packs contain fifty-two copies of the same card to make it easier for the forcer to guess which card has been picked; the dozen packs from Cincinnati were made up exclusively of queens of diamonds. Marco figured the time would come to try Raymond out as player of the ancient game of solitaire that very morning, and he didn't want to have to waste any time waiting for the queen of diamonds to show up in the play.

An hour after Chunjin had made his report to the Soviet security drop from the red telephone booth at the Fifty-ninth Street exit from

Central Park, a meeting was called between Raymond's American operator and a District of Columbia taxi driver who also served as chief of Soviet security for the region. As they drove around downtown Washington, with Raymond's operator as passenger, the conversation seemed disputatious.

Raymond's operator told the hackman emphatically that they would be foolish to panic because of what was obviously a ten-thousand-to-one happenstance by which some idiot had unknowingly stumbled upon the right combination of words in Raymond's presence.

"If you please."

"What?"

"This is a professional thing on which I cannot be fooled. Cannot. They have been working over him. He has broken. They have chosen this contemptuous and insulting way of telling us that he has cracked and is useless to us."

"You people are really insecure. God knows I have always felt that the British overdo that paternal talk about this being a young country but, my God, you really *are* a young country. You just haven't been at it long enough. Please understand that if our security people knew what Raymond had been designed to do they would not let you know they knew. Once they find out what Raymond is up to, which is virtually impossible, they'll want to nail whoever is moving him. Me. Then, through me, you. Certainly you people do enough of this kind of thing in your own country, so why can't you understand it here?"

"But why should such a conservative man jump in a lake?"

"Because the phrase 'go jump in the lake' is an ancient slang wheeze in this country and some boob happened on the trigger accidentally, that's how."

"I am actually sick with anxiety."

"So are they," Raymond's operator said blandly, enjoying the bustle of traffic all around them and thinking what a hick town this so-called world capital was.

"But how can you be so calm?"

"I took a tranquillizer."

"A what?"

"A pill."

"Oh. But how can you be so sure that is what happened?"

"Because I'm smart. I'm not a stupid Russian. Because Raymond is at large. They allow him to move about. Marco is tense and frightened. Read the Korean's reports, for Christ's sake, and get hold of yourself."

"We have so little time and this is wholly my responsibility as far as my people are concerned."

"Heller," Raymond's operator said, reading the name from the identification card which said that the driver's name was Frank Heller, "suppose I prove to you that Raymond is ours, not theirs."

"How?" The Soviet policeman had to swerve the cab to avoid a small foreign car that hurtled across from a side street at his left; he screamed out the window in richly accented, Ukrainian-kissed English. "Why dawn't you loo quare you are gung, gew tsilly tson of a bitch?"

"We certainly have a severe case of nerves today, don't we?" Raymond's operator murmured.

"Never mind my nerves. To be on the right of an approaching vehicle is to have the right of way! He broke the law! How can you prove Raymond is not theirs?"

"I'll have him kill Marco."

"Aaaaah." It was a long, soft, satisfaction-stuffed expletive having a zibeline texture. It suggested the end of a perfect day, a cause well served, a race well run.

"Marco is in charge of this particular element of counterespionage," Raymond's operator said. "Marco is Raymond's only friend. So? Proof?"

"Yes."

"Good."

"When?"

"Tonight, I think. Let me off here."

x. *Some Losers*

The salient characteristic of spy fiction, as of other adventure stories, is that the hero must win and the enemy must be bested. Also the hero must not only successfully complete his mission but he must survive. One reason for this is that the public wants a happy and successful hero. Another is that if our particular hero makes a hit, he ought to be available for a whole series of novels. Someone once pointed out that the popularity of much successful mystery fiction depended as much upon the distinctive and intriguing detective who dominates the scene—Maigret, Poirot, Nero Wolfe, Lord Peter Wimsey—as upon the detection he accomplishes. Some of our spies have also become fixtures—Tommy Hambledon, Hugh North, Peter Ward, and, of course, the most popular of them all, James Bond. It is therefore a bit of a shock for more reasons than one when the hero of a spy story loses the battle and, worst of all, doesn't come home.

I have included two rare samples of losers here. Le Carré's novels do not attempt to fulfill the ordinary reader's desire for a mere adventure story but are concerned with human character and moral issues. Given le Carré's aim, it is not surprising that his spies fail, because in his somewhat Puritanical view of things spying is a misbegotten profession in an imperfect world. If people were good and nations decent, there would be no need for it. Which is quite true.

Fleming's reason for turning James Bond into a loser had a somewhat different basis. But more of that later.

I have also included in this section a Somerset Maugham classic. His hero, Ashenden, survives and is, in fact, in no real danger, but he is outwitted, which is another kind of losing.

JOHN LE CARRÉ

▼

1 Taylor's Run

This is the opening chapter of what I consider to be John le Carré's best book—despite the immense and deserved popularity of The Spy Who Came in from the Cold. *But as the traitor and spy Kim Philby said about the latter book in a letter to his wife: "The whole plot from beginning to end is basically implausible, at any rate, to anyone who has any real knowledge of the business." And who should know better than Philby?*

The Looking Glass War is quite another matter. To anyone who has ever been associated with an intelligence service, its jumble of unusual personalities, their speech and behavior, their daily business, and even the awful scheme which carries them in their enthusiasm far from reality—all ring true. It is perhaps for this very reason that the nonprofessional reader may miss much that is outstanding in the book and thus likes it less than The Spy Who Came in from the Cold. *I must also admit that the rather special circumstances of* The Looking Glass War *would probably leave many readers cold.*

The situation is this: A special unit of British intelligence, which during the war was engaged in parachute drops and operations behind enemy lines, has gone somewhat to seed and has been relegated to purely analytical and documentary matters. Suddenly the unit develops some evidence about an area of East Germany which appears to be of great intelligence significance (the reason for the overflight in our excerpt). Its chiefs manage to wangle permission from a busy War Office to undertake agent operations again. The whole unit is immediately galvanized into action on a wartime footing. Superannuated spymasters take to sleeping at the office, mystifying their wives, and a caricature of wartime super-

FROM *The Looking Glass War.*

security descends upon the place. The operation, of course, comes to grief in a ridiculous and pathetic manner, having been mounted according to World War II methods and techniques in a world twenty years more sophisticated and complex.

Snow covered the airfield. It had come from the north, in the mist, driven by the night wind, smelling of the sea. There it would stay all winter, threadbare on the gray earth, an icy, sharp dust; not thawing and freezing, but static like a year without seasons. The changing mist, like the smoke of war, would hang over it, swallow up now a hangar, now the radar hut, now the machines; release them piece by piece, drained of color, black carrion on a white desert.

It was a scene of no depth, no recession and no shadows. The land was one with the sky; figures and buildings locked in the cold like bodies in an ice floe.

Beyond the airfield there was nothing; no house, no hill, no road; not even a fence, a tree; only the sky pressing on the dunes, the running fog that lifted on the muddy Baltic shore. Somewhere inland were the mountains.

A group of children in school caps had gathered at the long observation window, chattering in German. Some wore ski clothes. Taylor gazed dully past them, holding a glass in his gloved hand. A boy turned around and stared at him, blushed and whispered to the other children. They fell silent.

He looked at his watch, making a wide arc with his arm, partly to free the sleeve of his overcoat and partly because it was his style; a military man, he wished you to say, decent regiment, decent club, knocked around in the war.

Ten to four. The plane was an hour late. They would have to announce the reason soon over the loudspeaker. He wondered what they would say: delayed by fog, perhaps; delayed takeoff. They probably didn't even know—and they certainly would not admit—that she was two hundred miles off course, and south of Rostock. He finished his drink, turned to get rid of the empty glass. He had to admit that some of these foreign hooches, drunk in their own country, weren't at all bad. On the spot, with a couple of hours to kill and ten degrees of frost the other side of the window, you could do a lot worse than Steinhäger. He'd make them order it at the Alias Club when he got back. Cause quite a stir.

The loudspeaker was humming; it blared suddenly, faded out and began again, properly tuned. The children stared expectantly at it.

First, the announcement in Finnish, then in Swedish, now in English. Northern Air Services regretted the delay to their charter flight two-nine-zero from Düsseldorf. No hint of how long, no hint of why. They probably didn't know themselves.

But Taylor knew. He wondered what would happen if he sauntered over to that pert little hostess in the glass box and told her: two-nine-zero will be a bit of time yet, my dear, she's been blown off course by heavy northerly gales over the Baltic, bearings all to Hades. The girl wouldn't believe him, of course, she'd think he was a crank. Later she'd know better. She'd realize he was something rather unusual, something rather special.

Outside it was already growing dark. Now the ground was lighter than the sky; the swept runways stood out against the snow like dykes, stained with the amber glow of marking lights. In the nearest hangars neon tubes shed a weary pallor over men and airplanes; the foreground beneath him sprang briefly to life as a beam from the control tower flicked across it. A fire engine had pulled away from the workshops on the left and joined the three ambulances already parked short of the center runway. Simultaneously they switched on their blue rotating lights, and stood in line patiently flashing out their warning. The children pointed at them, chattering excitedly.

The girl's voice began again on the loudspeaker; it could only have been a few minutes since the last announcement. Once more the children stopped talking and listened. The arrival of flight two-nine-zero would be delayed at least another hour. Further information would be given as soon as it became available. There was something in the girl's voice, midway between surprise and anxiety, which seemed to communicate itself to the half-dozen people sitting at the other end of the waiting room. An old woman said something to her husband, stood up, took her handbag and joined the group of children. For a time she peered stupidly into the twilight. Finding no comfort there, she turned to Taylor and said in English, "What is become of the Düsseldorf plane?" Her voice had the throaty, indignant lilt of a Dutchwoman. Taylor shook his head. "Probably the snow," he replied. He was a brisk man; it went with his military way.

Pushing open the swing door, Taylor made his way downstairs to the reception hall. Near to the main entrance he recognized the yellow pennant of Northern Air Services. The girl at the desk was very pretty.

"What's happened to the Düsseldorf flight?" His style was confiding; they said he had a knack with little girls.

She smiled and shrugged her shoulders. "I expect it is the snow. We are often having delays in autumn."

"Why don't you ask the boss?" he suggested, indicating with a nod the telephone in front of her.

"They will tell it on the loudspeaker," she said, "as soon as they know."

"Who's the skipper, dear?"

"Please?"

"Who's the skipper, the captain?"

"Captain Lansen."

"Is he any good?"

The girl was shocked. "Captain Lansen is a very experienced pilot."

Taylor looked her over, grinned and said, "He's a very *lucky* pilot anyway, my dear." They said he knew a thing or two, old Taylor did. They said it at the Alias on Friday nights.

Lansen. It was odd to hear a name spoken out like that. In the outfit they simply never did it. They favored circumlocution, cover names, anything but the original: Archie boy, our flying friend, our friend up North, the chappie who takes the snapshots; they would even use the tortuous collection of figures and letters by which he was known on paper; but never in any circumstances the name.

Lansen. Leclerc had shown him a photograph in London: a boyish thirty-five, fair and good-looking. He'd bet those hostesses went mad about him; that's all they were, anyway, cannon fodder for the pilots. No one else got a look in. Taylor ran his right hand quickly over the outside of his overcoat pocket just to make sure the envelope was still there. He'd never carried this sort of money before. Five thousand dollars for one flight; seventeen hundred pounds, tax free, to lose your way over the Baltic. Mind you, Lansen didn't do that every day. This was special. Leclerc had said so. He wondered what she would do if he leaned across the counter and told her who he was; showed her the money in that envelope. He'd never had a girl like that, a real girl, tall and young.

He went upstairs again to the bar. The barman was getting to know him. Taylor pointed to the bottle of Steinhäger on the center shelf and said, "Give me another of those, d'you mind? That's it, the fellow just behind you; some of your local poison."

"It's German," the barman said.

He opened his wallet and took out a banknote. In the cellophane compartment there was a photograph of a girl, perhaps nine years old, wearing glasses and holding a doll. "My daughter," he explained to the barman, and the barman gave a watery smile.

His voice varied a lot, like the voice of a commercial traveler. His phony drawl was more extravagant when he addressed his own class, when it was a matter of emphasizing a distinction which did not exist; or as now, when he was nervous.

He had to admit: he was windy. It was an eerie situation for a man of his experience and age, going over from routine courier work to operational stuff. This was a job for those swine in the Circus, not for his outfit at all. A different kettle of fish altogether, this was, from the ordinary run-of-the-mill stuff he was used to; stuck out on a limb, miles from nowhere. It beat him how they ever came to put an airport in a place like this. He quite liked the foreign trips as a rule: a visit to old Jimmy Gorton in Hamburg, for instance, or a night on the tiles in Madrid. It did him good to get away from Joanie. He'd done the Turkish run a couple of times, though he didn't care for wogs. But even that was a piece of cake compared to this: first-class travel and the bags on the seat beside him, an Allied pass in his pocket; a man had status, doing a job like that; good as the diplomatic boys, or nearly. But this was different, and he didn't like it.

Leclerc had said it was big, and Taylor believed him. They had got him a passport with another name. Malherbe. Pronounced Mallaby, they said. Christ alone knew who'd chosen it. Taylor couldn't even spell it; made a botch of the hotel register when he signed in that morning. The subsistence was fantastic, of course: fifteen quid a day operational expenses, no vouchers asked for. He'd heard the Circus gave seventeen. He could make a good bit on that, buy something for Joanie. She'd probably rather have the money.

He'd told her, of course: he wasn't supposed to, but Leclerc didn't know Joanie. He lit a cigarette, drew from it and held it in the palm of his hand like a sentry smoking on duty. How the hell was he supposed to push off to Scandinavia without telling his wife?

He wondered what those kids were doing, glued to the window all this time. Amazing the way they managed the foreign language. He looked at his watch again, scarcely noticing the time, touched the envelope in his pocket. Better not have another drink; he must keep a clear head. He tried to guess what Joanie was doing now. Probably having a sit-down with a gin and something. A pity she had to work all day.

He suddenly realized that everything had gone silent. The barman was standing still, listening. The old people at the table were listening too, their silly faces turned toward the observation window. Then he heard it quite distinctly, the sound of an aircraft, still far away but approaching the airfield. He made quickly for the window, was halfway there when the loudspeaker began; after the first few words of German the children, like a flock of pigeons, fluttered away to the reception lounge. The party at the table had stood up; the women were reaching for their gloves, the men for their coats and briefcases. At last the announcer gave the English. Lansen was coming in to land.

Taylor stared into the night. There was no sign of the plane. He waited, his anxiety mounting. It's like the end of the world, he thought, the end of the bloody world out there. Supposing Lansen crashed? Supposing they found the cameras? He wished someone else were handling it: Woodford, why hadn't Woodford taken it over, or sent that clever college boy Avery? The wind was stronger; he could swear it was far stronger; he could tell from the way it tore at the flares; the way it made white columns on the horizon, dashing them vehemently away like a hated creation. A gust struck suddenly at the windows in front of him, making him recoil, and there followed the rattle of ice grains and the short grunt of the wooden frame. Again he looked at his watch; it had become a habit with Taylor. It seemed to help, knowing the time.

Lansen will never make it in this, never.

His heart stood still. Softly at first, then rising swiftly to a wail, he heard the klaxons, all four together, moaning out over that god-forsaken airfield like the howl of starving animals. Fire . . . the plane must be on fire. He's on fire and he's going to try and land. . . . He turned frantically, looking for someone who could tell him.

The barman was standing beside him, polishing a glass, looking through the window.

"What's going on?" Taylor shouted. "Why are the sirens going?"

"They always make the sirens in bad weather," he replied. "It is the law."

"Why are they letting him land?" Taylor insisted. "Why don't they route him further south? It's too small, this place; why don't they send him somewhere bigger?"

The barman shook his head indifferently. "It's not so bad," he said, indicating the airfield. "Besides, he is very late. Maybe he has no petrol."

They saw the plane low over the airfield, her lights alternating above the flares; her spotlights scanned the runway. She was down, safely down, and they heard the roar of her throttle as she began the long taxi to the reception point.

The bar had emptied. Taylor was alone. He ordered a drink. He knew his drill: stay put in the bar, Leclerc had said; Lansen will meet you in the bar. He'll take a bit of time; got to cope with his flight documents, clear his cameras. Taylor heard the children singing downstairs, and a woman leading them. Why the hell did he have to be surrounded by kids and women? He was doing a man's job, wasn't he, with five thousand dollars in his pocket and a phony passport.

"There are no more flights today," the barman said. "They have forbidden all flying now."

Taylor nodded. "I know. It's bloody shocking out there, shocking."

The barman was putting away bottles. "There was no danger," he added soothingly. "Captain Lansen is a very good pilot." He hesitated, not knowing whether to put away the Steinhäger.

"Of course there wasn't any danger," Taylor snapped. "Who said anything about danger?"

"Another drink?" the barman said.

"No, but you have one. Go on, have one yourself."

The barman reluctantly gave himself a drink, locked the bottle away.

"All the same, how do they do it?" Taylor asked. His voice was conciliatory, putting it right with the barman. "They can't see a thing in weather like this, not a damn thing." He smiled knowingly. "You sit there in the nose and you might just as well have your eyes shut for all the good they do. I've seen it," Taylor added, his hands loosely cupped in front of him as though he were at the controls. "I know what I'm talking about . . . and they're the first to catch it, those boys, if something *does* go wrong." He shook his head. "They can keep it," he declared. "They're entitled to every penny they earn. Specially in a kite that size. They're held together with string, those things; string."

The barman nodded distantly, finished his drink, washed up the empty glass, dried it and put it on the shelf under the counter. He unbuttoned his white jacket.

Taylor made no move.

"Well," said the barman with a mirthless smile, "we have to go home now."

"What do you mean, *we?*" Taylor asked, opening his eyes wide and tilting back his head. "What do you mean?" He'd take on anyone now; Lansen had landed.

"I have to close the bar."

"Go home indeed. Give us another drink, come on. You can go home if you like. I happen to live in London." His tone was challenging, half playful, half resentful, gathering volume. "And since your aircraft companies are unable to *get* me to London, or any other damn place until tomorrow morning, it's a bit silly of you to tell me to go there, isn't it, old boy?" He was still smiling, but it was the short, angry smile of a nervous man losing his temper. "And next time you accept a drink from me, chum, I'll trouble you to have the courtesy—"

The door opened and Lansen came in.

This wasn't the way it was supposed to happen; this wasn't the way they'd described it at all. Stay in the bar, Leclerc had said, sit at the corner table, have a drink, put your hat and coat on the other chair as if you're waiting for someone. Lansen always has a beer when he clocks in. He likes the public lounge, it's Lansen's style. There'll be people milling about, Leclerc said. It's a small place but there's always something going on at these airports. He'll look around for somewhere to sit—quite open and aboveboard—then he'll come over and ask you if anyone's using the chair. You'll say you kept it free for a friend but the friend hadn't turned up: Lansen will ask if he can sit there. He'll order a beer, then say, "Boy friend or girl friend?" You'll tell him not to be indelicate, and you'll both laugh a bit and get talking. Ask the two questions: height and airspeed. Research Section must know the height and airspeed. Leave the money in your overcoat pocket. He'll pick up your coat, hang his own beside it and help himself quietly, without any fuss, taking the envelope and dropping the film into your coat pocket. You finish your drinks, shake hands, and Bob's your uncle. In the morning you fly home. Leclerc had made it sound so simple.

Lansen strode across the empty room toward them, a tall, strong figure in a blue mackintosh and cap. He looked briefly at Taylor and spoke past him to the barman: "Jens, give me a beer." Turning to Taylor he said, "What's yours?"

Taylor smiled thinly. "Some of your local stuff."

"Give him whatever he wants. A double."

The barman briskly buttoned up his jacket, unlocked the cupboard and poured out a large Steinhäger. He gave Lansen a beer from the cooler.

"Are you from Leclerc?" Lansen inquired shortly. Anyone could have heard.

"Yes." He added tamely, far too late, "Leclerc and Company, London."

Lansen picked up his beer and took it to the nearest table. His hand was shaking. They sat down.

"Then you tell me," he said fiercely, "which damn fool gave me those instructions?"

"I don't know." Taylor was taken aback. "I don't even know what your instructions were. It's not my fault. I was sent to collect the film, that's all. It's not even my job, this kind of thing. I'm on the overt side—courier."

Lansen leaned forward, his hand on Taylor's arm. Taylor could feel him trembling. "I was on the overt side too. Until today. There were kids on that plane. Twenty-five German schoolchildren on winter holidays. A whole load of kids."

"Yes." Taylor forced a smile. "Yes, we had the reception committee in the waiting room."

Lansen burst out, "What were we *looking* for, that's what I don't understand. What's so exciting about Rostock?"

"I tell you I'm nothing to do with it." He added inconsistently: "Leclerc said it wasn't Rostock but the area south."

"The triangle south: Kalkstadt, Langdorn, Wolken. You don't have to tell me the area."

Taylor looked anxiously toward the barman.

"I don't think we should talk so loud," he said. "That fellow's a bit anti." He drank some Steinhäger.

Lansen made a gesture with his hand as if he were brushing something from in front of his face. "It's finished," he said. "I don't want any more. It's finished. It was O.K. when we just stayed on course photographing whatever there was; but this is too damn much, see? Just too damn, damn much altogether." His accent was thick and clumsy, like an impediment.

"Did you get any pictures?" Taylor asked. He must get the film and go.

Lansen shrugged, put his hand in his raincoat pocket and, to Taylor's horror, extracted a zinc container for thirty-five-millimeter film, handing it to him across the table.

"What was it?" Lansen asked again. "What were they after in such a place? I went under the cloud, circled the whole area. I didn't see any atom bombs."

"Something important, that's all they told me. Something big. It's got to be done, don't you see? You can't make illegal flights over an area like that." Taylor was repeating what someone had said. "It has to be an airline, a registered airline, or nothing. There's no other way."

"Listen. They picked us up as soon as we got into the place. Two MIGs. Where did they come from, that's what I want to know? As soon as I saw them I turned in to cloud; they followed me. I put out a signal, asked for bearings. When we came out of the cloud, there they were again. I thought they'd force me down, order me to land. I tried to jettison the camera but it was stuck. The kids were all crowding the windows, waving at the MIGs. They flew alongside for a time, then peeled off. They came close, very close. It was bloody dangerous for the kids." He hadn't touched his beer. "What the hell did they want?" he asked. "Why didn't they order me down?"

"I told you: it's not my fault. This isn't my kind of work. But whatever London is looking for, they know what they're doing." He seemed to be convincing himself; he needed to believe in London. "They don't waste their time. Or yours, old boy. They know what they're up to." He frowned, to indicate conviction, but Lansen might not have heard.

"They don't believe in unnecessary risks either," Taylor said. "You've done a good job, Lansen. We all have to do our bit . . . take risks. We all do. I did in the war, you know. You're too young to remember the war. This is the same job: we're fighting for the same thing." He suddenly remembered the two questions. "What height were you doing when you took the pictures?"

"It varied. We were down to six thousand feet over Kalkstadt."

"It was Kalkstadt they wanted most," Taylor said with appreciation. "That's first-class, Lansen, first-class. What was your airspeed?"

"Two hundred . . . two forty. Something like that. There was nothing there, I'm telling you, nothing." He lit a cigarette.

"It's the end now," Lansen repeated, "however big the target is." He stood up. Taylor got up too; he put his right hand in his overcoat pocket. Suddenly his throat went dry: the money, where was the money?

"Try the other pocket," Lansen suggested.

Taylor handed him the envelope. "Will there be trouble about this? About the MIGs, I mean?"

Lansen shrugged. "I doubt it, it hasn't happened to me before. They'll believe me once: they'll believe it was the weather. I went off course about half way. There could have been a fault in the ground control. In the hand-over."

"What about the navigator? What about the rest of the crew? What do they think?"

"That's my business," said Lansen sourly. "You can tell London it's the end."

Taylor looked at him anxiously. "You're just upset," he said, "after the tension."

"Go to hell," said Lansen softly. "Go to bloody hell." He turned away, put a coin on the counter and strode out of the bar, stuffing carelessly into his raincoat pocket the long buff envelope which contained the money.

After a moment Taylor followed him. The barman watched him

push his way through the door and disappear down the stairs. A very distasteful man, he reflected; but then he never had liked the English.

Taylor thought at first that he would not take a taxi to the hotel. He could walk it in ten minutes and save a bit of subsistence. The airline girl nodded to him as he passed her on his way to the main entrance. The reception hall was done in teak; blasts of warm air rose from the floor. Taylor stepped outside. Like the thrust of a sword the cold cut through his clothes; like the numbness of an encroaching poison it spread swiftly over his naked face, feeling its way into his shoulders. Changing his mind, he looked around hastily for a taxi. He was drunk. He suddenly realized: the fresh air had made him drunk. The rank was empty. An old Citroën was parked fifty yards up the road, its engine running. He's got the heater on, lucky devil, thought Taylor, and hurried back through the swing doors.

"I want a cab," he said to the girl. "Where can I get one, do you know?" He hoped to God he looked all right. He was mad to have drunk so much. He shouldn't have accepted that drink from Lansen.

She shook her head. "They have taken the children," she said. "Six in each car. That was the last flight today. We don't have many taxis in winter." She smiled. "It's a very *little* airport."

"What's that up the road, the old car? Not a cab, is it?" His voice was indistinct.

She went to the doorway and looked out. She had a careful balancing walk, artless and provocative.

"I don't see any car," she said.

Taylor looked past her. "There was an old Citroën. Lights on. Must have gone. I just wondered." Christ, it went past and he'd never heard it.

"The taxis are all Volvos," the girl remarked. "Perhaps one will come back after he has dropped the children. Why don't you go and have a drink?"

"Bar's closed," Taylor snapped. "Barman's gone home."

"Are you staying at the airport hotel?"

"The Regina, yes. I'm in a hurry, as a matter of fact." It was easier now. "I'm expecting a phone call from London."

She looked doubtfully at his coat; it was of rainproof material in a pebble weave. "You could walk," she suggested. "It is ten minutes, straight down the road. They can send your luggage later."

Taylor looked at his watch, the same wide gesture. "Luggage is already at the hotel. I arrived this morning."

He had that kind of crumpled, worried face which is only a hairsbreadth from the music halls and yet is infinitely sad; a face in which the eyes are paler than their environment, and the contours converge upon the nostrils. Aware of this, perhaps, Taylor had grown a trivial moustache, like a scrawl on a photograph, which made a muddle of his face without concealing its shortcoming. The effect was to inspire disbelief, not because he was a rogue but because he had no talent for deception. Similarly he had tricks of movement crudely copied from some lost original, such as an irritating habit which soldiers have of arching his back suddenly, as if he had discovered himself in an unseemly posture, or he would affect an agitation about the knees and elbows which feebly caricatured an association with horses. Yet the whole was dignified by pain, as if he were holding his little body stiff against a cruel wind.

"If you walk quickly," she said, "it takes less than ten minutes."

Taylor hated waiting. He had a notion that people who waited were people of no substance: it was an affront to be seen waiting. He pursed his lips, shook his head, and with an ill-tempered "Good night, lady," stepped abruptly into the freezing air.

Taylor had never seen such a sky. Limitless, it curved downward to the snowbound fields, its destiny broken here and there by films of mist which frosted the clustered stars and drew a line round the yellow half-moon. Taylor was frightened, like a landsman frightened by the sea. He hastened his uncertain step, swaying as he went.

He had been walking about five minutes when the car caught him up. There was no footpath. He became aware of its headlights first, because the sound of its engine was deadened by the snow, and he only noticed a light ahead of him, not realizing where it came from. It traced its way languidly over the snowfields and for a time he thought it was the beacon from the airport. Then he saw his own shadow shortening on the road, the light became suddenly brighter, and he knew it must be a car. He was walking on the right, stepping briskly along the edge of the icy rubble that lined the road. He observed that the light was unusually yellow and he guessed the headlights were masked according to the French rule. He was rather pleased with this little piece of deduction; the old brain was pretty clear after all.

He didn't look over his shoulder because he was a shy man in his way and did not want to give the impression of asking for a lift. But it did occur to him, a little late perhaps, that on the Continent they actually drove on the right, and that therefore strictly speaking he was walking on the wrong side of the road and ought to do something about it.

The car hit him from behind, breaking his spine. For one dreadful moment Taylor described a classic posture of anguish, his head and shoulders flung violently backward, fingers extended. He made no cry. It was as if his entire body and soul were concentrated in this final attitude of pain, more articulate in death than any sound the living man had made.

The car carried him for a yard or two then threw him aside, dead on the empty road, a stiff, wrecked figure at the fringe of the wilderness. His trilby hat lay beside him. A blast seized it, carrying it across the snow. The shreds of his pebble-weave coat fluttered in the wind, reaching vainly for the zinc capsule as it rolled gently with the camber to lodge for a moment against the frozen bank, then to continue wearily down the slope.

IAN FLEMING

▼

2 The End of James

I knew Ian Fleming well and I liked him. If you were an extrovert
you could hardly help liking him, and if you didn't bore him he
would probably like you. He was no snob, but he couldn't stand
bores and hypocrites. Everything for him had to be exciting, even his
food. Ian was a real gourmet, particularly in exotic dishes from the
Orient. He felt society owed him an interesting life and he went
about to get it. In many ways it was through creating James Bond
that he achieved it.

Also, I liked Ian Fleming's books. Until John F. Kennedy—then
Senator Kennedy—took him up, I think my friends felt that I was a bit
soft-headed in my interest in Fleming and my praise of James Bond.
But when I found myself in such august company—together with a
few million other addicts not so august—my hobby was then tolerated,
although some of the pros working for me in the Central Intelligence
Agency never could quite understand this weakness of The Boss.

I was introduced to Fleming's books some seven years ago by the
then Mrs. Jacqueline Kennedy herself. She gave me a copy of *From
Russia with Love*. "Here is a book *you* should have, 'Mr. Director,'"
she said. To my mind, *From Russia* is one of the best of Fleming's
thrillers, though here I may well be prejudiced because much of the
action takes place in Istanbul, in areas that I knew so intimately. For a
couple of years in post World War I days, I lived in Constantinople
(as it was then called), next door to the well-known hotel that figures
prominently in the book. It was then infamous mainly for its bedbugs
rather than its blondes, however. Also, I was very familiar with the
fantastic underground catacombs of Stamboul where Bond almost
ended his days. Later, for a time, I kept Mrs. Kennedy supplied with
new Bond thrillers as they came along.

It was a few years after this that I came to know Fleming per-

FROM *From Russia with Love.*

sonally. A score of my British colleagues, in the days when I was Director of Central Intelligence, invited me to a dinner in London with Ian and we had quite a night of it. Fleming was a brilliant and witty talker, with ideas on everything. Before we got through, we had pretty well torn orthodox Intelligence to pieces. We talked of new tools that would have to be invented for the new era. The U-2 was already making its top-secret flights, but Fleming's imagination could go even higher. After all, he was trained in the great tradition of British Naval Intelligence. Ever since that night, I kept in constant touch with him— and he kindly kept sending me his books.

In 1962, just as I retired as Director of Central Intelligence, came *The Spy Who Loved Me*—his worst book, in my opinion—with this inscription: "To Allen, who had been such a strong arm for so long. Ian Fleming." Then came *On Her Majesty's Secret Service*, to which he added a teasing inscription as a reminder of the fact that I was no longer to receive classified information: "To Allen, although he is denied access to similar material. From Ian."

As our acquaintanceship grew, Fleming condescended to include in his books references to the CIA and its people. Occasionally CIA personnel even joined James Bond in his exploits—in a subordinate role, of course, but after all with a good by-line. He wrote many of his books in Jamaica as he liked the Caribbean isles as background scenes for Bond's adventures. Here the helping hand of the CIA and its chief often received honorable mention.

The Kennedy interest in James Bond gave Fleming's books a great lift, and Ian well knew it. But there is something more than that in his success. This generation seems to be attuned to spy stories, and I wonder why. It is true that, as never before, great governments have gone into the spy business—among others this government of ours. Large organizations have been built up and they are engaged in a kind of conflict that seems to intrigue people, as they try to get each other's secrets first. The Soviets really initiated this duel when, though allied with us in war, they used Klaus Fuchs and others to steal the secrets of the atomic bomb.

Possibly it was public interest in this kind of struggle that caused Fleming to write about "SMERSH"—the Kremlin's "death to spies" organization. This he did in *From Russia with Love*. At the time, many of his readers thought that SMERSH was just another bit of James Bond fiction, but it was in fact a very real Soviet terror organization. When he thought his audience had had enough of the Soviet theme, he moved on to international gangsters who, among other things, stole a couple of atomic bombs and tried to use them for massive blackmail. After what we have read of the great $7 million British train robbery, this seems not so far removed from reality either. James Bond's last antagonist, "SPECTRE," was the Special Executive for Counterintelligence, Terrorism, Revenge, and Extortion—also in the gangster class.

People always want to know what relation James Bond has to the secret service agent of today or, if you prefer, the modern spy. The fact is that there is very little resemblance. In my book *The Craft of Intelligence,* I drew a comparison of Bond with Colonel Rudolph Abel, the highly trained secret Soviet agent in the United States who was exchanged a few years ago for our U-2 pilot Francis Gary Powers. I contrasted Abel's retiring and cautious behavior in Brooklyn with James Bond's abandon and I pointed out that the modern intelligence officer does not usually carry weapons, concealed cameras, or coded messages sewn into the lining of his pants—although Abel did carelessly leave behind in his quarters too many of these telltale articles.

The modern spy could not permit himself to become the target of luscious dames who approach him in bars or come out of closets in hotel rooms. In fact, most of the great spies of World War II were modest in appearance, careful in their actions and in their contacts, and hence not likely to be smoked out on their first mission. Good spies are too valuable, their training is too long and costly, and they are too hard to find to warrant undue exposure. I fear that James Bond in real life would have had a thick dossier in the Kremlin after his first exploit and would not have survived the second. But some of the Bond characteristics like courage, resourcefulness, and ingenuity—all used somewhat differently—are elements for anyone, whether in Her Majesty's Secret Service or that of the United States or any other nation whose security depends upon sound knowledge of what the enemy is up to. But there are exceptions to all rules, and Richard Sorge, the great Soviet spy in the Far East during the first part of World War II, was much more like Bond in his personal behavior than the typical spy I have described.

I often said when I was director of Central Intelligence that I would be glad to hire several James Bonds. I did not mean by this that I lacked men and women with Bond's qualities, because I had many of them. But I was always looking for more—to be used, as I say, somewhat differently from Bond.

I was also always interested in the novel and secret "gadgetry" Fleming described from time to time in the Bond books. I recall, in particular, one device: it was a special kind of homing radio outfit which Bond installed in cars his opponents were using and which permitted him, with an appropriate radar type of gadget, to follow the hostile car and home in on it from his own car even at many miles distance. James Bond used this to track his quarry across France and into Switzerland. I put my people in CIA to work on this as a serious project but they came up with the answer that it had too many bugs in it. The device really didn't work very well when the enemy got into a crowded city. The same may be true of many of Bond's gadgets, but they did get one to thinking and exploring, and that was worth while because sometimes you came up with other ideas that *did* work.

The last time I saw Ian Fleming, he didn't look well to me. I knew that he had had a slight heart attack some three years before and had been told to take it easy. But that is something that neither James Bond nor his creator, Fleming, could ever do. Then came Fleming's last published story, *You Only Live Twice*. The setting of the book is Japan and the inscription on the flyleaf was in keeping. It read: "To Celestial Dulles-san, from Miserable Fleming-san."

I have already apologized in my foreword for making use here of the very last chapter of From Russia with Love. *The fact is that this final chapter is not, as in many tales of suspense, a revelation of a mystery that has been burgeoning for the previous two hundred pages. The* smersh *plot to lure Bond to his death has been foiled. Bond and Tatiana, the girl who was to have been his undoing, reach Paris more or less intact, with a top-secret Soviet code machine. The mission is successful. Bond's fatal visit to Rosa Klebb is merely a bonus. Why not capture the boss herself?*

But smersh *has the last word. Fleming intended to surprise (and dismay) his readers with the unexpected demise of his hero—and to break all the rules of the adventure story.*

From Russia with Love, *published in 1956, was the fifth of the Bond books. The fame and fortune which Fleming had hoped to reap from the Bond tales had not yet begun to come his way. He was sick of Bond, didn't think he had any more tales to tell about him, and was convinced that the time had come to invent something new. He killed him off—or meant to. But just after he had done so, there was an upswing in the Bond market on the part both of certain critics whose opinions Fleming esteemed and of the movie and television producers. So it was that at the beginning of the next book,* Doctor No, *we find the indestructible Bond recovering from what happened to him at the end of* From Russia with Love. *Bond went on for six more volumes, but was never quite the same man again. In Fleming's own opinion, and certainly in mine, From* Russia with Love *was his best.*[*]

[*] Most of this introductory note has been adapted from an article by Allen Dulles, "Our Spy-Boss Who Loved Bond," which originally appeared in *Life* for August 28, 1964.

The taxi drew up at the Rue Cambon entrance to the Ritz Hotel.

Bond looked at Nash's watch. 11:45. He must be dead punctual. He knew that if a Russian spy was even a few minutes early or late for a rendezvous the rendezvous was automatically cancelled. He paid off the taxi and went through the door on the left that leads into the Ritz bar.

Bond ordered a double vodka martini. He drank it half down. He felt wonderful. Suddenly the last four days, and particularly last night, were washed off the calendar. Now he was on his own, having his private adventure. All his duties had been taken care of. The girl was sleeping in a bedroom at the Embassy. The Spektor, still pregnant with explosive, had been taken away by the bomb-disposal squad of the Deuxième Bureau. He had spoken to his old friend René Mathis, now head of the Deuxième, and the concierge at the Cambon entrance to the Ritz had been told to give him a pass-key and to ask no questions.

René had been delighted to find himself again involved with Bond in *une affaire noire*. "Have confidence, *cher* James," he had said. "I will execute your mysteries. You can tell me the story afterwards. Two laundry-men with a large laundry basket will come to Room 204 at 12:15. I shall accompany them dressed as the driver of their camion. We are to fill the laundry basket and take it to Orly and await an R.A.F. Canberra which will arrive at two o'clock. We hand over the basket. Some dirty washing which was in France will be in England. Yes?"

Head of Station F had spoken to M. on the scrambler. He had passed over a short written report from Bond. He had asked for the Canberra. No, he had no idea what it was for. Bond had only shown up to deliver the girl and the Spektor. He had eaten a huge breakfast and had left the Embassy saying he would be back after lunch.

Bond looked again at the time. He finished his martini. He paid for it and walked out of the bar and up the steps to the concierge's lodge.

The concierge looked sharply at him and handed over a key. Bond walked over to the lift and got in and went up to the third floor.

The lift door clanged behind him. Bond walked softly down the corridor, looking at the numbers.

204. Bond put his right hand inside his coat and on to the taped butt of the Beretta. It was tucked into the waistband of his trousers. He could feel the metal of the silencer warm across his stomach.

He knocked once with his left hand.

"Come in."

It was a quavering voice. An old woman's voice.

Bond tried the handle of the door. It was unlocked. He slipped the pass-key into his coat-pocket. He pushed the door open with one swift motion and stepped in and shut it behind him.

It was a typical Ritz sitting-room, extremely elegant, with good Empire furniture. The walls were white and the curtains and chair covers were of a small patterned chintz of red roses on white. The carpet was wine-red and close-fitted.

In a pool of sunshine, in a low armed chair beside a Directoire writing desk, a little old woman sat knitting.

The tinkle of the steel needles continued. The eyes behind light-blue tinted bi-focals examined Bond with polite curiosity.

"*Oui, Monsieur?*" The voice was deep and hoarse. The thickly powdered, rather puffy face under the white hair showed nothing but well-bred interest.

Bond's hand on the gun under his coat was taut as a steel spring. His half-closed eyes flickered round the room and back to the little old woman in the chair.

Had he made a mistake? Was this the wrong room? Should he apologize and get out? Could this woman possibly belong to SMERSH? She looked so exactly like the sort of respectable rich widow one would expect to find sitting by herself in the Ritz, whiling the time away with her knitting. The sort of woman who would have her own table, and her favourite waiter, in a corner of the restaurant downstairs—not, of course, the grill-room. The sort of woman who would doze after lunch and then be fetched by an elegant black limousine with white side-walled tyres and be driven to the tea-room in the Rue de Berri to meet some other rich crone. The old-fashioned black dress with the touch of lace at the throat and wrists, the thin gold chain that hung down over the shapeless bosom and ended in a folding lorgnette, the neat little feet in the sensible black-buttoned boots that barely touched the floor. It couldn't be Klebb! Bond had got the number of the room wrong. He could feel the perspiration under his arms. But now he would have to play the scene through.

"My name is Bond, James Bond."

"And I, Monsieur, am the Comtesse Metterstein. What can I do for you?" The French was rather thick. She might be German Swiss. The needles tinkled busily.

"I am afraid Captain Nash has met with an accident. He won't be coming today. So I came instead."

Did the eyes narrow a fraction behind the pale-blue spectacles?

"I have not the pleasure of the Captain's acquaintance, Monsieur. Nor of yours. Please sit down and state your business." The woman inclined her head an inch towards the high-backed chair beside the writing desk.

One couldn't fault her. The graciousness of it all was devastating. Bond walked across the room and sat down. Now he was about six feet away from her. The desk held nothing but a tall old-fashioned telephone with a receiver on a hook, and, within reach of her hand, an ivory-buttoned bellpush. The black mouth of the telephone yawned at Bond politely.

Bond stared rudely into the woman's face, examining it. It was an ugly face, toadlike, under the powder and under the tight cottage-loaf of white hair. The eyes were so light brown as to be almost yellow. The pale lips were wet and blubbery below the fringe of nicotine-stained moustache. Nicotine? Where were her cigarettes? There was no ashtray—no smell of smoke in the room.

Bond's hand tightened again on his gun. He glanced down at the bag of knitting, at the shapeless length of small-denier beige wool the woman was working on. The steel needles. What was there odd about them? The ends were discoloured as if they had been held in fire. Did knitting needles ever look like that?

"*Eh bien, Monsieur?*" Was there an edge to the voice? Had she read something in his face?

Bond smiled. His muscles were tense, waiting for any movement, any trick. "It's no use," he said cheerfully, gambling. "You are Rosa Klebb. And you are Head of Otdyel II of SMERSH. You are a torturer and a murderer. You wanted to kill me and the Romanov girl. I am very glad to meet you at last."

The eyes had not changed. The harsh voice was patient and polite. The woman reached out her left hand towards the bellpush. "Monsieur, I am afraid you are deranged. I must ring for the *valet de chambre* and have you shown to the door."

Bond never knew what saved his life. Perhaps it was the flash of realization that no wires led from the bellpush to the wall or into the carpet. Perhaps it was the sudden memory of the English "Come in" when the expected knock came on the door. But, as her finger reached the ivory knob, he hurled himself sideways out of the chair.

As Bond hit the ground there was a sharp noise of tearing calico. Splinters from the back of his chair sprayed around him. The chair crashed to the floor.

Bond twisted over, tugging at his gun. Out of the corner of his eye he noticed a curl of blue smoke coming from the mouth of the "telephone." Then the woman was on him, the knitting needles glinting in her clenched fists.

She stabbed downwards at his legs. Bond lashed out with his feet and hurled her sideways. She had aimed at his legs! As he got to one knee, Bond knew what the coloured tips of the needles meant. It was poison. Probably one of those German nerve poisons. All she had to do was scratch him, even through his clothes.

Bond was on his feet. She was coming at him again. He tugged furiously at his gun. The silencer had caught. There was a flash of light. Bond dodged. One of the needles rattled against the wall behind him and the dreadful chunk of woman, the white bun of wig askew on her head, the slimy lips drawn back from her teeth, was on top of him.

Bond, not daring to use his naked fists against the needles, vaulted sideways over the desk.

Panting and talking to herself in Russian, Rosa Klebb scuttled round the desk, the remaining needle held forward like a rapier. Bond backed away, working at the stuck gun. The back of his legs came against a small chair. He let go the gun and reached behind him and snatched it up. Holding it by the back, with its legs pointing like horns, he went round the desk to meet her. But she was beside the bogus telephone. She swept it up and aimed it. Her hand went to the button. Bond leapt forward. He crashed the chair down. Bullets sprayed into the ceiling and plaster pattered down on his head.

Bond lunged again. The legs of the chair clutched the woman round the waist and over her shoulders. God she was strong! She gave way, but only to the wall. There she held her ground, spitting at Bond over the top of the chair, while the knitting needle quested towards him like a long scorpion's sting.

Bond stood back a little, holding the chair at arm's length. He took aim and high-kicked at the probing wrist. The needle sailed away into the room and pinged down behind him.

Bond came in closer. He examined the position. Yes, the woman was held firmly against the wall by the four legs of the chair. There was no way she could get out of the cage except by brute force. Her arms and legs and head were free, but the body was pinned to the wall.

The woman hissed something in Russian. She spat at him over the chair. Bond bent his head and wiped his face against his sleeve. He looked up and into the mottled face.

"That's all, Rosa," he said. "The Deuxième will be here in a minute. In an hour or so you'll be in London. You won't be seen leaving the hotel. You won't be seen going into England. In fact very few people will see you again. From now on you're just a number on a secret file. By the time we've finished with you you'll be ready for the lunatic asylum."

The face, a few feet away, was changing. Now the blood had drained out of it, and it was yellow. But not, thought Bond, with fear. The pale eyes looked levelly into his. They were not defeated.

The wet, shapeless mouth lengthened in a grin.

"And where will you be when I am in the asylum, Mister Bond?"

"Oh, getting on with my life."

"I think not, *Angliski spion.*"

Bond hardly noticed the words. He had heard the click of the door opening. A burst of laughter came from the room behind him.

"*Eh bien,*" it was the voice of delight that Bond remembered so well. "The 70th position! Now, at last, I have seen everything. And invented by an Englishman! James, this really is an insult to my countrymen."

"I don't recommend it," said Bond over his shoulder. "It's too strenuous. Anyway, you can take over now. I'll introduce you. Her name's Rosa. You'll like her. She's a big noise in SMERSH—she looks after the murdering, as a matter of fact."

Mathis came up. There were two laundry-men with him. The three of them stood and looked respectfully into the dreadful face.

"Rosa," said Mathis thoughtfully. "But, this time, a Rosa Malheur. Well, well! But I am sure she is uncomfortable in that position. You two, bring along the *panier de fleurs*—she will be more comfortable lying down."

The two men walked to the door. Bond heard the creak of the laundry basket.

The woman's eyes were still locked in Bond's. She moved a little, shifting her weight. Out of Bond's sight, and not noticed by Mathis, who was still examining her face, the toe of one shiny buttoned boot pressed under the instep of the other. From the point of its toe there slid forward half an inch of thin knife blade. Like the knitting needles, the steel had a dirty bluish tinge.

The two men came up and put the big square basket down beside Mathis.

"Take her," said Mathis. He bowed slightly to the woman. "It has been an honour."

"*Au revoir,* Rosa," said Bond.

The yellow eyes blazed briefly.

"Farewell, Mister Bond."

The boot, with its tiny steel tongue, flashed out.

Bond felt a sharp pain in his right calf. It was only the sort of pain you would get from a kick. He flinched and stepped back. The two men seized Rosa Klebb by the arms.

Mathis laughed. "My poor James," he said. "Count on SMERSH to have the last word."

The tongue of dirty steel had withdrawn into the leather. Now it was only a harmless bundle of old woman that was being lifted into the basket.

Mathis watched the lid being secured. He turned to Bond. "It is a good day's work you have done, my friend," he said. "But you look tired. Go back to the Embassy and have a rest because this evening we must have dinner together. The best dinner in Paris. And I will find the loveliest girl to go with it."

Numbness was creeping up Bond's body. He felt very cold. He lifted his hand to brush back the comma of hair over his right eyebrow. There was no feeling in his fingers. They seemed as big as cucumbers. His hand fell heavily to his side.

Breathing became difficult. Bond sighed to the depth of his lungs. He clenched his jaws and half closed his eyes, as people do when they want to hide their drunkenness.

Through his eyelashes he watched the basket being carried to the door. He prised his eyes open. Desperately he focused Mathis. "I shan't need a girl, René," he said thickly.

Now he had to gasp for breath. Again his hand moved up towards his cold face. He had an impression of Mathis starting towards him.

Bond felt his knees begin to buckle.

He said, or thought he said, "I've already got the loveliest . . ."

Bond pivoted slowly on his heel and crashed headlong to the wine-red floor.

W. SOMERSET MAUGHAM

▼

3 Giulia Lazzari

It would be unthinkable for a collection of spy stories to omit Somerset Maugham. The distinction of Giulia Lazzari *lies, I think, in the fact that while the spy plot is excellent and without blemish from a professional point of view, the real force of the story stems from the characterization of the female protagonist herself, right up to that last punch line after which the scene closes over her shabby venality. Yet in her frailty she is unforgettable. One has the feeling, moreover, that Maugham has drawn the lady from life.*

Maugham tells us in The Summing Up, *when he speaks of the year he spent at Geneva during World War I as a British agent, that it was "all doubtless very necessary but so reminiscent of what was then known as the shilling shocker that for me it took most of its reality away from the war and I could not but look upon it as little more than material that might one day be of use to me." This is a passage that is easily misunderstood. He is speaking here of the techniques of espionage, the surveillances, the clandestine transmissions of information, the paroles and passwords, and the complicated arrangements for secret rendezvous with agents. I imagine he felt that while these may be exciting for the persons involved in them, especially if there is danger of discovery, they do not make for literature. The "material" for him was doubtless the human material, and this is what makes* Guilia Lazzari *the outstanding fiction it is.*

Ashenden knew that R. had not sent for him to talk about the weather and the crops, and wondered when he was coming to the point. He did not wonder long.

FROM *Ashenden.*

"You've been doing pretty well in Geneva," he said.

"I'm glad you think that, sir," replied Ashenden.

Suddenly R. looked very cold and stern. He had done with idle talk.

"I've got a job for you," he said.

Ashenden made no reply, but he felt a happy little flutter somewhere about the pit of his stomach.

"Have you ever heard of Chandra Lal?"

"No, sir."

"A frown of impatience for an instant darkened the Colonel's brow. He expected his subordinates to know everything he wished them to know.

"Where have you been living all these years?"

"At 36 Chesterfield Street, Mayfair," returned Ashenden.

The shadow of a smile crossed R.'s yellow face. The somewhat impertinent reply was after his own sardonic heart. He went over to the big table and opened a despatch-case that lay upon it. He took out a photograph and handed it to Ashenden.

"That's him."

To Ashenden, unused to Oriental faces, it looked like any of a hundred Indians that he had seen. It might have been the photograph of one or other of the rajahs who come periodically to England and are portrayed in the illustrated papers. It showed a fat-faced, swarthy man, with full lips and a fleshy nose; his hair was black, thick and straight, and his very large eyes even in the photograph were liquid and cow-like. He looked ill-at-ease in European clothes.

"Here he is in native dress," said R., giving Ashenden another photograph.

This was full-length, whereas the first had shown only the head and shoulders, and it had evidently been taken some years earlier. He was thinner and his great, serious eyes seemed to devour his face. It was done by a native photographer in Calcutta and the surroundings were naïvely grotesque. Chandra Lal stood against a background on which was a rubber-plant in a flower-pot. But in his turban and long, pale tunic he was not without dignity.

"What d'you think of him?" asked R.

"I should have said he was a man not without personality. There is a certain force there."

"Here's his dossier. Read it, will you?"

R. gave Ashenden a couple of typewritten pages and Ashenden sat down. R. put on his spectacles and began to read the letters that awaited his signature. Ashenden skimmed the report and then read it a second time more attentively. It appeared that Chandra Lal was a dangerous agitator. He was a lawyer by profession, but had taken up politics and was bitterly hostile to the British rule in India. He was a partisan of armed force and had been on more than one occasion responsible for riots in which life had been lost. He was once arrested, tried and sentenced to two years' imprisonment; but he was at liberty at the beginning of the war and, seizing his opportunity, began to foment active rebellion. He was at the heart of plots to embarrass the British in India and so prevent them from transferring troops to the seat of war, and with the help of immense sums given to him by German agents he was able to cause a great deal of trouble. He was concerned in two or three bomb outrages which, though beyond killing a few innocent bystanders they did little harm, yet shook the nerves of the public and so damaged its morale. He evaded all attempts to arrest him, his activity was formidable, he was here and there; but the police could never lay hands on him, and they only learned that he had been in some city when, having done his work, he had left it. At last a high reward was offered for his arrest on a charge of murder, but he escaped the country, got to America, from there went to Sweden and eventually reached Berlin. Here he busied himself with schemes to create disaffection among the native troops that had been brought to Europe. All this was narrated dryly, without comment or explanation, but from the very frigidity of the narrative you got a sense of mystery and adventure, of hairbreadth escapes and dangers dangerously encountered. The report ended as follows:

"C. has a wife in India and two children. He is not known to have anything to do with women. He neither drinks nor smokes. He is said to be honest. Considerable sums of money have passed through his hands and there has never been any question as to his not having made a proper (!) use of them. He has undoubted courage and is a hard worker. He is said to pride himself on keeping his word."

Ashenden returned the document to R.

"Well?"

"A fanatic." Ashenden thought there was about the man something rather romantic and attractive, but he knew that R. did not want any nonsense of that sort from him. "He looks like a very dangerous fellow."

"He is the most dangerous conspirator in or out of India. He's done more harm than all the rest of them put together. You know that there's a gang of these Indians in Berlin; well, he's the brains of it. If he could be got out of the way I could afford to ignore the others; he's the only one who has any guts. I've been trying to catch him for a year, I thought there wasn't a hope; but now at last I've got a chance and, by God, I'm going to take it."

"And what'll you do then?"

R. chuckled grimly.

"Shoot him and shoot him damn quick."

Ashenden did not answer. R. walked once or twice across the small room and then, again with his back to the fire, faced Ashenden. His thin mouth was twisted by a sarcastic smile.

"Did you notice at the end of that report I gave you it said he wasn't known to have anything to do with women? Well, that was true, but it isn't any longer. The damned fool has fallen in love."

R. stepped over to his despatch-case and took out a bundle tied up with pale blue ribbon.

"Look, here are his love-letters. You're a novelist, it might amuse you to read them. In fact you should read them, it will help you to deal with the situation. Take them away with you."

R. flung the neat little bundle back into the despatch-case.

"One wonders how an able man like that can allow himself to get besotted over a woman. It was the last thing I ever expected of him."

Ashenden's eyes travelled to the bowl of beautiful roses that stood on the table, but he said nothing. R., who missed little, saw the glance and his look suddenly darkened. Ashenden knew that he felt like asking him what the devil he was staring at. At that moment R. had no friendly feelings towards his subordinate, but he made no remark. He went back to the subject in hand.

"Anyhow that's neither here nor there. Chandra has fallen madly in love with a woman called Giulia Lazzari. He's crazy about her."

"Do you know how he picked her up?"

"Of course I do. She's a dancer and she does Spanish dances, but she happens to be an Italian. For stage purposes she calls herself La Malagueña. You know the kind of thing. Popular Spanish music and a mantilla, a fan and a high comb. She's been dancing all over Europe for the last ten years."

"Is she any good?"

"No, rotten. She's been in the provinces in England and she's had a few engagements in London. She never got more than ten pounds a week. Chandra met her in Berlin in a Tingel-tangel, you know what that is, a cheap sort of music-hall. I take it that on the Continent she looked upon her dancing chiefly as a means to enhance her value as a prostitute."

"How did she get to Berlin during the war?"

"She's been married to a Spaniard at one time; I think she still is though they don't live together, and she travelled on a Spanish pass-port. It appears Chandra made a dead set for her." R. took up the Indian's photograph again and looked at it thoughtfully. "You wouldn't have thought there was anything very attractive in that greasy little nigger. God how they run to fat! The fact remains that she fell very nearly as much in love with him as he did with her. I've got her letters too, only copies, of course, he's got the originals and I dare say he keeps them tied up in pink ribbon. She's mad about him. I'm not a literary man, but I think I know when a thing rings true; anyhow you'll be reading them, and you can tell me what you think. And then people say there's no such thing as love at first sight."

R. smiled with faint irony. He was certainly in a good humour this morning.

"But how did you get hold of all these letters?"

"How did I get hold of them? How do you imagine? Owing to her Italian nationality Giulia Lazzari was eventually expelled from Germany. She was put over the Dutch frontier. Having an engagement to dance in England she was granted a visa and"—R. looked up a date among the papers—"and on the twenty-fourth of October last sailed from Rotterdam to Harwich. Since then she has danced in London, Birmingham, Portsmouth and other places. She was arrested a fortnight ago at Hull."

"What for?"

"Espionage. She was transferred to London and I went to see her myself at Holloway."

Ashenden and R. looked at one another for a moment without speaking and it may be that each was trying his hardest to read the other's thoughts. Ashenden was wondering how much of it he could advantageously tell him.

"How did you get on to her?"

"I thought it odd that the Germans should allow her to dance quite quietly in Berlin for weeks and then for no particular reason decide to put her out of the country. It would be a good introduction for espionage. And a dancer who was not too careful of her virtue might make opportunities of learning things that it would be worth somebody's while in Berlin to pay a good price for. I thought it might be as well to let her come to England and see what she was up to. I kept track of her. I discovered that she was sending letters to an address in Holland two or three times a week and two or three times a week was receiving answers from Holland. Hers were written in a queer mixture of French, German and English; she speaks English a little and French quite well, but the answers were written entirely in English; it was good English, but not an Englishman's English, flowery and rather grandiloquent; I wondered who was writing them. They seemed to be just ordinary love-letters, but they were by way of being rather hot stuff. It was plain enough that they were coming from Germany and the writer was neither English, French nor German. Why did he write in English? The only foreigners who know English better than any Continental language are Orientals, and not Turks or Egyptians either; they know French. A Jap would write English and so would an Indian. I came to the conclusion that Giulia's lover was one of that gang of Indians that were making trouble for us in Berlin. I had no idea it was Chandra Lal till I found the photograph."

"How did you get that?"

"She carried it about with her. It was a pretty good bit of work, that. She kept it locked up in her trunk, with a lot of theatrical photographs, of comic singers and clowns and acrobats; it might easily have passed for the picture of some music-hall artist in his stage dress. In fact, later, when she was arrested and asked who the photograph represented, she said she didn't know, it was an Indian conjuror who had given it to her and she had no idea what his name was. Anyhow I put a very smart lad on the job and he thought it queer that it should be the only photograph in the lot that came from Calcutta. He noticed that there was a number on the back, and he took it, the number, I mean; of course the photograph was replaced in the box."

"By the way, just as a matter of interest how did your very smart lad get at the photograph at all?"

R.'s eyes twinkled.

"That's none of your business. But I don't mind telling you that he was a good-looking boy. Anyhow it's of no consequence. When we got the number of the photograph we cabled to Calcutta and in a little while I received the grateful news that the object of Giulia's affections was no less a person than the incorruptible Chandra Lal. Then I thought it my duty to have Giulia watched a little more carefully. She seemed to have a sneaking fondness for naval officers. I couldn't exactly blame her for that; they are attractive, but it is unwise for ladies of easy virtue and doubtful nationality to cultivate their society in wartime. Presently I got a very pretty little body of evidence against her."

"How was she getting her stuff through?"

"She wasn't getting it through. She wasn't trying to. The Germans had turned her out quite genuinely; she wasn't working for them, she was working for Chandra. After her engagement was through in England she was planning to go to Holland again and meet him. She wasn't very clever at the work; she was nervous, but it looked easy; no one seemed to bother about her, it grew rather exciting; she was getting all sorts of interesting information without any risk. In one of her letters she said: 'I have so much to tell you, *mon petit chou* darling, and what you will be *extrêmement intéressé* to know,' and she underlined the French words."

R. paused and rubbed his hands together. His tired face bore a look of devilish enjoyment of his own cunning.

"It was espionage made easy. Of course I didn't care a damn about her, it was him I was after. Well, as soon as I'd got the goods on her I arrested her. I had enough evidence to convict a regiment of spies."

R. put his hands in his pockets and his pale lips twisted to a smile that was almost a grimace.

"Holloway's not a very cheerful place, you know."

"I imagine no prison is," remarked Ashenden.

"I left her to stew in her own juice for a week before I went to see her. She was in a very pretty state of nerves by then. The wardress told me she'd been in violent hysterics most of the time. I must say she looked like the devil."

"Is she handsome?"

"You'll see for yourself. She's not my type. I dare say she's better when she's made up and that kind of thing. I talked to her like a Dutch uncle. I put the fear of God into her. I told her she'd get ten years. I think I scared her, I know I tried to. Of course she denied everything, but the proofs were there, I assured her she hadn't got a chance. I spent three hours with her. She went all to pieces and at last she confessed everything. Then I told her that I'd let her go scot-free if she'd get Chandra to come to France. She absolutely refused, she said she'd rather die; she was very hysterical and tiresome, but I let her rave. I told her to think it over and said I'd see her in a day or two and we'd have another talk about it. In point of fact I left her for a week. She'd evidently had time to reflect, because when I came again she asked me quite calmly what it was exactly that I proposed. She'd been in a gaol a fortnight then and I expect she'd had about enough of it. I put it to her as plainly as I could and she accepted."

"I don't think I quite understand," said Ashenden.

"Don't you? I should have thought it was clear to the meanest intelligence. If she can get Chandra to cross the Swiss frontier and come into France she's to go free, either to Spain or to South America, with her passage paid."

"And how the devil is she to get Chandra to do that?"

"He's madly in love with her. He's longing to see her. His letters are almost crazy. She's written to him to say that she can't get a visa to Holland (I told you she was to join him there when her tour was over), but she can get one for Switzerland. That's a neutral country and he's safe there. He jumped at the chance. They've arranged to meet at Lausanne."

"Yes."

"When he reaches Lausanne he'll get a letter from her to say that the French authorities won't let her cross the frontier and that she's going to Thonon, which is just on the other side of the lake from Lausanne, in France, and she's going to ask him to come there."

"What makes you think he will?"

R. paused for an instant. He looked at Ashenden with a pleasant expression.

"She must make him if she doesn't want to go to penal servitude for ten years."

"I see."

"She's arriving from England this evening in custody and I should like you to take her down to Thonon by the night train."

"Me?" said Ashenden.

"Yes, I thought it the sort of job you could manage very well. Presumably you know more about human nature than most people. It'll be a pleasant change for you to spend a week or two at Thonon. I believe it's a pretty little place, fashionable too—in peace-time. You might take the baths there."

"And what do you expect me to do when I get the lady down to Thonon?"

"I leave you a free hand. I've made a few notes that may be useful to you. I'll read them to you, shall I?"

Ashenden listened attentively. R.'s plan was simple and explicit. Ashenden could not but feel unwilling admiration for the brain that had so neatly devised it.

Presently R. suggested that they should have luncheon and he asked Ashenden to take him to some place where they could see smart people. It amused Ashenden to see R., so sharp, sure of himself and alert in his office, seized as he walked into the restaurant with shyness. He talked a little too loud in order to show that he was at his ease and made himself somewhat unnecessarily at home. You saw in his manner the shabby and commonplace life he had led till the hazards of war raised him to a position of consequence. He was glad to be in that fashionable restaurant cheek by jowl with persons who bore great or distinguished names, but he felt like a schoolboy in his first top-hat, and he quailed before the steely eye of the maître d'hôtel. His quick glance darted here and there and his sallow face beamed with a self-satisfaction of which he was slightly ashamed. Ashenden drew his attention to an ugly woman in black, with a lovely figure, wearing a long row of pearls.

"That is Madame de Brides. She is the mistress of the Grand Duke Theodore. She's probably one of the most influential women in Europe, she's certainly one of the cleverest."

R.'s clever eyes rested on her and he flushed a little.

"By George, this is life," he said.

Ashenden watched him curiously. Luxury is dangerous to people who have never known it and to whom its temptations are held out too suddenly. R., that shrewd, cynical man, was captivated by the vulgar glamour and the shoddy brilliance of the scene before him. Just as the advantage of culture is that it enables you to talk nonsense with distinction, so the habit of luxury allows you to regard its frills and furbelows with a proper contumely.

But when they had eaten their luncheon and were drinking their coffee Ashenden, seeing that R. was mellowed by the good meal and his surroundings, went back to the subject that was in his thoughts.

"That Indian fellow must be a rather remarkable chap," he said.

"He's got brains, of course."

"One can't help being impressed by a man who had the courage to take on almost single-handed the whole British power in India."

"I wouldn't get sentimental about him if I were you. He's nothing but a dangerous criminal."

"I don't suppose he'd use bombs if he could command a few batteries and half a dozen battalions. He uses what weapons he can. You can hardly blame him for that. After all, he's aiming at nothing for himself, is he? He's aiming at freedom for his country. On the face of it it looks as though he were justified in his actions."

But R. had no notion of what Ashenden was talking.

"That's very far-fetched and morbid," he said. "We can't go into all that. Our job is to get him and when we've got him to shoot him."

"Of course. He's declared war and he must take his chance. I shall carry out your instructions, that's what I'm here for, but I see no harm in realizing that there's something to be admired and respected in him."

R. was once more the cool and astute judge of his fellows.

"I've not yet made up my mind whether the best men for this kind of job are those who do it with passion or those who keep their heads. Some of them are filled with hatred for the people we're up against and when we down them it gives them a sort of satisfaction like satisfying a personal grudge. Of course they're very keen on their work. You're different, aren't you? You look at it like a game of chess and you don't seem to have any feeling one way or the other. I can't quite make it out. Of course for some sort of jobs it's just what one wants."

Ashenden did not answer. He called for the bill and walked back with R. to the hotel.

The train started at eight. When he had disposed of his bag Ashenden walked along the platform. He found the carriage in which Giulia Lazzari was, but she sat in a corner, looking away from the light, so that he could not see her face. She was in the charge of two detectives who had taken her over from English police at Boulogne. One of them worked with Ashenden on the French side of Lake Geneva and as Ashenden came up he nodded to him.

"I've asked the lady if she will dine in the restaurant-car, but she prefers to have dinner in the carriage so I've ordered a basket. Is that quite correct?"

"Quite," said Ashenden.

"My companion and I will go into the diner in turn so that she will not remain alone."

"That is very considerate of you. I will come along when we've started and have a chat with her."

"She's not disposed to be very talkative," said the detective.

"One could hardly expect it," replied Ashenden.

He walked on to get his ticket for the second service and then returned to his own carriage. Giulia Lazzari was just finishing her meal when he went back to her. From a glance at the basket he judged that she had not eaten with too poor an appetite. The detective who was guarding her opened the door when Ashenden appeared and at Ashenden's suggestion left them alone.

Giulia Lazzari gave him a sullen look.

"I hope you've had what you wanted for dinner," he said as he sat down in front of her.

She bowed slightly, but did not speak. He took out his case.

"Will you have a cigarette?"

She gave him a glance, seemed to hesitate, and then, still without a word, took one. He struck a match and, lighting it, looked at her. He was surprised. For some reason he had expected her to be fair, perhaps from some notion that an Oriental would be more likely to fall for a blonde; but she was almost swarthy. Her hair was hidden by a close-fitting hat, but her eyes were coal-black. She was far from young, she might have been thirty-five, and her skin was lined and sallow. She had at the moment no make-up, and she looked haggard. There was nothing beautiful about her but her magnificent eyes. She was big, and Ashenden thought she must be too big to dance gracefully; it might be that in Spanish costume she was a bold and flaunting figure, but there in the train, shabbily dressed, there was nothing to explain the Indian's infatuation. She gave Ashenden a long, appraising stare. She wondered evidently what sort of man he was. She blew a cloud of smoke through her nostrils and gave it a glance, then looked back at Ashenden. He could see that her sullenness was only a mask, she was nervous and frightened. She spoke in French with an Italian accent.

"Who are you?"

"My name would mean nothing to you, madame. I am going to Thonon. I have taken a room for you at the Hotel de la Place. It is the only one open now. I think you will find it quite comfortable."

"Ah, it is you the Colonel spoke to me of. You are my gaoler."

"Only as a matter of form. I shall not intrude upon you."

"All the same you are my gaoler."

"I hope not for very long. I have in my pocket your passport with all the formalities completed to permit you to go to Spain."

She threw herself back into the corner of the carriage. White, with those great black eyes, in the poor light her face was suddenly a mask of despair.

"It's infamous. Oh, I think I could die happy if I could only kill that old Colonel. He has no heart. I'm so unhappy."

"I am afraid you have got yourself into a very unfortunate situation. Did you not know that espionage was a dangerous game?"

"I never sold any of the secrets. I did no harm."

"Surely only because you had no opportunity. I understand that you signed a full confession."

Ashenden spoke to her as amiably as he could, a little as though he were talking to a sick person, and there was no harshness in his voice.

"Oh, yes, I made a fool of myself. I wrote the letter the Colonel said I was to write. Why isn't that enough? What is to happen to me if he does not answer? I cannot force him to come if he does not want to."

"He has answered," said Ashenden. "I have the answer with me."

She gave a gasp and her voice broke.

"Oh, show it to me, I beseech you to let me see it."

"I have no objection to doing that. But you must return it to me."

He took Chandra's letter from his pocket and gave it to her. She snatched it from his hand. She devoured it with her eyes, there were eight pages of it, and as she read the tears streamed down her cheeks. Between her sobs she gave little exclamations of love, calling the writer by pet names French and Italian. This was the letter that Chandra had written in reply to hers telling him, on R.'s instructions, that she would meet him in Switzerland. He was mad with joy at the prospect. He told her in passionate phrases how long the time had seemed to him since they were parted, and how he had yearned for her, and now that he was to see her again so soon he did not know how he was going to bear his impatience. She finished it and let it drop to the floor.

"You can see he loves me, can't you? There's no doubt about that. I know something about it, believe me."

"Do you really love him?" asked Ashenden.

"He's the only man who's ever been kind to me. It's not very gay, the life one leads in these music-halls, all over Europe, never resting, and men—they are not much, the men who haunt those places. At first I thought he was just like the rest of them."

Ashenden picked up the letter and replaced it in his pocket-book.

"A telegram was sent in your name to the address in Holland to say that you would be at the Hotel Gibbons at Lausanne on the 14th."

"That is to-morrow."

"Yes."

She threw up her head and her eyes flashed.

"Oh, it is an infamous thing that you are forcing me to do. It is shameful."

"You are not obliged to do it," said Ashenden.

"And if I don't?"

"I'm afraid you must take the consequences."

"I can't go to prison," she cried out suddenly, "I can't, I can't; I have such a short time before me; he said ten years. Is it possible I could be sentenced to ten years?"

"If the Colonel told you so it is very possible."

"Oh, I know him. That cruel face. He would have no mercy. And what should I be in ten years? Oh, no, no."

At that moment the train stopped at a station and the detective waiting in the corridor tapped on the window. Ashenden opened the door and the man gave him a picture-postcard. It was a dull little view of Pontarlier, the frontier station between France and Switzerland, and showed a dusty place with a statue in the middle and a few plane-trees. Ashenden handed her a pencil.

Will you write this postcard to your lover? It will be posted at Pontarlier. Address it to the hotel at Lausanne."

She gave him a glance, but without answering took it and wrote as he directed.

"Now on the other side write: 'Delayed at frontier but everything all right. Wait at Lausanne.' Then add whatever you like, *tendresses*, if you like."

He took the postcard from her, read it to see that she had done as he directed and then reached for his hat.

"Well, I shall leave you now, I hope you will have a sleep. I will fetch you in the morning when we arrive at Thonon."

The second detective had now returned from his dinner and as Ashenden came out of the carriage the two men went in. Giulia Lazzari huddled back into her corner. Ashenden gave the postcard to an agent who was waiting to take it to Pontarlier and then made his way along the crowded train to his sleeping-car.

It was bright and sunny, though cold, next morning when they reached their destination. Ashenden, having given his bags to a porter, walked along the platform to where Giulia Lazzari and the two detectives were standing. Ashenden nodded to them.

"Well, good morning. You need not trouble to wait."

They touched their hats, gave a word of farewell to the woman and walked away.

"Where are they going?" she asked.

"Off. You will not be bothered with them any more."

"Am I in your custody then?"

"You're in nobody's custody. I'm going to permit myself to take you to your hotel and then I shall leave you. You must try to get a good rest."

Ashenden's porter took her hand-luggage and she gave him the ticket for her trunk. They walked out of the station. A cab was waiting for them and Ashenden begged her to get in. It was a longish drive to the hotel and now and then Ashenden felt that she gave him a sidelong glance. She was perplexed. He sat without a word. When they reached the hotel the proprietor—it was a small hotel, prettily situated at the corner of a little promenade and it had a charming view—showed them the room that had been prepared for Madame Lazzari. Ashenden turned to him.

"That'll do very nicely, I think. I shall come down in a minute."

The proprietor bowed and withdrew.

"I shall do my best to see that you are comfortable, madame," said Ashenden. "You are here absolutely your own mistress and you may order pretty well anything you like. To the proprietor you are just a guest of the hotel like any other. You are absolutely free."

"Free to go out?" she asked quickly.

"Of course."

"With a policeman on either side of me, I suppose."

"Not at all. You are as free in the hotel as though you were in your own house and you are free to go out and come in when you choose. I should like an assurance from you that you will not write letters without my knowledge or attempt to leave Thonon without my permission."

She gave Ashenden a long stare. She could not make it out at all. She looked as though she thought it a dream.

"I am in a position that forces me to give you any assurance you ask. I give you my word of honour that I will not write a letter without showing it to you or attempt to leave this place."

"Thank you. Now I will leave you. I will do myself the pleasure of coming to see you to-morrow morning."

Ashenden nodded and went out. He stopped for five minutes at the police-station to see that everything was in order and then took the cab up the hill to a little secluded house on the outskirts of the town at which on his periodical visits to this place he stayed. It was pleasant to have a bath and a shave and get into slippers. He felt lazy and spent the rest of the morning reading a novel.

Soon after dark, for even at Thonon, though it was in France, it was thought desirable to attract attention to Ashenden as little as possible, an agent from the police-station came to see him. His name was Felix. He was a little dark Frenchman with sharp eyes and an unshaven chin, dressed in a shabby grey suit and rather down at heel, so that he looked like a lawyer's clerk out of work. Ashenden offered him a glass of wine and they sat down by the fire.

"Well, your lady lost no time," he said. "Within a quarter of an hour of her arrival she was out of the hotel with a bundle of clothes and trinkets that she sold in a shop near the market. When the afternoon boat came in she went down to the quay and bought a ticket to Évian."

Évian, it should be explained, was the next place along the lake in France, and from there, crossing over, the boat went to Switzerland.

"Of course she hadn't a passport, so permission to embark was denied her."

"How did she explain that she had no passport?"

"She said she'd forgotten it. She said she had an appointment to see friends in Évian and tried to persuade the official in charge to let her go. She attempted to slip a hundred francs into his hand."

"She must be a stupider woman than I thought," said Ashenden.

But when next day he went about eleven in the morning to see her he made no reference to her attempt to escape. She had had time to arrange herself, and now, her hair elaborately done, her lips and cheeks painted, she looked less haggard than when he had first seen her.

"I've brought you some books," said Ashenden. "I'm afraid the time hangs heavy on your hands."

"What does that matter to you?"

"I have no wish that you should suffer anything that can be avoided. Anyhow, I will leave them and you can read them or not as you choose."

"If you only knew how I hated you."

"It would doubtless make me very uncomfortable. But I really don't know why you should. I am only doing what I have been ordered to do."

"What do you want of me now? I do not suppose you have come only to ask after my health."

Ashenden smiled.

"I want you to write a letter to your lover telling him that owing to some irregularity in your passport the Swiss authorities would not let you cross the frontier, so you have come here where it is very nice and quiet, so quiet that one can hardly realize there is a war, and you propose that Chandra should join you."

"Do you think he is a fool? He will refuse."

"Then you must do your best to persuade him."

She looked at Ashenden a long time before she answered. He suspected that she was debating within herself whether by writing the letter and so seeming docile she could not gain time.

"Well, dictate and I will write what you say."

"I should prefer you to put it in your own words."

"Give me half an hour and the letter shall be ready."

"I will wait here," said Ashenden.

"Why?"

"Because I prefer to."

Her eyes flashed angrily, but controlling herself she said nothing. On the chest of drawers were writing materials. She sat down at the dressing-table and began to write. When she handed Ashenden the letter he saw that even through her rouge she was very pale. It was the letter of a person not much used to expressing herself by means of pen and ink, but it was well enough, and when towards the end, starting to say how much she loved the man, she had been carried away and wrote with all her heart, it had really a certain passion.

"Now add: 'The man who is bringing this is Swiss, you can trust him absolutely. I didn't want the censor to see it.'"

She hesitated an instant, but then wrote as he directed.

"How do you spell absolutely?"

"As you like. Now address an envelope and I will relieve you of my unwelcome presence."

He gave the letter to the agent who was waiting to take it across the lake. Ashenden brought her the reply the same evening. She snatched it from his hands and for a moment pressed it to her heart. When she read it she uttered a little cry of relief.

"He won't come."

The letter, in the Indian's flowery, stilted English, expressed his bitter disappointment. He told her how intensely he had looked forward to seeing her and implored her to do everything in the world to smooth the difficulties that prevented her from crossing the frontier. He said that it was impossible for him to come, impossible, there was a price on his head, and it would be madness for him to think of risking it. He attempted to be jocular, she did not want her little fat lover to be shot, did she?

"He won't come," she repeated, "he won't come."

"You must write and tell him that there is no risk. You must say that if there were you would not dream of asking him. You must say that if he loves you he will not hesitate."

"I won't. I won't."

"Don't be a fool. You can't help yourself."

She burst into a sudden flood of tears. She flung herself on the floor and seizing Ashenden's knees implored him to have mercy on her.

"I will do anything in the world for you if you will let me go."

"Don't be absurd," said Ashenden. "Do you think I want to become your lover? Come, come, you must be serious. You know the alternative."

She raised herself to her feet and changing on a sudden to fury flung at Ashenden one foul name after another.

"I like you much better like that," he said. "Now will you write or shall I send for the police?"

"He will not come. It is useless."

"It is very much to your interest to make him come."

"What do you mean by that? Do you mean that if I do everything in my power and fail, that . . ."

She looked at Ashenden with wild eyes.

"Yes, it means either you or him."

She staggered. She put her hand to her heart. Then without a word she reached for pen and paper. But the letter was not to Ashenden's liking and he made her write it again. When she had finished she flung herself on the bed and burst once more into passionate weeping. Her grief was real, but there was something theatrical in the expression of it that prevented it from being peculiarly moving to Ashenden. He felt his relation to her as impersonal as a doctor's in the presence of a pain that he cannot alleviate. He saw now why R. had given him this peculiar task; it needed a cool head and an emotion well under control.

He did not see her next day. The answer to the letter was not delivered to him till after dinner, when it was brought to Ashenden's little house by Felix.

"Well, what news have you?"

"Our friend is getting desperate," smiled the Frenchman. "This afternoon she walked up to the station just as a train was about to start for Lyons. She was looking up and down uncertainly so I went to her and asked if there was anything I could do. I introduced myself as an agent of the Sûreté. If looks could kill I should not be standing here now."

"Sit down, *mon ami*," said Ashenden.

"*Merci.* She walked away, she evidently thought it was no use to try to get on the train, but I have something more interesting to tell you. She has offered a boatman on the lake a thousand francs to take her across to Lausanne."

"What did he say to her?"

"He said he couldn't risk it."

"Yes?"

The little agent gave his shoulders a slight shrug and smiled.

"She's asked him to meet her on the road that leads to Évian at ten o'clock to-night so that they can talk of it again, and she's given him to understand that she will not repulse too fiercely the advances of a lover. I have told him to do what he likes so long as he comes and tells me everything that is of importance."

"Are you sure you can trust him?" asked Ashenden.

"Oh, quite. He knows nothing, of course, but that she is under surveillance. You need have no fear about him. He is a good boy. I have known him all his life."

Ashenden read Chandra's letter. It was eager and passionate. It throbbed strangely with the painful yearning of his heart. Love? Yes, if Ashenden knew anything of it there was the real thing. He told her how he spent the long hours walking by the lakeside and looking towards the coast of France. How near they were and yet so desperately parted! He repeated again and again that he could not come, and begged her not to ask him, he would do everything in the world for her, but that he dared not do, and yet if she insisted how could he resist her? He besought her to have mercy on him. And then he broke into a long wail at the thought that he must go away without seeing her, he asked her if there were not some means by which she could slip over, he swore that if he could ever hold her in his arms again he would never let her go. Even the forced and elaborate language in which it was written could not dim the hot fire that burned the pages; it was the letter of a madman.

"When will you hear the result of her interview with the boat-man?" asked Ashenden.

"I have arranged to meet him at the landing-stage between eleven and twelve."

Ashenden looked at his watch.

"I will come with you."

They walked down the hill and, reaching the quay, for shelter from the cold wind stood in the lea of the Customs-house. At last they saw a man approaching and Felix stepped out of the shadow that hid them.

"Antoine."

"Monsieur Felix? I have a letter for you; I promised to take it to Lausanne by the first boat to-morrow."

Ashenden gave the man a brief glance, but did not ask what had passed between him and Giulia Lazzari. He took the letter and by the light of Felix's electric torch read it. It was in faulty German.

"On no account come. Pay no attention to my letters. Danger. I love you. Sweetheart. Don't come."

He put it in his pocket, gave the boatman fifty francs, and went home to bed. But the next day when he went to see Giulia Lazzari he found her door locked. He knocked for some time, there was no answer. He called her.

"Madame Lazzari, you must open the door. If you are ill I will send for a doctor."

"No, go away. I will see no one."

"If you do not open the door I shall send for a locksmith and have it broken open."

There was a silence and then he heard the key turned in the lock. He went in. She was in a dressing-gown and her hair was dishevelled. She had evidently just got out of bed.

"I am at the end of my strength. I can do nothing more. You have only to look at me to see that I am ill. I have been sick all night."

"I shall not keep you long. Would you like to see a doctor?"

"What good can a doctor do me?"

He took out of his pocket the letter she had given the boatman and handed it to her.

"What is the meaning of this?" he asked.

She gave a gasp at the sight of it and her sallow face went green.

"You gave me your word that you would neither attempt to escape nor write a letter without my knowledge."

"Did you think I would keep my word?" she cried, her voice ringing with scorn.

"No. To tell you the truth it was not entirely for your convenience that you were placed in a comfortable hotel rather than in the local gaol, but I think I should tell you that though you have your freedom to go in and out as you like you have no more chance of getting away from Thonon than if you were chained by the leg in a prison cell. It is silly to waste your time writing letters that will never be delivered."

"*Cochon.*"

She flung the opprobrious word at him with all the violence that was in her.

"But you must sit down and write a letter that will be delivered."

"Never. I will do nothing more. I will not write another word."

"You came here on the understanding that you would do certain things."

"I will not do them. It is finished."

"You had better reflect a little."

"Reflect! I have reflected. You can do what you like; I don't care."

"Very well, I will give you five minutes to change your mind."

Ashenden took out his watch and looked at it. He sat down on the edge of the unmade bed.

"Oh, it has got on my nerves, this hotel. Why did you not put me in the prison? Why, why? Everywhere I went I felt that spies were on my heels. It is infamous what you are making me do. Infamous! What is my crime? I ask you, what have I done? Am I not a woman? It is infamous what you are asking me to do. Infamous."

She spoke in a high shrill voice. She went on and on. At last the five minutes were up. Ashenden had not said a word. He rose.

"Yes, go, go," she shrieked at him.

She flung foul names at him.

"I shall come back," said Ashenden.

He took the key out of the door as he went out of the room and locked it behind him. Going downstairs he hurriedly scribbled a note, called the boots and despatched him with it to the police-station. Then he went up again. Giulia Lazzari had thrown herself on her bed and turned her face to the wall. Her body was shaken with hysterical sobs. She gave no sign that she heard him come in. Ashenden sat down on the chair in front of the dressing-table and looked idly at the odds and ends that littered it. The toilet things were cheap and tawdry and none too clean. There were little shabby pots of rouge and cold-cream and little bottles of black for the eyebrows and eyelashes. The hairpins were horrid and greasy. The room was untidy and the air was heavy with the smell of cheap scent. Ashenden thought of the hundreds of rooms she must have occupied in third-rate hotels in the course of her wandering life from provincial town to provincial town in one country after another. He wondered what had been her origins. She was a coarse and vulgar woman, but what had she been when young? She was not the type he would have expected to adopt that career, for she seemed to have no advantages that could help her, and he asked himself whether she came of a family of entertainers (there are all over the world families in which for generations the members have become dancers or acrobats or comic singers) or whether she had fallen into the life accidentally through some lover in the business who had for a time made her his partner. And what men must she have known in all these years, the comrades of the shows she was in, the agents and managers who looked upon it as a perquisite of their position that they should enjoy her favours, the merchants or well-to-do tradesmen, the young sparks of the various towns she played in, who were attracted for the moment by the glamour of the dancer or the blatant sensuality of the woman! To her they were the paying customers and she accepted them indifferently as the recognized and admitted supplement to her miserable salary, but to them perhaps she was romance. In her bought arms they caught sight for a moment of the brilliant world of the capitals, and ever so distantly and however shoddily of the adventure and the glamour of a more spacious life.

There was a sudden knock at the door and Ashenden immediately cried out:

"*Entrez.*"

Giulia Lazzari sprang up in bed to a sitting posture.

"Who is it?" she called.

She gave a gasp as she saw the two detectives who had brought her from Boulogne and handed her over to Ashenden at Thonon.

"You! What do you want?" she shrieked.

"*Allons, levez vous,*" said one of them, and his voice had a sharp abruptness that suggested that he would put up with no nonsense.

"I'm afraid you must get up, Madame Lazzari," said Ashenden. "I am delivering you once more to the care of these gentlemen."

"How can I get up! I'm ill, I tell you. I cannot stand. Do you want to kill me?"

"If you won't dress yourself, we shall have to dress you, and I'm afraid we shouldn't do it very cleverly. Come, come, it's no good making a scene."

"Where are you going to take me?"

"They're going to take you back to England."

One of the detectives took hold of her arm.

"Don't touch me, don't come near me," she screamed furiously.

"Let her be," said Ashenden. "I'm sure she'll see the necessity of making as little trouble as possible."

"I'll dress myself."

Ashenden watched her as she took off her dressing-gown and slipped a dress over her head. She forced her feet into shoes obviously too small for her. She arranged her hair. Every now and then she gave the detectives a hurried, sullen glance. Ashenden wondered if she would have the nerve to go through with it. R. would call him a damned fool, but he almost wished she would. She went up to the dressing-table and Ashenden stood up in order to let her sit down. She greased her face quickly and then rubbed off the grease with a dirty towel, she powdered herself and made up her eyes. But her hands shook. The three men watched her in silence. She rubbed the rouge on her cheeks and painted her mouth. Then she crammed a hat down on her head. Ashenden made a gesture to the first detective and he took a pair of handcuffs out of his pocket and advanced towards her.

At the sight of them she started back violently and flung her arms wide.

"*Non, non, non. Je ne veux pas.* No, not them. No. No."

"Come, *ma fille*, don't be silly," said the detective roughly.

As though for protection (very much to his surprise) she flung her arms around Ashenden.

"Don't let them take me, have mercy on me, I can't, I can't."

Ashenden extricated himself as best he could.

"I can do nothing more for you."

The detective seized her wrists and was about to affix the handcuffs when with a great cry she threw herself down on the floor.

"I will do what you wish. I will do everything."

On a sign from Ashenden the detectives left the room. He waited for a little till she had regained a certain calm. She was lying on the floor, sobbing passionately. He raised her to her feet and made her sit down.

"What do you want me to do?" she gasped.

"I want you to write another letter to Chandra."

"My head is in a whirl. I could not put two phrases together. You must give me time."

But Ashenden felt that it was better to get her to write a letter while she was under the effect of her terror. He did not want to give her time to collect herself.

"I will dictate the letter to you. All you have to do is to write exactly what I tell you."

She gave a deep sigh, but took the pen and the paper and sat down before them at the dressing-table.

"If I do this and . . . and you succeed, how do I know that I shall be allowed to go free?"

"The Colonel promised that you should. You must take my word for it that I shall carry out his instructions."

"I should look a fool if I betrayed my friend and then went to prison for ten years."

"I'll tell you your best guarantee of our good faith. Except by reason of Chandra you are not of the smallest importance to us. Why should we put ourselves to the bother and expense of keeping you in prison when you can do us no harm?"

She reflected for an instant. She was composed now. It was as though, having exhausted her emotion, she had become on a sudden a sensible and practical woman.

"Tell me what you want me to write."

Ashenden hesitated. He thought he could put the letter more or less in the way she would naturally have put it, but he had to give it consideration. It must be neither fluent nor literary. He knew that in moments of emotion people are inclined to be melodramatic and stilted. In a book or on the stage this always rings false and the author has to make his people speak more simply and with less emphasis than in fact they do. It was a serious moment, but Ashenden felt that there were in it elements of the comic.

" 'I didn't know I loved a coward,' " he started. " 'If you loved me you couldn't hesitate when I ask you to come.' . . . Underline 'couldn't' twice." He went on. " 'When I promise you, there is no danger. If you don't love me, you are right not to come. Don't come. Go back to Berlin where you are in safety. I am sick of it. I am alone here. I have made myself ill by waiting for you and every day I have said he is coming. If you loved me, you would not hesitate so much. It is quite clear to me that you do not love me. I am sick and tired of you. I have no money. This hotel is impossible. There is nothing for me to stay for. I can get an engagement in Paris. I have a friend there who has made me serious propositions. I have wasted long enough over you and look what I have got from it. It is finished. Good-bye. You will never find a woman who will love you as I have loved you. I cannot afford to refuse the proposition of my friend, so I have telegraphed to him and as soon as I shall receive his answer I go to Paris. I do not blame you because you do not love me, that is not your fault, but you must see that I should be a stupid to go on wasting my life. One is not young for ever. Good-bye, Giulia.'"

When Ashenden read over the letter he was not altogether satisfied. But it was the best he could do. It had an air of verisimilitude which the words lacked because, knowing little English, she had written phonetically, the spelling was atrocious and the handwriting like a child's; she had crossed out words and written them over again. Some of the phrases he had put in French. Once or twice tears had fallen on the pages and blurred the ink.

"I leave you now," said Ashenden. "It may be that when next you see me I shall be able to tell you that you are free to go where you choose. Where do you want to go?"

"Spain."

"Very well, I will have everything prepared."

She shrugged her shoulders. He left her.

There was nothing now for Ashenden to do but wait. He sent a messenger to Lausanne in the afternoon, and next morning went down to the quay to meet the boat. There was a waiting-room next to the ticket-office and here he told the detectives to hold themselves in readiness. When a boat arrived the passengers advanced along the pier in line and their passports were examined before they were allowed to go ashore. If Chandra came and showed his passport, and it was very likely that he was travelling with a false one, issued probably by a neutral nation, he was to be asked to wait and Ashenden was to identify him. Then he would be arrested. It was with some excitement that Ashenden watched the boat come in and the little group of people gathered at the gangway. He scanned them closely but saw no one who looked in the least like an Indian. Chandra had not come. Ashenden did not know what to do. He had played his last card. There were not more than half a dozen passengers for Thonon, and when they had been examined and gone their way he strolled along the pier.

"Well, it's no go," he said to Felix, who had been examining the passports. "The gentleman I expected hasn't turned up."

"I have a letter for you."

He handed Ashenden an envelope addressed to Madame Lazzari on which he immediately recognized the spidery handwriting of Chandra Lal. At that moment the steamer from Geneva which was going to Lausanne and the end of the lake hove in sight. It arrived at Thonon every morning twenty minutes after the steamer going in the opposite direction had left. Ashenden had an inspiration.

"Where is the man who brought it?"

"He's in the ticket-office."

"Give him the letter and tell him to return to the person who gave it to him. He is to say that he took it to the lady and she sent it back. If the person asks him to take another letter he is to say that it is not much good as she is packing her trunk and leaving Thonon."

He saw the letter handed over and the instructions given and then walked back to his little house in the country.

The next boat on which Chandra could possibly come arrived about five and having at that hour an important engagement with an agent working in Germany he warned Felix that he might be a few minutes late. But if Chandra came he could easily be detained; there was no great hurry since the train in which he was to be taken to Paris did not start till shortly after eight. When Ashenden had finished his business he strolled leisurely down to the lake. It was light still and from the top of the hill he saw the steamer pulling out. It was an anxious moment and instinctively he quickened his steps. Suddenly he saw someone running towards him and recognized the man who had taken the letter.

"Quick, quick," he cried. "He's there."

Ashenden's heart gave a great thud against his chest.

"At last."

He began to run too and as they ran the man, panting, told him how he had taken back the unopened letter. When he put it in the Indian's hand he turned frightfully pale ("I should never have thought an Indian could turn that colour," he said), and turned it over and over in his hand as though he could not understand what his own letter was doing there. Tears sprang to his eyes and rolled down his cheeks. ("It was grotesque, he's fat, you know.") He said something in a language the man did not understand and then in French asked him when the boat went to Thonon. When he got on board he looked about, but did not see him, then he caught sight of him, huddled up in an ulster with his hat drawn down over his eyes, standing alone in the bows. During the crossing he kept his eyes fixed on Thonon.

"Where is he now?" asked Ashenden.

"I got off first and Monsieur Felix told me to come for you."

"I suppose they're holding him in the waiting-room."

Ashenden was out of breath when they reached the pier. He burst into the waiting-room. A group of men, talking at the top of their voices and gesticulating wildly, were clustered round a man lying on the ground.

"What's happened?" he cried.

"Look," said Monsieur Felix.

Chandra Lal lay there, his eyes wide open and a thin line of foam on his lips, dead. His body was horribly contorted.

"He's killed himself. We've sent for the doctor. He was too quick for us."

A sudden thrill of horror passed through Ashenden.

When the Indian landed Felix recognized from the description that he was the man they wanted. There were only four passengers. He was the last. Felix took an exaggerated time to examine the passports of the first three, and then took the Indian's. It was a Spanish one and it was all in order. Felix asked the regulation questions and noted them on the official sheet. Then he looked at him pleasantly and said:

"Just come into the waiting-room for a moment. There are one or two formalities to fulfil."

"Is my passport not in order?" the Indian asked.

"Perfectly."

Chandra hesitated, but then followed the official to the door of the waiting-room. Felix opened it and stood aside.

"*Entrez*."

Chandra went in and the two detectives stood up. He must have suspected at once that they were police-officers and realized that he had fallen into a trap.

"Sit down," said Felix. "I have one or two questions to put to you."

"It is hot in here," he said, and in point of fact they had a little stove there that kept the place like an oven. "I will take off my coat if you permit."

"Certainly," said Felix graciously.

He took off his coat, apparently with some effort, and then he turned to put it on a chair, and then before they realized what had happened they were startled to see him stagger and fall heavily to the ground. While taking off his coat Chandra had managed to swallow the contents of a bottle that was still clasped in his hand. Ashenden put his nose to it. There was a very distinct odour of almonds.

For a little while they looked at the man who lay on the floor. Felix was apologetic.

"Will they be very angry?" he asked nervously.

"I don't see that it was your fault," said Ashenden. "Anyhow, he can do no more harm. For my part I am just as glad he killed himself. The notion of his being executed did not make me very comfortable."

In a few minutes the doctor arrived and pronounced life extinct.

"Prussic acid," he said to Ashenden.

Ashenden nodded.

"I will go and see Madame Lazzari," he said. "If she wants to stay a day or two longer I shall let her. But if she wants to go to-night of course she can. Will you give the agents at the station instructions to let her pass?"

"I shall be at the station myself," said Felix.

Ashenden once more climbed the hill. It was night now, a cold, bright night with an unclouded sky and the sight of the new moon, a white shining thread, made him turn three times the money in his pocket. When he entered the hotel he was seized on a sudden with distaste for its cold banality. It smelt of cabbage and boiled mutton. On the walls of the hall were coloured posters of railway companies advertising Grenoble, Carcassonne and the bathing places of Normandy. He went upstairs and after a brief knock opened the door of Giulia Lazzari's room. She was sitting in front of her dressing-table, looking at herself in the glass, just idly, despairingly, apparently doing nothing, and it was in this that she saw Ashenden as he came in. Her face changed suddenly as she caught sight of his and she sprang up so vehemently that the chair fell over.

"What is it? Why are you so white?" she cried.

She turned round and stared at him and her features were gradually twisted to a look of horror.

"*Il est pris*," she gasped.

"*Il est mort*," said Ashenden.

"Dead! He took the poison. He had the time for that. He's escaped you after all."

"What do you mean? How did you know about the poison?"

"He always carried it with him. He said that the English should never take him alive."

Ashenden reflected for an instant. She had kept that secret well. He supposed the possibility of such a thing should have occurred to him. How was he to anticipate these melodramatic devices?

"Well, now you are free. You can go wherever you like and no obstacle shall be put in your way. Here are your ticket and your passport and here is the money that was in your possession when you were arrested. Do you wish to see Chandra?"

She started.

"No, no."

"There is no need. I thought you might care to."

She did not weep. Ashenden supposed that she had exhausted all her emotion. She seemed apathetic.

"A telegram will be sent to-night to the Spanish frontier to instruct the authorities to put no difficulties in your way. If you will take my advice you will get out of France as soon as you can."

She said nothing, and since Ashenden had no more to say he made ready to go.

"I am sorry that I have had to show myself so hard to you. I am glad to think that now the worst of your troubles are over and I hope that time will assuage the grief that I know you must feel for the death of your friend."

Ashenden gave her a little bow and turned to the door. But she stopped him.

"One little moment," she said. "There is one thing I should like to ask. I think you have some heart."

"Whatever I can do for you, you may be sure I will."

"What are they going to do with his things?"

"I don't know. Why?"

Then she said something that confounded Ashenden. It was the last thing he expected.

"He had a wrist-watch that I gave him last Christmas. It cost twelve pounds. Can I have it back?"

XI. *Gimmickry*

Since the beginning spies have needed and used gadgets in their work, and often spy fiction has outrun technology and invented gadgets which do not yet exist. One of the earliest of the popular authors of spy tales, William Le Queux, writing around the turn of the century, specialized in lethal devices with which his heroes and villains tried to dispose of each other—poisoned pins in freshly laundered shirts, explosive cigars that discharged a missile into the smoker, reading lamps that blew up, and many more.

As science and technology continually come up with new discoveries, the intelligence services of the world study them to see if there is, in fact, a use for them in the business of espionage. Often there is, not in order to blow up the opposition but rather in the acquisition of information itself. One of the best spies in the world today is the inanimate electronic eye of an orbiting satellite. But these unparalleled achievements of technology—radar, high-altitude photography, orbiting spy-missiles—are not, for obvious reasons, going to keep up the reader's interest for long. For him the spy's paraphernalia itself, the tricky gadgets like the magnetic deflecting belt in James Leasor's story or the hidden contents of James Bond's attaché case, are far more fun.

For an imaginative combination of gadgets to be used in an espionage operation, I don't think you can beat David St. John's invention in the selection which follows. In order to get the safe open in an important Ministry in a short time and in such a way that it shows no sign of having been opened, the sound of the tumblers inside the locking device as the dial is twirled is broadcast by short-wave transmitter. This sound is fed into a computer at a remote post which at lightning speed analyzes the state of affairs inside the lock and figures out the combination, which is then radioed back to the safecrackers. To the best of my knowledge, this is not yet being done by the intelligence services of the world.

DAVID ST. JOHN

▼

1 All's Well

David St. John has made it a specialty in his books to write about the "operations" of the CIA and its agents abroad, which, however, is not why I chose this selection. He boldly has his indomitable hero, Peter Ward, step in and out of the CIA headquarters building at Langley to pick up his assignments, but the resemblance between reality and imagination usually ceases shortly after he leaves the building. As I said in my foreword, no intelligence service in its right mind sends its regular officers on missions of derring-do into enemy territory, certainly not on the kind of second-story job we are regaled with in the excerpt which follows.

But this episode, from the beginning of his novel On Hazardous Duty, *has a great deal of dash, and the gimmickry, which was what primarily appealed to me, is impressive.*

The room's grimed window framed distant mountain foothills purpling in the late-evening haze. Across the cobbled street a light burned in a window.

The three men in the room had entered the country separately and illegally, documented as a merchant seaman, a tourist, and a functionary in the Communist party of France. They were ordinary-looking men, shabbily dressed, in keeping with the drabness of the country, and they had been watching the lighted window for nearly five days.

The room was not ideal for their work, but it was the only one obtainable, procured from a prostitute for gold and a forged exit cachet.

One man lay on the sagging bed, another stood watch by the

FROM *On Hazardous Duty.*

window, and the third lay on the floor, an earphone plugged into a gray metal box. On its face a ruby light glowed briefly, and the man glanced up.

"They're moving again," he said.

Without turning, the lookout said, "Check with Base." He was a well-built man somewhat over six feet tall, with a high forehead, angular cheekbones, and sandy hair. His eyes were as gray as the twilight that filtered through the window.

The communicator pressed a button and spoke toward the gray transceiver. "Field to Base. Over."

While he listened the man on the bed sat up and shook himself. "Did I miss anything?"

"They're stirring, Harry," the lookout told him. "This could be it."

"I hope to hell it is." Cracking his knuckles, he eased off the bed to move stiffly across the room and kneel beside the parcel of concentrated food: tubes, pellets, and powders. They were compressed and dehydrated for minimum bulk, but with water added they could be warmed into palatable nourishment over a briquette of ashless fuel. In all there was enough remaining to last them another five days.

Selecting a banded tube, he squeezed meat paste into his mouth, ate some high-protein crackers, and began heating water over a stand bent from a wire coat hanger. When it was hot he sifted instant coffee into glasses and carried them to the other men.

Still watching the lighted window, the lookout said, "Thanks, Harry. These boys are dedicated types. This month they make their norm."

"They've got that big Five Year Plan to fulfill," Harry said dryly and glanced down at the communicator. "Who knows, Ellis, one day the workers may be able to buy shoes, soap, and ball-point pens."

"Easy," the lookout said and studied his wristwatch.

The communicator said, "Base wants you, Peter."

Harry took over as lookout while Peter Ward knelt beside the UHF and plugged in an auxiliary earphone. "Seraph speaking," he said.

Through the small plastic plug crackled a voice: *"How does it look, Seraph?"*

"Too early to tell. I think I'd move the car into position, though."

"Will do. Lonely?"

"More bored than lonely." He looked up at Harry and saw that the gray of the sky was deepening.

"If it doesn't go tonight, want to cancel out?"

He shook his head. "No. Too much has gone into it to scrub. And we agreed on a ten-day try."

"Okay, Seraph," the voiced rasped; *"you're in charge."*
"We'll check chronometers now, " he said. "Mark at five after."
"Ready."
He watched the second hand skip around the stopwatch dial, said, "Mark," and heard Base verify. "Good," he said then. "We'll move into Commo Plan, check on the half hour, and after the hour check every fifteen minutes until midnight."

Base said laconically, *"I'll have the car call in. By the way, we read you well, Seraph."*

Peter stood up. Ellis detached the auxiliary plug, flicked switches on the box, and tested the mobile unit of the car that was now moving slowly around the periphery of the city.

Peter went over to the bed, reached under it, and pulled up the equipment bag. From it he laid out three piles of gear: large squares of black plastic for the windows, coshes, a suction-cup high-impedance microphone, a small lucite box that held the key-maker, the special high-intensity flashlight, the automatic sixteen-millimeter document camera, the tranquilizer gun, masking tape, plastic gloves, the Polaroid camera, spare film cassettes . . .

And as he worked methodically, almost automatically, he reflected that this was the first second-story job he had ever run behind the Curtain, the first in the Heartland. If the mission succeeded, if the take was what they were after, it would form a page or so in the next National Estimate of the target country. Beautifully bound, he told himself, handsomely done with colored maps that were the apogee of cartographic art. "Top Secret" printed at the top and bottom of every page in large bold-face type.

"Target light out," Harry whispered, and Peter felt a brief chill as he saw Harry pick up the night binoculars and focus them on the exit door of the target building. To the communicator he said, "Notify the car to move in."

"Roger."

This could be it, he thought as he pulled off his coat and wrapped the black plastic around his shirt. It all depended on the next half hour—whether the office chief and deputy went to their homes or dallied in a bar over slivovitz and coffee, whether the radio circuits stayed operative, and whether the computer at Base did its job. And, then, there was always the unexpected, the unforeseeable.

Harry said, "They're out, Peter—both of them—walking together in the same direction."

"Relay that," Peter told the communicator, who was sitting up now, tense, no longer sprawled.

The car should spot them two blocks away, escort them home, and maintain fixed surveillance to guard against their returning to the office. Peter wiped slick palms on his thighs, fitted equipment into special coat-liner pockets, and pulled on his coat.

Ellis said, "Car's heading for contact point. All clear in the office."

Either that or the mike's gone dead, Peter told himself. The energizer was certified for a month, but he had known them to die in less than a week. Taking the binoculars from Harry, he focused on the target window. The blinds were up and the room was dark—what he could see of it.

The haunting thought returned that the team had been spotted and that the target would become a trap, that in the darkness men would be concealed waiting for them to open the door. He wet his lips and looked down at the communicator. "Give me contact verification, Ellis."

"I don't have it. Not yet."

Grimacing, he visualized the old car angling across the city, heading for the rendezvous with the two walking men. I should have vectored it nearer, he told himself, no more than two or three blocks away. But he had kept it outside the zone of police patrols, and now his caution might abort the whole effort. He swore under his breath, peered out of the window, and saw the night watchman opening the target door with a large old-fashioned key.

A month ago the key had been photographed through a telescopic lens and duplicated at Langley; one facsimile was in Harry's change pocket, chemically aged and commonplace-looking. The agent who had planted the mike in the target office had tested the key, so the first barrier would yield. But the lock on the office door was a later model—pin and tumbler—and they would have to make its key on the spot.

"Visual contact," the communicator reported.

Peter swallowed. "Tell the car not to report again unless there's trouble."

Ellis bent over to relay the order.

Harry was checking his gear, fitting equipment around his waist and into liner pockets. To Peter he said, "Go?"

"It looks that way."

He glanced down at the exit door and saw that it was closed now, locked. The watchman was inside. According to routine the watchman went to the basement first, made tea for himself, and listened to his radio for an hour before making his first round.

In that hour of grace they should be well along to opening the Ministry safe.

Gesturing Harry over, Peter spoke to his teammates. "We've gone over the emergency procedures, but this looks like the real thing, so we'll do it again. Harry?"

Reaching inside his coat, Harry held out a coil of black nylon cord and a telescoping cosh. "Slug 'em and out the window," he said. "Head for the boat. If I can't make the boat, try the Embassy. If the Embassy's ringed—" He swallowed. "Maybe I can make the safehouse."

"Want the L-pill?"

Harry shook his head. "I don't even want to see it."

"Ellis?"

The communicator's face tightened. "I'd better take one," he said. "I know too damn much."

From a small box Peter took out two capsules, each attached to a curving plastic flap and colored to simulate mouth membrane. He gave one to the communicator and fitted the other inside the rear of his mouth, the capsule resting in the groove between jaw and cheek. It felt slick and as cruelly large as a torpedo.

His L-pill in place, Ellis said, "In emergency circumstances I cut the building power after warning Base. Then I go to the roof to give the car time to come in. When I see it I talk it into position and scale down when I can."

"All right," Peter said curtly. "I don't want heroes, just the contents of the safe. If the watchman starts moving early, you're to notify me. If anything else seems the slightest out of routine, let me know at once. I want the target mike on, and keep your transmitter live so I can check progress. If the computer can't solve the combination in four hours, we've had it. But almost anything could foul up—if there's rust in the safe tumblers or they've greased it recently . . ." He shrugged. "We'll have our try."

Harry looked down at his spread hands with their stubby, powerful fingers. "If there's a rumble, Peter, how will you get out?"

"I'll look for a skyhook."

Ellis said, "Foolish question, Harry." He spread a drop of glycerin over the concave surface of the mike's suction cup, pressed it to the lower flesh of his throat, and buttoned his shirt collar to conceal it. From the mike a wire led around his body to a miniature transceiver taped over his left kidney. In a low voice he tested it, and on the floor the master unit glowed.

Moving to the window, Peter fitted the binoculars to his eyes and scanned the street in both directions. Harry and Ellis went to the door and unlocked it noiselessly. Below, a small car bumped over the cobbles; an old woman in a babushka trudged slowly past the Ministry.

From the doorway Harry said, "Maris advances to second on a bunt. Mantle picks up the bat, swings—it's a liner to right field, where it's fumbled, and now the bases are loaded. Whaddaya think of that, sports fans?"

The tension breaker, Peter thought, and forced a smile. "All's clear. Move out."

Turning, he saw the door close behind his teammates, heard the creak of hall flooring as the old boards took the weight of their gum-soled shoes. Then he placed the UHF transceiver unit on a chair near the window, pressed the Base button, and spoke. "They're on their way."

"*Great, Seraph,*" the oddly disembodied voice replied, the voice of a man Peter had never seen. "*Car maintaining visual contact. Target personnel now entering their apartment building. Shall we warm the computer?*"

"Warm it," he said in a dry voice. "Team's crossing the street."

He could see Harry and Ellis below, walking across the cobble-stones, two men who appeared to be worker-citizens of the country. Ellis paused on the steps to tie a shoelace, and Harry stepped to the door and inserted the key. Before turning it, both men glanced up and down the street, then entered. The door closed so quickly it seemed never to have been open at all.

In Peter's ear Ellis' voice spoke. "*We're in the lobby, starting up the stairs. No lights, no personnel visible. Do you read me, Seraph?*"

"I read you. Proceed."

The mike on Ellis' throat was so sensitive that a muffled cough in Peter's ear was like the crash of a missile. "Easy, Ellis."

"*Second floor, Seraph. No lights, no one moving.*"

"Proceed to target floor."

Base broke in. "*Will the key-maker work, Seraph?*"

"It'll work," Peter replied; "now clear the circuit."

"*Roger. Sorry.*"

Back at Base, he knew, men were monitoring police frequencies for unusual activity, any sign of alarm, any converging of police vehicles in the target zone. Two months before, Base had detonated a noise bomb to provoke police-radio activity, intercept their procedures and call signs.

Headquarters and the Pentagon had agreed that the Defense Ministry was the optimum target, but the Special Group had vetoed because of heavy military guarding. Instead, the Ministry of Economy had been selected. Its building was old and vulnerable, and from the secret budget figures in its safe, headquarters could determine what percentage of the national budget was allocated for offensive and defensive weapons and for nuclear and missile research, how much help was forthcoming from the Soviet Union, and so estimate the hostile intentions and capabilities of this satellite nation.

Ellis' voice: *"Working on the key. Everything quiet."*

Peter wet his lips again, visualizing Harry the tech squirting plastic into the narrow keyhole, waiting for it to harden, then withdrawing the flexible key, trimming sprues and rough spots, clamping it into a bed of soft amalgam, investing the mold with quick-hardening metal compound, and taking out a tough, finished key.

Through the earphone came the harsh rasp of quickened breathing. Peter rubbed damp palms across his shirt. The ruby dot on the gray box was dark; inside the office there was no sound for the mike to transmit.

Glancing at his watch, he said quietly, "I missed the check call, Base, but we've moved into phase two."

"Understood, Seraph," Base acknowledged.

Below, a streetlight burned dimly at the end of the block. Five days ago there had been one in front of the Ministry door, but an air pellet fired by Harry had broken the bulb and it would be weeks or months before it would be replaced. Life moved slowly in the satellites; without drive, enthusiasm, or incentive; just days that varied in shades of monotonous gray. Existence rather than life.

"Impression taken," Ellis reported. *"All quiet."*

"You're so quiet, there's no mike pickup," Peter told him. "I'll hear you open the door."

"If it opens. How are we for time?"

"Fat. Seven minutes gone." Mentally he saw them opening the door, masking the windows with black plastic and tape, setting the suction mike near the safe dial, and feeding its output into the Base computer as Harry went through dial-rotation procedures. With the safe open they would Polaroid-photograph the interior to guide them in replacing the contents. Then the laborious work of photographing page after page of documents by the illumination of the argon flashlight, methodically repositioning documents by the Polaroid picture, locking the safe, undraping the windows, and moving out.

The job had been calculated at a six-hour maximum, giving them until just before dawn to exit and return to the op room. The six hours allowed four hours for trial solutions to the safe combination and two for photography and cleanup. Harry was not likely to waste time copying unimportant documents, for he spoke and read the language of the country and could scan the sheets for content.

"Fitting key into lock," Ellis said tightly. *"Uh—it's opening."*

Peter's hands clenched. On the gray box the ruby glowed very faintly. It brightened as the office door closed.

"Inside," Ellis reported. *"Three windows to mask."*

"Proceed."

By now Harry would have fitted a small device of spring steel into the door jamb to prevent surprise opening from the outside.

Looking through the window, Peter picked up the binoculars and saw a shadow flit past the target window; then the background darkness deepened. The first one was blacked out.

They were a precise team, Peter reflected, well-drilled and operating like a professional backfield, without unnecessary words. Each knew his job thoroughly, the communicator and the technician, and they joked about leaving the agency and going into the bank business—after dark. They were backed by every technological resource of modern scientific warfare, but technology wasn't enough. Special devices were inanimate appurtenances devised in labs. They depended on human beings for activation. In the end it came down to men—to nerves and knowledge, resourcefulness and courage.

To Base Peter said, "In target area now. Windows draped."

"Roger. Computer's purring like a panther."

To Ellis he said, "Does the layout jibe with the casing report?"

"Perfect. We could work in the dark." He chuckled then. *"Hell, we are in the dark."*

The job was scoring points for Biskra, the agent who had tested the outside key and cased the office. Biskra was a penetration of the government, a man known perhaps not even to Base itself. Peter knew he was valued highly by headquarters, and the fact that Biskra had been preëmpted for the entry operation was evidence that the job held at least class-two priority. Peter did not know who procured the op room for Base; perhaps Biskra, though leaving it to another agent would have been more secure. It was hazardous enough to let Biskra, a local, know the target, without letting him know the location of the command post. Need to Know, Peter told himself; we live and die on Need to Know, absorbing scraps and bits of isolated information, hoping the opposition isn't picking them up to form a meaningful whole.

The thought nagged him that Biskra was a double putting out middle-level intelligence that seemed hot in the absence of any other for comparison. In that case, whatever documents the team photographed would be deception material and horribly dangerous.

As he sat there staring into the outside darkness he found himself wishing he had been allowed to review Biskra's file, see his polygraph report and intel output over the years. But even that was not always enough; you had to see the man himself, drink with him and maneuver him into response-provoking situations, to appraise his motives and judge his reliability.

These were senses developed over a period of time, by handling agents, good and bad, by learning what motivates men—the enemy— to do what they do: for pay, for "idealism," for credit with our side. And Peter remembered an instructor ten years before who had told his class, "Give me the mercenary agent over the idealist any time; the mercenary has a price, terms we can meet. The idealist is basically unreliable. One day he persuades himself to work for us, the next he shrinks from the ethical impact of betrayal and turns himself in. That's how reverse-double-agent cases begin."

He wiped his face and looked at the UHF transceiver. The ruby spot was glowing, picking up whatever sounds the men were making in the target area.

Biskra, he thought. I'm team leader Seraph, but I have to rely on estimates of Biskra made by others, when it's *our* three lives at stake.

"*Positioning mike by safe dial,*" came Ellis' voice.

"Delay procedures until okayed," Peter countered and went back to Base. "Ready for phase three?"

"*Ready and waiting,*" said Base cheerfully. "*Feed us the clicks, Seraph.*"

He merged the circuits and told the team to proceed. Relay lights glowed on the UHF panel, as now in the target office the suction mike began transmitting the calibrations of the safe dial as Harry turned it in prescribed patterns.

How different, Peter thought, from the stethoscope and sanded fingertips of Jimmy Valentine. And he supposed that the application of a mathematical computer to safecracking represented progress of a sort.

To relax his muscles he left his chair, surveyed the dark street, and went over to the food parcel. His mouth was dry and he had no appetite, but he sucked on a piece of crystal candy, looked with distaste at the desiccated, compressed biscuits, and longed for a thick steak swimming in mushroom sauce. That and a bottle of Beaujolais plus a tossed salad.

He knew the place to get them, too—in a two-star restaurant just off Boulevard Haussmann, where Marcel, the owner, knew the rites of wild strawberries and kirsch. With luck he could spend a day in Paris, he told himself; a day, and of course a long sleepless night.

Going back to the window, he stared down at the street until some sixth sense drew his attention to the UHF. The ruby indicator was dark; the mike had ceased transmitting. To Ellis he said, "Report."

Then, very faintly, came the communicator's breathing, but no words, no reply. To Base he said, "Something's wrong—I've lost contact."

"*Roger.*"

No lights in the building, Peter saw; from the team circuit, only the quickened rhythm of Ellis' breath. They must have heard something, he thought; something beyond the locked door.

"Shutting down," he told Base. "I'm going in."

"*No, Seraph!*"

"I'm in charge," he snapped, detached the earphone, and strode to the bed, mentally checking the gear he had and what additional gear he would need. Grabbing a hat, he pulled it on, felt for the spare key, and went out, setting the spring catch.

Through hallway and stairwell drifted a miasma of odors, steam from boiling cabbage, the nose-prickling savor of cooking sausage, the moldy stench of damp plaster. He hurried down the staircase to the street level and saw the caretaker's door begin to open. An old woman came out, gazed quizzically at him, and unfurled a mop. Slowing as he passed her, Peter stepped into the dark street, paused, and glanced along it. Then he crossed the cobbles, one hand readying the key so that no seconds would be lost when he reached the door.

It opened into a dark lobby; he closed the door and moved stealthily toward the foot of the staircase, listening, searching the darkness for light or motion. Gripping the railing, he trod worn padding to the first level, where he halted and listened again.

Still nothing.

He moved on and upward, his breathing quickened by the enforced idleness of a five-day vigil, feeling the jump of his heart. His right hand closed around the butt of a gas gun, his left entered the cosh wristlet, and now he was nearing the target floor.

Inching upward, he raised his eyes to the floor level, then slightly above, and breath caught in his throat.

Kneeling in the darkness, ear pressed to the target door, was the watchman.

Slowly Peter drew the gas gun from his pocket, steadied it against the flooring, and sighted along the short, stubby barrel.

He was squeezing the trigger when the watchman rose, jabbed a key into the lock, and put his shoulder to the door. The jammer would hold, Peter knew, but the watchman would realize something was amiss. There was only the grayness of the watchman's shirt to aim at, and the man was moving. Abruptly he stopped, set one foot against the door panel, and kicked.

In that moment Peter fired.

A soft, whispering sigh escaped the muzzle as the pattern of tiny darts sped at their target. The watchman grunted in surprise, stiffened, and began slapping at the back of his shirt. There were twenty soluble needles embedded in his flesh, some paralyzers derived from curare, others a powerful hypnotic.

With a curse the watchman clicked on a flashlight and waved it wildly around the hall. The beam caught Peter's eyes and he heard the watchman roar; feet pounded toward him, Peter swung out the cosh, crouched, and sprang toward the oncoming man.

The startled watchman had expected Peter to bolt, and he was unprepared for the weighted weapon that slashed across his shins. Yelping, he doubled forward to grasp his legs, and Peter swung the cosh again. This time the flexible metal struck the back of the man's head, and impetus hurtled him past Peter onto the stair edge, where he sprawled, inert.

Scooping up the light, Peter clicked it off and ran to the door. Rapping on it, he said, "Harry, I'll need help."

Then he went back to the unconscious man, felt his carotid pulse, and dragged the body clear of the stairs.

Behind him a door opened. Harry husked, "Peter?" and strode to him. "*My God!*"

"Have Ellis stay where he is while we move this fellow."

"Roger," Harry said shakily. He went back to the room and returned. Lifting the watchman's shoulders, Peter waited until Harry had his ankles; then together they carried the man down the stairway to the room Biskra's casing report had located in the basement.

The door was ajar, a light glowed dimly, and as they carried the body to the narrow cot, Peter saw a radio on its face, tubes and parts beside it as though the watchman had been tinkering.

Tonight's incalculable factor, he thought as they lowered their burden. If the radio had been working the watchman wouldn't have heard the team above. Turning the man on his back, Peter said, "Get back to Ellis; I'll finish here."

Harry looked at him doubtfully.

"Beat it. I'll call you from the room."

Nodding, Harry went out. Peter surveyed the little room, sniffed, and knelt to search drawers in a rickety desk.

One held a bottle labeled in Cyrillic letters. The language was close enough to Russian that Peter knew it was a kind of brandy, raw and strong. He uncorked the bottle, turned the man's face, and drained some of the liquor into his mouth. He sprinkled the pillow and blanket with more brandy, stifling a cough as the fumes began to rise. Setting the cork on the desk, he laid the bottle on the floor beside the cot and lowered the man's hand near it for final effect.

Pent-up breath left him suddenly; he filled his lungs and slid the cosh up his left sleeve. From his coat liner he took another needle-charged gas cartridge and fitted it into the odd-looking gun. Then he left the room.

At the street door he listened for footsteps, for cars, for any trace of outside motion. He opened it a crack, peered out, and exited quickly. Breathing deeply to slow his pulse, he crossed the street again and entered the building.

On the second floor a couple passed him; he nodded briefly and went on without looking back. He climbed the last flight slowly, readied the room key, and when he realized that he was alone in the hallway, he keyed the lock and went inside.

Seating himself, he bent toward the transceiver, pressed the circuit button, and said, "Seraph to Base."

"*Reading you, Seraph.*" The voice bore a harmonic of relief. "*For your information, the computer's come through. How are things in target?*"

"All's well," he said as, settling back in his chair, he watched the steady glow of the ruby eye.

XII. *Spoofs*

And, lastly, the spoofs. No anthology of spy fiction could dare omit them. They are usually written—the good ones—by people who have really seen the inside of an intelligence service, and it is more often in the spoofs, rather than in the unfunny fiction, that we catch a glimpse of the business from the inside. What is held up to ridicule is, of course, the bureaucracy and its bureaucrats. Most bureaucracies are funny to anyone with a sense of humor. The intelligence bureaucracy can be funny because it is so very secret and takes itself very seriously. Unfortunately these spoofs are therefore also most appreciated and understood by people who have worked in intelligence. It is a little like the office party at which a skit is presented which takes off the personalities of the establishment. The jokes are lost on the guests.

Water on the Brain, which used to be almost impossible to procure in this country, was "must" reading in the wartime OSS. It is actually a useful casebook of "do"s and "don't"s in intelligence work. Chiefly "don't"s. I recall that a photostat copy of it was circulated in OSS and in great demand. There was a waiting list. Through some error on the part of the technicians who had photostated and bound the office copy, the pages had been set in the binding in reverse order, so that one had to read from back to front. Perhaps it was intentional, considering the nature of the contents.

411

SIR COMPTON MacKENZIE

▼

1 The Recruitment of Major Blenkinsop

Sir Compton Mackenzie, now in his eighties, is the author of some forty or so books. He served in British intelligence in World War I and when, some fifteen years after the event, in 1933, he attempted to publish his memoirs of this period, he ran afoul of the Official Secrets Act, stood trial in the Old Bailey, and was sentenced to a brief term in prison. This experience prompted his classic burlesque of intelligence services, Water on the Brain, *which was suppressed by the British government immediately upon publication and was not available in England until it was reprinted twenty years later in 1953. That a burlesque should have been suppressed because it was too disrespectful of such a serious calling as professional espionage, or perhaps because it was thought to reveal secret operations and techniques, would seem to bear out Sir Compton's statement "It has indeed become impossible for me to devise any ludicrous situation the absurdity of which will not soon be surpassed by officialdom."*

On learning Major Blenkinsop's business the janitor almost hustled him into a waiting-room, where he remained until a furtive little man came in and looked at Blenkinsop as if he expected him to blow up at any moment.

"Major Blenkinsop?"

"Yes, I have an appointment with Sir William Westmacott at noon. He wrote to me."

FROM *Water on the Brain.*

"Quite. Quite. We always have to be a little careful of course . . ." he lowered his voice . . . "in our work. Will you follow me, and I'll take you up to Sir William's room."

No sooner was Major Blenkinsop in the corridor than he and his guide were surrounded by six very tall orderlies.

"My idea," said the furtive little man complacently. "We shan't be noticed by anybody on the way up."

Major Blenkinsop felt less confident of inconspicuousness. It seemed to him that to go tramping along the corridors of the War Office surrounded by six outsize orderlies partook of the nature of a public ceremony.

"And you'd better keep your head down," the furtive little man advised him. "Of course, we consider the War Office itself fairly safe, but these bloody Communists are everywhere now and we can't afford to deport them."

"Why not?"

"Why, because when war breaks out we want to arrest them. We can deal with them much better here than we can deal with them in Russia."

"I suppose you are in the . . ."

"I'm a Civil Assistant at the War Office," the furtive little man interrupted quickly. "And this is Sir William's room." He opened the door and after murmuring, "Major Blenkinsop, sir," he faded away into the smoke-screen of orderlies.

"Excuse me a minute," said the General. "I've three or four things to sign. Take a chair."

Blenkinsop saw seated at a desk a spare grizzled man of middle age, the most conspicuous feature of whose countenance were the large dark horn-rimmed spectacles which made his aquiline nose look absolutely owlish. Before long Blenkinsop was to learn that all senior Intelligence officers wore large dark horn-rimmed spectacles and that the first step of advancement in Intelligence work was a pair of dark horn-rimmed spectacles.

Presently the General pushed aside the heap of papers he had been signing. Putting his elbows on the desk, he balanced his face between his hands and stared long and fixedly at his visitor.

"You've not mentioned a word to anybody about the communication you received from me, Major Blenkinsop?" the Director of Extraordinary Intelligence asked at last.

"Not a word, sir."

"You realized of course that the matter on which I wished to see you was extremely secret?"

"Yes, sir, I certainly gathered that."

"Good! I'm glad to see you are not afraid to form your own conclusions. That's what we expect in Intelligence work. We want officers who can think for themselves."

Blenkinsop shifted on his chair. He was a modest Englishman, and beyond the natural desire of promotion which every officer possesses, be he dragoon, rifleman, or gunner, he had never been in the habit of pushing himself forward when he was still on the active list.

"You served for four years on the Commission for determining the boundaries of Mendacia under the terms of the Treaty of Versailles?"

"I did, sir."

"And after that you spent over six years looking after the island of Parvo off the coast of Mendacia?"

"I did, sir."

"And of course you have an extensive acquaintance with the country?"

"I know a little about it, sir, particularly the South. That was our pigeon. I mean to say we had to be rather careful of poking about too much in the North because that was the Venetians' pigeon, and the Burgundians didn't much like our poking about in the East because that was their pigeon. But I had a good week's shooting at Gassowitz once."

"That's on the Czecho-Slavian frontier?"

"Yes, sir. I see you know the country as well as I do."

"No, no, Blenkinsop," the General disclaimed. "But I know my geography pretty well."

"By Jove, sir, you certainly do."

It was idle for the Director of Extraordinary Intelligence to attempt any longer to conceal his pleasure at the unmistakable admiration of his visitor. He smiled, and on a sudden impulse of expansive good-fellowship he removed his spectacles.

"Do you speak the language well, Blenkinsop?" he asked.

Blenkinsop shook his head.

"It was too much for me, sir. Of course I can say 'good morning' and 'good night' and a few things like that, but all the waiters and fellows on Parvo spoke English."

"What's Mendacian like?"

Blenkinsop felt inclined to say that the language was very like ducks sneezing; but he feared this would make the General suppose him flippant.

"I believe it's related to Albanian, sir."

"Quite," said Sir William sagely. "Well, I'm not sure that your not speaking the language will be a handicap in the work I have in mind for you. Very few of our fellows in control of things at home know any languages, except a bit of French and German. And that brings me to my reason for asking you to come and see me this morning. Have you ever heard of a Captain Hubert Chancellor?"

"He wasn't in the cavalry, sir?"

"No, I think he was in the Cambridge Light Infantry."

Blenkinsop looked vague.

"Well, the point is that he was looking after Mendacia for us, but he's had to resign. Yes, the silly fellow has written some damned novel or something, and we've had to make a rule that nobody who writes novels can be employed by M.Q.99(E), and—er—vice versa, of course, if you follow me."

"Quite. I should think it was a very good rule, sir."

"It's a vital rule," said Sir William Westmacott, hurriedly putting on his glasses to create an atmosphere of intellectual authority. "What these writing fellows don't realize is that we may be at war again next week."

"Rather not!" Blenkinsop agreed enthusiastically, for this was the best news he had heard since, three years after the British Commission for Mendacia had been sitting, the impossibility of finding a satisfactory formula to reconcile Burgundian and Venetian aims in Mendacia had made it certain that the Commission would have to sit for at least another year and possibly for two.

"I was rather anxious at first to give Chancellor another chance. No joke intended," the General interposed quickly, with a suspicious glance at Blenkinsop, who murmured, "Oh, rather not." "But I told N that E.I. wouldn't hear of it."

Blenkinsop's face began to wear the same strained expression it had worn when, in the first flush of pleasure at being appointed to the Mendacian Boundary Commission, he had engaged a native to give him an hour's daily instruction in the language.

"E.I. Extraordinary Intelligence," the General explained.

"Quite, quite," Blenkinsop hastily acknowledged. He had smelt a job in the offing. He must not appear dull. He was relieved when the General said that of course he did not know who N was, and when by admitting his ignorance he could evidently please him.

"Ever hear of Henry Nutting?" asked Sir William, with a piercing look.

"Henry Nutting of the 13th Lancers?"

"That's the man. Know what he's doing now?"

"I know he commanded the 13th before he retired. He was with them in Cologne. I've played polo with him."

"You don't know what he's doing now?"

"No idea, sir."

"And that," said Sir William triumphantly, "is the answer to those fellows in the S.R.D.M."

"S.R.D.M.?"

"Safety of the Realm Division (Military). That's a recent development. We found there was a certain amount of friction between Scotland Yard and the War Office. So we formed S.R.D. (Military) and S.R.D. (Civil) and put them both under P——,* which taught the Admiralty a lesson. Yes, we showed our friends there that co-ordination of Intelligence activities could be achieved without them if they wouldn't co-operate with us. They'll be sorry they didn't come in with us when hostilities break out, for between you and me, Blenkinsop, I've absolutely no opinion of Naval Intelligence. Absolutely none at all. You'd think Nelson was still stumping about on his wooden leg to hear some of them. Prehistoric, that's my opinion of Naval Intelligence."

Blenkinsop, who when he had nothing better to do sometimes read a book that his wife had taken out from the library, wondered if he ought to correct Sir William's idea of Nelson's appearance, but decided it was not his business.

"I haven't a word to say against the S.R.D. people," the General continued. "I believe that the co-ordination, for which, between ourselves, I was largely responsible, is working well. I don't believe that we shall have any repetition in Scotland of that dismal mismanagement of the Irish business. But in some ways P is an alarmist. He told me the other day he was convinced a large number of people knew that Nutting was the head of M.Q.99(E). He said it was dangerous to print Nutting's name in the *War Office Guide,* because it can be bought by anybody for seven shillings and sixpence."

"Oh, but people never buy books," Blenkinsop put in hopefully. "They get them out of lending libraries."

"Exactly," said the General. "I pointed that out to P. I said that the *War Office Guide* was an absolute necessity for the people in the War Office. Otherwise we should be wasting all our time—and I reminded him that our time was the nation's time—wasting all our time in finding out where everybody was. After all, the War Office is a very big building. 'So long as nobody knows what M.Q.99(E) is,' I said,

---

* Although Sir William Westmacott mentioned the name and rank of this officer, it was decided to withhold it from the public in a work which will certainly be eagerly read by foreign agents.

'M.Q.99(E) is a convenient cover.' You don't know what M.Q.99(E) is, Blenkinsop?"

"Not in the least, sir."

"Exactly! P's a splendid chap, but he is a bit of an alarmist. I think these flying people often get like that when they give up flying. They don't realize they're on terra firma again. Well, to get back to our particular business, Blenkinsop, how would you like to tackle Mendacia again?"

"Well, frankly, sir, I think the unfortunate rumours that have gone round about the disturbed state of the country have for the time being spoilt our chances. People feel safer on the Riviera, in spite of the exchange."

To Blenkinsop's immense surprise Sir William rose from his chair, walked rapidly round his desk, and patted him on the back. He was not accustomed to seeing generals a prey to cordial and benevolent emotions.

"You're the very man we want," Sir William declared. "You're discreet. You knew I was offering you the charge of Mendacian espionage, but you never batted an eyelid. By gad, Blenkinsop, you've got an instinct for this work. I thought a good deal of Chancellor until he broke out as a confounded novel writer, but you'll go further than Chancellor. Well, what's your answer now to my question?"

"I should like to have a shot at it, sir. I had a little practice when I was running the Hotel Multum for my brother. I mean to say, I had to find out more or less what was going on in the hotel, but of course I don't know what I could do on a larger scale. The political situation in Mendacia is very tricky just now."

"It's an absolute powder-magazine. It may go off at any moment. I believe war's more likely to come from there than anywhere else. Well, the next thing is for you to see N. I suppose Paris is the place."

"Paris?"

"Yes. N makes a great point of all preliminaries being settled as far away as convenient from his headquarters, which naturally are in London. You'd better disguise yourself of course. Nothing much. Say an imperial. You've got the type of chin for an imperial. Only be sure you fix it firmly. One of our fellows put on a false moustache to meet a foreign agent in Seville, and not having allowed for the heat in Spain it fell off in the soup on the first night at dinner in the hotel."

"A bit awkward that, sir."

"It might have been, but he had the presence of mind to call the waiter and say 'Take this soup away, waiter, there are a lot of hairs in it,' and he did it so well that the waiter apologized. You want to think quickly in our work, Blenkinsop, and act at once in even the most trifling emergency. So if you do stick on an imperial, stick it on firmly, though of course the climate of Paris is much the same as ours. You'd better go to the Plonplon. We always find it less conspicuous to do our work in the better-class hotels. When N goes abroad he's usually known as Captain W. S. Churchill. A rumour goes round that Winston has arrived. Other guests all stare. Realize at once it isn't Winston. Take no more interest in him. That's what we call a convenient cover. Nobody asks who he is. He's not Winston, and that's enough."

"Shall I call myself Captain Chamberlain?"

"No, I don't think you'd better start an alias right away. I think that's a matter that should be decided between you and N. I think he might resent your going ahead quite so fast."

"Shall I go back on the active list, sir?"

"Not apparently," said the General, his eyes glittering with what might be called an expression of diabolical cunning. "Not openly. You will receive full pay, but for the sake of a convenient cover you will remain to the world at large apparently on the retired list. Besides your pay you will receive a generous allowance for incidental expenses. We're finding it a little easier to get money nowadays. There's so much of this bloody Communism about. The people at the top are frightened. They think that we're the only thing that stands between them and the first lamp-post. I will say this for P: he may be an alarmist, but he knows how to put the fear of God into those dam' politicians. In fact, one of the fellows at the Foreign Office said to me the other day that in his opinion P was either a lunatic or a criminal and probably both. That shows they're beginning to realize that P means business. It's a pity he wasted his talents in the Flying Corps during the war. He didn't take up Intelligence work till fairly recently, and since the S.R.D. was organized we've doubled the Secret Vote. You can't do this kind of work without money."

"Of course you can't, sir," Blenkinsop agreed fervidly, for there are few things which arouse so much enthusiasm in the human breast as the prospect of spending other people's money.

"And now you mustn't keep me any longer, Blenkinsop. I've got three or four things to sign and a long report to read through about a steel wall which the Poles are said to be building right along the top of the Carpathians. It sounds almost incredible when you read it, but the agent from whom we have received the information is very highly paid and he ought to be reliable."

"When shall I hear where I am to meet Colonel Nutting, sir?"

Sir William Westmacott took off his spectacles and shook his head reproachfully at Blenkinsop.

"N, Blenkinsop, N. We never allude to N by his name."

"I'm sorry, sir."

"I know you won't do it again. Of course, in one way it doesn't matter in my room at the War Office. But it's against the principles of the Secret Service. You do it once in private, and then before you know where you are you'll go and do it in the middle of Piccadilly. After all, the whole point of the Secret Service is that it should be secret."

"Quite, quite, sir. I'm very sorry."

"Of course I wouldn't go so far as to say that the secrecy was more important than the service, but it's every bit as important. Well, it stands to reason that if the Secret Service was no longer secret it would cease to be the Secret Service. After all, we're not cabinet ministers. We can't afford to talk. Now, let me see, you were asking where you were to meet N. Look here, on second thoughts, I think you'd better not wear an imperial. If it happened to come off, N mightn't recognize you. How would it be if you wore a white malmaison in your buttonhole?"

"I should think that could be managed, sir, and anyway I daresay Colonel—I daresay N will recognize me. We played polo together quite a lot. Besides, I shall certainly recognize him."

"Ah, but will you?" said the D.E.I. "Don't you be too sure, Blenkinsop. Some time ago N went over to Paris disguised as an opera singer, and he looked the part so well that the agent whom he was to meet thought he really was an opera singer and never went near him for a week. In fact, it turned out a little awkwardly, because one evening this agent saw a member of the French Cabinet dining at the Ritz and he looked so much like somebody disguised as an opera singer that this dam' fool of an agent went up and spoke to him. He was at once arrested by the French secret police, and there was very nearly a most unpleasant scandal. However, I'll warn N not to disguise himself too elaborately this time. In fact I think he'd better go as Captain Churchill, and you can just meet as brother officers who have not seen each other for some time. You could say, 'Hullo, Churchill, I haven't seen you since we met in that German pillbox in the summer of 'eighteen.' Yes, that's it. We'll arrange that definitely. You won't forget, will you, because N is a tremendously cautious chap and if we arranged for you to have met him in a pillbox and you said you'd met him last at a forward observation-post he'd be off like an arrow and you'd have to meet him all over again. And don't forget 'eighteen. He won't answer to any other year. German pillbox 'eighteen. G.P.E. Ever do Pelmanism? If you think of G.P.O., General Post Office, or G.P.I., General Paralysis of the Insane, you won't forget G.P.E. G for German, P for pillbox, E for eighteen."

"I won't forget, sir."

"Now the only thing left to arrange is where you are to meet N. I can't say that until I know when N can manage to run over to Paris. You're on the telephone?"

"Yes, sir. Double five double seven double eight Whitehall."

"I must make a note of that. When I was younger I used to be able to remember telephone numbers by Pelmanism, but I have such a lot to remember nowadays that I find it safer to write them down. Double five double seven double eight, you said? Good. Then you'll get a message. 'Please tell Major Blenkinsop if he's not in that the appointment is on such and such an afternoon or evening at such and such a time.' I'll arrange with N that the place is to be the Palm Court at the Hotel Plonplon. You know the Palm Court at the Plonplon, I suppose?"

"No, but I can easily find it, sir."

"Well, there's only one thing you want to watch. Up till six the women are perfectly respectable. In fact it's the fashionable place for tea. But after six the fashionable women all go away, and it becomes a little—er—lively. I thought I'd just warn you, because personally I find it very difficult nowadays to distinguish one kind of woman from another. Post-war. You know the sort of thing I mean? And now, Blenkinsop, I really must get on with my work. Just walk out of my room quite naturally, and if you call a taxi outside the War Office don't give your address to the driver right off. I don't suppose anybody will be looking out for you, but you can never be absolutely sure. From now on you want to remember that 'secrecy and caution' is your motto. I never go either to N's headquarters or P's headquarters without changing taxis at least twice on the way. Don't be afraid of the expense. We never question anybody's expenses if he can satisfy us they were incurred on behalf of secrecy. Well, good-bye, Blenkinsop. We may meet some time at an Intelligence Conference. But not here. So long as you are in the Secret Service I would rather you did not even walk past the War Office. And of course in no circumstances must you ever go inside it. We've spent several months now in perfecting a system of communication between M.Q.99(E) and the S.R.D. and by both of them with the War Office and Scotland Yard, which is regarded even by P as absolutely impenetrable by foreign agents. However, N will explain lots of things that I haven't time to explain. I really must sign three or four letters before I go to lunch. I'm glad you've made up your mind to join us, Blenkinsop. You'll find the work fascinating even in peace time, and after all there's a jolly good chance of another war soon. A jolly good chance! All our information points that way."

With these cheering words the Director of Extraordinary Intelligence sped Major Blenkinsop on his way.

GRAHAM GREENE

▼

2 The Inventive Mr. Wormold

Graham Greene has written many serious tales of spies and international intrigue. He knows the business, having served in British intelligence in World War II (in the same office as Kim Philby and Malcolm Muggeridge). It was not until 1958, however, that he decided to have some fun with it—in Our Man in Havana. *In this book, he put his finger on a never-failing source of amusement both inside and outside intelligence services, though it may sometimes have disastrous consequences—the fabrication of reports by agents, usually for the purpose of robbing the exchequer. That this happens in intelligence services is no secret. It is funny—as many kinds of crookedness and swindles are funny—because it shows imagination on the part of the swindler and unfortunate gullibility on the part of the victim. In the case of intelligence services, the inclination of the staff officer at headquarters to believe what is reported, even when it is somewhat improbable-sounding, results from the fact that much real intelligence is improbable-sounding, and for that reason an intelligence officer cannot risk rejecting a source of information out of hand.*

With this theme, Greene sets out to augment the fortunes of Mr. Wormold, the modest little vacuum-cleaner salesman, an Englishman who lives in pre-Castro Cuba. At the opening of the excerpt, Mr. Wormold is being given his instructions by Hawthorne, the British intelligence officer, who partially recruited Mr. Wormold a short time before in the men's room of a Havana bar. The "Lamb" which Hawthorne mentions is Charles Lamb's Tales from Shakespeare *which is to be used as the key in the encoding and decoding of Mr. Wormold's spy messages. López is Wor-*

FROM *Our Man in Havana.*

mold's Cuban helper in his store. The Turbo Jet and the Atomic Pile are the names of vacuum-cleaner models. Milly is Wormold's teen-age daughter.

I haven't even said I was willing. . . ."

"London agrees to $150 a month, with another hundred and fifty as expenses; you'll have to justify those, of course, payment of sub-agents, et cetera. Anything above that will have to be specially authorized."

"You're going much too fast."

"Free of income tax, you know," Hawthorne said and winked slyly. The wink somehow didn't go with the royal monogram.

"You must give me time. . . ."

"Your code number is 59200 stroke 5." He added with pride, "Of course *I* am 59200. You'll number your sub-agents 59200 stroke 5 stroke 1 and so on. Got the idea?"

"I don't see how I can possibly be of use to you."

"You are English, aren't you?" Hawthorne said briskly.

"Of course I'm English."

"And you refuse to serve your country?"

"I didn't say that. But the vacuum cleaners take up a great deal of time."

"They are an excellent cover," Hawthorne said. "Very well thought out. Your profession has quite a natural air."

"But it *is* natural."

"Now if you don't mind," Hawthorne said firmly, "we must get down to our Lamb."

The Chief sat behind a desk on which an enormous green marble paper weight held down a single sheet of paper. A half-drunk glass of milk, a bottle of grey pills, and a packet of Kleenex stood by the black telephone. (The red one was for scrambling.) His black morning coat, black tie, and black monocle hiding the left eye gave him the appearance of an undertaker, just as the basement room had the effect of a vault, a mausoleum, a grave.

"You wanted me, sir?"

"Just a gossip, Hawthorne. Just a gossip." It was as though a mute were gloomily giving tongue after the day's burials were over. "When did you get back, Hawthorne?"

"A week ago, sir. I'll be returning to Jamaica on Friday."

"All going well?"

"I think we've got the Caribbean sewn up now, sir," Hawthorne said.

"Martinique?"

"No difficulties there, sir. You remember at Fort-de-France we are working with the Deuxième Bureau."

"Only up to a point?"

"Oh yes, of course, only up to a point. Haiti was more of a problem, but 59200 stroke 2 is proving energetic. I was more uncertain at first about 59200 stroke 5."

"Stroke 5?"

"Our man in Havana, sir. I didn't have much choice there, and at first he didn't seem very keen on the job. A bit stubborn."

"That kind sometimes develops best."

"Yes, sir. I was a little worried too by his contacts. However he seems to be going ahead. We got a request for extra expenses just as I was leaving Kingston."

"Always a good sign."

"Yes, sir."

"Shows the imagination is working."

"Yes. He wanted to become a member of the Country Club. Haunt of the millionaires, you know. Best source for political and economic information. The subscription's very high, about ten times the size of White's, but I've allowed it."

"You did right. How are his reports?"

"Well, as a matter of fact, we haven't had any yet, but of course it will take time for him to organize his contacts. Perhaps I rather overemphasized the need of security."

"You can't. No use having a live wire if it fuses."

"As it happens, he's rather advantageously placed. Very good business contacts—a lot of them with government officials and leading ministers."

"Ah," the Chief said. He took off the black monocle and began to polish it with a piece of Kleenex. The eye that he disclosed was made of glass; pale blue and unconvincing, it might have come out of a doll which said "Mama."

"What's his business?"

"Oh, he imports, you know. Machinery, that sort of thing." It was always important to one's own career to employ agents who were men of good social standing. The petty details on the secret file dealing with the store in Lamparilla Street would never, in ordinary circumstances, reach this basement room.

"Why isn't he already a member of the Country Club?"

"Well, I think he's been rather a recluse of recent years. Bit of domestic trouble."

"Doesn't run after women, I hope?"

"Oh, nothing of that sort, sir. His wife left him. Went off with an American."

"I suppose he's not anti-American? Havana's not the place for any prejudice like that. We have to work with them—only up to a point of course."

"Oh, he's not at all that way, sir. He's a very fair-minded man, very balanced. Took his divorce well and keeps his child in a Catholic school according to his wife's wishes. I'm told he sends her greeting telegrams at Christmas. I think we'll find his reports when they do come in are a hundred per cent reliable."

"Rather touching, that about the child, Hawthorne. Well, give him a prod, so that we can judge his usefulness. If he's all you say he is, we might consider enlarging his staff. Havana could be a key spot. The Communists always go where there's trouble. How does he communicate?"

"I've arranged for him to send reports by the weekly bag to Kingston in duplicate. I keep one and send one to London. I've given him the book code for cables. He sends them through the Consulate."

"They won't like that."

"I've told them it's temporary."

"I would be in favour of establishing a radio unit if he proves to be a good man. He could expand his office staff, I suppose?"

"Oh, of course. At least—you understand it's not a big office, sir. Old-fashioned. You know how these merchant adventurers make do."

"I know the type, Hawthorne. Small scrubby desk. Half a dozen men in an outer office meant to hold two. Out-of-date accounting machines. Woman secretary who is completing forty years with the firm."

Hawthorne now felt able to relax; the Chief had taken charge. Even if one day he read the secret file, the words would convey nothing to him. The small shop for vacuum cleaners had been drowned beyond recovering in the tide of the Chief's literary imagination. Agent 59200/5 was established.

"It's all part of the man's character," the Chief explained to Hawthorne, as though he and not Hawthorne had pushed open the door in Lamparilla Street. "A man who has always learnt to count the pennies and to risk the pounds. That's why he's not a member of the Country Club—nothing to do with the broken marriage. You're a romantic, Hawthorne. Women have come and gone in his life; I suspect they never meant as much to him as his work. The secret of successfully using an agent is to understand him. Our man in Havana belongs—you might say—to the Kipling age. Walking with kings— how does it go?—and keeping your virtue, crowds and the common touch. I expect somewhere in that ink-stained desk of his there's an old penny notebook of black wash leather in which he kept his first accounts—a quarter gross of indiarubbers, six boxes of steel nibs . . ."

"I don't think he goes quite as far back as steel nibs, sir."

The Chief sighed and replaced the black lens. The innocent eye had gone back into hiding at the hint of opposition.

"Details don't matter, Hawthorne," the Chief said with irritation. "But if you are to handle him successfully you'll have to find that penny notebook. I speak metaphorically."

"Yes, sir."

"This business about being a recluse because he lost his wife—it's a wrong appreciation, Hawthorne. A man like that reacts quite differently. He doesn't show his loss, he doesn't wear his heart on his sleeve. If your appreciation were correct why wasn't he a member of the Club before his wife died?"

"She left him."

"Left him? Are you sure?"

"Quite sure, sir."

"Ah, she never found that penny notebook. Find it, Hawthorne, and he's yours for life. What were we talking about?"

"The size of his office, sir. It won't be very easy for him to absorb many in the way of new staff."

"We'll weed out the old ones gradually. Pension off that old secretary of his. . . ."

"As a matter of fact . . ."

"Of course this is just speculation, Hawthorne. He may not be the right man after all. Sterling stuff, these old merchant kings, but sometimes they can't see far enough beyond the counting house to be of use to people like ourselves. We'll judge by his first reports, but it's always well to plan a step ahead."

López was demonstrating the Turbo Jet Cleaner to a priest's housekeeper who had rejected the Atomic Pile. Wormold's worst fears about the new model had been justified, for he had not succeeded in selling a single specimen. He went upstairs and opened the telegram; it was addressed to a department at the British Consulate, and the figures which followed had an ugly look like the lottery tickets that remained unsold on the last day of the draw. There was 2674 and then a string of five-figure numerals: 42811 79145 72312 59200 80947 62533 10605 and so on. It was his first telegram and he noticed that it was addressed from London. He was not even certain (so long ago his lesson seemed) that he could decode it, but he recognized a single group—59200—which had an abrupt and monitory appearance as though Hawthorne that moment had come accusingly up the stairs. Gloomily he took down Lamb's *Tales from Shakespeare*—how he had always detested Elia and the essay on roast pork. The first group of figures, he remembered, indicated the page, the line, and the word with which the coding began. "Dionysia, the wicked wife of Cleon," he read, "met with an end proportionable to her deserts." He began to decode from "deserts." To his surprise something really did emerge. It was rather as though some strange inherited parrot had begun to speak. "Number 1 of January 24. Following from 59200 begin paragraph A."

After working for three-quarters of an hour at adding and subtracting he had decoded the whole message, apart from the final paragraph, where something had gone wrong either with himself or 59200, or perhaps with Charles Lamb. "Following from 59200 begin paragraph A nearly a month since membership Country Club approved and no repeat no information concerning proposed sub agents yet received stop trust you are not repeat not recruiting any sub agents before having them properly traced stop begin paragraph B economic and political report on lines of questionnaire left with you should be despatched forthwith to 59200 stop begin paragraph C cursed galloon must be forwarded kingston primary tubercular message ends."

The last paragraph had an effect of angry incoherence which worried Wormold. For the first time it occurred to him that in their eyes—whoever *they* were—he had taken money and given nothing in return. This troubled him. It had seemed to him till then that he had been the recipient of an eccentric gift which had enabled Milly to ride at the Country Club and himself to order from England a few books he had coveted. The rest of the money was now on deposit in the bank; he half believed that some day he might be in a position to return it to Hawthorne.

He thought: I must do something—give them some names to trace, recruit an agent, keep them happy. He remembered how Milly used to play at shops and give him her pocket money for imaginary purchases. One had to play the child's game, but sooner or later Milly always required her money back.

He wondered how one recruited an agent. It was difficult for him to remember exactly how Hawthorne had recruited *him*—except that the whole affair had begun in a lavatory, but surely that was not an essential feature. He decided to begin with a reasonably easy case.

"You called me, Señor Vormell." For some reason the name Wormold was quite beyond López' power of pronunciation, and, as he seemed unable to settle on a satisfactory substitute, it was seldom that Wormold went by the same name twice.

"I want to talk to you, López."

"Sí, Señor Vomell."

Wormold said, "You've been with me a great many years now. We trust each other."

López expressed the completeness of his trust with a gesture towards the heart.

"How would you like to earn a little more money each month?"

"Why, naturally . . . I was going to speak to you myself, Señor Ommel. I have a child coming. Perhaps twenty pesos?"

"This has nothing to do with the firm. Trade is too bad, López. This will be confidential work, for me personally, you understand."

"Ah yes, señor. Personal services I understand. You can trust me. I am discreet. Of course I will say nothing to the señorita."

"I think perhaps you *don't* understand."

"When a man reaches a certain age," López said, "he no longer wishes to search for a woman himself, he wishes to rest from trouble. He wishes to command, 'Tonight yes, tomorrow night no.' To give his directions to someone he trusts . . ."

"I don't mean anything of the kind. What I was trying to say— well, it had nothing to do . . ."

"You do not need to be embarrassed in speaking to me, Señor Vormole. I have been with you many years."

"You are making a mistake," Wormold said. "I had no intention . . ."

"I understand that for an Englishman in your position places like the San Francisco are unsuitable. Even the Mamba Club."

Wormold knew that nothing he could say would check the eloquence of his assistant now that he had embarked on the great Havana subject; the sexual exchange was not only the chief commerce of the city, but the whole *raison d'être* of a man's life. One sold sex or one bought it—immaterial which, but it was never given away.

"A youth needs variety," López said, "but so too does a man of a certain age. For the youth it is the curiosity of ignorance, for the old it is the appetite which needs to be refreshed. No one can serve you better than I can, because I have studied you, Señor Venell. You are not a Cuban; for you the shape of a girl's bottom is less important than a certain gentleness of behaviour. . . ."

"You have misunderstood me completely," Wormold said.

"The señorita this evening goes to a concert."

"How do you know?"

López ignored the question. "While she is out, I will bring you a young lady to see. If you don't like her, I will bring another."

"You'll do nothing of the sort. Those are not the kind of services I want, López. I want . . . well, I want you to keep your eyes and ears open and report to me. . . ."

"On the señorita?"

"Good heavens no."

"Report on what then, Señor Vommold?"

Wormold said, "Well, things like . . ." But he hadn't the faintest idea on what subjects López was capable of reporting. He remembered only a few points in the long questionnaire and none of them seemed suitable: "Possible Communist infiltration in the armed forces. Actual figures of coffee and tobacco production last year." Of course there were the contents of waste-paper baskets in the offices where López serviced the cleaners, but surely even Hawthorne was joking when he spoke of the Dreyfus case—if those men ever joked.

"Like what, señor?"

Wormold said, "I'll let you know later. Go back to the shop now."

What was the good of playing a game with half a heart? At least let him give them something they would enjoy for their money, something to put on their files better than an economic report. He wrote a rapid draft: "Number 1 of February 8 paragraph A begins in my recent trip to Santiago I heard reports from several sources of big military installations under construction in mountains of Oriente Province stop these constructions too extensive to be aimed at small rebel bands holding out there stop stories of widespread forest clearance under cover of forest fires stop peasants from several villages impressed to carry loads of stone paragraph B begins in bar of Santiago hotel met Spanish pilot of Cubana air line in advanced stage drunkenness stop he spoke of observing on flight Havana Santiago large concrete platform too extensive for any building paragraph C 59200/5/3 who accompanied me to Santiago undertook dangerous mission near military HQ at Bayamo and made drawings of strange machinery in transport to forest stop these drawings will follow by bag paragraph D have I your permission to pay him bonus in view of serious risks of his missions and to suspend work for a time on economic report in view disquieting and vital nature of these reports from Oriente paragraph E have you any traces Raul Domínguez Cubana pilot whom I propose to recruit as 59200/5/4."

Wormold joyfully encoded. He thought, I never believed I had it in me. He thought with pride: 59200 stroke 5 knows his job. His good humour even embraced Charles Lamb. He chose for his passage page 217, line 12: "But I will draw the curtain and show the picture. Is it not well done?"

Wormold called López from the shop. He handed him 25 pesos. He said, "This is your first month's pay in advance." He knew López too well to expect any gratitude for the extra five pesos, but all the same he was a little taken aback when López said, "Thirty pesos would be a living wage."

"What do you mean, a living wage? The agency pays you very well as it is."

"This will mean a great deal of work," López said.

"It will, will it? What work?"

"Personal service."

"What personal service?"

"It must obviously be a great deal of work or you wouldn't pay me twenty-five pesos."

He had never been able to get the better of López in a financial argument.

"I want you to bring me an Atomic Pile from the shop," Wormold said.

"We have only one in the store."

"I want it up here."

López sighed. "Is that a personal service?"

"Yes."

When he was alone Wormold unscrewed the cleaner into its various parts. Then he sat down at his desk and began to make a series of careful drawings. As he sat back and contemplated his sketch of the sprayer detached from the hose-handle of the cleaner—the needle jet, the nozzle, and the telescopic tube, he wondered, Am I perhaps going too far? He realized he had forgotten to indicate the scale. He ruled a line and numbered it off: one inch representing three feet. Then for a better measure he drew a little man two inches high below the nozzle. He dressed him neatly in a dark suit, and gave him a bowler hat and an umbrella.

"Had a good flight?" the Chief asked.

"A bit bumpy over the Azores," Hawthorne said. On this occasion he had not had time to change from his pale-grey tropical suit—the summons had come to him urgently in Kingston and a car had met him at London Airport. He sat as close to the steam radiator as he could, but sometimes he couldn't help a shiver.

"What's that odd flower you're wearing?"

Hawthorne had quite forgotten it. He put his hand up to his lapel.

"It looks as though it had once been an orchid," the Chief said with disapproval.

"Pan American gave it to us with our dinner last night," Hawthorne explained. He took out the limp mauve rag and put it in the ashtray.

"With your dinner? What an odd thing to do," the Chief said. "It can hardly have improved the meal. Personally I detest orchids. Decadent things. There was someone, wasn't there, who wore green ones?"

"I only put it in my buttonhole so as to clear the dinner tray. There was so little room, what with the champagne and the sweet salad and the tomato soup and the chicken Maryland and ice cream . . ."

"What a terrible mixture. You should travel B.O.A.C."

"You didn't give me enough time, sir, to get a booking."

"Well, the matter is rather urgent. You know our man in Havana has been turning out some pretty disquieting stuff lately."

"He's a good man," Hawthorne said.

"I don't deny it. I wish we had more like him. What I can't understand is how the Americans have not tumbled to anything there."

"Have you asked them, sir?"

"Of course not. I don't trust their discretion."

"Perhaps they don't trust ours."

The Chief said, "Those drawings—did you examine them?"

"I'm not very knowledgeable that way, sir. I sent them straight on."

"Well, take a good look at them now."

The Chief spread the drawings over his desk. Hawthorne reluctantly left the radiator and was immediately shaken by a shiver.

"Anything the matter?"

"The temperature was ninety-two yesterday in Kingston."

"Your blood's getting thin. A spell of cold will do you good. What do you think of them?"

Hawthorne stared at the drawings. They reminded him of something. He was touched—he didn't know why—by an odd uneasiness.

"You remember the reports that came with them?" the Chief said. "The source was stroke 3. Who is he?"

"I think that would be Engineer Cifuentes, sir."

"Well, even he was mystified. With all his technical knowledge. These machines were being transported by lorry from the army headquarters at Bayamo to the edge of the forest. Then mules took over. General direction those unexplained concrete platforms."

"What does the Air Ministry say, sir?"

"They are worried, very worried. Interested too, of course."

"What about the atomic research people?"

"We haven't shown them the drawings yet. You know what those fellows are like. They'll criticize points of detail, say the whole thing is unreliable, that the tube is out of proportion or points the wrong way. You can't expect an agent working from memory to get every detail right. I want photographs, Hawthorne."

"That's asking a lot, sir."

"We have got to have them. At any risk. Do you know what Savage said to me? I can tell you, it gave me a very nasty nightmare. He said that one of the drawings reminded him of a giant vacuum cleaner."

"A vacuum cleaner!" Hawthorne bent down and examined the drawings again, and the cold struck him.

"Makes you shiver, doesn't it?"

"But that's impossible, sir." He felt as though he were pleading for his own career. "It couldn't be a vacuum cleaner, sir. Not a vacuum cleaner."

"Fiendish, isn't it?" the Chief said. "The ingenuity, the simplicity, the devilish imagination of the thing." He removed his black monocle and his baby-blue eye caught the light and made it jig on the wall over the radiator. "See this one here—six times the height of a man. Like a gigantic spray. And this—what does this remind you of?"

Hawthorne said unhappily, "A two-way nozzle."

"What's a two-way nozzle?"

"You sometimes find them with a vacuum cleaner."

"Vacuum cleaner again. Hawthorne, I believe we may be on to something so big that the H-bomb will become a conventional weapon."

"Is that desirable, sir?"

"Of course it's desirable. Nobody worries about conventional weapons."

"What have you in mind, sir?"

"I'm no scientist," the Chief said, "but look at this great tank. It must stand nearly as high as the forest trees. A huge gaping mouth at the top, and this pipe-line—the man's only indicated it. For all we know it may extend for miles—from the mountains to the sea, perhaps.

You know the Russians are said to be working on some idea—something to do with the power of the sun, sea evaporation—I don't know what it's all about, but I do know this thing is Big. Tell our man we must have photographs."

"I don't quite see how he can get near enough. . . ."

"Let him charter a plane and lose his way over the area. Not himself personally, of course, but stroke 3 or stroke 2. Who is stroke 2?"

"Professor Sánchez, sir. But he'd be shot down. They have Air Force planes patrolling all that section."

"They have, have they?"

"To spot for rebels."

"So they say. Do you know, I've got a hunch, Hawthorne."

"Yes, sir?"

"That the rebels don't exist. They're purely notional. It gives the government all the excuse it needs to shut down a censorship over the area."

"I hope you are right, sir."

"It would be better for all of us," the Chief said with exhilaration, "if I were wrong. I fear these things—I fear them, Hawthorne."